Date Due

SEP 2 2 1966			
NOV 24 1966			
MAY 4 1940			

J. Hill Martin.

1872.

2v

HISTORICAL SKETCH

OF

BETHLEHEM

IN

PENNSYLVANIA,

WITH SOME ACCOUNT OF THE

Moravian Church,

BY

JOHN HILL MARTIN,

Of the Philadelphia Bar,

A Member of the "Moravian Historical Society."
And of the "Historical Society of Pennsylvania."
And author of "Sketches in the Lehigh Valley."

SECOND EDITION.

PHILADELPHIA:

Printed for THE AUTHOR,

By JOHN L. PILE, at No. 422 Walnut Street.

1873.

Kc

A782758

Entered according to the Act of Congress, by
JOHN HILL MARTIN,
In the Office of the Clerk of the District Court
of the United States in and for the
Eastern District of Pennsylvania,
in the year 1869.

First Edition, 350 copies printed.
Second Edition, 150 copies only printed, with corrections.

INTRODUCTION.

~~~~~~~~~~~~

THIS work is not a full history of Bethlehem, but simply an historical Sketch, for the use of the traveller. It is intended to supply a want which is felt by those people who desire to know something of the origin of the Town, the character of the peculiar people who first settled and built it, and of the different Institutions they founded in it.

No one can visit the Town without desiring to know more of it than can be derived from mere enquiry; and to render such information is the object of this sketch.

It was written entirely for amusement, but from the most authentic information that could be obtained by the Author; who became much interested in the Town, its people, its institutions, and its historic mementoes.

<div align="right">JOHN HILL MARTIN.</div>

PHILADELPHIA, March 1st, 1869.

Table of Contents.

CHAPTER I.

Settlement of Bethlehem; building of the first house; origin of name of the town; some account of the Moravian Church; sketch of Count Zinzendorf and his family; Anna Nitschmann, - - - - - 5

CHAPTER II.

The descendants of Zinzendorf, Louis David de Schweinits; the Old Indian Chapel; the Unity, Doctrine and Missions of the Moravian Church; a list of the Inhabitants of Bethlehem; the Indian Troubles, - - - 12

CHAPTER III.

The Married People's House; the Indian Wars of 1755; Benjamin Franklin as a General; his account of Bethlehem; Penn's Walking Purchase the cause of the Indian Troubles; Longfellow's Burial of the Minisink, - - 19

CHAPTER IV.

The Old Mill, built in 1751, burned in 1869; the Bethlehem Water Works; Revolutionary times of 1776; Washington and Bishop Ettwein; Pulaski's Banner; Longfellow's Poem; Visit of Washington; Lafayette; Mrs. Reidesel's Account; Mrs. Friday; Cotton; the Fishery; Manufacturers; Main Road to Ohio; the Stone Ridge; Views and Scenery, - - - 26

CHAPTER V.

The "Crown Inn;" the Sun Hotel; Marriages in Olden Times; the Choirs; Dr. John Schopf's Account of his Visit; a Sketch from the Boston Magazine of 1784; Extract from a Paper read before the Historical Society of Pennsylvania, 36

CHAPTER VI.

The Schnitz House; the Farmers in Old Times; the Object of the Establishment of the Moravian Church in America; Rochefoucault's Description of Bethlehem; the Bethlehem Souvenir; Simplicity of Moravian Life in the Last Century; Music; Bishop Spangenberg; The Fifty Year's Celebration, June 25, 1792; The Old Bridge over the Lehigh, 1792; Sketch from the American Gazetteer, - 44

CHAPTER VII.

The First Moravian Store; Bethlehem in 1797, from Ogden's Excursion into Bethlehem and Nazareth in 1800; the Ancient Institutions of the Brethren's Church, - 50

CHAPTER VIII.

Description of the large Moravian Church, erected in 1803; The Bethlehem Archives; The Gemein Haus, or Congregation House; The First Moravian Church in Bethlehem; The Old Chapel, or Second Church; The Old School, or the First Moravian Seminary for Females; The Official Seal of the Church of the United Brethren; The

Addition to the Old School; "The Sister's House;" The "Widows' House;" Origin of the Sisters' Houses; Marriage by Lot; Lieut. Aubery's Opinion; Explanation of the Lot; Account of it in the Historical Collections of New Jersey; The "Great Marriage Act" in Bethlehem, April 20th, 1757; Miss Mortimer's Novel of the Marrying by Lot; Married Women, and Ancient Customs; Remarks in Stroud's History of Pennsylvania; Act of Parliament of 20 George 2d, C. 44, for the Naturalization of Foreign Protestants, &c.,   ·   57

CHAPTER IX.

The Bethlehem Alphabet; the Old Water Works; Dr. Mease's Sketch of the Moravians; Derby's Gazetteer, 1827; Mrs. Royal's Account, 1829; Prince Maxamilian of Neuwied's Visit, 1832; James N. Beck's Sketches; Gordon's Gazetteer of Pennsylvania, 1832: The Centennial Celebration; U. S. Gazatteer, 1843; Incorporation of the Borough, 1845; "God Save the Luckenbach's;" Act of Parliament Recognizing the "Unitas Fratrum," as a Protestant Episcopal Church in 1749; Origin of the Moravians; Some Account of the Settlement at Hope, New Jersey, from the Historical Collections of that State,   ·   68

CHAPTER X.

Moravian Memories; Modern Bethlehem; the Old Grave Yard; Funeral Ceremonies of the Moravians; Tschoop; Tadeuskung, Anecdote of the Chief, the Figure on Indian Rock, on the Wissahicon; David Nitschmann; Dr. Robert Dudley Ross; Mourning Dress not Worn by the Moravians; the Passing Bell; Easter Morning Celebration; Drives, Walks, and Places of Interest near Bethlehem; Dr. Maurice C. Jones and the Fremdendiener's; Moravians in Early Times,   81

CHAPTER XI.

The Moravian Parochial School; the Moravian College, founded, A. D., 1807, charted April 3, 1863; the Bethlehem Male Boarding School; Nisky Hill Male Seminary; the Old Barn of the Congregation Farm; Sketch of the Bethlehem Seminary for Young Ladies; the Military Record of Bethlehem during the Rebellion,   -   97

CHAPTER XII.

The Enterprise of the Moravian Church; their schools; their Publications; the Text-Book; Birth Days, and their Celebration; the First Printing Office; the Newspapers of Bethlehem in the Past and Present; "Pennsylvania Dutch;" "Love-Feasts;" the Moravian Christmas Putz; the "Young Men's Missionary Society," and Christian Association of Bethlehem,   110

CHAPTER XIII.

The Society for Propagation the Gospel among the Heathen; Statistics of the Unity of the Brethren, January 1, 1869; List of the Churches and Missions in the Northern Diocese of the Church of the United Brethren in America; an Old Passport; Christian Frederick Post; Sister "Polly Heckewelder;" Rev. John Heckewelder, and his Writings; the Horsfield Papers; History of Northampton County, from a Pamphlet; Official Seal of the Moravian Church, a Correction; Travels of the Marquis de Chastellux in America, 1780; Chas. Thompson's Theory of the Formation of the Wind-Gap; Curiosities; the Old Iron Stove Plates; Indian Corn Grinder; the Old Sun Dial; Old Tiles; Old Water Pipes; the First Market House; Old Grave Yard, South of the Lehigh; Zinzendorf's visit to Wyoming; Formation of Northampton County,   -   -   - 127

CHAPTER XIV.

The Litany of the Moravian Church; "Bartow's Path;" Niskey Hill; Friedenshuetten; the Indian House; the German Barns; Tecumseh; the Indian Missionary Stations; Haidte's Painting of the First Fruits; Seheussle's Picture of Zeisberger Preaching to the Indians; The Lehigh, its Freshets and Fisheries; A ride on the Switch-

back; American Tea; The Old Perseverance and the Fire Apparatus of Bethlehem; The Hotels; The Streets; The Old Tannery; Social Life; Census of 1870;
Powder Magazine; Height of the Lehigh Hills; May-day; The Masonic Societies
of Bethlehem,   -   -   -   -   141

CHAPTER XV.

Music in Bethlehem, by Rufus A. Grider, of the Bethlehem Moravian Congregation, - 157

CHAPTER XVI.

Borough Authorities; Lawyers and Doctors; The choice of Bishops by Lot; An Account of a "Vesper" of the Moravian Historical Society; Old Map of Bethlehem in
the Historical Society of Pennsylvania; The Married Peoples' Houses; Mano-
kasy; The Apothecary Shop; Pottery; Tobacco; Silk; Public Buildings; The
Vineyards; The Pennsylvania and Lehigh Zinc Co.; South Bethlehem; The Pa-
per Bag Manufactury; New Street Bridge; Volunteer Companies; The Lehigh
University; The Freshet of October 4, 1869; The First Public Roads; David
Nitschman and His Company; The Great Minnisink Trail; The First Post Office;
The Mode of Travel in the Olden Times; The "Crown Inn"; Stage Route, Wind
Gap to Philadelphia,   -   -   -   -   174

First House, Bethlehem, built 1741.

HISTORICAL SKETCH

OF

BETHLEHEM,

Pennsylvania,

WITH SOME ACCOUNT OF THE MORAVIAN
CHURCH.

—•+✕+•—

BETHLEHEM.

A quiet town, embowered by patriarch trees,
Around which sleeps an atmosphere, as sweet
As airs of Paradise: where tiny feet
Tinkle, at twilight, on a balmier breeze,
Than ever blew from Ceylon's spicy seas—
And where throughout the long and languid days
Poised on the Sycamore's silver-rinded sprays,
The Oriole swings his nest, and flutes his glees.
Far statelier spots may beam beneath the sun,
But none so bland in beauty—none so bright
With Eden's own Asphodel, that, exhaling light,
Blooms in her paths, while, like a kneeling nun
Hearing High Mass, she looks with reverent eyes,
Through clasping greenery, on smiling skies!
—Henry B. Hirst.

CHAPTER I.

Settlement of Bethlehem.—Building of
the First House.—Origin of Name of
the Town.—Some Account of the Moravian Church.—Sketch of Count Zinzendorf and his Family.—Anna Nitschmann.

Bethlehem, Northampton County,
Pennsylvania, is situated on the southern side of a declivity rising from the northern bank of the Lehigh River, twelve miles
from its mouth at Easton, on the river Delaware, and fifty-two miles from, and connecting with the city of Philadelphia by the
North Pennsylvania Railroad; which forms
a junction with the Lehigh Valley Railroad
at that point; thus placing Bethlehem within
two hours ride by railroad of Philadelphia,
and three hours from Harrisburg and New
York.

Bethlehem was settled in 1741 by Moravians
from Germany. It is a place of great resort
in the summer season for the inhabitants of
Philadelphia and New York, and is chiefly
celebrated for its dry and salubrious climate.
It is particularly adapted as a place of residence for invalids, especially for those suffering from weakness of the lungs, being at the
southern end of an extensive plain called
the "Dry lands," and sheltered on the west
and north by the Blue Ridge Mountains,
twenty miles distant. It is famous for its
schools, its beautiful walks and drives, and
the open-hearted hospitality of its Anglo-
German population, numbering at this time,
about 7,000.

To the better understanding of the appearance of the town of Bethlehem, and the customs of the people, it will be necessary to give
a short sketch of the rise and progress of the
Moravian Society.

In the early part of the year 1741, a small party of German Moravians, seventeen in number, under the leadership of Peter Boehler, left Ephrata now Nazareth, in Northampton County, Pennsylvania, and settled at that point on the Lehigh or *Lecha* river, (as it was named by the Indians) where a small creek called the Manockasy empties into that stream. This place is now called BETHLE-HEM, the Society having purchased there 4100 acres of land for the purpose of forming a settlement.

The first house, with a stable attached, was erected that year, and within its walls were assembled on Christmas Eve, 1741, the pious inhabitants of the little settlement, (added to whom were Count Nicholas *Louis Von Zinzendorf and his daughter Be-nigna*, who had just arrived in this country from Germany,) for the purpose of celebrating the coming anniversary of the birth-day of our Saviour, and from the coincidence that the celebration was partly performed in the stable, *the name of Bethlehem was given to* the infant town ; the proposed name had been Bethlechem, or the " *house upon the Lecha*," but in commemoration of this eventful evening it was changed to Bethlehem.

The following interesting sketch concerning the settlement of Bethlehem, was written by John Martin Mack, a Moravian Missionary to the American Indians. He was born in 1715 and died in 1784. "On the 13th of April, 1740, we concluded to break up our settlement in Georgia, on account of the war, as we had no religious liberty, and remove to Pennsylvania, where we arrived the same month, and were engaged as mechanics and day-labourers by Mr. Whitefield at Nazareth, in order to build a house for him at that place, as he had purchased the land for converted people in England. We had a pleasant household, every one laid hold where they could, and the Lord was with us.

"In Dec. 1740, Bishop David Nitschman Father Nitschman, and his daughter Anna, Sister, Mother, and Charles Fröhlich arrived from Europe with a commission to locate a settlement for the Brethren, and they did so in 1741. The ground whereon Bethlehem stands was purchased, and in the spring *I assisted in cutting down the first tree and founding* the place. In the fall of the same year came the blessed follower (Zinzendorf), several days before Christmas. He came to our new built place ere it had a name ; it so happened that we celebrated Christmas Eve in memory of the birth of our dear Saviour, and as there was only a wall between our dwelling and our cow and horse stable—so the *Selige Jünger* went into the stable in the tenth hour with us, and sang with feeling, so that our hearts were melted.

'Nicht aus Jerusalem, sondern Bethlehem
    Aus dem Komt was mir fromet.'

And thus the place received the name of Bethlehem. The impression which it made upon my heart will remain to my latest hour."

Geo. Whitefield purchased 5,000 acres of land A. D. 1740, in Upper Nazareth Township, which he transferred to the Brethren in 1743. This domain was known as the 'Barony of Nazareth,' and was nominally the property of the Countess Zinzendorf; it had the right of Court Baron, and was the only manor sold by the Penns with the privilege of rendering service to them and their heirs, of a *Red Rose* in June of each year.

The first house was a large log house, such as are common in the wilds of Pennsylvania, even in these days. It was intended as a temporary residence for the settlers, until a more substantial building could be erected. It stood upon the site of the present stables of the "Eagle Hotel." Numerous drawings of it have been made, in which it is represented as a one-story log house with attic rooms or garrets, having two doors and two windows in the front of the house, and two windows in each gable end of the first story, and two irregular windows in the gable ends of the garrets. When the house was torn down some of the wood was preserved, from which canes, rules, and pen-holders have been made, and are highly prized.

The existence of the religious society of the Moravians, or the church of the United Brethren, the ancient " *Unitas Fratrum*," is now a matter of history. They are the oldest known Apostolic and Protestant church, coming from Bohemia and Moravia; its Bishops justly claiming Apostolic succession, authoritatively recognized by the Established Church of England, and by the Protestant Episcopal Church in the United States.

To sketch briefly a history of the rise of the United Brethren, it will be necessary to begin in the year 1176, when the Waldenses, a religious and primitive people, first made their appearance in Bohemia, and settled on the borders of the Eger, where they soon united in friendly and religious communion with the Bohemians and Moravians. The early history of these persecuted people is involved in much obscurity, although their origin is dated from the eighth century, and sometimes earlier; they inhabited the valley of Peidmont and took their name from a celebrated leader of their sect, Peter Waldo.

They were undoubtedly, however, the earliest advocates of Christian Truth, and suffered the most terrible persecutions; their descendants are still found in Peidmont, Switzerland and France. They traced their Episcopal ordination to the Apostles, and on settling in Bohemia, finding their doctrines and practices assimilating with those of that country, they finally became united into one church.

From these united people, sprung the Bohemian John Huss, who about the year 1400, brought the doctrines of his people before the world; and in consequence suffered the persecutions of the Church of Rome, and was finally burnt at the stake as a Heretic, on the 6th of July, 1415. Then followed the great Hussite war.

Finally, after many persecutions and secret worshipping in caves, George Podiebrad, of Bohemia, about the year 1456, permitted the Bohemians and Moravians to form themselves into an association, (the " Unitas Fratrum,") and to settle in the principality of Litiz.

In the year 1467, a deputation of seventy of the most respectable members of the Moravian brethren met at Lahota. Nine of these were chosen, from whom three were selected by lot, to be the spiritual advisers of the people; those chosen were Mathias of Kunewold, Thomas Pizelaucius and Elias Krenovins, and as it was necessary these Presbyters should properly administer the rites of Ordination, they decided on seeking Episcopal ordination from some pure source accordingly, some time after, the Brethren resolved on sending three of their priests to the Waldenses, (who still had their churches and bishops in Austria,) to receive their sacred ordination, one of whom was Michael Bradacius, who was with two others, ordained by Stephen, one of the last remaining Waldensian bishops, who, within a year thereafter, was burned at the stake, and his followers fugitives.

About the same time the persecutions of the Brethren began anew, and they struggled on long weary years against civil and ecclesiastical power, until at last a patron and a protector was raised up for them, under whose influence, bravery and goodness, the society has become great and prosperous in this country and in Europe; where they have built many pleasant towns, from which they send out numerous missionaries, who go about the world doing good to all mankind.

Nicholas Louis, Count von Zinzendorf, to whose protection, fraternal friendship and pious exertions the Moravians owe so much, and which they repay so fully by cherishing and keeping ever green his memory amongst them, was born in the city of Dresden, on the 26th of May, 1700. His father was minister of State to the king of Saxony, and a nobleman much esteemed, he married the Countess Reuss Von Ebeisdorf, by whom he had this one son, and died soon after. His widow then retired to the residence of her mother (at Hennersdorf, in upper Lusatia, Saxony,) Henrietta, Baroness de Gersdorf, a learned and pious lady, who devoted herself to the education of her grandson. When quite young he was sent to the University of Halle, then under the direction of of its founder, Francke; and afterwards in 1716, he went to the University of Wittenburg, to complete his studies. He left there in 1719, resolved to embrace the Ecclesiastical profession, and traveled throughout Northern Europe, including France and Holland; having spent most of his time during his journey, with the most eminent theologians of the countries through which he passed. He wrote and published his travels under the title of "The Pilgrimage of Atticus through the World."

On returning from his travels, the .Count purchased the manor and estates of Berthelsdorf. About this time the society of the United Brethren in Moravia were again being much persecuted for the practice of their religious belief. Zinzendorf becoming acquainted with the fact, extended to them through Christian David, an invitation to come and settle on his estates; and in acceptance thereof, there arrived on the 17th of June, 1722, a little company of ten persons, who immediately commenced to erect a house for their own accommodation, upon the estate of the Count. Such was the beginning of "Hernhut," meaning, "The protection of the Lord." The number of settlers soon increased, and within five years the town had a population of 500 souls. Zinzendorf took great interest in the infant settlement; and assisted by a Lutheran minister, Rothe, instructed the settlers and educated their children: He conceived the idea of founding a religious community, embracing the doctrines of the martyred Huss, which was soon accomplished; and it is from this time that the Moravians date the renewal of the church of the United Brethren.

John Huss, the great reformer, was born in the village of Hussinitz, in Bohemia, in the year 1373, and is regarded by the Moravians as the founder of their faith. As early as the year 1500, the United Brethren had over 200 churches in Bohemia; they had published their confession of faith, their editions of the Bible, their hymn book and catechism. Luther, with great justice, styled them "The reformers before the Reformation." It was the descendants of these United Brethren, the remnants of that once large religious community, to whom Zinzendorf gave an asylum at Hernhut; and convinced that their doctrines were of the true faith, he became a member of their church, passed his examination as a theological candidate at Stralsund, and preached there his first ser-

mon. He was subsequently consecrated a bishop of the Moravian Church at Berlin; and in 1732 he was married to the Countess Erdmuth Dorothea Von Reuss; by the marriage contract he transferred to her all his property, and they entered into a mutual covenant, that they would both be ready at a moment's warning, to enter upon the task of converting the heathen. The Brethren soon began to establish foreign missions, and their churches are now found in nearly all parts of the known world; the conversion of the heathen to the true faith, being one of the first objects of the society. It may be stated, that the belief, and the forms and ceremonies of the Moravian Church, assimilate to those of the Protestant Episcopal Church, of which they claim to be the oldest known member, saying that they are a branch of the Greek Church, and have preserved the Episcopal succession. Crantz, the great Moravian historian, has written fully on all these points, and his work is one of great interest. It is said to have been Zinzendorf's wish that the Moravians should adopt the liturgy of the Episcopal Church, instead of the one now in use; but he found himself so violently opposed by his Brethren, that he abandoned the idea.

In the year 1737, Zinzendorf visited England, in order to confer with Doctor Potter, the Archbishop of Canterbury, concerning Moravian affairs, and the Episcopal ordination. It was there that he met General Oglethorpe, and other gentlemen interested in the settlement of Georgia; they solicited the Count to send missionaries to that colony; he objected on the ground that his Brethren were not acknowledged as duly ordained by the Established Church. The Arch-Bishop was consulted, and replied: "That the Moravian Brethren were an Apostolic and Episcopal Church, not sustaining any doctrines repugnant to the thirty-nine articles of the Church of England; that they could not therefore with propriety, nor ought they to be hindered from preaching the gospel among the heathen." He also said: "That no Englishman who had any notion of Ecclesiastical history, could doubt their Apostolic succession." The bench of Bishops in England in the year 1749, agreed that these Brethren (referring to the present Moravian Church—then known by the name of the "Unitas Fratrum at Hernhut") were an Episcopal Church, and an act of parliament was passed June 6, 1749, which granted and secured to them certain solicited privileges. Copies of the act were printed in English, Latin, French and German, and distributed among the Brethren; one of the original printed copies in English, is now in possession of B. E. Lehman, of Bethlehem, Pa.

In the list of Bishops of the Unity of the Bohemian and Moravian Brethren, commencing with Michael Bradacius, consecrated in 1467, by Stephen, Bishop of the Waldenses; and ending in 1644, we find fifty-five names, adding to these the Bishops of the Unity in Poland, taken from Jablonsky's letter to Arch-bishop Wake, in 1717, down to David Nitschman, (consecrated in 1735, by Jablonsky, at Berlin,) the first Bishop of the renewed Moravian Church, we have sixty-seven Bishops; and from that time till the ordination of Samuel Reinke in 1858, no less than eighty-nine more bishops were added to the list. Making the entire number of Bishops of the Moravian Church to that time, one hundred and sixty-six. Some writers increase the number, but Crantz makes David Nitschman the sixty-seventh Bishop, and he has been followed as the best authority.

The Rev. Edward De Schweinitz, in the Moravian Manual, gives a list of the Bishops of the church, constituting the Episcopal succession of the *Unitas Fratrum:* In the ANCIENT CHURCH from 1467 to 1734, he makes the number of Bishops to be 70. Since then, up to 1866, he gives 97 Bishops of the

RENEWED CHURCH.

No.	Year of Consecration.	Bishops.
71	1735	David Nitschman.
72	1737	Lewis Count de Zinzendorf.
73	1740	Polycarp Mueller.
74	1741	John Nitschman, sen.
75	1743	Frederick Baron De Watteville.
76	1744	Martin Dober.
77	1745	Augustus G. Spangenberg.
78	1746	David Nitschman, jun.
79	"	Frederick W. Neisser.
80	"	Christian F. Steinhofer.
81	"	J. F. Camerhof.
82	1747	John Baron de Watteville.
83	"	Leonard Dober.
84	"	A. A. Vieroth.
85	1748	Frederick Martin.
86	"	Peter Boehler.
87	1750	George Waiblinger.
88	1751	Matthew Hehl.
89	1754	John Gambold.
90	1756	Andrew Grasman.
91	1758	John Nitschman.
92	"	Nathaniel Seidel.
93	1770	Martin Mack.
94	1773	Martin Graf.
95	1775	John F. Reichel.
96	"	Paul E. Layritz.
97	"	P. H. Melther.
98	1782	Henry de Brueningk.
99	"	George Clemens.
100	"	Jeremiah Risler.
101	1783	George Tranecker.
102	1784	John Etwein.
103	1785	John Schaukirch.
104	1786	Benjamin G. Mueller.
105	1789	Christian Gregor.
106	"	Samuel Liebisch.
107	"	C. Duvernoy.
108	"	Benjamin Rothe.
109	1790	John A. Huebner.
110	"	John D. Koehler.
111	1801	Thomas Moore.
112	"	Christian Dober.
113	"	Samuel T. Benade.
114	"	Gotthold Reichel.
115	1802	George H. Loskiel.
116	1808	John G. Cunow.
117	"	Herman Richter.
118	1811	John Herbst.
119	1814	William Fabricius.
120	"	Charles G. Hueffel.
121	"	Charles A. Baumister.
122	"	John Baptiste de Albertini.
123	1815	Jacob Van Vleck.
124	1818	George M. Schneider.
125	"	F. W. Foster.
126	"	Benjamin Reichel.
127	1822	Andrew Benade.
128	1825	John Wied.
129	"	Lewis Fabricius.
130	"	Peter F. Curie.
131	"	John Holmes.
132	1827	John D. Anders.
133	1835	Frederick L. Koelbing.

134	1835	John C. Bechler.
135	1836	C. A. Pohlman.
136	"	H. L. Halbeck.
137	"	Jacob Levin Reichel.
138	"	Daniel F. Gambs.
139	"	William Henry Van Vleck.
140	"	John King Martyn.
141	"	John Ellis.
142	1843	John M. Nitschman.
143	"	C. C. Ultsch.
144	"	John Stengaerd.
145	1844	William Wisdom Essex.
146	1845	Peter Wolle.
147	1846	John G. Herman.
148	"	Benjamin Seifferth.
149	1848	C. W. Matthiesen.
150	1852	F. Joachim Nielsen.
151	"	John Rogers.
152	1853	John C. Breutel.
153	"	Henry T. Dober.
154	"	George Wall Westerby.
155	1854	John Christian Jacobson.
156	1857	Godfrey Andrew Cunow.
157	"	William Edwards.
158	"	Charles William Jahn.
159	"	Henry Rudolph Wullschlaegel.
160	1858	Samuel Reinke.
161	1860	Geo. Fred'k Bahnson.
162	1862	Ernest F. Reichel.
163	"	E. W. Croeger.
164	1863	James Latrobe.
165	1864	Henry A. Shultz.
166	"	David Bigler.
167	1866	G. T. Tietzen.

Since 1866 there has been no new Bishops appointed in the church.

In March 1736, Count Zinzendorf was banished from Saxony, under the pretext of his disseminating false doctrines on religion, and having given protection to the community at Hernhut, against whom there were many like complaints. Driven from his home, he visited England and the missions of the Society in America, during which time he visited Bethlehem, and was present at the ever memorable celebration at that place on Christmas Eve, 1741. In 1743, he returned to Europe, and in 1747 obtained permission from the King of Saxony to return to Hernhut. During his absence the government had sent a commission to investigate charges against the community of the Breth-

ren, but their report proving favorable to the usages, social forms and religious practices of the people there, they were not disturbed. In 1756 the Countess Von Zinzendorf died, and the Count, in about a year after her death married Anna Nitschman, who had accompanied him and his daughter in their travels in America. The Count and his wife both died in 1760, within twelve days of each other; and were buried side by side in the cemetery at Hutberg.

Anna Nitschman was a daughter of "Old father Nitschman," one of the original emigrants from Moravia, who died at Bethlehem, and is interred in the cemetery there. She was a very remarkable woman, and attracted as much attention and respect from those who were acquainted with her, as did the celebrated Zinzendorf. At the early age of fifteen she was an Eldress of the Sisters at Hernhut, and became quite eminent in the performance of ministerial duties. It was not uncommon at that time for women to speak and pray in unofficial life.

Many of the hymns used by the Moravians in their religious services were composed by Zinzendorf, and he has so completely identified himself with their Society, that it has become impossible to make even a brief sketch of it, such as this, without a continual reference to him, and in a great measure, giving a history of his life.

The Count's eldest daughter, the Countess Henrietta Benigna Justina de Zinzendorf, who accompanied her father during his visit to America, was married in 1747, to Johannes Baron de Watteville, a Bishop of the Moravian Church. The Count had twelve children by his first marriage, six sons, and six daughters.

The Countess Erdmuth took as much interest as her husband in the little community at Hernhut, and during his banishment she was the chief counsel and recourse of the Society there. "The family of Zinzendorf appears to have been of very remote antiquity in the Duchy of Austria. As early as the eleventh century, it was numbered among the twelve noble houses, which were the chief support of the Austrian dynasty. From its founder Ehrenhold, to his descendant, the subject of this sketch, were reckoned twenty-two generations. The dignity of Count of the Holy Roman Empire was conferred on it by the Emperor Leopold in the year 1662. The first member of the family who embraced the doctrines of the Reformation, was John, the second of the name who died in 1552. Of his descendants, several families remained in the Austrian dominions, and were distinguished by their adherence to the Protestant faith, not less than by their civil and military services. It is a remarkable fact, that Luke Bakeneister, Doctor and Professor of Theology, who in the reign of the Emperor Rudolph II, held a visitation of the Churches in Austria adhering to the Augsberg Confession, found four flourishing Protestant congregations, duly provided with Pastors established on the estates of Zinzendorf family at Lung, Charlsutten, Pottendorf and Orth, near Markfeld. The grandfather of the Count, Maximilian Erasmus, emigrated from his native land and settled at Oberberg near Nuremberg, esteeming the loss of all his estates more than counterbalanced by the superior liberty of conscience which he thus obtained. His son George Lewis, the father of the Count, having moved to Dresden, entered into the service of the elector of Saxony, and died as stated in the narrative, in the year 1700. The head-ship of the family which fell to the Count in 1756, on the decease of his elder brother, he ceded with all his rights and immunities to his nephew, as soon as the necessary forms could be gone through.

The motto of the house of Zinzendorf, derived from Count Albert the Prime Minister of the Emperor Leopold, was: " I yield to no one, not even to the whole world." See a note to a poem by Count Zinzendorf, on his brother Frederick Christian's second marriage, German Poems No. 63, page 176, in which he makes a striking allusion to this motto.

THE OLD INDIAN CHAPEL,
BETHLEHEM, PA., 1765.

CHAPTER II.

THE DESCENDANTS OF ZINZENDORF, LOUIS DAVID DE SCHWEINITZ.—THE OLD INDIAN CHAPEL.—THE UNITY, DOCTRINE AND MISSIONS OF THE MORAVIAN CHURCH.—A LIST OF THE INHABITANTS OF BETHLEHEM.—THE INDIAN TROUBLES.

OUNT ZINZENDORF left behind him three daughters, the only survivors of a family of twelve children, (six sons and as many daughters,) most of whom departed in infancy. The eldest, Henrietta Benigna Justina, became the consort of Baron John de Watteville; the second, Maria Agnes, of Maurice Count Dohna; the third, Elizabeth, of Baron Frederick de Watteville. By the two alliances last mentioned, the Count has no surviving descendant; the only son of Count Dohna, Henry Lewis, having died without issue in 1833.

To Baron John de Watteville, and his lady, were born two sons and two daughters; the sons died unmarried; the elder of the daughters, Anna Dorothy Elizabeth, was married to Hans Christian Alexander von Schweinitz; the younger, Maria Justina, to Henry the 55th, Count Reuss, of the house of Kostritz. By these marriages there are now living four great grand-children of Count Zinzendorf.

Louis David De Schweinitz, Doctor of Philosophy and the celebrated Botanist, was born in Bethlehem, Northampton County, Pennsylvania, on the 13th of February, A. D. 1780. He was the eldest son of Hans Christian Alexander De Schweinitz, and his wife Anna Dorothea Elizabeth de Watteville. His father was of an ancient and very distinguished family in Silesia, in Germany; he came to this country in 1770, and filled at Bethlehem, the office of Superintendent of the fiscal and secular concerns of the Moravian Brethren in North America.

On the 4th of July, 1787, Louis David De Schweinitz was placed at Nazareth Hall, to be educated, and remained there as a scholar *eleven* years. About the year 1822, he became the *Senior Civilis* of the Society, and also took charge of the Boarding School for young girls, at Bethlehem. He died February 8th, 1834, and his remains are interred in the old Cemetery. He left a widow and four sons, namely, the Rev'd Emil A. De Schweinitz, Fiscal Agent of the Moravian Church in North Carolina; Rev'd Robert De Schweinitz, President of the Provincial Elders' Conference of the Moravian Church; Edmund De Schweinitz, Minister of the Church, and President of the Theological College at Bethlehem; and Bernard De Schweinitz, deceased, who at the time of his death in 1854, was Minister of the Moravian Church, on Staten Island, New

York. These, and their issue, are the only living descendants of the Count in America; in Europe there are living, some four or five cousins of the De Schweinitz family.

In Hazard's Register of Pennsylvania, of June 13th, 1835, page 369, it is alleged that "Count Zinzendorf in a Latin speech at Philadelphia in 1742, formally renounced his title of Count, and resumed his original family name of Von Thurnstein." Be this as it may, Zinzendorf did, certainly, during his visit to America in 1841-42, go by the name of S. Lewis Thurnstein, Knight. There can be no valid objection to a nobleman using, or travelling under, his family name, if he feels so disposed; and, although the Count may have honestly intended to renounce his rank and title, he will always be known in history, and in the Moravian Church, as Count Zinzendorf; and his eccentricities and peculiarities can in no way alter the fact, that in his life and actions he did much good in the world; and that his memory is revered and fondly cherished in the Church, and by the descendants of the people among whom he lived and labored.

On the monument erected to his memory in the famous and beautiful cemetery at *Hernhut*, is the following: "Here rests the remains of that never-to-be-forgotten man of God, Nicholas Ludwig, Count and Lord of ZINZENDORF and POTTENDORF, who by God's grace and his own faithful untiring efforts, in this the 17th century, most worthily revived and re-organized the UNITED BRETHREN.

"He was born in Dresden, the 21st of May, 1700, and entered into the joy of his Lord on the 9th of May, 1760.

"He was appointed to bring forth fruit, and fruit that remains."

The Old Indian Chapel, a view of which illustrates this chapter, was an old log house, torn down in the fall of the year 1868, to make room for the erection of a new structure. It stood in Market street, on the south side, the second house west of the Old Graveyard, and was occupied by William Busch. It was formerly used as a Chapel for the Indian Congregation at Nain; which was a village of Christian Indians, established by the

Moravians. And in this old chapel, they were taught, and preached to in their own language. The village was situated about three miles north-west of Bethlehem, in Hanover township; and upon the removal of the Indians in 1765, from Nain to the Susquehanna, the old chapel and a number of the houses erected there for their use, were moved to Bethlehem, and all traces of Nain soon became obliterated; its site is however yet pointed out on the "Geisinger Farm." The next building to the west, owned, and at present occupied by Ambroise J. Erwin, is another of these old log houses. There is a third, standing at the south-west corner of Cedar Alley and Market Street. These old houses were objects of great interest and curiosity, and it is to be regretted that the Old Chapel, and the one beside it, had to give place to a more suitable modern residence.

It is related of the Christian Indians residing at NAIN, that whenever a child was baptised in the Bethlehem Church, they always claimed the right to kiss the babe after the ceremony. So, many of the old inhabitants had the honor of being kissed by the Red people when they were christened. The rite of Baptism was then invariably performed in the Church.

The proper title of the Moravian Church, so called, is "*The Unitas Fratrum*," which was the name adopted by the Ancient Society of the Brethren, and is retained by the renewed Church. It includes all the provinces, and missions, of the Church, wherever they may be situated, as one confederated ecclesiastical body.

During Zinzendorf's lifetime, the government of the Church depended in a great measure upon him, and his two distinguished assistants, his son-in-law, John Baron de Watteville, and Augustus Spangenberg, both bishops of the Moravian Church. Since his death, a more positive ecclesiastical constitution has been adopted. The Synods receiving the supreme power; and the executive administrations of affairs being committed to an elective college of bishops and elders, which, in 1769, took the title of "The Unity's Elders Conference;" and subordinate

Boards were appointed for the superintendance of the affairs of the American and British Provinces.

The Moravian Brethren's Unity is at present divided into three distinct Provinces. The *American*, comprising the Moravian Churches in the United States; the Continental, including those on the Continent of Europe; and the British, embracing those of Great Britain and Ireland.

The American province is sub-divided into two districts, the Northern and Southern. To the latter, belong the Moravian Churches in North Carolina, and to the former, all the rest of the Churches of the Brethren in America. Each district has a government of its own, consisting of a Synod and a Provincial Board.

Formerly, there were several Church settlements in the United States, in which all real property was held in common by the Brethren; this was especially necessary in the infant state of the Church in this country, when poverty, persecutions, public wars and civil tumults, required a union of labor to provide for the support of each little Society, as well as to enable them to perpetuate the customs and regulations of their religion. This peculiar feature has however been abandoned, the common property has been sold or divided, and the towns are now thrown open to all who choose to settle in them. The Moravian Churches are now without exception, ordinary churches like those of any other Protestant denomination.

All the Congregations receive the Holy Scriptures of the Old and New Testament, as the only standard rule, both of the doctrine and practice of the church. And they have agreed that no doctrines shall be delivered in any assembly of the Brethren, which are repugnant to the Augustine or Augsburg Confession.

One of the most laudable objects of the United Brethren, and their chief aim, is the conversion of the Heathen, by the establishment of missions in all parts of the world. Their first appearance on the American Continent was in Georgia and North Carolina; the settlers in the latter place were not disturbed, but those who settled in Georgia suffered so many persecutions from their refusal to bear arms, (which was then one of the tenets of their faith) that most of them finally came to Pennsylvania; although it was admitted that they did much good among the slaves.

The establishment of Foreign Missions by the Church, was begun in 1732, ten years after the first house was built at Hernhut, and when the entire congregation there numbered but six hundred. The first mission was among the negro slaves on the island of St. Thomas, in the West Indies. Leonard Dober, and David Nitschman, the first bishops of the renewed church, were the pioneers in the good work. They have founded missions in Greenland, Sweden, and Russia; among the Hottentots in Southern Africa; in Persia; in Australia; in Surinam; and in many other places.

The pious intentions of the Moravian Brethren, seem to have had their effect upon numerous other branches of the Protestant Church. Many of the followers of Wickliff left England and joined the Society, as did the Waldenses in earlier days, and as many other religious sects have done since.

All these things have been enumerated here to show how old and honorable a Church is that of the United Brethren, and how praiseworthy are its objects.

In the Pennsylvania Archives, volume 3d, page 70, under the date of November 29, 1756, will be found "a catalogue of all the men, women and children who, for the present, belong to the Bethlehem Economy."

BETHLEHEM, Nov. 29th, 1756.

I. OF THE MARRIED PEOPLE.

Aug. Gottlieb Spangenberg	Abraham Buninger,
Peter Bohler,	Joseph Powel,
Matthæus Hehl,	John Christoph Francke,
Anton Lawatsch,	Jaspar Payne,
David Nitschmann,	Robt. Hussey,
Abraham Reincke,	Nic. Sangerhausen,
Martin Mack,	Christian Gottfr. Engel,
Joh. Michel Graff.	George Partsch,
David Heckewælder,	Peter Mordyk,
Matthæus Schropp,	Michel Mucksch,
Christian Henrich,	Jacob Eyerle,
Thomas Benzien,	Ephraim Coulver,
Bernh. Adam Grube.	Rud. Christ,
Frank Christian Lembke,	Peter Brown,
George Neuser,	Joh. Christian Richter,
John Jacob Schmick,	Gottlieb Bernt,
John Edwin,	George Kaske,
Jacob Rogers,	Hartman Verdries,
George Weber,	John Levering,

John Bohner,
Ernst Gambold,
Albrecht Russmeyer,
George Ohneberg.
Timothy Horseneld,
John Bechtel,
Philip Christian Bader,
John Okely,
Henry Beck,
Frederik Otto,
Matthæus Otto,
Frank Blum,
Tobias Hirte,
Paul Dan. Bryzelius,
George Klein,
Wm. Thorne,
Joh. Valentin Haidt,
John Jorde,
Wm. Dixon,
Christian Stoz,
Wm. Edmonds,
Christian Eggert,
Thomas Fisher,
Daniel Kunckler,
Carl Schulze,
John Schmidt,
Melchior Schmidt,
Bernhard Muller,
Gottfried Roemelt,
George Pitshmann,
Wm. Werner,
Joh. Georg Geitner,
John Stoll,
Anton Schmidt,
Michel Schnall,
David Digeon,
Christian Werner,
Andreas Horne,
Samuel Maw.
David Tanneberger, sen.,
David Tanneberger, Jun.,
John Schebosch,
Frederik Boeckel,
Matthæus Wittke,
John Brandmuller,
Chr. Fr. Steinmann,
Abraham Hessler,
Ludwig Stoz,
Christian Fritsche,
Joh. Jacob Hafner,
Peter Schuert,
Christian Anton,
Andreas Kremser,
Matth. Hancke,
Phil. Transou,
Martin Bohmer,
Andreas Schober,
Joh. George Jungmann,
Jno. H. Moeller,
Anton Wagner,

Henrich Deutel,
Richd. Utley,
Peter Gotje,
Christ. Fr. Oerter,
Joseph Muller,
Thomas Schauf,
Martin Luck,
Nicol. Schæfer,
George Schneider,
George Christ,
Henry Frey,
Joh. Nic. Weinland,
John Christian Weinert,
Martin Liebsch,
Joseph Moller,
Adam Schneider,
Paul Fritsche,
Henrich Fritsche,
Melch. Schmidt, morav.,
Elias Flex,
Wenzel Bernhard,
Enert Eaerson,
Joh. Henry. Segner,
Joh. Matthew Spohn,
Frank Steap,
Valentin Fuhrer,
Joh. Burstler,
Abraham Bouper,
Michel Haberland,
John Brucker,
Samuel Isles,
Thomas Yarrel,
Nic. Garrison, Sen.,
Salomon Schumann,
David Bischoff,
Mathi. Krause,
Joh. Fredr. Beyer,
Andreas Brocksch,
Albrecht Kloz,
Henrich Muller,
George Zeisberger,
Gottfr. Schulze,
George Gold,
Daniel Oesterlein,
Rudolph Stræhle,
G. Stephan Wolson,
Philip Meurer,
Daniel Neubert,
Michel Jahm,
George Nixdorff,
Fredr. Schlegel,
Joh. Hantsch,
Joh. Chr. Loepfner,
Henrich Biefel,
Carl Opir,
Wm. Graps,
Christoph. Schmidt,
Kunast,
George Schmidt.

No. of Married People, 157.
No. of Children, 288.

II. WIDOWERS.

David Nitschmann, Sen.,
Jacob Till,
Joachim Sensemann,
Wolfgang Michler,
Mickel Mucke,
Daniel Kliest,
Jonas Nilson,

Andreas Shout,
Joh. Fr. Post,
Matth. Weiss,
David Richard,
Rubel,
John Michler,
Gotlieb Haberecht,

No. of Widowers, 14.
No. of Children, 16.

III. WIDOWS.

Catharine Huber,
Gertraud Bonn,
Cathorine Brownfield,
Rosina Endtean,
Ana. Mar. Lehnert,
Elizabeth Ronner,

Magd. Elis. Reissin,
Maria Hausin,
Elizabeth Herzerin,
Judith Schurer,
Regina Hautsch,
Rosina Munster,

Catharina Weber,
Sarah Lighton,
Rosina Shutsin,

A. Mar. Demuth,
A. Elis. Leinbach.

No. of Widows, 17.
No. of Children, 18.
188 persons, 322 Children.—Total, 510.

Nota. There are 96 children more with us, some Orphans, others belonging to some Brethren and Friends, who are not of the Bethlehem Oeconomy, and therefore their Names are not mentioned.

IV. SINGLE MEN.

Nathaniel Seidel,
Gottlieb Bezold,
David Zeisberger,
Otto Krogstry.
George Solle,
Frederic Weber,
Joseph Haberland,
John Schwie-shaupt,
Gottfried Roesler,
Carl Friederich,
Samuel Herr,
George Meiser,
Andreas Hoger,
Gottfried Ruud,
Jacob Herr,
George Schindler,
Christoph. Kioze,
Andreas Albrecht,
Ludwig Hubner,
Joseph Lemmert,
Gottlieb Lange,
Christian Petersen,
Adam Hossfeld,
Andreas Weber,
Andreas Seifert,
Christian Hoppner,
Jonh Seiffert,
Richd. Poppelwell,
John Merck,
Paul Schneider,
Michel Odenwald,
John Musch,
Joseph Hopsch,
Daniel Sydrich,
Andreas Rillmann,
Peter Drews,
Paul Hennig,
G. Wenzel Golkobsky,
Christian Wedstadt,
Jacob Rister,
Joseph Boeleu,
Joh. Andr. Borlnock,
Christ. Steiner,
John Heur. Grunewald,
Melchior Conrad,
Abraham Hasselberg,
Heurich Schoen,
H. Wm. Schemes,
Christ. H. Lolher,
Nic. Matthiesen,
Heurich. Lindemeyer,
Joh. H. Richling,
Phillips Meyer,
Johanes Ortlieb,
Abraham Andres,
John Stadtner,
Jens Sherbeck,
George Walter,
Phil. Wesa,
Marc. Kiefer,
Edward Thorpe,
Joseph Willis,
Christ. H. Baremeyer,
Samuel Saxon,
P. Christian Stauber,
Samuel Johannes,
Peter Jurgensen,

Carl August Ludwig,
Andreas Jæncke,
Just. Jansen,
Matth. Dacher,
Detloff Delffs,
Mich. Lindstrœhm,
Anton Stiemer,
Joseph Hubsch,
Aug. H. Francke,
Carl Weineke,
Martinus,
Henrich Zillman,
Jens Wittenberg,
Peter J. Pell,
Jacob Schneider,
Curtus Ziegler,
John Thomas,
Clau Colln,
Samuel Lank,
Jacob Meyer,
John Knecht,
Lucas Fus,
Lorenz Nilson,
Joh. H. Herbst,
Jacob Ernst,
John Klein,
Wm. Okely,
Wm. Edwards,
Michel Ruch,
John Jag,
John Rogers,
Abraham Bless,
Caspar Fischer,
Joseph Giersch,
John Wurtele,
Henr. Gerstberger,
Zach. Eckart,
Jens Kolkier,
Michel Munster,
Andreas Hotter,
Fredr. Ziegler,
Jacob Schœn,
Benjamin Brown,
Christian Giersch,
Henrich Seidel,
Schmaling,
Hans Jac. Schmidt,
Ernst Mensinger,
Casper Hellermann,
Ellert Korts,
Joh. Mich. Rippel,
John Rothe,
John B. Bœnighæus,
John Muller,
Michel Ruch,
James Staal,
Henr. Ollringshaw,
Jacob Frus,
John Nic. Funck,
Gottfr. Schwarz,
Lorenz Bage,
George Huber,
Joh. Mich. Bizmann,
Joh. G. Starck,
Martin Schenck,
Joh. G. Green,
Nic. H. Eberhard,

Peter Worbas,
Jacob Herrmann,
Adam Koffler,
Phil. H. Ring,
Matth. Gimmell,
Joh. G. Kriegbaum,
Jacob Heidecker,
David Kuntz,
John Hirst,
Martin Heckedorn,
Joh. Adam Wageneell,
Jon. G. Bitterlich,
Joh. H. Merck,
Abraham Steiner,
Martin Hirte,
Franz Chr. Diemer,
Joh. Theobald Kornman,
Carl Jac. Dreyspring,
Nic. Anspach,
Christian Schmidt,
George Lash,
Nic. Fleissner,
Matheus Kremser,
Joh. G. Masner,
Fr. Tollner,
Ludw. Dehne,
Marc. Ralfs,
Christoph Bambey,
Christoph Schmid,
Peter Wenzzl,
Dan. Kamm.
George Caries,
John Kalberlan,
Herman Loesch,
John Nagel,
Thomas Hofman,
George Holder,
Jacob Kapp,
Abraham Strauss,
George Goeptert,
Wm. Angel,
Ludwig Chr. Bachoff,
Michel Sauter,
Hans Petersen,
Gottlieb Fockel,
Jeremias Shaaf,

Adam Weidel,
Dorffer,
Henr. Strauss,
Stephen Nicholaus,
Christian Seidel,
Jacob Loesh,
Gottleb Hofmann,
Adam Van Erd,
Joseph Bulitschek,
Balthasar Hoge,
Jacob Prising,
Henr. Sproge,
Chr. Matthiesen,
Martin Fryhube,
Andreas Brocksh,
Johannes Schiffler,
Joh. H. Lenzner,
John Lisher,
Christian Pfeiffer,
Jacob Lung,
Fr. Pfeil,
Ehrhard Heckedorn,
Samuel Wutke,
Andreas Gros,
Christian Merkly,
Henr. Feldhausen,
Erich Ingergretsen,
John Berosh,
Christian Triebel,
Melchior Munster,
Melch. Rasp,
Johannes Ranke,
Andreas Bez,
Jacob Steiner,
Nic. Anspach,
Michel Rancke,
George Baumgarten,
John Richter,
George Renner,
Gottfr. Aust,
Adam Kramer,
Christoph Kirschner,
Stephan Meyer,
Jac. Van der Merk,
Joseph Muller.

V. SINGLE WOMEN.

Anna Rosina,
Anna Ramsberg,
Hannah Sperbach,
Rosina Schulius,
Juliana Weekler,
Catharina Beuder,
Anna Antes,
Christina Morhard,
A. Mar. Krause,
Margaretha Wernhamer,
A. Mar. Schnuter,
Margaretha Seidner,
Catharina Slingastiu,
Catharini Koonln,
Martha,   } Indians.
Theodora,   }
Anna Burnet,
Barbara Krausin,
Henrietta Peterman,
Martha Mans,
Mariana Beyerle,
Gertraud Peterson.
Elizabeth Burstier,
Anna Vander Bit,
A. Mar. Beyer,
Mar. Elis. Loesch,
Ana Schæfer,
Felicitas Schuster,
Magd. Mingo,
Catharina Heil,
Catharina Hotter,
Mar. Barbara Bierlch,
Maria Zerb,
Elizabeth Palmer,

Maria Pfingstag,
Elizabeth Cornwell,
Maria,   } Indians.
Christina, }
Mar. Elis. Minier,
Ana Merz,
Magdalena Schmidt,
Elizabeth Steiner,
Salome Burstier,
Catharina Biez,
A. Mar. Schemel,
Johanna Burnet,
Maria Loesh,
Regina Neumann,
Elizabeth Burnet,
Maria Beroth,
Mar. Barb. Hændel,
Rosina Schwarz,
Magdalena Rederberg,
Agnes Meyer,
Cathar. Klingenstein,
Christina Loesh,
Anna Bender,
Sarah Preis,
Cath. Elis. Neumann,
Magd. Steiner,
Cathar. Gerhard,
Johanetta Salterbach,
Magdalena Negro,
Ana Rebecca Langly,
Salome Dock,
Cornelia,
Anna Wright.

The single men and single women are
counted in the total 510, as children.

Prepared at Request of Gov. Denny, by
Rev. Mr. Spangenberg;—see Min. Dec. 8,
1756, Vol. VII. p. 353.

Memorandum.

1. Bethlehem makes out a certain Religious
Society intended for the Furtherance of the
Gospel, as well among the Heathen as Chris-
tians.

2. Forty-eight of the above mentioned
Brethren and Sisters are actually employed
for that End among the Heathen, not only
on the Continent of America, as Pensilvania,
New England, Barbice, Suriname, &c., but
also in Several Islands, as Thomas's, Crux,
John's, Jamaica, &c.

3. Besides them mention'd just now, there
are Fifty-four of them employ'd in the Pensilvania, New York, New England, Jersey &
Carolina Gevernments in preaching of the
Gospel, keeping of Schools, & the like.

4. Sixty-two of them are meerly employ'd
in the Education of our Children at Bethlehem & Nazareth as Attendants and Tutors.

5. Fourty-five Single men & 8 Couples of
married people, are gone to Carolina to make
a new Settlement there, and fifty-more, who
have come for that End from Europe, will
go there Soon.

6. There are Seventy-two of the above
mentioned Brethren in Holy Orders, viz:
Four Bishops, twelve Ordinaries (Priests,)
and the rest Deacons; And as many Acoluthi,
who are preparing for the Ministry in the
Congregation, and now and then are made
use of like Deacons.

7. About 90 of the Children at Bethlehem
& Nazareth have their Parents abroad, mostly
on the Gospel's Account.

8. 425 of those in the foregoing List are
under Age.

9. Not all who are named in this Catalogue
live in Bethlehem Township, but some in
Sackona, Some in Liehy, and Some in another Township joining Bethlehem Township.

10. There are 82 Indians besides those
young Indian Women who live with our
young Women, and besides the Savages who
are going and coming and Staying longer or
Shorter with us.

TIMOTHY HORSFIELD TO GOV. DENNY, 1756.

BETHLEHEM, Nov. 29, 1756.

May it Please Your Honour,

SIR :—According to your Commands, I herewith Inclose a list of the United Brethren & Sisters & Children, &c., &c., Now residing in Bethlehem, Nazareth, &c., &c., with proper Notes to Explain the Same, which I hope will be agreeable.*

I beg leave to mention to your honour, that a few Days Since as one of our Indians was in the Woods a small distance from Bethlehem, with his gun, hopeing to meet with a Deer, on his return home he met with two men, who (as he Informs) he saluted by takeing off his Hat; he had not gone far before he heard a gun fired, and the Bullet whistled near by him, which terrified him very much, and running thro' the thick Bushes his gun lock Catched fast, and went off, he dropt it, his Hat, Blanket, &c., and came home much frighted. The Indians came to me complaining of this treatment, Saying they fled from Amongst the Murthering Indians, and came here to Bethlehem, and Adresst his Honour the Late Governor, and put themselves under his protection, which the Governor Answered to their Satisfaction, Desireing them to sit Still amongst the Brethren, which they said they had done, and given offence to none. I told them I would do all in my Power to prevent such Treatment for the future, and that I would write to the Governor and Inform him of it, and that they might be Assured the Governor would use proper measures to prevent any mischief hapening. I thought at first to write a few Advertisements to warn wicked people for the future how they Behave to the Indians, for if one or more of them should be kill'd in such a manner, I feer it would be of very bad consequence; but I have since considered it is by no means proper for me to advertise, for as the Late Governor's proclamation of War against the Indians I conceive is still in force. I thought it my Duty to

* The remarks are recorded in Colon. Records, Dec. 8, Vol. VII., p. 353, but the names and letter are not, it is thought best to keep them together. This was prepared at Gov. Denny's request.

Inform your Honor of this Affair, and Doubt not you will take the matter into your wise Consideration.

I am with all Due Respect,

Your Honour's most Obed't,

Humble Servant,

TIMO. HORSFIELD.

To the Hon. Wm. Denny, Esquire.

TIMOTHY HORSFIELD TO GOV. DENNY, 1756.

BETHLEHEM, Nov. 30th, 1756.

John Holder came here this Evening from Allemangle, and Informed me that last Sunday Evening, ye 28th Inst. three Indians Came to the House of a certain Man Named Schlosser, and Nockt at the Door, the People within called who is there? Answer was made, A Good Friend; they Within not Opening the Door, they Nockt Again, they within not Opening the Door, they Nockt Again, they Within Answer'd Who is there? No Answer being made from Without, Then one of the Men Named Stonebrook, Lookt Out of the Window, When an Indian Discharged a gun and Kill'd him on the Spot. They then Open'd the Door, the Woman & 2 Children Endavering to Escape, and the Indians pursued & took Both the Children; One of the Men Fired at the Indians, and Saw One of them fall, when one of the Gairls he had possession of, Made her escape from him, but the other they took away; the Indian yt was fired at which fell Cryed out very Much, but in a Short time he got up and made off.

The above said Holder Informs me he had this Acco't from good Authority, said Schlosser's House is situated in Allemangle.

TIMO. HORSFIELD.

An old chronicler says that "During the Indian troubles in 1756 and 1757, Bethlehem was in great danger from the savages, every precaution was taken to guard against it. The town was surrounded by palisades, which were made by putting poles from 15 to 20 feet long, into the ground, close together and secured above by hickory withes. Watch towers were also erected, built of logs; one of these was back of Louis F. Beckel's store, and another north of the graveyard. Bethlehem was then the frontier town of the white settlements. Those settlers further north and west, came to the town for protection, in addition to several hundred christian Indians, making the number of stranger in our town about seven hundred, all of whom had to be fed and clothed. The whole male population took turns in watching, and everything was conducted as if the place were besieged; excellent discipline was kept up by bishop Spangenberg, and the preservation of the town was altogether owing to the precautions taken. One dark night, a sentinel fired at an object which refused to answer his hail, it proved to be an ox, but it was afterwards ascertained that his alarm had driven off a hostile band of Indians, who were approaching to assault the place.

The Moravians seemed to have had some lingering doubts, about even taking up arms to defend themselves, for the sentinels were ordered to fire at the legs of an approaching object. They were to wound and capture, and not to kill their foes.

THE MARRIED BRETHREN AND SISTERS' HOUSE, AND WATER TOWER,

BETHLEHEM, PA.

CHAPTER III.

THE MARRIED PEOPLE'S HOUSE.—THE INDIAN WARS OF 1755.—BENJAMIN FRANKLIN AS A GENERAL.—HIS ACCOUNT OF BETHLEHEM.— PENN'S WALKING PURCHASE THE CAUSE OF THE INDIAN TROUBLES.—LONGFELLOW'S BURIAL OF THE MINISINK.

THE picture at the head of this chapter, is a representation of the Married People's House, with the Water Tower attached, at its west end, which once stood on the knoll, now the site of the present large Moravian Church, at the corner of Main and Church Streets, in Bethlehem. The drawing, of which the wood cut is an exact copy, was made by Mr. Rufus A. Grider, of Bethlehem, from the original sketch of Mr. Oerter, now in possession of the Moravian Historical Society at Nazareth, Pa.

The Married People's House, was erected among the first buildings in the place, and built of logs, as was the Water Tower also. It was constructed for the use and occupation of the Married Brothers and Sisters, who were not permitted, during the first days of the settlement, to reside anywhere else. The Ministers and their wives lived together in the Gemein Haus. The house was also called by some, "the Ancestor's House;" although the German words were used, that is the correct meaning in English. Yet it was more generally called "the Married People's House." In Rondthaler's life of Heckewelder, page 33, it is referred to, thus, "The old School House has disappeared; it was a log building, erected on the spot where the church now stands; and this house and the apothecary's shop, were at that time the only buildings on the east side of Main Street. On the west side, was the "Farm," with its stables, and several other houses; the rest of the hill, and the whole of the site of the present town being covered with a dense forest." This was in the year 1754.

The Water Tower, which stood at the west end of the Married People's House, was the principal reservoir into which the water was forced from the celebrated spring, situated on Water Street, at the foot of the hill near the old Mill, to give it a head for distribution. From this tower all the lower part of the village was supplied with water. The same spring still furnishes all the water distributed in the town, by the Bethlehem Water Company. The Tower is said to have been as high as the steeple of the present church, but the statement is evidently erroneous, as can easily be seen from the copy of Mr. Oerter's drawing, and from the fact, that the water works were only calculated to raise the water seventy feet in perpendicular height, when first erected, in 1764, although the power was afterwards increased to one hundred and fourteen feet; besides which, the spring was at the foot of the hill, on the banks of the Menokasy, at least forty feet below the foundation of the Tower.

Crantz says, that Pennsylvania was very much desolated by the Indian War, which began in the year 1755. The first event which materially affected the Moravians, occurred on the evening of November 24, 1755, when the savages made an attack upon the house and plantation of the European Brethren, on the *Mahony*, near Gnadenheutten; eleven persons were killed in all, some of them shot and scalped, and the rest burnt. The buildings, cattle, furniture, implements and stock, were entirely destroyed. The Christian Indians, who lived on the other side the Lehigh, took flight, and most of them got safely to Bethlehem.

There was formerly a large Log house, standing on the west side of the Manokasy, opposite the old Tannery, in Water Street, which was called the "*Indian House.*" It was built in the early days of the settlement, as a lodging place for the Indian visitors, great numbers of whom constantly visited the town. In 1752, six hundred and eighty Indians visited the place, at different times during the year. In 1756 and '57, the number was much greater. Bishop Spangenberg, in a letter to Governor Denny, says:

"May it please your Honour,.

These are to return your Hnr, our most humble thanks, for the Favour of so kind a visit of yr Hnrs at Bethlehem. As we are a people, more used to the country, then to cities, we hope yr Hnr will excuse what may have been amiss. So much I can say, and this from the Bottom of my Heart, that yr Hnrs Person and Place or Station, is sacred unto us. We all do wish unanimously that yr Hnr may prosper, and meet with a blessed success in all undertakings for the good of this Province.

Mr. Horsefield having told us, that yr Hnr. wants a compleat catalogue of all men, women and children belonging to our oeconomy; I have ordred one to be made, and have added some Memorandums or observations, whch I hope will give you a clear idea thereof. I recommend my Self, and all my Brethren, who live in this Province, again in yr Hnrs Protection.

As for our circumstances, we are at a loss how to act with those Indians, that come out of the woods, and want to stay at Bethlehem. They are very troublesome guests, and we should be glad to have your Hnrs Orders about them. Our Houses are full already, and we must be at the Expences of building Winter-Houses for them, if more should come; which very likely will be the case, according to the account we have from them who are come. And then another difficulty arises, viz., we hear that some of our neighbors are very uneasy at our receiving such murdering Indians; for so they stile them. We therefore, I fear, shall be obliged to set watches, to keep of such of the Neighbours who might begin Quarrels with or attempt to hurt any of them.

Now we are willing to do any thing that lays in our power, for the Service of that Province, where we have enjoyed sweet pease for several years past. But we want yr Hnrs Orders for every step we take, and we must humbly beg not to be left without them; the more so, as we have reason to fear, that some how an Indian may be hurt or killed, which certainly would breed new Troubles of war. We had at least a case last week, that some one fired at an Indian of Bethlehem but a little way from Bethlehem in the woods.

I hope Mr. Horsefield will give y^r Hnr a particular account thereof, and so I will add no more.

Y^r Hnrs
Most humble and
Most obedient Servant,
SPANGENBERG.

Bethl., Nov. 20, 1756."

As the Bishop feared, so many Indians afterwards took refuge at Bethlehem, that it became necessary to assign them a piece of land, where, with the Brethren's assistance, they built themselves huts. The settlement was called *Nain*. The first house was erected June 10, 1757, and on the 18th of October, 1758, all the Indians were removed from Bethlehem to the town, and the "Old Indian Chapel" was consecrated. The war had retarded the progress of the buildings at first, but by the year 1760, the Indian inhabitants of Nain, had increased so rapidly that they could not all be supported there, and the Brethren were obliged to send a portion of them to a tract of land on the north side of the Blue Mountains, on the *Wechquatank*, about thirty miles from Bethlehem, where they could live by hunting, and dwell together under the direction of a missionary.

In January, 1757, public religious services began to be performed at Bethlehem, in the Indian language, the liturgy having been translated into the Mohican, by *Jacob Schmick*, the missionary. Part of the Scriptures, and many hymns, were translated into the Delaware Indian, for the use of the churches and schools.

The Moravian towns were great obstacles to the designs of the hostile savages, in their warfare upon the whites, because they could not prevail upon the friendly Indians to destroy the missionary establishments, nor prevent them from informing the Brethren when any attempt was to be made upon the settlements by the warriors, and thus many schemes were frustrated. Great numbers of whites, also, took refuge in the different Moravian places, being driven from their homes

by the fear of the Indians; most of these people were entirely destitute. Not only Bethlehem, but Nazareth, Friedensthal, Christiansbrunn and the Rose, were asylums for these fugitives; the houses of the Brethren were crowded, and the empty school-houses, mills and barns, were alloted to them for residences.

The Moravians, and their Indian converts, were peculiarly situated about this time. The hostile tribes were burning and destroying the white settlements on the Lehigh, while, on the other hand, the Irish inhabitants of the Kittatinny Valley, were exasperated at the Brethren for protecting the Indian refugees, and giving them an asylum; they also charged the Brethren with being in league with the French, because they would not take up arms, and engage in offensive warfare. They abused the missionaries, and threatened to kill the Indian converts, so that it was dangerous for the friendly Indians to leave the towns.

In the fall of the year 1756, the Government sent proposals of peace to the Indians, and a proclamation was issued at the same time, that all who were peaceably inclined, should have a safe escort to Bethlehem, Col. Croghan was very desirous that the Indians should be accommodated at Bethlehem, and the treaties held there, but the Brethren justly fearing that all kinds of disorders might take place among so many savages of different nations collected together, by which the Indian Brethren might be led astray, and their young people contaminated, they persistently refused, and induced the authorities to order that the treaty be held at Easton. Accordingly, in July and August, 1757, conferences were held with the Indians at *East-town*, and a treaty made in the name of the Ten Nations, with *Teedyuseung*, king of the Delawares, and three hundred other Indians, most of whom belonged to the Munsys and the Delawares.

During the time, however, that the Indians were at Easton, they made many visits to Bethlehem, and proved very troublesome visitors.

A gentlemen of Bethlehem has an old Day-book, of the " *Crown Inn*," in which the charges against some of the Indians, and the credits given them, are very amusing.

In the Penna. Archives, 3d volume, 242, will be found a list of the alterations in the return of the Brethren, dated July 26, 1757; but they are not of material interest; but the concluding part of the statement has a direct bearing upon the events of the times; it is signed by Matth. Schropp, and is as follows :

" The Widow Benezet, since the last Tax, has sold her two five hundred acre Tracts of Land, adjoining Bethlehem, to the Brethren for a £1000, and has taken a Mortgage on the same for the whole Consideration Money, they paying her yearly 6 ℔ cent. Interest, &c., as may be seen in the Publick Records. This the Brethren were induced to do that they might have a convenient Place, near Bethlehem, to place the Indians upon next Spring.

In these times of Trouble and Danger, being become the Frontier, the Brethren for the Defence of themselves and neighbours, have, under the Governor's Commission for that Purpose, established Military Watches in all their Places, and been at a very great Expense in providing themselves with Arms and Ammunition, and in strengthening and securing all their Houses and Plantations against any sudden Attack and Surprize from the Enemy.

In Bethlehem there are 5 Persons, namely, 2 Married, and 3 Singlemen constantly kept as a Night Watch, and thereby rendered wholly unfit for any Labour in the Day Time.

Besides the above there are 44 Singlemen and 25 married, who have Arms, and are always ready by night or Day in case of any Alarm.

In Nazareth there are 3 Persons who are kept as a constant Night Watch, Besides whom all the Inhabitants, mentioned in the return, except 7 Persons, are provided with Arms and Ammunition, and are always in Readiness for the Defence of themselves and neighbors.

In Gnadenthal there are 2 People employed as a Night Watch.

All the Inhabitants, except 5, have Arms and are kept in Readiness as aforesaid.

In Christian's Brun, there is one Singleman kept as a Night Watch, and 18 of the Singlemen have Arms as aforesaid, and frequently go out with some of the Indians, who are paid for that Purpose, in ranging Parties, for several miles round the neighborhood and in the Barrens, to see that no Indians are lurking about, if possible to prevent their coming upon them by Surprize.

In Friedensthal-Mill, They have all Arms and are constantly on their Guard and Watch by Turns.

Besides the above, the Brethren, for the Summer Season, have for the most Part thirteen of their Indians in Pay, whose Business it is with some of the white Brethren to range from Place to Place and be a Guard to their People in their Harvest and other work where they might otherwise be exposed to the Incursions of the Enemy.

Now, considering the above and the present helpless and exposed condition our poor Country has been and still is in, it may with modesty and Justice be said, that it is owing, in great measure, to this care and prudent Circumspection of the Brethren, that the whole Fort has not long ago been over run by the Indians; and therefore it is presumed a Relaxation of Tax proportioned to the Trouble and great Expence they have been at, cannot be contrary to the Sense of the Law, which expressly directs the making Allowances in *Extraordinary Cases*.

Added to this, the extraordinary Expence the Brethren are and must still be at, in maintaining the Indians, who fled to them from Gnaden-Hutten (now wholly thrown upon their Hands and left unprovided for by the Government,) for whose Subsistance alone, this year, they have been obliged to let them have upwards of 50 Acres of their best Land, (cleared and fenced for them at the Brethren's own Expence,) to plant their

Indian Corn, &c. Moreover the Badness of the Times and almost Total Stagnation of Business, are Hardships, which constrain the Brethren to declare, that they find themselves utterly unable to bear the Weight of the Tax as they have hitherto been rated, and therefore humbly beg the Hon'ble, the Commissioners and Assessors, will please to consider them accordingly, in laying the Tax not yet raised."

Benjamin Franklin, in his autobiography, writing of the eventful occurrences of the Indian Wars of that period, says :

" The Governor prevailed upon me to take charge of the North-western frontier, which was infested by the enemy, and provide for the defence of the inhabitants, by raising troops, and building a line of forts. I undertook this military business, although I did not conceive myself well qualified for it. He gave me a commission, with full powers, and a parcel of blank commissions for officers, to be given to whom I thought fit. I had but little difficulty in raising men, having soon 560 under my command. My son, who had in the preceding war, been an officer in the army raised against Canada, was my aid-de-camp, and of great use to me. The Indians had burned Gnadenheutten, a village settled by the Moravians, and massacred the inhabitants ; but the place was thought a good situation for one of the forts.

" In order to march thither, I assembled the companies at Bethlehem, the chief establishment of those people. I was surprised to find it in so good a posture of defence, the destruction of Gnadenheutten, had made them apprehend danger. The principal buildings were defended by a stockade; they had purchased a quantity of arms and ammunition from New York, and had even placed large quantities of small paving stones between the windows of their high stone houses, for their women to throw upon the heads of any Indians that should attempt to force into them. The armed Brethren, too, kept watch, and relieved as methodically as in any garrison town. In conversation with Bishop Spangenberg, I mentioned this to my sur-

prise, for, knowing they had obtained an act of Parliament, exempting them from military duties in the colonies, I had supposed they were conscientiously scrupulous of bearing arms. He answered me, that it was not one of their established principles, but that, at the time of their obtaining the act, it was thought to be a principle of many of their people ; on this occasion, however, they, to their surprise, found it adopted but by a few. It seems they were either deceived in themselves, or deceived the Parliament, but common sense, aided by present danger, will sometimes be too strong for whimsical opinions.

" It was the beginning of January, when we set out on this business of building forts. * * The Moravians procured me five wagons for our tools, stores, baggage, &c. * * * While at Bethlehem, I enquired a little into the practice of the Moravians, some of them had accompanied me, and all of them were very kind to me. I found that they worked for a common stock, eat at common tables, and slept in common dormitories, great numbers together. In the dormitories, I observed loopholes, at certain distances, all along under the ceiling, which I thought judiciously placed for change of air. I was at their church, where I was entertained with good music, the organ accompanied with violins, hautboys, flutes, clarinets, &c. I understood that their sermons were not usually preached to mixed congregations of men, women and children, as is our common practice, but that they assembled sometimes the married men, at other times their wives, then the young men, the young women, and the little children, each division by itself. The sermon I heard was to the latter, who came in and were placed in rows on benches, the boys under the conduct of a young man, their tutor, and the girls conducted by a young woman. The discourse seemed well adapted to their capacities, and was delivered in a pleasing, familiar manner, coaxing them, as it were, to be good.

" I enquired, concerning the Moravian marriages, whether the report was true, they were by *Lot*, and was told, that lots were used only in particular cases; that generally, when a young man found himself disposed to marry, he informed the Elders of his class, who consulted the Elder ladies, that governed the young women. As these Elders of the different sexes, were well acquainted with the tempers and dispositions of their respective pupils, they could best judge what matches were suitable, and their judgments were generally acquiesced in, but if, for example, it should happen that two or three young women were found to be equally proper for the young man, the lot was then recurred to. I objected, that if these matches are not made by natural choice of the parties, some of them may chance to be very unhappy. 'And so they may,' answered my informer, 'if you let the parties choose for themselves,' which, indeed, I could not deny."

The Indian troubles and wars, which began in 1755, were caused by the dissatisfaction of the *Minsi* and other Indian tribes, at the result of the " Walking Purchase," so called, and the encroachments of the whites upon their hunting grounds north of the Blue Mountains. Conrad Weiser, in a letter to the Governor, as early as April 22d, 1749, called his attention to the matter, saying : "The Indians are very uneasy about the white people settling beyond the *endless mountains.*"

Longfellow has written one of his characteristic effusions, (which, by kind permission of Messrs. Fields, Osgood & Co., of Boston, Mass., the publishers of Mr. Longfellow's Poems, is inserted here :) entitled

THE BURIAL OF THE MINISINK.

On sunny slope and beachen swell,
The shadowed light of evening fell;
And when the maple's leaf was brown,
With soft and silent lapse came down
The glory, that the wood receives
At sunset in the brazen leaves.

Far upwards in the mellow light,
Rose the *Blue Hills*, one cloud of white;
Around a far uplifted cone;
In the warm blush of evening shone;
An image of the silver lakes,
By which the Indian soul awakes.

But soon a funeral Hymn was heard,
When the soft breath of evening stirred
The tall gray forest; and a band
Of stern in heart, and strong in hand,
Came winding down beside the wave,
To lay the red chief in his grave.

They sang that by his native bowers,
He stood in the last moon of flowers;
And thirty snows had not yet shed
Their glory on the Warrior's head,
But as the summer fruit decays,
So died he in those naked days.

A dark cloak of Roebuck's skin
Covered the Warrior, and within
Its heavy folds the weapons made,
For the hard toil of war were laid,
The Cuirass woven of plaited reeds,
And the broad belt of shells and beads.

Before, a dark haired virgin train,
Chanted the death-dirge of the slain ;
Behind the long procession came
Of hoary men and chiefs of fame,
With heavy hearts and eyes of grief,
Leading the war horse of their chief.

Stripped of his proud and martial dress
Uncurbed, unreined and riderless,
With darting eye and nostril spread,
And heavy and impatient tread,
He came, and oft that eye so proud,
Asked for his rider in the crowd.

They buried the dark chief; they freed
Beside the grave his battle steed,
And swift an arrow cleaved its way
To his stern heart, one piercing neigh
Arose—and on the dead man's plain,
The rider grasps his steed again.

The history of the " Walking Purchase" is this :—William Penn, in 1686, bought of the Indians a tract of land, commencing on the line of his former purchases, and extending northwestwardly as far as a man could ride on horseback in two days; this was not carried out until 1737; when, at a Treaty held with Indians by the Proprietaries, Thomas and John Penn, on the 25th day of August, of that year, at Durham, near Easton, it was stipulated, that the purchase of 1686, be consummated by commencing at Wrights', in Bucks County, and terminating at a spot a man could reach in one and a-half day's walk. Edward Marshall, one of the walkers, started from Wrightstown at sunrise, on September 10th, 1737, and at sunset, had reached the foot of the Blue Mountains, and next day at noon had reached *Tobihanna* Creek. He walked 50 miles the first day. Although not an extraordinary performance, the Indians were terribly exasperated, as they had no idea of selling their land beyond the Endless Mountains; as it was, a rectangular line, drawn from the terminating point of the walk to the Delaware River, robbed them of nearly all the Minisink country, their favorite hunting ground. Their dissatisfaction at last ended in open warfare on the whites, in 1755, and Marshall's entire family were among the first victims.

Bethlehem is therefore within the limits of the Walking Purchase

In 1763, the frontiers were again overrun by the Indians. The massacre of the New England people at Wyoming, increased the fury of the white people against the Indians settled at Nain. On the 8th of November, 1763, the Moravian Indians there were sent to Philadelphia by order of the Governor, for protection. And the Indians from the Mission at Wyalusing, were also sent to the same place, for the same reasons, and all lodged in the Barracks.

Wechquatank was burnt by the white people on the night of November 18, 1763, and some incendiaries endeavored to destroy Bethlehem. The Oil Mill was set on fire, and entirely consumed, and the fury of the flames was such, that the adjoining Water Works were with difficulty saved.

Peace was finally concluded with the hostile Indians, in 1764, when the Moravian Indians returned in safety to Nain, Wyalusing and Bethlehem; but were soon after, in 1765, removed to the Susquehanna.

TꞮE "OLD MILL."—BUILT, 1751.—BURNED IN 1869.

BETHLEHEM, PA.

CHAPTER IV.

THE OLD MILL, BUILT 1751, BURNED IN 1869.
—THE BETHLEHEM WATER WORKS.—REVO-
LUTIONARY TIMES OF 1776.— WASHINGTON
AND BISHOP ETTWEIN.—PULASKI'S BANNER
—LONGFELLOW'S POEM.—VISIT OF WASHING-
TON.—LAFAYETTE.—MRS. REIDESEL'S AC-
COUNT.—MRS. FRIDAY.—COTTON.—THE FISH-
ERY.—MANUFACTURES.—MAIN ROAD TO OHIO.
—THE STONE RIDGE.—VIEWS AND SCENERY.

A T the head of this chapter will be seen
a correct view of the "Old Mill,"
lately destroyed by fire, which was considered, very justly, one of the most interesting curiosities in Bethlehem. It was made
from a photograph, taken by Moulton A.
Kleckner, residing in the town. He has
taken excellent pictures of all the old buildings of the place, and handsome stereoscopic
views of all the beautiful spots in the vicinity. He deserves much credit for the love of
art, and pride of place, which have induced
him to take and preserve for the future, so
many objects of interest.

The following pleasing account of the "Old
Mill," and the more ancient structure, erected by the Moravian Brethren, on the same
spot, is copied from *The Bethlehem Daily Times*,
of January 27th, 1869, a newspaper edited by
David J. Godshalk and Wm. Hackett, Jun.,
gentlemen who appreciate the historical
mementoes connected with the venerable
old town in which they live; and who take
pleasure in recording in their spirited daily,
all matters of interest concerning its antiquities, and its local history.

"*The Old Mill.—Built* 1751.—*Burned Jan.* 27,
1869.

The Moravians who settled in the Forks of
Delaware, in 1741, had the harvests of that
and the following year ground for bread, at
Nathaniel Irish's Mill, on Saucon Creek,
near its confluence with the Lehigh, (now
the site of Shimersville.) Mr. Irish was a man
of some note on the borders, an agent for William Allen, Esq., merchant of Philadelphia,
in the sale of lands, and a Justice of the
Peace of the county of Bucks.

The erection of so important a building as a grist mill, for an agricultural people, engaged in the establishment of an exclusive settlement, was taken in hand by the Moravians of Bethlehem, in 1743; and on the 25th of January of that year, a site for the structure was selected. In April the work was already under roof; on the 24th of June the machinery was put in running order, and on the 28th of June the first grist was ground. The wheaten loaf, eaten next day by the brotherhood, was altogether of their make. This achievement was a matter of congratulation to the infant settlement, as well as to the neighborhood, which in those days of scattered farms, embraced a wider area than at present. For, we are told, in February of 1847, there came *neighbors* from beyond the Blue Mountain, (adventurous German farmers who had hewed them farms in the very heart of the Indian country, on the borders of the Aquarishiccola and the Pocopoco,) to have the fruit of their toil converted into bread at the Moravian Mill. One Adam Schaus, else unknown to fame, was the first miller. He ran but one pair of stones; but they ground well, and won Adam a goodly reputation; and many came from the East and from the West, and most came from the ' North Countrie,' from the land of pines, and swamps, and scrub-oaks, to have their grain made into flour; and in 1744 there was taken from these barbarians, as the Greeks would say, toll as follows:

Of wheat, 222 bushels; of rye, 170 bushels; of Indian corn, 27 bushels; of buckwheat, 12 bushels; of barley, 2 bushels.

Mr. Henry Antes, of Frederic, (now Montgomery County,) descendants of whom are still residing in and about Pottstown, was the millwright employed by the Moravians in the construction of the mill in 1743. It was built of stone, and well-built, too, as was the fashion of those days; yet its walls gave way under the pressure of the swollen Manocasy, in the freshet of March 30, 1747; and although repaired, in the course of a few years it was thought advisable to supersede it by a new and large building.

Preparations for the erection of the second Moravian Mill, were made early in 1751. The masons began with the foundation-wall on the 14th of June, selecting the best of the limestone that was quarried on Nisky Hill, for this part of the work. As harvest was at the door, and the entire force of the settlement would be needed during its continuance, every nerve was strained to make headway in the important undertaking just initiated. By the end of August, the building was under roof, the works in running order, and on the 2nd of September, 1751, the first grist was ground by the mill, that ground its last, on the 27th of January, 1869.

The structure was 90 x 31 feet, and contained in addition to one run of stones for grinding grain, and a granary, a fulling mill, a clothiers shop, and a dye-house, all under one roof. The limestone was quarried in the Nisky quarries, and the laths sawed at the Gnadenhoch (now Christianbrun,) saw mill. Durham Furnace supplied the iron work of the machinery. The water wheel and mill stones were new. Above the former was the mill room. In May, 1753, a second run of stones was added. The ground floor was laid in tiles, the roof covered with the same material, and the building furnished with a sun dial and elevator.

Mr. John Jungmann, a well known missionary among the Indians, who died in Bethlehem on the 17th of July, 1808, tells us in his autobiography, he was the first miller in the mill of 1754.

During the French and Indian war, in 1755, and again in 1758, when the part of Bethlehem, long and still known as Water Street, and the workshops and institutes on Main Street, were palisaded and put into a state of defense from fear of surprises by hostile Indians, the old mill was the citidal within the city, crowded with panic stricken refugees from the unprotected frontiers.

When, in 1769, the Moravians in North America abolished the quasi communistic system of which Bethlehem had been the central point since 1741, the mill was worked for the benefit of the settlement solely, being one of a number of industrial pursuits retained as sources of revenue.

In 1830 it was purchased by Charles Augustus Luckenback, of the Bethlehem congregation of the United Brethren, and of him by Jacob Luckenback. The late proprietors, David & Andrew Luckenback, have the sympathy of the community in the calamity so suddenly befallen them.

In the sad loss of property occasioned by the disastrous conflagration of last night, is involved the destruction of another of the few remaining monuments of early Moravian domination in the forks of Delaware. The old mill carried us back further into the past than perhaps any other remaining old time landmark here, excepting the ' stone row' on Church Street. It weathered the storms of one hundred and eighteen years, and outlived the changes that have since then came over the country in which, and the association by which it was erected in 1751. Pennsylvania was then a loyal province of the British crown, and the Moravians in North America a society, in an extraordinary sense of the word, organized to a man for missionary activity. Its erection supplied the urgent want of the settlement, and proved a benefaction to the country around. It was always a busy place, the old mill down by the creek, with its face to the sunny South, and yet cool in the shadow of willows. It was always busy within with its whirring stones, and dripping wheel, and trembling hopper, that poured out untold wealth of golden grain, to be transformed into the staff of life; and I can even now see how busy the scene without already in the times of Adam Schues, the first of a long line of ' dusty millers,' where, on ' mill days,' a cavalcade of settlers from the outskirts of Pennsylvania civilization would dismount, and, tying their jaded beasts with rope halters, each shouldered his grist, and, as he crossed the threshold within the precincts of the famous Moravian Mill, did homage to the mysterious dial that stood sentinel above; and thus each succeeding generation repeated the busy scene without, with only a change of masks. But the life *within* the mill was the same; and this ceased when its restless hour glass, from which the golden grain of over a hundred years had poured in one continuous stream, was at last run out.

And because the life of the mill was a long life of good to the family of man, hence these chronicles and hence this pious requiem.

The original mill-stones, used in the ' old mill' when it was first erected, in 1743, were found by the Messrs. Luckenback, in removing the ruins left by the late fire."

The Water Works of Bethlehem, are celebrated as the first of the kind erected in this country. They were planned and constructin the year 1762, by a Danish Moravian, a resident of the village; *Hans Christian Christianson*, a shoemaker, and a native of the city of Copenhagen; and were first put in operation on the 21st of January, 1764. The machinery consisted of three single acting force pumps, four inch calibre, and eighteen inch stroke, worked by a triple crank, geared to the shaft of an undershot water wheel, eighteen feet in diameter, and two feet clear in the buckets. The total head of water was two feet. On the water wheel shaft was a wallower of thirty-three rounds, and gearing into a spin-wheel of fifty-two cogs, attached to the crank. The three pistons were attached each to a frame cross-head, working in grooves, to give them a parallel motion with the pump, the cross-head was wood, as well as the part containing the grooves, as guides. These works were in operation until 1832, when the present works were erected, and remodelled, upon the principle of the present Water Works at Fairmount, Philadelphia, where the *horizontal double forcing pump*, the design of Frederick Graeff, was first used in this country.

The first raising main of the Bethlehem works, was made of *Gum wood* as far as it was subject to great pressure, the rest of pitch pine. The first forcing pumps were made of *Lignum Vitæ*, the water was forced up into the Receiver, in the High Tower, at the west end of the " Brothers' and Sisters' House;" from thence it was distributed into *Water Boxes* or Cisterns, partly above ground, from which it was drawn off for use. The water-boxes mentioned, were six in number, and were situated at the following places.

1. In the yard of the Brethren's House.
2. In the yard of the Sisters' House, on Church Street, and still in use.
3. At Simon Rau's, still used.
4. In Market Street, opposite the Old Graveyard, and still in use.
5. In the Old Farm House Yard.
6. At the "Sun Hotel."

The first pipes laid for the conveyance of water, were of leather, but not proving very serviceable, wooden ones were soon substituted; in 1786 leaden pipes were introduced in their stead, and in 1813 these were changed for pipes made of iron, which are now used all over the town.

In constructing the first Water Works, a very curiously made *crank* had to be invented, in order to work the three pistons, it was at first thought to be impossible to make it, but a celebrated blacksmith of the place, named *Stephen Blum*, accomplished it, and gained great credit thereby.

The Spring from which the supply of water is obtained, is quite a curiosity in its way, and that it is able to furnish the constant demand, is a matter of astonishment to all who examine it, for it is a very small affair, not more than three feet square, and two feet deep, situated near the "Old Mill," on Water Street, opposite the "Old Tannery," yet, small as it is, and despite the constant use of its waters, there is never, even in summer time; any perceptible diminution in the quantity of water in the Spring; there being a constant, and almost imperceptible flow into it from some unseen source. And although in 1868, steam power was introduced to supply the increasing demand of the growing town, the Spring still continues full, without any signs of inability to meet all the wants of the inhabitants, except in cases of fires.

The lower Mill, where the forcing power is located, is the Mill where the celebrated Bethlehem buckwheat flour is made, which is in such demand in the cities of Philadelphia and New York. The forcing power was, previous to the year 1868, furnished by the water of the Manockasy Creek, which runs through that part of the town.

The water of the Spring is very cool and clear, slightly impregnated with lime, but not enough so as to affect its taste; it is perfectly healthful, very pleasant to the palate, and has no perceptible effect upon the human system, that is at all injurious. A large frame building is erected over the Spring, which is used by the people of the neighborhood, for the purpose of keeping cool and preserving their meats and butter, during the summer season, the water passing through it, keeping the building as cold as an ice house. The reservoirs in the town, into which the water is conveyed for distribution, are covered from the sun and dirt, so that it is carried to the houses, free from all impurities, and comes out of the supply pipes as clear as crystal, and does not need ice to cool it, even in the hottest days of summer.

Before the Water Works were erected there were many attempts made to obtain water, by digging wells, but as the hill on which the town is built, is formed of rotten lime-stone, all was labor in vain. There exists at present, in the middle of Broad Street near Main, one of those wells arched over, instead of being filled up; its exact position will be discovered unexpectedly some day.

The Rev. C. F. Seidel, thus speaks of the Revolutionary Times of 1776. "During the Revolutionary War, the Moravians were divided in opinion. The clergy mostly sided with the Tories, but a portion of the Brethren, and nearly all the Sisters, sided with the Whigs. Brother Ettwein, leader of the congregation, sided with the Whigs, and was a great friend of Washington. He was frequently consulted by the noble General, and the Bishop ever found a ready and a steadfast friend and protector in him.

"The people were prejudiced against the Brethren because they refused to bear arms. (The Moravians held it against their conscience to engage in offensive war, resisting armed force was regarded as a duty,) but when their position was explained, and their honest intentions made known to reasonable persons, no objection could be made to their course. They nursed the sick and wounded, gave up their houses for hospitals, and many even died from the contagious camp fever. They visited the sick, supplied them with clothing, and showed them every act of kindness. Religious services were held twice every week; but arms they would not bear, deeming it wrong to kill their fellow creatures."

"Bishop Ettwein, says: ' In those years, when the chief Hospital of the United States army was located at Bethlehem, I was a visitor to the sick, and a preacher in the Hospital, and preached twice each week to five or six hundred soldiers, and had the pleasure to observe good fruits.'

"Washington admired the character of the Moravians, and during an interview with Ettwein, expressed himself to that effect, saying : ' I wish I were a simple Moravian.' —'Bleib du wo du bist !'—stay where you are, answered the Bishop, ' you can do more good where you are.' The Bishop had great influence with Washington, he spoke in such a blunt, straight forward way, that he gained the General's good opinion. Washington detested unnecessary fuss.

"The Bishop was the first *Fremdindiener*, (i. e., Guide or Strangers' Friend,) in Bethlehem, from 1776 to 1779. An anecdote is told of him, which shows his active measures in religious affairs. While speaking to the congregation, during the Revolutionary War, on their duties to their God and their country, he remarked that they should not forget to pray for the Government, and ' Wir besser tathens gleich,' i. e., ' We had better do so at once !' and fell on his knees and poured out a fervent prayer for the protection of the Almighty over our country. Then, as now, the whole congregation done as their minister did, fell on their knees also. In prayer, none but those who are sick or disabled, are allowed to keep their seats."

Among the Archives of the Society, are preserved many original and valuable papers and letters; a copy of one of the letters is inserted here, as confirming the foregoing statements, and redounding to the credit of this ancient Church.

" BETHLEHEM, September 22, 1777.

Having observed a humane and diligent attention to the sick and wounded, and a benevolent desire to make necessary provision for the relief of the distressed, as far as the powers of the Brethren enable them ; we desire that all Continental officers may refrain from disturbing the persons or property of the Moravians in Bethlehem, and particularly, that they do not disturb or molest the Houses where the Women are assembled.

Given under our hands, at the time and place above mentioned.

JOHN HANCOCK,	RICHARD HENRY LEE,
NATHAN BROWNSON,	HENRY LAURENS,
NATHANIEL FOLSOM,	WILLIAM DUER,
CORNELIUS HARNETT,	RICHARD LAW,
BENJ. HARRISON,	SAMUEL ADAMS,
JOHN ADAMS,	JAMES DUANE,
HENRY MARCHANT,	ELIPHALET DYER,
JOSEPH JONES,	WM. WILLIAMS.

Delegates to Congress."

The " Brethren's House" was taken as the Army Hospital, of course the Society objected, but in vain, and the Brethren had to live with their friends and relatives in the town, a necessity which finally led to the entire abandonment of the custom of the Single Brethren all living together in one establishment, although not till some time thereafter, for it was not till 1815, that the " Brethren's House" was handed over for the use of the Girls' School, and occupied that year for its new purpose, for which it is still used, being the centre building of the Seminary, fronting on Main Street.

It was on the 3rd of December, 1776, that the General Hospital of the American army was established at Bethlehem, and on the same day, Doctors Warren and Shippen arrived, and took possession of the " Brethren's House," and made arrangements for 250 sick soldiers, who came into town the next day, gaunt, destitute and famishing, and had not the people supplied them with food, many would have perished, no government supplies having arrived. During the winter, 110 of the soldiers died; and were buried near where Levin J. Krause's large barn now stands, on the west bank of the Manockasy, on the north side of the road leading to Allentown.

On the 17th of December, General Lee's division of the army, consisting of 3,000 men, reached Bethlehem, and encamped for the night on the south side of the river, General Sullivan in command.

On September 2d, 1777, " The Large Family House," was taken for quarters for 260 English prisoners; the Brethren objected, but without avail. On the 23rd, the whole of the heavy baggage of the army arrived at the place for winter quarters, the train consisted of 700 wagons, and an escort of 200 men, under the command of Colonel Polk. And the " Brethren's House" was again used as a hospital till June, 1778.

In the history of Lehigh Valley, it is written that, " In consequence of the removal of the hospital to Bethlehem, in 1776, the place was visited by many persons of distinction, among whom were General Washington, the Marquis de La-Fayette, Count Pulaski, Baron De Kalb, Generals Armstrong, Gates, Mifflin and Schuyler, John Hancock, Henry Laurens, Benjamin Franklin, John Adams and others."

" It was during this time that Count Pulaski was complimented for his gallantry, by a presentation of a banner, embroidered by the ' *Single Sisters*,' as a token of their gratitude for the protection he had afforded them, surrounded as they were, by rough and uncouth soldiery. The banner was made of crimson silk. On one side the capitals U. S. are encircled by the motto, ' *Unitas Virtus fortier*,' on the other side, the all-seeing eye of God, in the midst of thirteen stars of the Union, is surrounded by the motto, ' *Non alius regit.*' These designs were embroidered with yellow silk, the letters shaded with green. A deep green bullion fringe ornaments the edges; the size of the banner was twenty inches square. It was attached to a lance, when borne in the field. The banner was received by Pulaski with grateful acknowledgments, and borne by his regiment through the campaign, until he fell in the attack upon *Savannah*, in the autumn of 1779. It is now in the possession of the Maryland Historical Society at Baltimore. Longfellow has immortalized the incident in a beautiful poem, which is printed by permission of his publishers, Field, Osgood & Co., entitled the

HYMN

Of the Moravian Nuns at Bethlehem at the consecration of Pulaski's Banner.

" When the dying flame of day,
Through the chancel shot its ray,
Far the glimmering tapers shed,
Faint light on the cowled head;
And the censer burning swung,
Where before the Altar, hung
The blood red banner, that with prayer
Had been consecrated there,
And the nuns' sweet hymn was heard the while,
Sung low in the dim mysterious aisle.

" Take thy banner! May it wave
Proudly o'er the good and brave;
When the battle's distant wail,
Breaks the Sabbath of our vale;
When the clarion's music thrills
To the heart of these lone hills,
When the spear in conflict shakes,
And the strong lance shivering breaks.

" Take thy banner! and beneath
The battle cloud's encircling breath,
Guard it! till our homes are free!
Guard it! God will prosper thee!
In the dark and dying hour,
In the breaking forth of power,
In the rush of steeds and men,
His right hand will shield thee then.

" Take thy banner! but when night
Closes round the ghastly fight,
If the vanquished warrior bow,
Spare him! by our holy vow,
By our prayers and many tears
By the mercy that endears,
Spare him! he our love hath shared!
Spare him! as thou would'st be spared!

" Take thy banner! and if e'er,
Thou should'st press a soldier's bier,
And the muffled drum should beat
To the tread of mournful feet,
Then this crimson flag shall be
Martial cloak and shroud for thee.

" The warrior took that banner proud,
And it was his martial cloak and shroud."

The piece is very beautiful, but it is very certain that Longfellow never visited Bethlehem, or any other Moravian town.

An old Sister, writing of Revolutionary

times, says: "General Washington visited Bethlehem but once, he intended coming a second time, but did not do so. When here he visited the manufactories of the Society. The Woollen and Fulling Mill, (then in the old mill on Water Street,) the 'Brother's House,' the 'Sister's house,' and everywhere that manufactories were established. At the 'Sister's House,' he stood for some time in the southeast room, now occupied by Sister Sally Horsfield, he expressed himself much pleased with the product of their industry, and desired to purchase a dress for Lady Washington, but the Sisters presented him with the materials for one for her, a dress pattern of 'blue stripe.' His officers purchased finery, but the general supplied himself with useful articles, among which were two pairs of stockings."

James Hall, in his manuscript, says, he remembered Washington well, that he visited Bethlehem twice, and was welcomed by the music of trombones, playing in the belvedere on the "Brethren's House."

La-Fayette came to the town on the 20th of September, 1778. Charles Beckel, in his journal, says: "This young French general lodged at our house. He had been wounded in the foot at the battle of Brandywine. I had an aunt, who was then about 17 or 18 years of age. She was the Marquis' nurse. Being very handsome and lively, my grandfather became very uneasy for fear of her forming an intimacy with the volatile and witty Frenchman."

Mr. Beckel lived in the house now occupied by Rauch, as a confectionery store.

Frederica Von Massow, the beautiful wife of Major-General Riedesel, who commanded the German Auxiliaries, (Brunswicker's,) in Burgoyne's Army, at the time of its capture at Saratoga, during the Revolution, thus speaks of Bethlehem in her published Letters and Journals, page 163. "After leaving York, Pennsylvania, we rode through a magnificent country, and passed among others, a very well cultivated section inhabited by the Moravian Brethren; one place is called the Holy Sepulchre, and another district goes by the name of the

Holy Land, in which is a town called Bethlehem, where we found a right good tavern.

"In Bethlehem, as in all other Moravian communities, there are separate houses for the Brethren and Sisters. In the latter establishment they made magnificent embroidery, and other beautiful handiworks, and we bought at these places several articles. A Miss Girsdorff, a German, who afterwards resided at Hernhut, had taught the Sister's all these kinds of work. The houses of this community are well built, and there were at this place all sorts of manufactories. Among others there was one which dressed leather, which was as good as that of England, and half as cheap. The gentlemen of our party bought a quantity of it. There were also very clever cabinet makers, workers in steel and excellent smiths. While at Bethlehem we went to church, and enjoyed the splendid singing."

During, and after the Revolution, says Mrs. Friday; times were very hard, wages poor, little to do, and everything high; 4-4 chintz sold at $3 per yard. Tea was a luxury none could enjoy. The sisters collected herbs in order to test them as a substitute for the tea-plant. Tea was three dollars a pound, Continental money. A species of *Sumac* berries were used to flavor meats with, as salt was not to be had, and provisions were of a very bad quality; even as late as 1820.

"Cotton was not then raised in the United States, but was brought from Jamaica, and the best from St. Thomas, W. I. The price per pound paid for new cotton averaged about 50 cents; soon after the Revolutionary War. Among the Sisters, spinning, weaving and needle work, were the sources of revenue. West India cotton was spun for the city and home markets, the cotton had first to be pulled apart, and the seeds had to be picked out, then (secondly,) carded into flakes, and (thirdly,) into rolls by hand, by means of a spindle. Cotton so prepared, was much stronger than when machine manufactured. Working cotton, knitting cotton and thread were also made; to earn seven cents a day was considered much.

"Board at the "Sister's House" cost seven shillings and three pence per week; including board for dinner, rent, night watch, sick room, and the privilege of taking boiling water. Breakfast and tea they found for themselves."

Fish were caught in the Lehigh in great quantities. Shad were caught between the Islands and opposite Nisky Hill; they sometimes sold at two cents each, and very large fish; many were salted down in barrels. The Lehigh abounded in shad and bass. In the Church Diaries of Bethlehem there is frequent mention of the fact. In the year 1741, the statement is made, that, "at the end of August we were blessed with such abundance of Rock Fish, as to enable us to provide for our guests and friends in profusion." In May, 1752, one thousand shad were taken on the 10th of the month. May 18, 1785, nine hundred shad were caught. May 5, 1786, seven hundred. May 21, 1787, "fished for the last time this season and caught one hundred and eighty shad and thirty rock fish." The fishing ground used to be below the upper bridge, the fish being driven into a pond opposite Mr. Beckel's foundry; this mode of capturing the shad was learned from the Indians; and is described fully by Loskiel, in his "History of the Indian Mission."

The Manockasy and Saucon creeks were both at one time celebrated for their fine trout. Some are yet occasionally caught in both streams.

The Manockasy takes its name from the tribe of Minissink Indians who once hunted on its banks, and is a corruption of the name of that tribe.

Wafers seem to have been a scarce commodity in Revolutionary times, judging by the following order from the Honorable Executive Council of *Pensilvania.*

PHILADELPHIA, April 5, 1779.

SIR:—I must beg the favour of you to send by the first good opportunity, half a pound of common sized wafers, 500 for the Great Seal, and 500 or 1000 for the less seal of the State, and I will pay you, or your order for them on demand.

I am, with great respect, your F'd and Hon'ble Servant,

T'Y MATLOCK, Sec'y.

Directed.

Rev'd John Ettwein, at Bethlehem.

The manufactories of the Moravians in those early times, made them independent of the outside world. They raised hemp, flax and wool, grain of all kinds, from which they made starch, flour, and the buckwheat meal, which is celebrated even in this our day. From the flax they made Linseywoolsey, for the females to wear, and the woolen for winter, with the changeable stripe or plaid of two colors, blue and red. These same goods, when fulled, were worn by the men and boys. They had good weavers, even in the "Sister's House." Letters are still preserved, which contain orders from merchants in Philadelphia, directing goods to be made for their wives.

Sister Langley, an English Sister, had charge of the "Sister's House," and they produced some very handsome and superior needle-work. Dyeing, spinning, fulling, weaving, bleaching on grass, making glue and tanning were carried on to a much greater extent than at the present day.

The first Tile and Brick Manufactory was established soon after the settlement of the town, in 1742, at a place about a mile north of Bethlehem, on the Manockasy Creek, on the farm now owned by B. G. Unangst, on the opposite side of the creek from his mill, and near the Indian town; it was then known as Queer's place. The first bricks used in Bethlehem were made at this place; afterwards tiles were made in the town at the house now occupied by D. Henry Bishop, at the corner of the Main Street and the road leading to Allentown. Earthenware was also extensively made, and in great demand. An applicant was asked, "How many cows have you got?" and if more were asked for than deemed necessary, told, "You must do with less."

In those days an old finger post stood in the open space opposite Bishop's store, pointing down the hill along the narrow, winding road, between the two old stone houses, leading west to Allentown, with the following very indefinite direction inscribed upon it in quaint old fashions letters.

"MAIN ROAD TO OHIO."

A journey to Ohio in those days was a very serious matter, as it took from three weeks to a month's time, according to the mode of travel, on horseback, or by a Connestoga wagon. Now the guide post says, "To Reading 40 miles."

The stone used for erecting most of the old stone buildings, and for the Old Chapel and the Church, was brought from the mountain to the southwest of the "Islands," at the present day known as the *Stone-ridge;* it acquired that name from the German word to slide, (*Die stein rütscht.*) Immense quantities of good building stone were there lying loose on the side of the hill, and it was only necessary *to slide* them down to the water's edge, float them across the river on flat boats, and haul them into town for use.

Houses in the olden times were built with great labor, no saw mills existed, the heavy logs were all dressed by the axe, even the studs for the partition walls had to be cut and dressed in the same manner, the plastering laths were split with the axe, the boards and laths were sawed with a whip saw, the wood used for all purposes was oak. The excellence of the work of the mechanics even in those rude times, was surprising, no such substantial buildings are erected now. All the other necessary work was done in the town.

The mortar used in the old building has often created surprise, after over an hundred years, all of it is still in as good condition as when first put on, despite its exposure to the weather all that time, and the plastering inside the houses is smooth and hard, and has not chipped off, as it does in modern houses in a few years. This, however, is easily accounted for; in the old times people were not in a hurry, they made haste slowly. The mortar was prepared in the fall of the year, in a pit in the ground, where it remained all winter, covered only by a few boards to keep out the dirt, so that all the lime became *thoroughly slacked* by exposure to the weather, and when used, it became as soon as it was dry, a cement as hard almost as stone.

The view of Bethlehem and the surrounding country from Rauch's mountain farm, back of the *Stone-ridge,* is very fine. The Blue Mountains, about seventeen miles distant, lie in the form of an arc of a circle, distinctly visible, with that peculiar blue haze hanging over them, from which they derive their name, with indentations in their otherwise regular formation, known as the *Lehigh Water-Gap,* The *Little Gap,* and the *Delaware Water Gap.* In the centre of the picture looking north, half hid by a high projection of land, called the *Camel's rump,* lies slumbering the Moravian town of Nazareth, plainly visible to the naked eye. To the right, and almost at the foot of the mountain, lies Moravian Bethlehem, and her lovely islands; between and around which winds the clear waters of the beautiful Lehigh; on the north bank of which is seen the canal and railroad of the Lehigh Navigation Company; and on the south, the Lehigh Valley Railroad; while the broad expanse of the "Dry Lands," with its now richly cultivated fields, and its clumps of woodland, lie mapped out before the looker-on, forming a scene of surpassing beauty.

The high hills around Bethlehem in the month of October, present a scene of gorgeous beauty almost beyond description. The foliage of the trees contain all the tints of the rainbow, but are even more beautiful, if that is possible, because the colors are more diffused. Some trees, the pine, the hemlock and the laurel, still retain their vivid green. The sycamore, its sombre brown; the maple, the beauty of the wood and valley, is particolored, its leaves green at first, soon turn into a brilliant red and yellow; the sturdy oak is clothed in purple; the gum is dressed in brilliant red; the sumac bushes are covered with leaves of brightest crimson; the beech, with those of a delicate pale yellow, almost white; the chesnut, a buff;

while the noble hickory hangs with golden pendants; the dog-wood has its deep rich red leaves, and clusters of berries, of a brighter red.

Walking one day of perfect beauty, in the Old Cemetery, during the time when the Lehigh hills wore their glorious autumnal livery, and the sun threw his golden light upon them:

> —— " Through a smoke,
> As from a thousand wigwams tells,
> The Indian Summer." ——

and wanting some one to share my pleasure, I said to the Old Moravian grave-digger and overseer, Schmidt, busy at work near by, how beautiful the mountains look to day ? " Yah! Yah!" he replied, " They look just like calico."—and so they did.

The splendor of the sunsets at this season of the year, are only equalled by those of the spring months; and for a wonder, the inhabitants seem to enjoy those grand displays of nature as much as the visitors.

THE "CROWN TAVERN."
(From the North.)
BETHLEHEM, PA.

CHAPTER V.

THE "CROWN INN."—THE SUN HOTEL.—MAR-
RIAGES IN OLDEN TIMES.—THE CHOIRS.—
DR. JOHN SCHOPF'S ACCOUNT OF HIS VISIT.
—A SKETCH FROM THE BOSTON MAGAZINE
OF 1784.—EXTRACT FROM A PAPER READ
BEFORE THE HISTORICAL SOCIETY OF PENN-
SYLVANIA.

THE first Tavern in Bethlehem was the "Crown Inn," a view of which heads this chapter, made from a drawing by Mr. Rufus A. Grider. It was built in 1743, near where the old Lehigh bridge now spans that river, on the southern bank of the stream. In 1794, on the completion of the bridge, the Inn was converted into a farm house. It stood on the lands of the "Crown Farm," so called, which consisted of 1200 acres; and from that circumstance took its name. While a Tavern, it was kept by Ephraim Culver, in 1763, and afterwards by Valentine Fuehrer. The old Inn was torn down in 1854, and its former site is now occupied by the new Union depot of the North Pennsylvania and Lehigh Valley railroads. Previous to the erection of the bridge, there was a Rope Ferry over the river at this point, under the charge of Massy Warner.

The Ferry across the river was of such particular contrivance, that a flatboat, large enough to carry a team of six horses, run upon a strong rope, made fast on each bank, and stretched across the river; and by the mere force of the stream, without any other assistance, it crossed the river backwards and forwards; the *Flat* always being put in an oblique direction, with its foremost end verging towards the line described by the rope.

In the year 1760, the Brethren completed the erection of the "Sun Hotel." It was originally kept by Matthias Schropp, and its first license is dated June 20, 1760. There are many incidents connected with this famous hostelrie, that should not be forgotten. Nearly all the patriots who signed the Declaration of Independence, have eaten and slept beneath its roof. Washington, Lafayette, Pulaski, and many other great generals of our Revolutionary army, have partaken of its cheer; all of our Presidents have passed beneath its hospitable portals; Lincoln, Johnson, and Grant, only excepted; and the fairest and proudest daughters of America, have graced its halls with their charms. It is one of the most famous Inns in all this fair land of Liberty, and although little is left to remind the traveller of its appearance in ancient times, it is still as celebrated as in days of yore.

In 1777, Just Johnson was the landlord of the "Sun," and upon making application for the renewal of his license for the next year, it was granted on condition that he took the *Test Oath;* this he refused to do. The "Test law," which passed in 1777, rendered it obligatory on every man over 21 years of age, to take the oath of allegiance to the United States. About 60 of the Brethren refused to stand the test; professing to have conscientious scruples against taking an oath. The Ministers and the older Brethren opposed the taking of the obligation, while the younger members of the church subscribed willingly; this created great excitement in the church. In 1786, after the war was over, Johnson, and the other 68, took the oath; having forgotten that they were scrupulous.

Johnson was a man of a powerful frame, a host! within himself. Christian Grubb, an iron master of Lancaster County, having heard of Johnson, and being himself notorious for his great strength, and also a celebrated boxer, visited the "Sun," on purpose to get up a fight with the giant Moravian Brother; but it was not until he had been grossly insulted, that Just lost his good temper; then, suddenly seizing Grubb by his breeches and his coat collar, he threw him over the iron railing of the tavern porch, (which were some feet from the ground,) to

the pavement below, saying, "God bless meiner soul, I drows you over de bannisters." Grubb was quite a heavy man, and being very good natured in the main, was satisfied with Johnson's display of strength, told him who he was, and why he had visited Bethlehem, and so together they made themselves merry over the occurrence.

The "Sun" was also the "head-quarters" of that famous land speculator, Nicholas Kraemer, of Allentown; who held weekly "*courts*" there from 1800 to 1817. He bought and sold lands at exorbitant prices, and in immense quantities. Sellers and buyers met here in great numbers at the "Sun" on his meeting days. He was well acquainted with the value of all the lands in the surrounding counties, and his purchases were made at once; in selling he named his price instanter, and never varied. He was entirely uneducated, and could not write his name or even draw a figure, yet he could reckon up his purchases or calculate his loss or gain, mentally, in a few moments. His liberality was proverbial; on his *court days*, as they were called, he paid all the expenses at the Hotel, amounting often to hundreds of dollars. His bills at the "Sun" amounted to thousands every year. The moneyed troubles of 1817 entirely ruined him, and he died quite poor.

In 1835, a third story was added to the original structure; in 1850 it was further enlarged for the accommodation of the increased travel, by the addition of the present extensive back building, and in 1857, it was again enlarged, by adding a fourth-story to the entire building, so great was the demand for rooms by summer visitors to the town, and the growing travel arising from the opening the rich products of the Lehigh Valley to a market, by the different railroads built and projected through it.

The old building, as it appeared in former days, no longer greets the eye of the traveller; but the curious may see, neatly framed, and hanging in the reading-room of the hotel, the original plan and elevation of the ancient famous structure; this careful preservation of old relics, has been from the early

3

days of its settlement, a peculiar feature of the people of the ancient church who settled the town.

"Sister Sally Horsfield," thus describes a wedding in Bethlehem in 1780.

"The couple were married in the 'Old Chapel,' which was open to the whole congregation. After the ceremony, the friends and the invited guests proceeded to the small chapel, (*Kleine Saal*,) which was in the second-story of the '*Gemein Haus*.' The Brothers and Sisters walked in and sat down on benches without leans to them, each sex separate. The bride and groom proceeded to the minister's room, which was in the same house; where the bride was divested of her rose-colored ribbon, and a blue one placed instead. The newly married couple then proceeded to the Chapel again, taking their seats in the face of the congregation, when wine, diluted with water, into which nutmeg was grated, was handed to them and the guests. When they entered, all eyes were fixed on the bride, in order to see whether she had lost her ribbon. The cake eaten with the wine was pretzel."

The females were divided into five choirs, each choir having its distinctive ribbon, the order was as follows:

Children wore in their caps cherry or scarlet—girls wore coclico or crimson—single sisters pink or blossom—married sisters light blue—widows wore white ribbon. Thus, all classes could easily be distinguished by the color of the ribbon they wore on their caps. The Elders of the choir were called choir laborers.

Seats without leans to them were invented to keep the worshipers from going to sleep, an excellent remedy; yet improved upon in some churches in ancient days, by having the seats of the benches revolve on pivots, so that to slumber and nod, gave the sleepy victim a violent start, or if the only one on the seat, a fall over backwards.

The large Moravian church till 1868, had hard wooden benches, of unpainted pine, with backs to them, for the congregation to sit on, very primitive in style, very disa-

greeable to look at, and exceedingly uncomfortable to sit upon. But as there was no earthly reason for continuing the use of such back breaking machines, and it being admitted that true religion does not require us to do penance in church, more agreeable arrangements have been made, adding much to the beauty of the interior of the building, and giving more comfort to the congregation.

Dr. John Schopf, in his book entitled, "*Incidents of Travel, &c., in* 1783 *and* '84." Thus relates his visit to Bethlehem.

"From a distance it rises most impressively on the traveller's view, and after having passed the last half of the way from Philadelphia through a tedious sameness of forest and underwood, with only an occasional lowly cabin, the effect is almost overpowering, on suddenly seeing before him in an anticipated wilderness, stately buildings, rising aloft, side by side. There are upwards of fifty (50) houses in the village. The principal building is imposing, large, and has two wings. One of the latter contains a capacious place of worship, and furnishes a place of residence for the ministers.

"In the centre is the school for children, and in the right wing the sisters live. Opposite stands the Widow's House, and further down the street the Brethren's House. These, and all the other buildings, are constructed of the limestone of the neighborhood. An air of superlative cleanliness prevades the Sister's House, spinning, weaving, knitting and embroidery, occupy the time and attention of its inmates. The Single Brethren are employed with various trades. In short, the arrangement of these houses is the same as that adopted in similar institutions of the Moravian Brethren in Europe, bearing the impress of order and industry.

"The congregation numbers about 500 souls, the majority of whom are Germans. There are but few English; and yet almost every individual is conversant with both languages,—so much so, that a discourse in the English language is held each Sunday. As most of the Brethren, and especially their minister, are of Saxon origin, it is a matter of no surprise that the purest and most cor-

"THE OLD SUN TAVERN,"
BETHLEHEM, PA. (Rebuilt.)

rect German of which America can boast, is spoken here at Bethlehem, and in the other Moravian settlements.

"The Right Rev. John Etwein and the Rev. John Andrew Heubrer, are at present the acting clergymen. The former was absent. In the latter I found an agreeable and amiable gentleman. He is an ardent lover of botany, but his pastoral duties leave him little leisure for the prosecution of this science. Dr. Otto attends the community in the three-fold capacity of physician, surgeon and apothecary. There is only one INN, and it belongs to the congregation. Its accommodations are not inferior to those of the first hotels in America. Everything about the establishment is excellent, and the traveller is surprised at finding in this remote and secluded village, what he cannot obtain in towns as large, and even larger, on the public highways. The house is seldom without visitors, in addition to transient travellers. Philadelphians are wont to make excursions hither, with the two-fold object of viewing the institutions and social arrangements of the congregation, and also enjoying the superior entertainments afforded by this house. While sojourning under its hospitable roof, I made the acquaintance of Baron Hermelin, an able Sweedish mineralogist, who had come from Europe to examine American mines.

"In the spring of the year the Lehigh is wont to swell considerably, from heavy rains and sudden thaws,—according to the gauge at the Brewery, generally from seven to eight feet, and on one occasion, as much as eleven feet. These freshets frequently continue for some days, and aid flat-boats laden with grain and produce, to pass over the rocks and shallows, which usually render the river unnavigable for such craft. The Lehigh empties into the Delaware, and affords by these spring freshets a convenient communication with Philadelphia.

"In the Lehigh and its tributary creeks are found muscles, which occasionally contain tolerably large and pure pearls.   *   *   *   On the banks of the Lehigh, around which gather in bewildering beauty, all the fasci-nations of a truly delightful region, are crowded together a number of the most beautiful North American shrubs and trees, which, with their shadow and boughs overhanging the banks far into the stream, impart to the picture a glow of richest exuberance.   *   *   *   The river does not exceed a hundred yards in breadth—a gentle, clear and sparkling stream, flowing over a rocky bed.

"We visited the interesting factories and mills belonging to the Society, and among these was a well-arranged Oil Mill and Grist Mill. The former is newly built, on the site of an old one, which was destroyed by fire a few years ago. On the upper floor of the Grist Mill is a crane, in connection with the mill works, by which the heaviest burdens are raised aloft. There is besides, a profitable tannery, with the requisite bark-mill, and an extensive dyeing establishment.

"As Bethlehem lies high on a limestone ridge, it is supplied with water from a single spring, which, however, is never failing and pure. It lies far down in the valley, near the river. The Water Works are admirably contrived.   *   *   *   *   *   *   *

"Near the river is an ingeniously arranged brewery, erected under the superintendence of Sigmund Leshinsky. The water used in the brewery is pumped from the Lehigh. The boiler is at such an elevation, that the boiling water flows downward over the malt, and is thence pumped by hand into the vat which contains the hops, from here the infusion is drawn off in pipes leading to the cooling vat, and finally led by others into casks in the cellar immediately below; these arrangements, under one or two men, sufficed for all the necessary work. The malt is dried in the air. The beer is of superior quality.   *   *   *   *   *"

The author of the following sketch, copied from the Boston Magazine, for May, 1784, (lately reproduced in the Moravian,) not having properly understood the purposes of the different Moravian establishments at Bethlehem, has made it in many particulars almost as absurd as parts of Longfellow's imaginative poem on Pulaski's Banner.

There is no such a person as an Abbess, connected with the "Sister's Houses" of the Moravians, in any part of the world. They were of course, under the charge of an Eldress or Matron. They did not live in seclusion, and although the rules were strict in former days as regards the association with the other sex, they visited their relatives, received visits, walked out every day, and at a proper age got married, if they felt so disposed, which most of them did. The death-like paleness of the Sisters, existed in a great measures in the writer's imagination, although it is a well-known fact, that the complexions of the inhabitants of mountainous parts of North America, do not become tanned by exposure to the weather, like that of those who live in the lowlands, and on the river and seashores. And in regard to their want of exercise, the writer forgets how the Sisters worked in levelling the Minister's garden.

The peculiar dress which the women wore, was, in reality, one of the fashions of that day. Every religious Society in Continental Europe had then their own peculiar costume, or uniform dress. A fashion, rule of their order, or a custom, which is still adhered to, even in this, our day, in the United States, notwithstanding our republican simplicity of dress, by the Quakers, Shakers, and many other societies, not forgetting the many singular costumes of the different religious orders of the Roman Catholic Church. Now, however, in America, the Moravians dress, act and live as all other reasonable people. I believe it is now an admitted fact, that the dress worn by the members of the Society of Friends, was not adopted by them till after the death of William Penn. See Atlantic Monthly, October, 1868, page 488.

"My last informed you that we should proceed homeward by the shortest course, but the pleasing accounts which we heard of Bethlehem, greatly excited our curiosity, and to gratify it we altered our intended route to visit that *terestrial paradise*. On the afternoon of the second day from Philadelphia, as we were passing solitarily between two overhanging rocks, we suddenly found ourselves upon the banks of a winding river, and the beauty of the prospect that immediately presented itself to view, left us no room to doubt that we had arrived at the end of our excursion; in fact, Bethlehem was situated on the opposite side.

"The view of this place strikes the traveller very agreeably, it is in itself beautiful, and the pleasure arising from a view of its beauties, is not a little heightened by the reflection that you have attained the end of a very disagreeable ride.

"The town is built in a verdant valley, plentifully watered by the Delaware." The Lehigh River was originally called the west branch of the Delaware.

"The banks of this fresh water river afford a most romantic spectacle, as they are covered to the very water's edge with shrubs of myrtle, and other verdure, which shoot up in all their natural luxuriancy. The almost impenetrable woods on the surrounding hills, serve not only to give an idea of an entire seclusion from a wicked world, but restrain the eye and fix the attention upon the many beauties brought into one point of view. I believe there are few who reach this spot, but stop some minutes to regale the sight, that most delicious of the senses.

"These reflections occurred while crossing the river; during this short passage, strictest silence was observed, each seeming absorbed in the contemplation of the surrounding objects. Upon reaching the tavern, we could not help congratulating each other upon the full completion of our most sanguine expectations. This building, (the 'Sun Hotel,') is neatness itself, it is built wholly of stone, even the partitions between the apartments are of the same materials, these are plastered and whitewashed so exceedingly white, as makes looking upon them painful to the eyes. The house is divided into a great number of rooms for the accommodation of travellers. We were attended with a cheerfulness extremely pleasing, and had each wish gratified in so obliging a manner as to fully compensate for the bad entertainment on the road. After a refreshing night's sleep and a social breakfast, our whole party, conducted by one of the Ministers of the place, went out to view everything worthy of notice.

"The town contains about 100 houses, besides the public edifices, all built of very rough stone, in the simplest manner. The Church, Single Sisters' house, the Single Men's house, and the Minister's house are the most striking objects. We first visited the Single Sisters'. At the door of their house, we were met by the abbess, who with the truest politeness, conducted us into every chamber; we were much gratified with the sight of this temple of industry, each chamber, which is large and commodious, is set apart for some branch of useful manufactures; in one were five or six looms, at which the sisters were weaving linen of various qualities, in others, numbers were carding wool, spinning, knitting and making various parts of wearing apparel. After looking into these rooms, we visited the kitchen and bed-rooms; here neatness is most particularly observable. The kitchen, where two young women were preparing dinner for the whole sisterhood, was perfectly cool, clean and neat, a number of coppers built in brick, serve to dress each day's provisions, which are either boiled or baked; roast dishes I found they were utter strangers to. The bed-room extends over the whole house, and in it are placed about one hundred beds, regularly disposed in four ranges, two on each side, so as to leave a clear walk in the middle; this room has an open window at each end, which serve as ventilators; a large lamp is suspended from the centre of the ceiling, with an opening over it to let out the smoke. Two young women watch there every night; the duty is performed in rotation, so that each undergoes an equal share of fatigue.

"After your curiosity has been gratified by a sight of these apartments, it is their custom to lead you into a room, where a number of women are busied in embroidery and other delicate work; here they spread before you many neat and curious pieces of nuns' (the

sisters') work, and so great is the general admiration of every thing belonging to this enchanting spot, that few depart without purchasing something.

"Such is the Single Sisters' house; neatness and simplicity are its characteristics, and piety and industry distinguish its inhabitants; but notwithstanding the pleasure received from the visit, I cannot say that I formed a wish to partake of such a life.

"To the sisters, their luxuriant valley and romantic river, seem to have no charms; the want of exercise and continual sedentary occupation have given their countenances a deathlike paleness. Their dress, though perfectly neat, does not serve to adorn their persons. Their habit is a short waistcoat which covers the neck, and a petticoat of white linen: their hair is carried back from the forehead, and covered by a linen cap of most unbecoming form; contrived to cover the ears, and tie under the chin; their only ornament is a plain stripe of muslin about two inches wide, surrounding the head, and tied in a small bow behind; this I call their only ornament, for though the caps of the single women are tied under the chin with a *red ribbon*, and those of the married with a *blue*, I found that this was not intended as an ornament, but merely as a distinguishing badge.

"This particular account of the Sisters' house, has anticipated my observations upon that of the single men; as they are both built upon the same plan, and in general the same economy observed; what we most remarked in the latter, was the absence of that extreme neatness so much admired in the former. This want of neatness in the men's apartments arises principally from the exclusion of females, and I think, proves the advantage, if not the necessity of social intercourse between the sexes.

"We made a short visit to the Minister's house, there being nothing about it that merits special attention, except the garden; which was laid out on the declivity of a steep hill, but had been made quite level by the industry and indefatigable perseverance of the single sisters; who with their own hands raised the lower part many feet.

" Each of the public buildings has a large garden where nature maintains her place, and suffers no encroachment from her hand-maid art. We attended at their devotions in the church. This is built with the same disregard to ornamental architecture as the rest of the town. About twenty paintings representing the principal passages in our Saviour's life are hung upon the walls; but that it should not appear they were placed there with a view to ornament the building, they are without frames, even of the simplest kind. The service was in German, and consequently not very edifying to me, but the music was excellent; this being, if I may be allowed the expression, the language of nature, and addressed to the feelings, is intelligible to every nation. The church is built near the Single Sisters' house, and the passage between them enclosed with a very high wall that the sisters may go into church unobserved. The seats for the men are distinct from those of the women; and this attention to keep the sexes separate is observed even after death; for even the burying ground is divided into two parts, one for the males, and the other for the females. This repository of the dead is laid out with the most exact uniformity, into beds of seven feet in length. It is the custom on the death of a member of the society, to place the body in a small building at the corner of the burying ground, until marks of dissolution are perceptible, then the body is interred in one of these beds; the smallest infant being allowed the same space with the largest adult, to avoid breaking in upon the much loved regularity. Perhaps you have no idea of children in this society; or the distinction between the single and married sisters, the keeping of the sexes entirely separate, you look upon as an insuperable bar to marriage; indeed this is one of their most peculiar customs. Their ministers or priests rule over them with an unbounded sway, and their decisions are regarded as infallible, tending to the best. It is the custom of the abbess to enquire of the women if any of them wish to marry; the minister does the same with the men. The names of the candidates are placed in two lists, and the first of each list proposed as companions for life; if the parties do not approve of the proposed match, they have a right to dissent, but have no other choice till the next is formed. This privilege of refusal is seldom exercised. So great is the veneration of the commands of their superiors, and so firm is their reliance on Providence, that they think the persons pointed out, must be in every respect best suited to them. I am informed that there has never been an unhappy marriage. This must arise in a great measure from their high sense of duty; for we cannot suppose, that persons thus arbitrarily joined can feel any love for each other. As soon as a couple is married, the society build them a small house, and advance some money to enable them to maintain a family. Their children pass the first years of their life with their parents, and are instructed at the public school. At a proper age the girls are admitted among the single sisters, and the boys are apprenticed to various trades; or provision is made for them in the Young Men's house.

" Industry is no less a characteristic of the men than the women. They have established a brewery for strong beer, which they sell at a profit lower down the river; they have a Fulling Mill, and Oil Mill, and most handicraft trades are carried on here. They are exceedingly ingenious and well versed in the principles of mechanics; the water works are a proof of this. A stream of water turns a wheel with great rapidity, which working four forcing pumps, raises a body of water into a reservoir more than one hundred feet high, from this the water is conveyed by leaden pipes into every house in town. These useful works were contrived and executed by a German, one of the society, and so simple is the machinery, that they have been continued free from obstruction, and without needing repair, for upwards of thirty years."

In this connection the following extract made from papers in the office of the Secretary of the Commonwealth at Harrisburg, and read before the Historical Society of Pennsylvania, March 15, 1826, may not be without interest.

"The adult unmarried men and boys upwards of 12 years of age, in the settlement of the United Brethren, live mostly together in a house called 'The Choir house of the Single Brethren.' That also the adult unmarried women, and girls upwards of 12 years of age, inhabit 'The Choir house of the Single Sisters.' There are also choir houses for the Widows and Widowers.

"Marriages in the congregation of the United Brethren are made by general agreement, with the advice and approbation of the Elders. Whenever a Brother wishes to marry, he signifies his intention to the Elders. If they have no objection, his proposal is submitted to the Lot. If the question proves affirmative, and the Sister proposed, and her parents, all give their approbation, the wedding is performed.

"At the baptism of children, both the Witnesses and Ministers bless the infant with laying on of hands,

"The *pedilavium*, or washing of feet, is used by some agreeably to the command of Christ, 'Ye ought also to wash one another's feet.'

"The most singular custom, is the assembling of the congregations in their respective burying-grounds on EASTER Monday, at sunrise, when the Litany is performed.

"The United Brethren are remarkable for their honest simplicity of manners, industry, economy, and neatness in their habitations; kind and affectionate to each other, living as Brothers and Sisters. They are considered a great acquisition to the Province."

An emigrant passing through Bethlehem in 1788, says:

"We saw the young females just coming out of school, their dress was a short gown and petticoat, while their heads were covered with snug little white linen caps, giving them a very neat appearance. The school for the boys was kept entirely distinct, and no intercourse was allowed between the sexes, except through the intervention of the teachers.

"'The Bethlehem Seminary for Young Females,' was becoming quite celebrated, and was patronized by many Southern men, who sent their daughters there to be educated. It was one of the earliest schools established for the education of females in America.

"On leaving this pleasant and well-built village, we crossed the Lehigh by a *Rope-ferry*, which was the first of the kind we had ever seen."

THE SCHNITZ HOUSE,
BETHLEHEM, PA.

CHAPTER VI.

THE SCHNITZ HOUSE.—THE FARMERS IN OLD TIMES.—THE OBJECT OF THE ESTABLISHMENT OF THE MORAVIAN CHURCH IN AMERICA.—ROCHEFOUCAULT'S DESCRIPTION OF BETHLEHEM.—THE BETHLEHEM SOUVENIR. —SIMPLICITY OF MORAVIAN LIFE IN THE LAST CENTURY.—MUSIC.—BISHOP SPANGENBERG.—THE MORAVIAN HISTORICAL SOCIETY.—THE FIFTY YEAR'S CELEBRATION, JUNE 25, 1792.—THE OLD BRIDGE OVER THE LEHIGH, 1792.—SKETCH FROM THE AMERICAN GAZETTEER.

THE wood cut at the head of this chapter, is a correct representation of the "*Schnitz House*," so called from the German word, *schnitz*, to cut, or slice. It is a long, one-story log house, plastered over on the outside, in imitation of stone, and is still standing; back from the street, on the first lot east of the "Sister's House," on Church Street. It was erected in the early days of the settlement, and used by the Sisters as a place to cut and dry apples, which were then extensively used in the winter for *pies*, by the inhabitants. There was formerly a large orchard of apple trees surrounding the house, and in the rear of the "Sister's House." With the Germans of Pennsylvania, *pies* of all kinds seem to be considered one of the absolute necessaries of human life; they eat them at every meal; as well as cakes, preserves and pickels of all sorts. They also drink strong coffee three times a day, and are not a nervous people. The Bethlemites make many kinds of domestic wines, of a very superior quality, for family use, of which they are justly proud; all the fruits and berries of the country are *pressed* into service for this latter purpose.

The farmers who first took up the lands around Bethlehem, were very poor, not even able to buy harness for use on their horses. So they used ropes for that purpose, made out of their own hemp. Oxen were used to draw their wagons, which were made of wood, and entirely without using iron, for wheels they sawed logs cross-ways, and bored holes in the centre for the axles, and so they came into town. The women often came into town on horseback, without any saddles on their horses, and riding a-straddle, like men.

The European settlers were few however, and thinly scattered around the adjacent country. Some of these were Irish, who, says Bishop Spangenberg, the Moravians dreaded more than the Indians. It was by them that the Moravians were first called Hernhutters.

Mr. Henry, in his history of Lehigh Valley, says, that the establishment of the Moravian congregations in America, had in view the *single object* of the propagating the gospel among the Indians. No doubt that was one of the objects of the Society, but not by any means the only one. They were desirous of escaping the persecutions in Europe, and were induced to emigrate to Georgia. From there they came to Bethlehem as stated, and thus it became from its beautiful position, fine climate, and the rapid increase of its population, the chief town of the Society, and naturally its central station, and as the Moravian church was, and still is a Mission church for the conversion of the heathen, it was from this place that the Brethren took their instructions from their superiors, and set out to the different missions of the Society, on the Upper Lehigh, the Susquehanna, and finally into the distant wilds of the Juniata, and the Alleghany mountains, as well as the inhospitable regions of the Ohio. Many of these mission posts, " Huts of Grace," as they were called ; originally thinly scattered through the wilderness, have become in the present day, prosperous and largely populated towns.

The Duke de Rochefoucault, in his travels in America in 1785, volume II., page 397, &c., gives the following facts connected with the temporal government of the Church in Bethlehem, at that time.

" In 1740, Count Zinzendorf purchased of Mr. William Allen, who held of William Penn, the district now called Bethlehem, with the view of founding there an establishment for the Society of the Moravians. Although some trees were cut down in 1741,

it was not until 1742 that the settlement was begun. One hundred and forty Moravian Brothers and Sisters arrived from Germany and settled there. These families were poor, had no other dependence but their labor, and everything was to be done to form a settlement in this desert. They lived there in one general community, *contrary to the rules and usages of their Society*, but only from the necessity of circumstances, which would have rendered the general progress of the Society more slow, and the situation of the individual families more inconvenient, if their labors and productions had been divided. This deviation from the construction of the Unity, (for thus they call the whole Society,) was prescribed by the Synod, which makes and alters the laws of the Moravian people.

" Thus, under the orders of the chiefs of the congregation established at Bethlehem, they cleared the woods, made roads, and cultivated the lands ; the women spun, wove, made their clothes, and prepared their victuals. One single will animated the whole, and the product of each individual labor served indiscriminately to support the whole Brother and Sisterhood. The fathers and mothers being constantly employed in labor, could not, without inconvenience to the community, give their attention to the children. The Society therefore, set apart some of the Sisters to take charge of the whole. The authority, however, and the superintendence of the parents, was neither taken away nor diminished.

" At that time, even, notwithstanding their community of goods, the Brethren that received any money from their families or friends, had the predisposal of it. If any of them invested their property in the common stock, it was voluntary, and the effect of a zeal and disinterested act, of which there were few examples. The Brethren possessed of any private property, had frequently their children with them; they clothed them better, and the care which they took of their infancy—a charge considered a relief by the Society—was a proof that at Bethlehem the children were not, as has been alleged, the property of the community, and that it was no part of the constitution to make members renounce all private property.

" In proportion as the settlement advanced their labor became less urgent, and the virtues of man have nearly everywhere the same character. The active Brethren killed themselves with work, while the idle took little trouble. Those who reflected, discovered whatever fatigue they endured, their situation was nowise ameliorated, and that industry, the indisputable property of every man, afforded them not a single advantage. Reflection, then had the same effect upon the industrious, as natural disposition had on the idle; the ardor for labor no longer continued, and the society did not prosper, and most of its members were discontented. These joint considerations induced them, in 1762, to change the system of the Society. The Society at Bethlehem was now established on the rules of the societies in Europe, and, agreeably to the new system, it has been regulated since that epoch, as well as all the other Moravian congregations established elsewhere in America. By the present ordinances, the communism of property is done away in favor of the individuals, it only continues as to the government of the Society, and exists partially.

" The territorial property, as well as the profits of the tavern, the store, the farms, the saw mill, the oil mill, corn mill and fulling mill, the tannery and the dyeing manufactory, belong to the Society, which, from these funds is enabled to provide for the poor, for the payment of debts, and of the public taxes. In all other respects every Brother enjoys the absolute property of whatever he can earn by his labor, be it what it may, and of the gifts he may receive. The government of the Society is vested in the Bishop, the Minister, and the Intendant, and the Inspectors, male and female, of the different divisions of the Society, which are five in number; the young men unmarried, the unmarried Sisters, the widows, the married Brethren and Sisters, and the schools. The Intendant has the exclusive adminis-

tration of the property of the Society, but he must advise with a committee composed of from eight to ten members chosen by the Brethren at large; in the name of the Intendant they carry on all their transactions, grant leases of houses and lands, securities for borrowed money, discharges, &c. All the houses, however, erected in the town of Bethlehem, and the 4,000 acres belonging to it, are not the property of the Society, nor even the greater part of them; they belong to the Brethren who have built upon the land, for which they pay rent to the Society. The amount of this rent is two pence the foot in front, by twenty feet in depth. The house built by the Brother is his absolute property; he can leave it to his wife or children, in the same way he can his other effects, or he can sell it, only he cannot convey it but to a Brother who has obtained permission from the Directory to buy it, with the burthen of the rent attached to it, and which perpetually remains.

" The Directors having the government of the Society, must admit those only into their territory, who they think will not disturb the Society. In the contract of lease made by the Intendant with the advice of the committee, to those intending to build a house, or to those who purchase a house, it is always stipulated, that if the proprietors shall be desirous of quitting it, and shall not find a purchaser who may be agreeable to the Society, the Society is to purchase it at a price declared by law, which also fixes the terms of payment. Garden ground, or land in the country, is let at six shillings the acre.

" Besides the government farm appropriated to the benefit of the Society, there are six or seven smaller farms belonging to it. These are let to tenants who pay a third part of their produce, and who also pay six shillings rent for their garden grounds. These tenants are all at present Moravians. Sometimes the farms are let to other persons, only the Society must be satisfied as to their character and behavior. The town of Bethlehem is inhabited by between five and six hundred inhabitants, all of the Brother and Sisterhood."

In the Bethlehem Souvenir, "a History of the rise, progress and present condition of the Bethlehem Female Seminary, by Wm. C. Reichel," published in 1858, it is very justly remarked, that "the spirit of pious simplicity which characterised the social and religious regulations of the early Brethren, while it astonishes us at the present day, cannot fail to elicit admiration of their honesty of purpose and determination to live the life of 'every day' christians. No occasion, however trifling, but was sanctified with the ceremonies of religion."

"In connection with this pastoral simplicity mentioned, Spangenberg, in describing Nazareth farm, in 1746, in his own quaint style, says in regard to the Brethren and Sisters engaged there, 'Never, since the creation of the world, were there made and sung such lovely and holy shepherds, ploughing, reapers, thrashing, spinners, knitters, sewers, washers and other laboring hymns, as by these people. An entire farmers' hymn book might be made by them.'" See Risler's life of Spangenberg, page 221.

James Henry, in his sketches of Moravian life and character, page 137, writes on this subject, that, "When travelling, the Moravian of patriarchal times had his 'Reiselieder,' or travelling hymns. These, sung in the solitude of the chamber, before retiring or at rising in the morning, or performed in agreeable chorus by several pilgrims, added solace to the journey, and if on a mission of evangelical labor, assuaged its toils and hardships."

It will be observed that the Moravians are essentially a musical people, even at the present day; although in the olden times music was more generally cultivated and used by them than at present. Hymns and music were used not only in the church and on all festival occasions, but in the family, at meals, in the fields, the work shop, and while travelling; even yet the good customs in this regard have not passed away, and the *Wiege lieder*, or cradle hymns, may yet be heard sung by the sweet voices of the little ones, in the good old town of Bethlehem.

On the 18th of September, 1792, the venerable, beloved and celebrated Bishop Augustus (Gottlieb) Spangenberg, died in the 89th year of his age, having been born on the 15th of July, 1704. The Bishop was, during twenty years of his life, from 1742 to 1762, the virtual head and superintendant of the Moravian affairs in America; he was educated for the Lutheran Church, and became a Professor of Divinity at the University of Halle, in 1731, (having received his degree at the University of Jena, which he entered in 1722,) and was discharged the next year, his views in religious matters not being agreeable to the direction. He then attached himself at once to the Moravian church, and became Zinzendorf's assistant at Hernhut, and finally a Bishop of the Unity, and in influence second only to the Count. He was eminently qualified for the performance of the onerous duties devolving on him in the infant days of the Society in America, during the Indian troubles, and in the pecuniary difficulties with which the church had at first to struggle.

In a note to page 9, of the history of Nazareth Hall, it is alleged that, "A century ago it was the custom for its Bishops (of the Moravian church,) to take official names," and a note from Spangenberg to Brother Rogers, dated July 19th, 1760, and signed "Joseph," is given in evidence to prove the assertion; but no other instance is mentioned, and no other authority adduced for the statement. The learned author of that book has been led into an error by making the peculiar case of Spangenberg, a general one. The Moravian Bishops did not as a rule, nor even as a common practice, assume official names. The case of Spangenberg is an exception. He had generally acquired among all his Brethren the name of "Joseph," for the reason, "that he cared so well for his Brethren;" in this way, he became generally well known by his Brethren as "Brother Joseph;" and finally assumed it as an official name, signing himself simply

"Joseph." It was at that time very usual for the Brethren to use simply their first or given names in addressing each other by letter, as it is even now the custom among intimate friends. Joseph, is a Hebrew name, signifying, "He shall add." The name of *Gottlieb*, means in English, *God-love.* In Ritter's history of the Moravian church in Philadelphia, is a portrait of the eminent Bishop, "Brother Joseph," with a *fac simile* of his signature, thus, "*Joseph, alias, Augustus Gottlieb Spangenberg.*"

In the published transactions of the Moravian Historical Society, in the year 1868, page 72; in a note, it is said that the name of "Brother Joseph" was given to Spangenberg by Count Zinzendorf, as an affectionate appellation, "on account of the excellent care he always took of his Brethren." If this is so, it finally disposes of the statement that the Bishops of the Moravian church in former times took official names.

The printed transactions above referred to, are contained in a pamphlet of 80 pages. It is the first publication ever issued by the Society, which is located at Nazareth.

In the year 1857, a number of Moravian gentlemen met together at Nazareth, in Pennsylvania; and formed an association, to which they gave the name of "The Moravian Historical Society;" having for its object the elucidation of the history of the Moravian church in America, in particular, and the history of the church in general, and its missions, wherever situated.

In the month of November, A. D., 1858, the Nazareth congregation of the United Brethren, presented the Society with a room in the old stone mansion known as the "Whitefield House," erected in the year 1743, and in this building the Society have ever since held their annual and special meetings. Nothing can be more interesting or charming, than to attend the annual Vesper of the Historical Society at Nazareth. The members are accompanied by their wives and daughters; all partake of a meal; and after the cakes and coffee, a veritable "love feast," historical papers are read, during which the men smoke and listen, and the women sew or are quietly attentive; many pleasant stories of old times are told; and only darkness breaks up the happy circle.

On the 25th of June, 1792, Bethlehem having stood fifty years, or half a century, the occasion was celebrated by a "Love Feast," and a pyramid was placed in the enclosure where the reservoir of the "Sister's House" now stands, which was decorated with *scarlet, coelico, pink, blue* and *white* ribbons, emblematic of all the choirs in the congregation. In the evening a procession, consisting of the whole congregation, passed through all the streets of the town, accompanied by music. The settlement of the town was commenced, as is well known, before the 25th of June, 1842, but the complete organization of the congregation as such, dates from that time.

The Lehigh Bridge Company of Bethlehem was incorporated in the year 1792. The bridge then erected was an uncovered structure, made of wood, but built in the most substantial manner, resting on three stone piers, with a side walk, similar to the present ones; for foot passengers; and the old rope ferry was then abandoned. The view from this old bridge is represented to have been impressively beautiful, but few buildings were erected near the stream, none were on the south side of the river but the "Old Crown Inn;" so there was nothing to obstruct the vision, or to take away the beauty of the scene. The river, its banks covered with verdure; the surrounding hills and mountains, covered with the forest trees; the islands, so dear to every Bethlehemite, and Bartow's path winding along beside the rippling waters of the Lehigh, formed a picture of quiet repose and wild beauty, seldom, if ever equalled. Modern improvements have partially destroyed, but not entirely eradicated all traces of the former beauty of the scene. The freshet of the 8th of January, 1841, washed away the old structure, the wood work of which had become gray with age, and worn with travel. During the same year the present covered bridge was built, the southern half of which was washed away by the freshet of June 5th, 1862, caused by the breaking of the dams of the Lehigh Navigation Company, above Mauch Chunk; heavy and continuous rains occurred on the 3rd of the month, in the mountains, and the splendid dams used to feed the Lehigh Canal, gave way one after another, before the great pressure of the water, the dam No. 4, at White Haven, being the first to break. The destruction of property was enormous, and the loss of life very serious. The dams were never rebuilt. A very interesting pamphlet was printed in 1863, giving incidents of the freshets. That portion of the bridge destroyed was soon rebuilt, and the new part roofed with slate.

The American Gazeteer, printed in 1797, says of Bethlehem: "It is a celebrated settlement of the Moravians, or United Brethren, of the Protestant Episcopal church, as they term themselves. It is situated on the Lehigh River, a western branch of the Delaware, fifty-three miles northerly from Philadelphia, and eighteen southerly from the *Wind-gap.* The town stands partly on the lower banks of the Manakes, a fine creek, which affords trout and other fish. The situation is healthful and pleasant, and in the summer is frequented by gentry from different parts. In 1787 there were 60 dwelling houses of stone, well built, and 600 inhabitants. Besides the Meeting House, are three other public buildings, large and spacious; one for single Brethren, one for single

Sisters, and the other for the Widows. The literary establishments, as well as the religious regulations, here deserve notice. In a house adjoining the church, is a school for females; and since 1787, a boarding school for young ladies, who are sent here from different parts, and are instructed in reading and writing, (in the English and German tongues,) grammar, arithmetic, geography, needle-work, music, &c. The Minister of the place has the direction of this, as well as the boys' school, which is kept in a separate house, where they are initiated in the fundamental branches of literature. These schools, especially that for young ladies, are deservedly in high repute; and scholars more than can be accommodated, are offered from all parts of the United States.

"There is a genteel tavern at the north end of the town, the profit arising from which belongs to the Society. There is also a store, with a general assortment of goods, an apothecary's shop, a grist mill, and on the banks of the Lehigh, a brewery.

"The Lehigh River rises in Northampton County, Pa., about twenty-one miles east of Wyoming Falls, in the Susquehanna River, and taking a circular course, passing through the Blue Mountains, empties into the Delaware River on the south side of Easton, eleven miles northeast of Bethlehem. It runs about seventy-five miles."

C.SMITH.ENG   TAYLER

THE FIRST MORAVIAN STORE,
BETHLEHEM, PA.

CHAPTER VII.

THE FIRST MORAVIAN STORE.—BETHLEHEM IN 1797, FROM OGDEN'S EXCURSION INTO BETHLEHEM AND NAZARETH.—THE ANCIENT INSTITUTIONS OF THE BRETHREN'S CHURCH.

THE illustration which heads this chapter, is a correct representation of the *first store* belonging to the Moravian congregation of Bethlehem, copied from one of M. A. Kleckner's photographs. It was originally kept by William Edmonds, an Englishman, and a Moravian, who came to America in 1763. This ancient structure, erected in the substantial style of the last century, is still standing, and is situated on Market Street, immediately opposite to the western gate of the old Graveyard, on the north side of the Street; no information can be obtained as to the time when it was built, but it must have been during the earlier days of the settlement of the town, as the "*new store,*" now the Eagle Hotel, which was the second building occupied as a store by the Society, was erected in 1784. Christian R. Heckewelder was the store-keeper after the removal, for many years; then, Owen Rice, senior, had charge, and was succeeeded by his son, Owen Rice, junior. In 1822 the store was removed to the building now occupied by the firm of Wolle, Krause & Erwin, the successors of Augustus Wolle, to whom the church in 1838, sold the stock and business.

In the "first store," the salesroom was in the western apartment of the building, (the house being a double structure,) and can be easily recognized in the cut by its large window, with diamond-shaped panels of glass. Some of the nails and spikes used in the erection of the store, and which were taken out in altering it into a dwelling house, have been preserved as curiosities, from their immense size. The house, judging from the thickness of its walls, would have made a good fort in the olden times; it will now make a good stone quarry, for it has been allowed to go to ruin, although situated on one of the finest building sites in Bethlehem. It is a quaint old building, very picturesque and beautiful.

The old store room is now occupied temporarily as an office, by Captain Owen Luckenback, Collector of U. S. Internal Revenue for the 11th District of Pennsylvania.

The dwelling house next door to the east, adjoining the "old store," was built in 1750, and was the first building erected on Market Street. It was the residence of Timothy Horsfield, an English Moravian, a noted and influential man in his day, a Justice of the Peace, and an eccentric character. His remains repose in the northwestern part of the old Cemetery, in the third grave from the west path, in the first row, on the northern side of the second walk from Market Street; and upon the tombstone the following words are inscribed.

TIMOTHY HORSFIELD,

Born April 25, 1708,

IN LIVERPOOL, OLD ENGLAND,

Departed March 9, 1773.

Some of his descendants, (great-grandchildren, by the name of *Kummer*,) are at this time, living in Bethlehem, and his old residence is now occupied by the widow of the late John Oerter; and is a substantial old two-story stone house, with massive walls like the old building next door.

The following graphic account of Bethlehem and its inhabitants, is copied from an old work now out of print, entitled, "*An Excursion into Bethlehem and Nazareth, in Pennsylvania, in the year 1799, with a succinct History of the Society of the United Brethren, commonly called Moravians, by John C. Ogden, a Presbyter in the Protestant Episcopal Church in the United States, printed by Charles Cist, No. 104 North Second Street, near the corner of Race Street, Philadelphia, 1800.*"

The writer says "The town of Bethlehem is approached through a large wood, and we beheld it with agreeable surprise, and we beheld it with agreeable surprise, and at some distance from the summit and slope of high grounds, which are formed parallel to two rivers or streams. The bridge, built in 1791, across the Lehigh, being out of repair, it was needful to pass the ford, which is safe and easy. The flat grounds open a way to the hill, which is ascended by two principal streets, the road being adorned by trees. A large and acceptable inn was reached before the setting of the sun, and an interesting chain of objects presented to call forth curiosity and enquiry on our part.

"A venerable man, one of the fathers of this town, is devoted chiefly to attendance upon strangers, that the hours of business among the inhabitants may not be unnecessarily disturbed by visitants, or the stranger be under undue restraint and embarrassment for want of a guide who would give full indulgence to a prudent curiosity.

"The inn is a stone building, with four large rooms on the first, second and third floors. Those on the second and third floor, are in part sub-divided into two small, and one large room. In this way, parties or gentlemen with servants, are accommodated almost as separate families. Fifty persons may be quartered here conveniently.

"Mr. Thomas indulged us with his company around the village. This benevolent attendant upon visitors is possessed of a large share of that primeval simplicity which becomes an Israelite indeed. He is saluted with a smile, and soft word of affection, under the paternal title of *Daddy*. The morning after our arrival, he introduced me to the Bishop, an aged grave personage, of great suavity of manner, such as embellish a father in the Church, and become that primitive sincere Christianity, which is professed by this Society. Assuming no pomp, he appears to live only to do good, and make others happy. His residence is in the Congregational House, devoted to the Clergy, and united to the Chapel. Being a widower, his daughter is mistress of the family. His answers to enquiries were made with frankness and very acceptably. These related to the foundation, principles and economy of the Brethren, and the general state of their affairs throughout America.

"It appears that this is a branch of the Greek Church, which has preserved Episcopal succession, with care and circumspection holding an union with their Synods abroad. Three Bishops reside in the United States. This person's name is Ettwine.

"Obtaining permission to visit him whenever his time would permit, we parted. Not, however, before he had favored us with a view of the Chapel, and a contiguous Hall. The first is a plain arched room, furnished with paintings upon canvass, between the windows. These present the most distinguished events in the history of our Lord, beginning with the visitation of the Angel to Mary, and the Nativity, and ending with the Crucifixion, Resurrection, and Ascension.

"The seats for the attendants are movable and divided into two parcels, one for the men and another for the women. No pomp, no display of pride, ostentation or wealth, are attempted. An organ is in the gallery, and other instruments of music are often joined with it on festivals.

"The second apartment was a Hall adorned with portraits, a half length of Zinzendorf, and about twenty of the most distinguished ministers and missionaries of this fraternity, who have served among them, from their first establishment in America. Portraits of some of the wives of these deceased Ministers, who had attended them in their missions, are also seen in this Hall.

"From these scenes we passed into the house devoted to the single sisters. One of them being called to attend us, we saw their habitation. They have rooms in this 'Sister's House,' of about twenty feet square, in which six or eight women make their residence by day. The employments of spinning, reeling of cotton, embroidery, painting and schooling, are in separate rooms. In the needle work they excel in figure and shades, both with silk and cotton.

"The Chapel of this choir has an organ and several pieces of instrumental music, which are played upon by the Sisterhood at their devotions. Indeed, in almost every room we saw some musical instrument, an organ, harpsichord, or piano-forte. These are in many private families in this settlement and other villages.

"Devotions are attended every morning. An Eldress presides and officiates. She sometimes delivers a lecture upon piety and morals. We were permitted to see the dormitory, in which forty of these women sleep in an upper story. This is a large, lofty, airy room, with a lamp suspended in the centre, which burns during the night; over it is a ventilator in the wall, which causes the circulation of fresh air.

"Before we left this house, we visited a room called the Store, in which are deposited upon shelves, and in large drawers, collections of the specimens of female industry, which they constantly vend.

"Our design was to have seen the Female School, erected for, and devoted to the instruction of children from other parts of the States, and the West India islands; with the girls of the fraternity, who are of the same age. But the accustomed hour for this privilege had not arrived, and the friendly attendant took me to the great reservoir or conduit, which receives the water from the machinery at the bottom of the hill, and conveys it by pipes under ground, to many public places.

"In a building formed as a pyramid, about fifty feet in height, we saw the pipes which convey water to the tavern, the congregation, Sister's, Widow's, Brother's, and several other houses. We ascended by ladders to the upper part of this edifice, and saw the summit to which the water was, and yet might be conveyed. The constant current prevents freezing in the winter.

"From thence we went to the Common School for boys, who are under the care of masters in a house adjoining that of the Brothers. These children are taught reading, writing, arithmetic, and accounts, as well as the catechism, and music connected with the religion and devotion.

"Our next visit was to the Brothers' House, which is but a counterpart to that of the Sisters'. Its hall for prayers, apartments for tradesmen, and a dormitory, are in different stories of this building. They have their meals together, in general, some take their dinners only at the common table. Apprentices frequently board with their masters in the town. They all sleep in the common dormitory, and every one in a separate bed.

"Their morning and evening devotions are under the direction of a single Brother or a clergymen. The office of Warden, and that of this clergymen, are often united in one person, when the number of inhabitants in such houses is small, as is at present in Bethlehem, Nazareth and Lititz. All boys from the age of twelve, reside here, as well as all the unmarried men, unless the circumstances of a parent require the presence of his children.

"From a walk on the top of this house we were entertained with a view of the gardens, neighboring fields, mountains, and the rivers Lehigh and Manakasy. The mountain in the rear descending gradually to the lower grounds, and heightening the view by its verdure.

"The variety of walks, rows of trees, and the plenty with which the gardens and meadows were stored, displayed taste, industry, and economy. To preserve the banks the common willow is planted, and not suffered to grow to a great height.

"The Manakasy is crossed by four bridges, for the convenience of the gardens and other places, besides two others, one above and another below the road and gardens. The sloping banks formed by nature, and the walks by which we mount the hill, prepared by labor, join their varieties to convert this fertile spot into the appearance of a pleasure garden.

"In a plain gallery or summer house on the side of this hill, built for the shelter of the children, who may be permitted to recreate themselves in a rainy or sultry day, was an aged missionary busy in preserving certain seeds and medical herbs; retired from the labors of his functions for many years, among the Indians, he resides in a part of the Congregation House.

"The hour being convenient for visiting the Girls' School, so much celebrated, a pleasing groupe appeared in different rooms,

under the care of their tutresses, where they learn reading, writing, arithmetic, embroidery, drawing and music.

"Since the applications to receive pupils from abroad have become so frequent and numerous, a new building has been erected for their use, upon a similar model with the Sister's House. A small court yard or grass plot is between these buildings. In the rear of this is another small enclosure, which forms a broad grass walk, and is skirted on each side by beds devoted to flowers, which the girls cultivate as their own.

"In the vicinity of the Chapel is a Corpse House, designed to receive the body previous to the sepulchre, in order to relieve the poor, and those whose houses are small, or when the deceased fell a prey to some infectious disorder. After this, in suitable weather, it is attended with great solemnity to a grave yard upon the summit of a hill.

"That neatness and decency which mark everything here, are conspicuous in the place of burial. It is surrounded partly with a stone wall, towards the street, where it cannot be enlarged, partly with a neat wooden fence, on those sides where it may be extended from time to time. The graves are laid out in perfect order, and each forms a flat hillock. The grave stones are about fourteen inches square, and present only the name, age, and native country of the persons, without any other monumental epitaphs or ornaments. This stone lies upon the grave. The departed members of the different choirs or orders are buried together in separate rows. The funerals are attended with great decorum. The females are dressed in white, and black is not worn as mourning.

"My guide, Mr. Thomas, brought for my amusement, Mr. Brailsford's experimental dissertations on the chemical and medical properties of the *Nicotiana Tobaccum* of *Linnæus*, commonly known by the name of Tobacco.

"This disposition to oblige, has made Mr. Thomas very dear to all who are acquainted with him. In the Bishop's apartment in the Brothers' and Sisters' Houses, in the schools, and among the inhabitants and strangers he is saluted by all, with the greatest respect and affection. In the girls' school, in particular, he was received with peculiar attention by the instructresses and pupils. Upon the visits of their parents, he escorts them, that they may not pass the streets alone. This he punctually observes in the evenings.

" The cloistered life and single state of the nuns in the Roman Catholic countries have been subjects of many remarks. The institutions here are not of that nature, as the women marry, and the single sisters walk abroad and visit their friends and neighbors when they think proper.

" The instructresses are treated with due respect. All females are educated by them, but all do not leave their fathers' houses, and families, to enter the Sisters' House as residents.

" At one end of the room, in which we saw the portraits of Zinzendorf, the ministers and missionaries, a painting on canvass is hung, which presents the divine Saviour in the clouds, attended by angels, descending from the superior regions, and surrounded by the various converts among the heathen, who were the first fruits of the Brethren's missions.

" Among the varied enjoyments of this settlement, is a pleasant walk on the banks of the river Lehigh. Nature has furnished a shade by means of the trees which grow near the margin. But this is improved by a row of locust trees between them and the road or walk. Thus, a thick shade is made for almost the whole day. Seats are placed for rest, and to enable the visitors to view the river at leisure. An island also assists to give beauty and variety, as well as to afford a retired bathing place. Not far from these seats, and in full view, is a large bridge, supported by piers of stone, and some farm houses on the opposite shore. Canoes are stationed here, for conveying such as wish to visit the island, which is frequently done.

" Near the river is a large brew-house, and bathing-room, devoted to the female schools. This last is surrounded and sheltered by trees in every direction. No one goes into the water without suitable bathing clothes,

and attendants. A clear stream, convenient shoal and bottom render the place safe and useful.

" At some distance in the rear, behind the trees, is a distillery and saw mill, whose works are set in motion by the small stream of the Monakasy. The mechanism of these works is not peculiar.

" The Widows' House, we were told, was conducted upon the same plan with those of the single brethren and sisters. Retired from the world and in the decline of years, their quiet is seldom disturbed by the visit of strangers. This is signified as their wish.

" The following morning we visited the more laborious employments in this colony, such as those of the grist, oil, fulling, hulling, snuff and bark mills.

" These works are erected under the banks west of the town, upon the waters of the Monakasy, whose stream is not large, but the water is husbanded with great care, as it passes through the various reservoirs, pent stocks and wheel works ; the waters of this stream decrease yearly.

" The spring which furnishes the town is at the foot of this hill, and enclosed within a small stone vault or cellar. It affords a redundancy of water, which is raised to the height of one hundred and twenty-five feet, by forcing pumps, which are in constant movement, by means of a small water wheel supplied from the Manakasy. The main tube which conveys the water is of lead, and of the diameter of four inches. It is so cold that the hand cannot rest upon it but for a few seconds.

" The brewery is a large building, not far from the river and bridge. It furnishes two kinds of beer, which are purchased by the inhabitants of the neighboring settlements.

" While the society of the Brethren were few in number, and a combination of labors and interests were needful to make settlements, property was held in common. This rule is now broken down *in part*, and individuals may follow their private and separate business, retain a station with the Brotherhood, and receive the benefits resulting from the public property, and public institutions, according to known and established rules. They appear to be a prosperous, but not a rich people.

"The Widows' House is more immediately the object of public care. Forty are in it at present. Many of them were the wives of the Ministers and Missionaries. Funds are connected with this institution, which arise from deposits of a certain sum, paid annually by their late husbands, and as a fee at entering into the order of ministers.

"These women are industrious, and treated with great respect. Making Bethlehem the asylum for aged ministers, their wives, children and widows, affords an opportunity for gaining information from every quarter, and explanations of facts and events connected with the general welfare.

"Seasons are appropriated to the reading of letters and reports, from every part of the world, in order to cultivate a general regard for every branch of their church.

"The afternoon being pleasant, I visited the island above the bridge. It is not large, but affords fine walks and an area for exercise, as well as seats and shelters for visitors. Tea parties sometimes select this for an excursion on a pleasant day. The locust trees are planted here to assist in forming shade.

"It may contain twelve acres, and is capable of receiving many improvements which wealth and fancy might suggest and form for embellishment. A small school of boys with their preceptor, were on a ramble here, after their hours of study. Walking appears to be the principal recreation for all ages and both sexes. On our return to the main land, we met another party from the female school, with their tutresses, walking in the gardens on the banks of the Lehigh.

"This evening we went to devotions at the Chapel. Previous to the arrival of the minister, a voluntary was played upon the organ. While this was doing, the Bishop came and took his seat under the gallery, at the head of a number of elderly men, some of whom had been missionaries. This appeared to be the only seat of distinction for him and the clergy.

"We were placed as strangers on a similar seat, next the wall, on the right hand of the minister. One half of this chapel is devoted to men, and the other to women. Each choir or fraternity, and sisterhood, sit together. The children, both boys and girls, are placed in the seats in front of their respective sexes.

"The minister upon reaching his seat near a table, opposite the middle aisle, gave out a psalm in German, line by line, which was sung by the whole congregation. He then read a chapter in German, out of the Gospel, and a second hymn was sung, accompanied also by the organ, and the assembly was dismissed with a benediction. The whole congregation stood until the minister left the Chapel. He was followed by the Bishop and other old men, and then the congregation at large, the men passing out at one door and the women at the other. The gravity, decorum and melody in this place are more easily imagined than described.

"In the shop of the barber, who is also a shoemaker, were glass globes filled with water. In the evenings they are hung around a lamp, according to the number who want light. This increases the brightness occasioned by the lamp, the glass and water, equal almost to the light of day. These globes are used by the stocking weavers and other mechanics, and by such as sew by night.

"In the public buildings and most other houses, we find German stoves, made of tile, which are in general use. Some are totally formed of tile, and others are part of cast iron. These last are in greatest esteem on all accounts, as they are not so liable to be injured by putting in of wood by careless persons; the tiles upon the top are so placed as to form a species of flue, in perpendicular and horizontal forms, which retains the heat, while it circulates longer, and heats a room more pleasantly and more durably than sheet iron.

"In the building of the potter who makes the tile for this stove, he was employed in making cheap pipes of clay, which are in great use among the Germans, and ought to be extended for the purpose of putting an end to the importation of those articles.

"On Sunday I attended divine worship in the Chapel, and had an opportunity carefully to observe the mode of worship. Divine service began at nine o'clock. The members of the Society and different choirs were present, and in their respective seats. According to an universal practice, the organist played a voluntary previous to the arrival of the minister, and beginning with their church litany. This compendium of devotions is not unlike that of the English church, but bears a greater affinity to the Lutheran, it is composed of short sentences, versicles, and responses read or sung alternately by the minister and congregation, the responses made with the aid of the organ and singers.

"The congregation appeared in plain habits, the minister in his accustomed garb, without gown, robe, or surplice. The women were generally dressed in white, and different colored badges distinguished the respective orders or choirs. All of them wear a white cap, and under the chin a ribbon. That of the widows is *white*, of married women *blue*, and the single sisters *pink* or *red*.

"After the celebration of this litany, the congregation retired for the space of an half hour, when the bell was rung, which was the signal for the attendance of the children and schools upon a service in English. This was introduced by the organ and a psalm, followed by a sermon, and succeeded by another psalm.

"The female school now took the seats generally occupied by the single sisters, and the sermon was principally addressed to youth. After this the children gave place and took possession of the seats at the further end of the Chapel, and those who were present before the litany, with others, came to attend offices, which were in German. The order was an hymn, prayer, sermon, psalm, and benediction.

"This Society observes the accustomed festivals and solemn days of the church. Certain meetings are peculiarly set apart for reading a lesson out of the bible. After the sermon the meeting is concluded with the Lord's prayer, an hymn, and the usual blessing.

"Sunday is entirely devoted to religion. In the afternoon communications from distant congregations were read, and in the evening a sermon was delivered by a minister about to set out on a mission.

"Discourses are delivered from time to time, at these meetings, to married people, widowers, widows, single brethren, single sisters, and the children.

All the congregations call themselves *The Unitas Fratrum*, or Protestant United Brethren of the Augustan Confession. They receive the Holy Scriptures of the Old and New Testament, as the only standard, both of the doctrine and practice of the Unity.

"The first emigrants into England and America, removed from Moravia, from whence the have commonly obtained the name of Moravians."

It would not be within the scope of a work like the present, to go into any details regarding the government of the Church, their community of goods, and the reason therefor, in the early days of the settlement of Bethlehem; but the foregoing extracts have been made to give a general insight into the manners, habits and customs of the community of the Brethren in those ancient times. Many radical changes have since then been made in all these matters, but few of the old customs have been preserved entirely unchanged, and in manner of living, and habits of life, and in dress, the members of the Society in no wise differ from other people of our day in America.

Of the ancient institutions of the Church in Bethlehem, only the Widows' and Sisters' Houses remain in operation; and it is to be hoped that they will ever be continued as homes for the aged single sisters and widowed mothers of the Brethren, where, safe and secure from the cold charity of the world, they may live in quiet comfort, and pass their delining years in peace, happiness and contentment, carefully guarded and cherished.

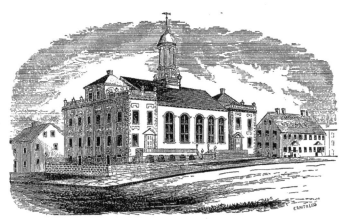

THE MORAVIAN CHURCH,
BETHLEHEM, PA.

CHAPTER VIII.

DESCRIPTION OF THE LARGE MORAVIAN CHURCH, ERECTED IN 1803.—THE BETHLEHEM ARCHIVES.—THE GEMEIN HAUS, OR CONGREGATION HOUSE.—THE FIRST MORAVIAN CHURCH IN BETHLEHEM.—THE OLD CHAPEL, OR SECOND CHURCH.—THE OLD SCHOOL, OR THE FIRST MORAVIAN SEMINARY FOR FEMALES.—THE OFFICIAL SEAL OF THE CHURCH OF THE UNITED BRETHREN.—THE ADDITION TO THE OLD SCHOOL.—"THE SISTERS' HOUSE."—THE "WIDOWS' HOUSE."—ORIGIN OF THE SISTERS' HOUSES.—MARRIAGE BY LOT.—LIEUT. AUBERY'S OPINION.—EXPLANATION OF THE LOT.—ACCOUNT OF IT IN THE HISTORICAL COLLECTIONS OF NEW JERSEY.—THE "GREAT MARRIAGE ACT" IN BETHLEHEM, APRIL 20, 1757.—MISS MORTIMER'S NOVEL OF THE MARRYING BY LOT.—MARRIED WOMEN, AND ANCIENT CUSTOMS.—REMARKS IN STROUD'S HISTORY OF PA.—ACT OF PARLIAMENT OF 20 GEORGE 2ND, C. 44, FOR THE NATURALIZATION OF FOREIGN PROTESTANTS, &c.

THIS chapter is illustrated with a fine view of the large and handsome *Moravian Church*, situated at the corner of Main and Church Streets, and the *Gemein Haus*, taken from an old drawing found among the papers of an old inmate of the " Sisters' House," lately deceased, Sister Sally Horsfield. In the drawing, the roof of the church is represented as it was originally constructed, but which was afterwards altered to its present form, as it leaked during all rain storms. The erection of the church was commenced in 1803, as is set forth on its vane, but it was not completed till 1806, when it was said to be the largest house for religious worship in Pennsylvania. The cost of the edifice was $60,000; and in 1803, when it was begun, the community had only a population of 580 souls. It is the third building in which the Moravians have held their religious services in Bethlehem. From the centre of the roof rises a belfry, containing a fine toned bell, the cupola is surmounted by a spire, the base of the belfry is occupied by a clock which strikes the hours and the quarters. In the eastern end of the building are several large apartments, one of which is for the use of the Ministers of the church, and in another there are preserved portraits of Count Zinzendorf, and other celebrated Fathers of the church, and their wives, together with the historical records relating to the Society, the church, and the town. In the centre of the building is the auditorium, with a pulpit at the eastern end, and in a gallery at the western end there is a fine organ, with ample room for the singers, and several rows of seats for the congregation, under this gallery are several rooms, used in preparing coffee for the "Love Feasts ;" in them can be seen some antique chairs and tables, that have done the church some service.

The Moravians of Bethlehem have carefully preserved all the records relating to the settlement of the town, as well as all books, papers and documents regarding the history of the Church, and its missions; these precious records are stored in a large room in the second story of the eastern portion of the large church just described, the apartment has a lofty arched ceiling, with four windows to admit the light; on one side of the room is the shelving which holds the library, estimated at about 2,000 volumes, of old, rich, rare, and curious works, all bearing upon the history of the "Unitas Fratrum." Those books are of inestimable value. Here are to be found all the publications of the Society ; a full collection of the writings of Count Zinzendorf, the Liturgies of the church, and the hymns used at different periods. A rare set of old Bibles, in several different languages, numerous works of the Fathers of the church of the United Brethren, and many valuable records relating to the History of Pennsylvania, and the treaties with the Indians. There is a large folio edition of the SACRA BIBLIA, in the German language, printed in Cologne, in 1630. But one of the most valuable works in the whole collection, is a thick little hymn book in English, bound in red morocco, with gold edges ; once the property of the Baroness Benigna de Watteville, Zinzendorf's eldest daughter. There is also a rare old quarto hymn book, in good preservation, which was printed in 1606, "By the Elders and servants of the Churches of the Brethren in Bohemia, Moravia and Poland ;" on one of the fly-leaves is the following entry, "This book our dear Brother PAUL MUENSTER, when he left all and fled for the Gospel's sake from his fatherland, Moravia, in 1729, brought to Hernhut, strapped upon his back, deeming it the greatest treasure which he owned. At Hernhut he gave it to Anna Nitschmann, (the celebrated Deaconess of Moravian History,) who presented it to Anna Joanna Seidel,) the wife of the Rev. C. F. Seidel,) from her Paul Muenster again obtained it, when he had come again to this place, (Bethlehem,) and at his death bequeathed it to our Church Library. He entered into the joy of his Lord on the 4th day of October, 1792. On the title page is the autograph of A. O. Nitschmann."

But the most valuable and interesting of all the records to the Bethlemite, are the DIARIES of the church, kept since the year 1742, written with great minuteness by the Ministers, giving a history of the Church affairs, of the town, and of the whole country, from day to day. Similar diaries have been kept in all the Moravian churches, missions, and settlements in America, from their earliest origin.

On one side of the library are neat closets, in which are kept with great care, many valuable and original letters and documents. Those of the Revolutionary period, from General Washington, and others in authority, during the time that the "Brethren's House" and other dwellings in Bethlehem, were used as the "General hospital of the American Army," give great praise to the Brethren for their attention to the sick and wounded soldiers, and are very interesting to the general reader, as well as extremely gratifying to the members of the Moravian Church.

The *Gemein Haus*, or more properly, "The

Congregation House," is situated at the corner of Cedar Alley and Church Street, immediately in the rear of the large church, and to the east of it. The corner stone of this, the second house, (and now the oldest,) in Bethlehem, was laid September 28th, 1741, and the building was completed the following year. It is a log-house, that is, it is built of hewn logs; it is two-stories high, with a steep roof, with two stories of garrets, and was formerly plastered over on the outside, with a heavy coating of mortar, made of lime and sand, and lined in imitation of stone, but in 1868, this coating was removed, and clapboarding substituted, much improving the looks of the building.

The *Gemein Haus* was erected as a dwelling place for the Ministers and their families, and is still used for that purpose. Father Nitschman was the master builder, as he was of the "First House." He is sometimes called the founder of Bethlehem, which is an error, as his nephew, Bishop Nitschman, was the founder, having been sent out from Europe expressly for that purpose, by the church authorities at Hernhut.

An old writer says: "The course of the Gemein was love and simplicity. Pride did not exist, and hence wants were few. The table was supplied with what they had, and what things they had not, they longed not to get; all were alike in the congregation. When the grandfather of doctor Huebener came to Bethlehem, he had to cross the Lehigh, and he hailed a person on the other side, who was watering linen on the bleach, (then linen was worn altogether,) the person came and took him across, it proved to be the noted Brother Petrus Boehler, who tended the bleach; all were required to be busy, he, as the minister of the congregation, set a good example to the others."

The first Moravian Church in Bethlehem, was a large room on the second floor of the "*Gemein Haus*," and was called "*Der Saal*," afterwards, "*Der Kleine Saal.*" Its low ceiling was supported by four wooden pillars, which are still to be seen in the partition walls of the four rooms into which it has been divid-ed. For nine years the congregation held their services in that room; and it was there the first Indian convert *David*, a *Mohican*, was baptised on the 16th of September, 1742. His remains repose in the old graveyard, where his tombstone can be seen, in the first compartment allotted to the men.

On the 19th of September, 1742, the corner stone of an enlargement of the "Gemein Haus" was laid, and the addition completed in 1743.

On the 5th of April, 1751, the town having a population of 200 souls, the community began the stone addition to the "Gemein Haus," now known as the "*Old Chapel.*" The first floor contained a *new hall* for the "married couples," the second floor being the chapel. The large buttresses of masonry on the outside of the building were put up at the time of the erection of the edifice, and not since, as is generally supposed. The dedication of this, the second Moravian Church in Bethlehem, took place July 10th, 1751, the ceremonies were performed by Bishop Nitschman, the building having been entirely completed. In the afternoon, at 1 o'clock, a general "Love Feast" was celebrated. Love feasts were held every Saturday in those times.

From May 10th, 1806, until 1815, the "Old Chapel" was used by the Boarding School for females, as a place to hold the examinations, exhibitions and daily worship. It was next used as a library, and a place for keeping the archives of the church; and afterwards as a concert room by the "Bethlehem Philharmonic Society;" and finally, in 1856, restored to its original purpose, a place for worship, and became then called, "The Old Chapel." In 1864, it was renovated, enlarged and improved, as it now appears; and on Sunday, April 2nd, 1865, it was re-dedicated by the Rev'd Edwin de Schwinitz, to the worship of God.

The "Old Chapel," when first erected, was provided with an organ, and at a later day, its walls were adorned by many interesting paintings, the works of the Moravian artist Haidt, representing incidents in the life of our Saviour. These valuable paintings for some unknown reason, were afterwards sold by the Rev'd Mr. Cunow.

Adjoining the "Old Chapel," immediately to the east, is the stone structure known as "The Old School," or the first Moravian Seminary for females, the erection of which was commenced in the year 1745, and completed in the year 1746. It had a door and two windows on the first story, and three windows in the second, fronting the open green space, in which now stands one of the old water-boxes employed for supplying the town with water, and which is still used. The lower floor of the building contained a kitchen for the "Married Couples," and "Single Brethren;" and a dining-room for the married people, who all took their meals at a common table. The upper floor was occupied by the married folks.

On the 9th of June, 1746, the belfry was completed in its present form. The base of the turret was occupied by a clock, made by *Augustus Neisser*, of Germantown, Pennsylvania; showing outside a brass face. In the cupola hung three bells, cast by Samuel Powell, one struck the hours, the others the quarters. The gilded emblem on the vane of the belfry, of a *Lamb with a Banner*, is the device on the official Episcopal Seal of the Moravian Church.

The official seal of the church of the United Brethren, is slightly oval, and three-fourths of an inch in diameter. In the centre, on a cartouche shield, which is enclosed by carved scroll work, is a Holy lamb, with a delicate tracery of vines and flowers encircling it. The whole surrounded by the motto: "*Vicit Agnus noster : eum sequamur,*" i. e., "Our lamb has conquered—him we will follow."

The Paschal or Holy-Lamb, passant, with a staff, cross and banner, is a typical figure of our Saviour, who is understood to be that Lamb mentioned in the Apocalypse of St. John, or the Revelations. The banner is always charged with a cross. See Clark's Introduction to Heraldry. The representation of the seal of the church on the reverse of the title page to De Schweinitz's Moravian Manual, published at Bethlehem in 1869, is drawn in utter disregard of all heraldic rules; it is unlike the seal it purports to represent; many things being omitted. The banner is a streamer, and the lamb faces to the right, instead of the left, which is the invariable rule.

In 1748, "The Old School" building had an addition made to its eastern end, and in 1749 one to its western gable, connecting it with the Old Chapel. In 1815 the Boarding School for females was removed to its present location on Church Street, and the "Single Sisters" took possession of the old edifice.

A school for girls was first commenced in Bethlehem, in the "Old School" building, on the 5th day of January, 1749, with sixteen scholars, daughters of the Moravian missionaries, ministers of the gospel, and of brethren of other Moravian settlements in America, forming a distinct household in the community, which was expected to defray its expenses by contributions from the church and individuals, and by the practice of a prudent economy.

On the 2nd of October, 1785, the school was closed, and arrangements made in the House for receiving pupils from abroad. The five remaining inmates of the school, viz: Anna and Maria Unger, Susan Bage, Rosina Friedman and Maria Heckewelder, daughter of the celebrated Indian Missionary, the Rev'd John Heckewelder, and the first white child born in the State of Ohio, and fifteen day scholars from the town were placed in charge of three Sisters, as teachers, and the room at the southwest corner of the second floor was assigned to them for a dwelling and recitations; all these continued at the school after the reception of scholars from other places.

On the 21st of May, 1786, the first scholar from abroad entered the Seminary, in the person of Miss Elizabeth Bedell, of Staten Island, New York. A full history of the school will be found in the *Bethlehem Souvenier*, printed by J. B. Lippincott & Co., of Philadelphia. The work is full of interesting information, and contains a full list of all the pupils entered in the institute since its foundation, with some beautiful views of Bethlehem, of the different buildings occupied by the school, and fine portraits of the principals, and other persons connected with the institution.

One of the regulations introduced in the school, was the ringing of the bell in the belfry of the "Sisters' House," for school in the mornings and afternoons, and a quarter before 12 o'clock M., for dinner, a custom which is still continued, and although the regulation is no longer applicable to the Seminary, it is to the scholars of the Moravian Day School, and most of the Moravian families, who still continue to dine at noon.

In 1789, finding that the number of applicants for admission to the school was increasing so rapidly, that the building used could not accommodate all who applied, it was determined to erect another building, to give additional room ; a site was selected in the rear of the old school, and on the 2nd of May, 1790, the corner stone of the new building was laid by the Rev'd Bishop Huebener, in the presence of a large assemblage, including the pupils of the school, and the children and members of the church.

The building then erected, afterwards known as the "OLD CASTLE," was a fine old stone edifice, an ornament to the town, and presenting an interesting and venerable appearance in a distant view of Bethlehem, and ought to have been carefully preserved, but it was torn down in 1857, and the present Moravian Day School, for the use of the children of the Bethlehem congregation, erected in its place.

The "Old Castle" was 52 by 40 feet, crowned by a heavy trip roof, whose lower pitch, overhanging the eves almost vertically, gave the building on the north side, where it was of one-story only, (being built on the declivity of the hill,) an air of uncommon strength and solidity. When vacated by the pupils of the Seminary, in 1815, it was occupied in part as a day school for the girls of the Moravian congregation; (the boys' school was in the Married People's House,) and partly as a dwelling place for the

families of several members of the church. There is a fine picture of the old building in the Souvenier.

THE "SISTERS' HOUSE."

The corner stone of the stone structure which forms the western end of the present "Sisters' House," was laid August 8th, 1742, and the edifice was completed in December of the same year. It was immediately occupied by the "Single Brethren," who lived there till November 15th, 1784, when they removed to their New House, the central building of the present Boarding School for Young Ladies. And the "Single Sisters," who had until then, lived at Nazareth, took possession of the old building, which has ever since borne its present name.

In 1752, the eastern wing of the "Sisters' House," opposite the "Old Chapel," and like it, supported outside by heavy stone buttresses, was finished, containing a large sleeping hall for the "Single Sisters." The wing was occupied for the first time, on the 10th of May, 1752, and the occasion celebrated by a *shad dinner*, to which one hundred blooming "Single Sisters" and "Great Girls" sat down.

In 1773, the western addition to the "Sisters' House," was erected, and the row completed as it now stands ; it was first occupied October 19th, A. D., 1773.

THE "WIDOWS' HOUSE."

On the south side of Church Street, directly opposite the "Sisters' House," stands the "Widows' House," erected in the year 1768, with an addition made to its eastern end in 1794. It is a large, long, two-story stone house, built in the most substantial manner. The building is, as its name imports, the residence of the widows of the members of the Moravian Church. The inmates of the Widows' and Sisters' houses, are not, however, supported by the church, but are dependent upon their own means, or the generosity of their relatives and friends. The church furnishes them with rooms at a nominal rent, in all else they are made to find themselves, if they can afford to do so, if not, they are supplied out of the Poor fund of the

Congregation. There used to be set apart in the "Widows' House," a room in which the Sisters and Widows exposed for sale, many beautiful articles of fancy works, of their own make, and from this source some of the more dependent added to their little means; now, however, the articles of their handiwork are sold at the "Eagle Hotel," through the motherly kindness of Mrs. Mary Yohe, wife of mine ancient host Caleb, who has presided now for nearly twenty-six years over the varying fortunes of the Eagle, ever ready "to welcome the coming, and speed the parting guest;" his hospitality is unbounded, and as one of the "Mystic Tie," he fraternally greets the Brethren of the craft, and gracefully does the honors of his Lodge.

> "When the Junior Warden to refreshment calls us,
> And the sun is at Meridian height,
> Let us merrily, unite most cheerily;
> In social harmony, new joys invite;
> One and all at his call
> To the feast repairing
> All around joys resound,
> Each the pleasure sharing."

Many of the Widows and Sisters who live in the Congregation Houses at Bethlehem, are in comfortable circumstances, and aid frequently the friends and companions of their youthful days, who are not so fortunate; so that they never want for anything; of course, the church authorities would extend assistance to inmates of the Houses in case of necessity; for these are the pet institutions of Bethlehem. Here, in their old age, free from poverty and care, live the "Single Sisters" and widowed mothers of this fine old town, and ancient church; many reside there from choice, whose families live in affluence in the town, there they receive the visits of their friends and relatives as at home; and surrounded as they are by the playmates of their youth, time glides not unhappily away; and we can but admire the affectionate care that is bestowed on those old ladies, and the loving attention of their children. May the winds of heaven deal gently with those time-honored walls, and may the more vandal hand of man long respect those venerable halls, built by the affectionate solicitude and labor of those who have gone home, yet have left behind them these monuments of their love for their wives, sisters, and daughters. When those old piles of masonry are no more, Bethlehem will have lost the most interesting objects within its limits; and the Moravian Church its crowning glory, which, more than aught else, wins our love and admiration.

The Sisters' Houses originated out of a voluntary act of the Sisters at Hernhut, in Germany, in the year 1750, who combined to live together under one roof, agreeing to serve the Lord, and receive no offer of marriage unless it were brought to them by their Ministers. The "Single Brethren" soon formed a similar association, and from the mutual agreement in respect to matrimony, in the two associations, arose the "Marriage by Lot." The sexes in the earlier days of the Moravian Church, were separated as much as possible; the Sisters were not permitted to pass the "Brethren's House;" nor the Brethren that of the "Sister's," if they accidentally met, they were not allowed to look at each other. The Sisters were forbidden to mention the name of any of the Brethren. Both sexes grew up in ignorance of each other, were timid in meeting with strangers, and the Moravians then were, indeed, a peculiar, religious people.

Lieutenant Aubery, in his "Travels in America," published in 1778, says of the Moravians. "They have adopted a sort of a marriage, but from the manner of its celebration, you cannot suppose those mutual, tender endearments and happiness, to subsist between the parties as with us. A young man feels an inclination to marry, which does not proceed from any object he is enamoured with, for he never sees his wife but once before the ceremony takes place, it being contrary to the principles of their religion, to suppose it is from the passions of their nature, but merely to uphold the Society, that it may not sink into oblivion. The young man communicates his inclination to the parent, who, consulting with the Superintendent, she produces her who is the next in rotation for marriage. The priest presents her to the young man, and leaves them together for an hour, when he returns. If they both consent, they are married the next day. If there is any objection, their cases are very pitiable, but especially the woman's, as she is put at the bottom of the list, which amounts to nearly sixty or seventy; nor does the poor girl stand the least chance of a husband till she arrives at the top, unless the man feels a second inclination for marriage, for he can never obtain any other woman than the one he had the first interview with. This, I am induced to think, is the reason of there being so many old women among the Single Sisters."

There are many absurd errors in the statement of Leiutenant Aubery, which have never been corrected. The parties marrying, were chosen by the consent of the Elder's Conference, with reference to their fitness for each other, and then submitted to Lot. The Brother had also the right to name a Sister, if he knew one personally, or through his friends; if not, one was chosen for him; in all cases the matter was determined by the Lot.

Mr. Henry, in his sketches of Moravian life, says: "It was the genius of Moravianism to submit all decisions to the Supreme will, and, in so doing, the Lot was the most available agent."

The Lot was not, however, used only in reference to the marriage tie by the Moravians, but is still resorted to on many important occasions to determine both worldly and religious matters. It is done after solemn prayer, asking the mediation and direction of the Lord and Saviour, in imitation of the Apostles, when choosing Matthias as one of the twelve, after the death of Judas. "*And they gave forth their lots, and the lot fell upon Matthias, and he was numbered with the eleven Apostles.*" See the Acts of the Apostles, 1st chapter and 26th verse.

In the historical collections of the State of New Jersey, edited by John W. Barber and Henry Hume, published in 1847, in the article upon Hope, New Jersey, once a Moravian settlement, page 495, it is stated: "The young of both sexes were not generally allowed to associate. When a young man wished to marry, he would hand in the name of the lady to the board of Elders. If judged improper from pecuniary disability, or other reasons, recourse was had to the lot to decide the question. This was always entered upon with solemnity, and preceded by prayer. If favorable, the young lady had the privilege of refusal. In extraordinary cases it is even now resorted to; for instance, when a young lady receives proposals of marriage from a missionary, and is undecided, she sometimes requests the lot to be taken."

It is undoubted that there were many impediments thrown in the way of the Brethren and Sisters marrying in the early days or the settlement of Bethlehem, why, is now a hidden mystery, yet there were some reasons for the restriction. Most of the Brethren were poor and unable to support a family. The Society only allowed one married couple of each trade to settle in the town, besides which, the church had not the means to build houses for all the married people.

The authorities at Hernhut, being informed that matrimony was not properly encouraged among the Brethren and Sisters in America; determined upon sending a visitation to the churches there; accordingly, the Rev'd Bishop, John, Baron de Watteville, was sent by the direction of the *Unity's Elder's Conference*," in Germany, to America, in the year 1756 or '57, his visit resulted in "THE GREAT WEDDING ACT," at Bethlehem, on the 20th day of April, 1757, when fourteen couple were married, at the same time, in the face of the whole congregation, in the old place of worship, "Der Kleine Saal," in the second story of the "GEMEIN HAUS," sometimes called the "Minister's House." The names of the couples married, and the ministers performing the ceremony, were as follows, viz:

1. Maria Redenberger to John Schweisshaught, by the Rev'd Anton Lawatsch.
2. Samuel Johannes to Magdaline Minga, by the Rev'd Frank Christian Lembke. This couple were Africans.
3. Elizabeth Cornwell to Richard Poppelwell, by the Rev'd I. Michael Graff.
4. John Henry Merck to Catharine Eliza-

beth Heil, by the Rev'd Paul Daniel Bryzelius.

5. Regina Neumann to Matthias Weiss, by the Rev'd Abraham Reincke.

6. George Meiser to Judith Schurer, by the Rev'd Augustus Gottleib Spangenberger.

7 Rosina Schultz to Jacob Till, by the Rev'd Bishop Augustus Gottleib Spangenberger.

8. Otto Krogstry to Anna Burnett, by the Rev'd Petrus Boehler.

.9. Barbara Krausin to Wolfgang Michler, by the Rev'd Bishop Petrus Boehler.

10. George Huber to Anna Maria Lehnert, by the Rev'd John Christopher Fancke.

.11. Salome Buerstler to Abraham Steiner, by the Rev'd John Ettwein.

12. Jacob Rubel to Catharina Hoetter, by the Rev'd Bernhardt Adam Grube.

13. Salome Dock to Philip Wesa, by the Rev'd Phillip Christian Bader.

14. Martin Hirte to Maria Beroth, by the Rev'd John Martin Mack.

The "Act" was preceded by the entrance of the fourteen couples, accompanied by the ministers, into the hall of worship, which the account says, "was a very respectable prospect;" while the trumpets and trombones were played. The Liturgy No. 92, from the Moravian Liturgy Book, was then sung.

"Wie bring ich's doch zu wege."

By the choir, till the second verse, when the whole congregation joined in. Then followed an address by "Brother Joseph," (Spangenberg,) upon the text of the day; "I am the Vine, you the branches." After which, the entire congregation arose, and sung the hymn

"Ach Gott du Keusches Lämmelein."

During the singing the fourteen couples were united in marriage, in the order given above, and Bishop Spangenberg then imparted the blessing of the Church upon the newly married people, to which the congregation responded, Amen!

Then followed congratulations, refreshments and an intermission; after which the newly married couples, and the married people of the congregation, assembled together, and were entertained by some musical performances. The Brother, Petrus Boehler, then sung an original ode, and Brothers Graff, Ettwein and Reineke, read original compositions; copies of all of which, are still carefully preserved by the Moravians of Bethlehem, as well as of the address delivered by Bishop Spangenberg.

This incident, one of the most remarkable that ever occurred in the Bethlehem congregation, is often spoken of by the older Moravians, as an event never to be forgotten. It was a triumph for the young people of both sexes, in favor of their marrying in greater numbers, a privilege which had been previously denied them.

"Marrying by Lot, a tale of the Primitive Moravians," is the title of a work by Charlotte B. Mortimer, the daughter of a Moravian minister, who was at one time a teacher in the Young Ladies' Seminary, at Bethlehem, it was published in New York, by G. P. Putnam & Son, in 1868. Perhaps some information can be derived from it in regard to this interesting subject, although it is not as clear and explicit as the curious reader could desire.

The married women were known by wearing light blue silk ribbons, as cap-ties under their chins. The cap fitted close to the face and head, was made of cambric, with a broad band of lace tied around the forehead, to keep it in place; it was called a *Schnepfen Haube*, owing to its being cut in the shape of a *snipe's bill*. This cap was worn by all the females over the age of twelve years; and remained in use in the American congregation till 1818, when it was abolished, to the great joy of the married women and sisters. The Great Girls wore dark red ribbons for their cap-ties. The Single Sisters used light pink in theirs; and the Widows wore white ribbons.

But all these restrictions to marriage, and all these ancient costumes are now but mementoes of the past. In those days nearly all the religious societies originating in Europe, had their monkish costumes, and peculiar dresses or uniforms; and those of the Moravians were no more singular than those of many other orders of Christians, some of which still exist; and who, unlike the Brethren, do good to no man, or woman either.

In Proud's History of Pennsylvania, volume 2nd, page 355, it is written, speaking of the *Unitas Fratrum*, or United Brethren, that, " By this name they were acknowledged by *Great Britain*, in the year 1737 and 1739, and by several other nations and states about the same period. In the latter of which years, they received a general toleration, by an act of the *British Parliament*, encouraging them to settle in the American plantations, &c., by allowing them to take a *solemn affirmation* instead of an oath, and dispensing with their not being concerned in *military affairs*, on payment of a rate assessed, &c."

The dates should be 1747 and 1749, respectively. The first mentioned Act is so interesting and curious, that it is given here entire. It was passed in the 20th year of the Reign of George the Second, 1747, and can be found in the Statutes at Large of England, 7th vol., chap. 44, p. 68, and is as follows:

ANNO REGNI, GEORGE II, REGIS.

Magnæ Brittanniæ, Franciæ and Hiberniæ.

VICESIMO.

At the Parliament begun and holden at Westminster, the first day of December, Anno Domini, 1741, in the fifteenth year of the Reign of our Sovereign Lord George the Second, by the Grace of God, of Great Britain, France and Ireland, King, Defender of the Faith, &c. *And from thence continued by several Prorogations to the eighteenth day of November, 1746, being the sixth session of this present Parliament.*

(The Royal Arms of Great Britain as they now are, 1869.)

LONDON.

Printed by Thomas Baskett, Printer to the King's most excellent Majesty; and of the Assigns of Thomas Baskett, 1747.

(935.)

Anno Vicesimo.

GEORGE II. REGIS.

An Act to extend the provisions of an Act made in the 13th year of His august Majesty's Reign, entituled, *An Act for Naturalizing Foreign Protestants, and others therein mentioned, as are settled, or shall settle in any of His Majesty's Colonies in America*, to other Foreign Protestants who conscientiously scruple taking an Oath.

WHEREAS, by an Act made in the thirteenth year of his present Majesty's reign, entituled " An Act for Naturalizing such Foreign Protestants, and others therein mentioned, as are settled, or shall settle in any of his Majesty's colonies in *America ;*" it was enacted, That from and after the first day of June, in the year of our Lord, 1740, all persons born out of the Ligeance of His Majesty, his Heirs or Successors, who had inhabited and resided, or should inhabit or reside for the space of seven years or more, in any of His Majesty's Colonies in America, and should not have been absent out of some of the said Colonies for a longer space than two months, at any one time during the said seven years, and should take and subscribe the oaths, and make, repeat and subscribe the Declaration appointed by an Act made in the first year of the Reign of His late Majesty, King George the I, entituled, an Act for the further security of his Majesty's person and Government, and the succession of the Crown in the Heirs of the late Princess *Sophia*, being Protestants, and for extinguishing the hopes of the present Prince of Wales, his open and secret abettors; or being of the people called Quakers, should make and subscribe the Declaration of fidelity, and take and affirm the effect of the Abjuration Oath, appointed and prescribed by an Act made in the eighth year of the Reign of his said late Majesty, entituled, an Act for granting the people called Quakers, such forms of affirmation or Declaration, as may remove the difficulties which many of them lie under; and also make and subscribe the Profession of his Christian Belief, appointed and prescribed by an Act made in the first year of the Reign of their late Majesties, King William and Queen Mary, entituled, an Act for exempting their Majesties' Protestant subjects for penalties of certain Laws, before the chief Judge or other Judge of the Colony wherein such Persons respectively had so inhabited and resided, or should so inhabit and reside, should be deemed, adjudged, and taken to be His Majesty's natural born Subjects of this Kingdom, to all Intents, Constructions, and Purposes, as if they, and every one of them, had been or were born within this Kingdom: And whereas, many of the People of the Congregation called the *Moravian Brethren*, and other Foreign Protestants not *Quakers*, who conscientiously scruple the taking of an Oath, are settled in his Majesty's Colonies in America, and demean themselves there as a sober, quiet and industrious People, and many others of the like Persuasion, are desirous to transport themselves thither; and if the Benefit of the said Act made in the thirteenth year of his present Majesty's Reign, were extended to them, they who are now there would thereby be encouraged to continue their Residence in his Majesty's Colonies, and others would resort thither in greater numbers, whereby the said Colonies would be improved, their strength increased, and their trade extended; be it therefore enacted by the King's most Excellent Majesty, by and with the advice and consent of the Lords Spiritual and Temporal and Commons, in this present Parliament assembled, and by the authority of the same. That from and after the 25th day of December, 1747, all Foreign Protestants, who conscientiously scruple the taking an Oath, and who are born out of the Ligeance of his Majesty, his Heirs or Successors, who have inhabited and resided, or shall inhabit and reside, for the space of seven years, or more, in any of his Majesty's Colonies in America, and shall not have been absent out of some of the said Colonies for a longer space than two months at any one time during the said seven years, and shall make and subscribe the Declaration of fidelity, and take and affirm the Effect of the Abjuration Oath, appointed and prescribed by the said recited Act, made in the eighth year of the Reign of his late Majesty, King George the first, and also make and subscribe the Profession of his Christian Belief, appointed and prescribed by the said recited Act, made in the first year of the Reign of their late Majesties, King William and Queen Mary, before the chief Judge, or other Judge of the Colony wherein such Persons respectively have so inhabited and resided, or shall so inhabit and reside, shall be deemed, adjudged, and taken to be his Majesty's natural born subjects of this Kingdom, to all Intents, Constructions, and Purposes, as if they and every of them had been and were born within this Kingdom; which said affirmation and subscription of the said Declaration, the said Chief or other Judge of every of the said respective Colonies, is hereby enable and empowered to administer and take; and the taking of every such affirmation, and the making and subscribing every such Declaration, shall be in such manner and Place, and at such Times and Hours, and such Entries made thereof, and for the same fees, and under the same Penalties, as in the said recited Act of the thirteenth year of his Majesty's Reign, are mentioned; and Lists of the Persons who shall take the Benefit of

this Act, shall be transmitted to the Commissioners of Trade and Plantations, in like Manner and under the same Penalties, as the Lists of the Persons taking the Benefit of the said Act are thereby directed to be transmitted.

Provided always, and be it enacted by the authority aforesaid. That no Person shall be naturalized by virtue of this Act, unless such person shall have received the Sacrament of the Lord's Supper, in some Protestant or Reformed Congregation, within some of the said Colonies in America, within Three months next before his taking such Affirmation, and making and subscribing such Declaration, and shall at the time of his taking such Affirmation, and making and subscribing such Declaration, produce a certificate signed by the Person administering the said Sacrament, and assisted by two credible witnesses, whereof an Entry shall be made in the Secretary's office of the Colony wherein such Person shall so inhabit and reside, and also in the Court where the said Affirmation shall be so taken as aforesaid, without any fee or Reward.

And be it further enacted by the authority aforesaid, That the Provisions contained in the said Act, made in the thirteenth year of his present Majesty's Reign, with Regard to the Certificates of Residence, and of having made and subscribed the said Declaration, and taken the said Affirmation, and as to such certificates being made evidence in the Courts of Great Britain and Ireland, and also in the said Colonies, and all other the Benefits of the said Act, shall extend to Foreign Protestants, who conscientiously scruple the taking of an Oath, and who shall be qualified as aforesaid.

Provided always, that the said Foreign Protestants shall enjoy the Privileges of natural born subjects, and all the Benefits of this Act, and the said Act of the thirteenth year of his Majesty's Reign

Provided always, and be it further enacted. That no Person who shall become a natural born subject of this Kingdom, by virtue of this Act, shall be of the Privy Council, or a member of either House of Parliament, or capable of taking, having, or enjoying any Office or Place of Trust within the Kingdoms of Great Britain and Ireland, either civil or military, or of having, accepting, or taking any Grant from the Crown to himself, or to any other in Trust for him, of any Lands, Tenements or Hereditaments, within the Kingdoms of Great Britain or Ireland, anything hereinbefore contained to the contrary thereof, in any wise notwithstanding.

Provided also, and it is hereby further enacted by the authority aforesaid, That nothing in this Act, or in the said recited Act of the thirteenth year of his Majesty's Reign contained, shall extend, or be construed to extend to naturalize any Person or Persons whatsoever, who, by virtue of an Act made in the fourth year of his Majesty's Reign, (intituled, *"An Act to explain a clause in an Act made in the Seventh Year of the Reign of Her late Majesty Queen Anne, for Naturalizing* Foreign Protestants, which relates to the children of natural born Subjects of the Crown of England, or of Great Britain,) are declared and enacted not to be intituled to the Benefit of the said Act of the Seventh year of her said late Majesty's Reign, but that all such Persons shall be and remain in the same State, Plight and Condition, to all Intents, Constructions and Purposes, whatsover, as they would have been in, if the said recited Act of the Thirteenth year of his Majesty's Reign, or this Act, had never been made; anything in this Act, or in the said recited Act of the Thirteenth year of his Majesty's Reign contained to the contrary, in anywise notwithstanding.

———

The following ancient and interesting Naturalization Paper, speaks for itself.

PENNSYLVANIA, SS.

I, EDWARD SHIPPEN, JUN: Prothonotary of the Supream Court of the Province of Pennsylvania, DO hereby certify, That at a Supream Court held at Philadelphia, for the said Province of Pennsylvania, the fifteenth day of April, in the year of our Lord, One thousand seven hundred and fifty-four, Before William Allen, Lawrence Growdon, and Caleb Cowpland, Esquires, Judges of said Court, between the hours of nine and twelve o'clock in the forenoon of the same day, GEORGE HOFFMAN, of Germantown, in the County of Philadelphia, being a Foreigner, and having inhabited and resided for the space of seven years in his Majesty's Colonies in *America*, and not having been absent out of some of the said Colonies for a longer time than Two months at any one time during the said seven years: And the said George Hoffman having produced to the said Court, a Certificate of his having taken the Sacrament of the Lord's Supper within three months before the said Court, took and subscribed the Oaths, and did make and repeat the Declaration, (appointed by an Act made in the first Year of the Reign of his late Majesty, King GEORGE, the First,) according to the Directions of an Act of Parliament, made in the thirteenth year of his present Majesty King GEORGE the Second, intituled, *An Act for Naturalizing such Foreign Protestants, and others, therein mentioned, as are settled in any of his Majesty's Colonies in America ;* and thereupon was admitted to be his Majesty's natural born Subject of the Kingdom of *Great Britain*, pursuant to the Direction and Intent of the said Act of Parliament. *In Testimony* whereof, I have hereunto set my Hand, and affixed the Seal of the Supream Court, the fifteenth Day of April, in the year first above mentioned.

EDW'D SHIPPEN, JR., *Prot.*

[Seal of the Court.]

THE OLD WATER WORKS,
BETHLEHEM, PA.

CHAPTER IX.

THE BETHLEHEM ALPHABET.—THE OLD WATER WORKS.—DR. MEASE'S SKETCH OF THE MORAVIANS.—DERBY'S GAZETEER, 1827.—MRS. ROYAL'S ACCOUNT, 1829.—PRINCE MAXAMILIAN OF NEUWEID'S VISIT, 1832.—JAMES N. BECK'S SKETCHES.—GORDON'S GAZETTEER OF PA., 1832.—THE CENTENNIAL CELEBRATION. U. S. GAZETEER, 1843.—INCORPORATION OF THE BOROUGH, 1845.—"GOD SAVE THE LUCKENBACK'S."—ACT OF PARLIAMENT RECOGNIZING THE "UNITAS FRATRUM," AS A PROTESTANT EPISCOPAL CHURCH.—ORIGIN OF THE MORAVIANS.—SOME ACCOUNT OF THE SETTLEMENT OF HOPE, NEW JERSEY, FROM THE HISTORICAL COLLECTIONS OF THAT STATE.

THE BETHLEHEM ALPHABET.

By the late Rev'd Louis David de Schweinitz.

A stands for *Anders,* both Bishop and Brewer.
B   "   *Boehler,* and *Bier* to secure.
C   "   *Crist,* whose lady keeps school.
D stands for *Doster,* the dyer in wool.
E   "   *Eggert,* who works with the saw.
F   "   *Friday,* his Father-in-law.
G   "   *Guetter,* who keeps the Wood-yard.
H   "   *Hillman,* who always works hard.
J   "   *John, Jacob, Jundt,* and his wife.
K   "   *Kampman,* the oldest in life.
L   "   *Lange,* both Father and Son.
M   "   *Maslick* and *Milchsack,* alone.
N   "   *Neisser,* whose house is but half.
O   "   *Oerter,* who binds books in calf.
P   "   *Pfeiffer,* who tends the bark-mill.
Q   "   *Quighy,* who married *Jake Till.*
R   "   *Rauch, Ricksecker* and *Rice.*
S   "   *Schneller,* who teaches for price.
T   "   *Tombler,* a Boat is his sign.
V   "   *Vugnitz,* his shop is his mine.
W   "   *Warner,* the maker of Combs.
X   "   a letter which nobody owns.
Y   "   *Youngman,* who has toys for sale.
Z   "   *Zoller,* who takes around the Ale.

The wood-cut at the head of this chapter, is a view of the "*Old Water Works of Bethlehem,*" or rather, of the old building in which the first works for forcing up the water were erected; taken from one of Kleckner's fine large photographs. The machinery was afterwards removed to the Oil Mill, so often spoken of in the accounts of the town, where the celebrated buckwheat meal is now made, and which is situated directly to the west of the old building, on the opposite side of Water Street, on the banks of the Manockasy.

A path runs along the south side of the house, up the hill into Main Street, between the residences of Captain Abbott and Mr. John Fitz. This old house was the last building held by the Moravian Society, when selling out their property in the town, and it was finally disposed of to Mr. Jedidiah Weiss, who still retains it; and whose son now occupies it as his residence.

The oil originally manufactured was *Linseed* oil, made from the seed of flax, which was raised in large quantities by the Moravians, previous to the Revolution, and before cotton came into use.

Heckewelder says in his Indian names, that the word "*Manockasy*, means in the Indian language, a stream with *long bends*, or many windings." And he spells it *Managassi*

Recently, in grading Market Street, the workman came upon the stone foundations of one of the old Water Towers, in use formerly to give a head to the water in supplying the village. The main tower stood in the rear of the "Married Peoples' Houses," as already stated; smaller towers were erected in different parts of the town; and the one above mentioned stood in Market Street opposite the site of the "Old Indian Chapel."

Morse's American Gazetteer, published in 1797, says, that Bethlehem in 1787, had 60 dwelling houses of stone, well built, and 600 inhabitants.

Dr. James Mease, in his work called "The Picture of Philadelphia," published in 1811 page, 209, says, in reference to the Moravians or United Brethren.

"The first congregation of this Amiable Sect, that settled in North America, came from Berthlesdorf, a village belonging to Count Zinzendorf, in upper Lusatia. When expelled from the Dominions of the Elector of Saxony, they resolved to go to America, and the Trustees of the Colony of Georgia having offered, through the Count, to grant them a tract of land, they set out in November, 1734.

"The written instructions given by the Count, were, 'That they should submit themselves to the wise direction and guidance of God in all circumstances; seek to preserve liberty of conscience; avoid all religious disputes, and always keep in view that call given them by God himself, to preach the Gospel of JESUS CHRIST to the *Heathen;* and further, that they should endeavor as much as possible to earn their own bread.' These principles they have ever strictly followed.

"Having met in London with General Oglethrope, the Governor of Georgia, they were provided with all the necessaries for the voyage to his beloved colony, where they safely arrived in 1735, and settled on the *Ogeeche* River: here they obtained the character which they so properly deserved, of a peaceful, pious people. Another colony arrived in the course of the following summer, and settled in *Savannah*. But in the following year, 1738, upon the attack of the Colony by the Spaniards from Florida, they were forced to leave their flourishing plantations, (*having early declared that they would not be concerned in war;*) and retired to Pennsylvania: part came in 1738, and the remainder in 1740. They settled in Bethlehem. In 1741, Count Zinzendorf arrived in Pennsylvania; and after much pious labor, particularly among the Indians, returned to Europe in 1743.

"In 1742, the Brethren erected a church in Philadelphia, in an alley running north and south from Mulberry Street to Sassafras Street, between Second and Third Streets, and hence called *Moravian* Alley. The church is 40 feet by 30 feet, and will hold about three hundred persons. It has an organ. Pastor, Rev. Joseph Zeslein.

"The principles of the Moravians are contained in 'An exposition of Christian doctrine, as taught in the Protestant Church of the United Brethren or *Unitas Fratrum*, by A.

G. Spangenberg, with a preface by Benjamin La Trobe.' They do not differ in the great cardinal points from other Protestant sects. They hold occasional ' Love Feasts' in their churches, for the purpose of promoting friendship, mutual love and kindness among one another. The aliment is of the most simple nature, wine is indeed sometimes used, but with the most rigid attention to temperance. They deem the propagation among the heathen, of the means of salvation by the Redeemer, a primary object of duty; and their zeal in this respect is truly astonishing. Every part of the Globe has been visited—nay, settled by their Missionaries; even the inhospitable shores of Greenland and Labrador; and the most unhealthy climates of Africa and Asia have received the benefit of their pious labors; the frontiers of North America, which, even at the present moment, are the hunting grounds of the savages, were settled by them more than half a century ago, by a colony under the venerable apostle, the late Rev. Mr. Zeisberger, and others. No danger, however great, no privations, or personal sufferings, however severe, deterred them from steadily pursuing their benevolent designs; and although the horrors of a predatory war carried on against the inoffensive converts from heathen darkness, by men who disgraced the name of Christians, often interrupted the tranquility of their settlements, and occasioned their persecution; yet they availed themselves of the first opportunity to recommence their labors, and have joyfully seen their example followed by other denominations of Christians.

"The members of this Society are few in number in Philadelphia, when compared with those of other sects. The head of their government is Hernhutt, in Germany: the subordinate power of their church, Bishop Loskiel, resides at Bethlehem in Pennsylvania.

"For a full account of the labors of the Moravians in North America, see ' The History of the Mission of the *Unitas Fratrum* among the Indians of North America, by the Rev. Mr. Loskiel, London, 1794.' "

In Buck's Theological Dictionary, printed in Philadelphia, in the year 1820, by Charles Buck, volume II, page 82, &c., there is an exhaustive article on the *Moravians*, the manner of their Church Government, Missions, &c., which, notwithstanding its great interest, would be out of place in the present work. It was compiled from *Crantz's Ancient and Modern History of the Church of the United Brethren*, 1780, *Spangenberg's Exposition of the Christian Doctrine*, 1784. *Dr. Haweis's Church History*, Vol. III, p. 184, &c.; *Crantz's History of the Missions in Greenland, Loskeil's History of the Missions to the North American Indians; and Oldendorp's History of the Brethren's Missions in the Danish West Indian Islands.*

In Derby's Universal Gazetter, issued in 1827, in the article on Bethlehem, it is stated among other things, that the population of the town in 1800, was only 543, and in the Township, 1343. In 1810, the number in the Township was 1436, and in 1820, the number in the Township had increased to 1860 individuals, nearly all Moravians. The number of *dwelling houses* in the town in 1820, was 72. The population of the town itself, is only given for the year 1800.

From *Mrs. Royal's Pennsylvania, printed in Washington, D. C., in* 1829, the following amusing and really entertaining sketch is extracted:

"Bethlehem is comparatively a large town and though mostly built of stone, has some handsome brick buildings. It is regularly laid off into handsome streets, and like Nazareth, stands on a considerable eminence. It, however, sinks in some places, and rises in others. The new buildings are showy, and built in the modern style; but the original buildings are roughly built of stone, and those where the Societies live, are huge masses of great size, small windows, and stone or brick floors, on the lower stories. The Church, however, and the Young Ladies' Academy, are two of the finest buildings in the United States.

"Their graveyards are peculiar; instead of putting the tombstone perpendicular, it is laid horizontally and loose on the top of the grave, as an emblem of death which levels all things. They have a house where the dead are placed and locked up till they are interred, and the friends of the deceased proceed from this house to the grave yard, with appropriate music.

"The Water Works of Bethlehem, by which water is conveyed through the town, are a great curiosity. It is forced from a spring 100 feet high into a deep well, and a number of pipes leading off from the well under ground, conveys the water wherever it is wanted. They keep large cisterns full in case of fire.

'Dr. Steckle, of Nazareth, recommended me to a Dr. Green, at Bethlehem, whom he said I would find at the stage house, kept by one Crist. Dr. Green, though he paid me a great deal of attention, was not the gentleman his friend represented him. Nor was I at all pleased with my quarters. The tavern keeper was from home, and his wife was an impertinent, disobliging woman.

"Bethlehem, as well as Nazareth, has long been distinguished for the excellence of its schools. The Young Ladies' Academy at Bethlehem, is so well known throughout, not only this country, but the world, that nothing I could say would be of any advantage to the Institution, its fame having reached all parts of the Union.

"I have seen numbers who were educated at Bethlehem, and have often seen the work done by the pupils, which, no doubt, has reached every part of the United States, and is doubtless superior to any needle work done in our country, at least.

"I unfortunately called at Bethlehem on Saturday, and the first thing I did after my arrival, was to inform the principal, Rev. Chas. F. Seidel, of my presence. He, very gentleman-like, waited on me in a few minutes, and, after communicating my views, Mr. S. said he would rather I would postpone my visit to the Academy till the next day, as the young ladies were always in undress on Saturday, preparing themselves for the ensuing week. That Saturday was the usual day for cleaning up. This being the case, I had to submit, as I was resolved upon seeing the pupils and the interior of the Academy. Mr. Seidel is a middle aged man,

heavy made, full round face and pleasing countenance. In his manners he excels, if possible, Rev. Van Vleck. He is a native of Germany, but has been in this country several years; no one, however, would perceive from his dialect that he was a foreigner. I have never seen an American whose demeanor and manners possessed the same ease and grace of Dr. Seidel, and it would be mockery to attempt a description of the man. His conversation bespoke him a man of high attainments, and upon the whole he is one of the most fascinating men I ever met with.

'The following day I went to Church in the first place, as I wished to see their mode of worship, and when the sermon was over I was to be admitted to the Academy, it having been so arranged. The Church is very large, and has a handsome organ. The men and women sit apart, the men taking off their hats. These sit on one side of the house, and the ladies of the place upon the other, face to face, and the pupils sit in the middle. The pupils have, however, a place of worship by themselves, their seats are at right angles with the others. The daughters of the citizens (single ones), sit with the pupils.

"This was a good opportunity to see the customs of the whole. Both men and women were fashionably dressed, excepting, as in other cases, the aged; but nothing could exceed the taste and neatness of the whole. They differ from all other people in countenance, manner and dress. They all have a smile on their countenance, and none of the sameness of the Quakers or the Shakers in their dress, nor the sadness of the Methodists, or the fripping flounces of other sects, and still less the studied grimness of the *Gray Coats*. Some of the citizen ladies were dressed in white, some in lead color, some in calico, some in bombazine, and some in silk; their hats or bonnets, (if you please), were neat, fine and small, and those of the young ladies were trimmed with ribbon, but chiefly they excel in that art which conceals art. For although most of them are learned, the most learned amongst them approach nearest to nature. The congregation accompanied the organ in singing, and both men and women have books in their hands. But nothing that has gone before can give any idea of the heavenly smile which sat upon the face of the preacher, and the beguiling ease of his gestures. If he is not perfection, there is none on earth. Though I am strongly prejudiced against priests, I could almost be brought to believe this man was a Christian, his face was never without a smile.

"They have none of that silly getting up and getting down, and continual motion of other churches, and if I were to believe, what I do not, that there were any Christianity in the United States, I would say it had fled to these Moravians for protection. In saying this, I wish to be understood that I have found a great deal of liberality, generosity, and good feeling, but no Christians agreeably to the requisites of the gospel. Those who have and are making so much noise about religion, as they call it, seem to be more upon the Jewish plan. But this is no more than an opinion,—to return, if there be any of the meek religion of the gospel in our land it is amongst these Moravians. It was not the Rev. Seidel who preached, nor do I know his name, he was quite an orator.

"The only singularity I saw was the men and women go out of the Church at opposite points, doubtless to prevent the young gentlemen from gallanting the young ladies. This was the only church in which I ever saw window curtains used. The windows are of amazing height and width, and every one has a large, fine, white curtain before it, with lead fastened to the bottom to keep it in its place, otherwise the Church is without ornament. The pulpit is very high, and the priest walks into it from another portion of the Church.

"After Church was out, Mrs. Seidel accompanied me through the Young Ladies' Academy, which, like that at Nazareth, does not consist of one entire large hall, like High schools or some Academies, but every class has a hall or class room to themselves. They dine in one great hall, and sleep in another ;

which plan of all sleeping in one room I do not approve, for though the room is high and airy, I am of the opinion that many human beings, inhaling, as they must do, each others breath, cannot be healthy. As respects this Academy, nothing would be more easy than to throw this large room into chambers.

"The cooking department is also in the same building ; this is the best constructed and in the neatest order of any I have visited in the Atlantic country, excepting that at the Hospital at Boston.

"As it was Sunday, I lost the pleasure of hearing the young ladies play, or of seeing them at work, though they were all in the rooms occupied in common for study.

"This was certainly the capstone of the climax, and what I had for many years back ardently longed to see, and though fancy was raised to the highest stretch, fell short of the burst of innocence, beauty, and elegance which met my eye at the opening of each door. The retiring modesty of some, the polished urbanity of others, the snowy arm, the delicate hand, the soft friendly smile, the spiral ringlet, the dimpled cheek. I lingered at each door, lost in admiration. As at Nazareth, they severally arose from their seats, and made a graceful courtesy as they were introduced. There were some from all parts of the United States, and some from the Islands, some were small girls and some were grown. I was much pleased to find Miss Bibbs there, from Alabama, with whose parents I had formerly a slight acquaintance.

"There was at this time a thin school, on account of a vacation, from sickness; if I recollect, the first time the institution was visited with sickness. There are, however, more applicants than can be accommodated. This is much to be lamented, as it is certainly the best female seminary in the United States. It is wholly under the control of the United Brethren of Germany, who, it appears, do not seek to enlarge it, though the profits go to establish other seminaries elsewhere.

"The young ladies showed me their frames with the unfinished work, which surpassed beauty. They have introduced what is called ribbon work, recently taught by a German lady. This is very ingenious, and has still a richer appearance than the common way with floss silk. The ribbon work is shaded like the floss, very narrow and curiously worked into flowers and figures of all sorts and shapes; it is richer and much easier done. The ebony work is a very useful work and a great curiosity; everything almost is made of it. The worsted work is also beautiful, hearth rugs, or anything you fancy is made of it. But the literary part of the education is by far the most important.

"Bethlehem is on the river Lehigh and a small creek called the Manakes, 54 miles from Philadelphia. The town begins on an eminence, and descends to the banks of the latter, a handsome stream. The prospect is not so handsome as that of Nazareth, as the Lehigh mountains approach too near the town, and confine the view within too narrow limits. It is, however, a lively town, the people pursuing a variety of business as in other towns. It owns a great number of mills, tanneries and breweries, and contains about 3000 inhabitants, (1828). There are also handsome flower gardens, shrubberies and pleasure grounds adjoining the academy, all of which, with pure air, fine water, and a rich surrounding soil, but above all the refined and pleasing manners of the inhabitants, render it a delightful summer retreat, and to which numbers of the Southern gentry resort during the warm months. All those who travel for amusement or curiosity ought to visit those interesting towns." ·

Mrs. Royal writes more at length about Nazareth and Bethlehem, and seems to have been much prepossessed in favor of the Moravians, which speaks well for them, as she handles "all the world, and the rest of mankind," without gloves. She, however, over estimates the population in 1828. In 1830, the town only contained 800 inhabitants; and in 1840, but 1,622 souls.

Prince Maxamilian, of Wied, in his travels in the interior of North America, in 1832 and 1833, (a fine work, handsomely illustrated with eighty-five superb engravings, translated from the German, printed in London in 1843, and sold at the rate of $200 per copy,) thus writes of the undergrowth of immense Mountain Laurel on the Lehigh Hills, on the south side of the Lehigh River, near Bethlehem. "We saw here a thick covert of the tall *Rhododendron Maximum*, which was still, (August 2nd, 1832,) adorned with magnificent tufts of flowers."

Neuwied, also calls attention to the *Cichorium Intybus*, with its beautiful flowers, white and blue, which grows so plentifully on the roadsides in the vicinity of Bethlehem; it would make a handsome garden flower.

Prince Maxamilian remained for some time at Bethlehem, at what is now known as "Fetter's Hotel," then kept by Captain Woehler, an old soldier of the great Napoleon, and a Westphalian by birth. The veteran's remains now repose in the Old Grave Yard. In his life-time, the Captain often spoke of "Prince Max," whom he drove all over the surrounding country, during his visit to Bethlehem and its vicinity.

Captain Woehler occupied the fine old stone house in Water Street, opposite the Tannery. He was a Moravian, and his house was kept with true German neatness, and there he dispensed to his guests Lager beer, wine and pretzles only. His liquids were kept as cool as ice, by the waters of the celebrated Spring that supplies the town with water, and which was on his premises. The massive walls, the solid oak floorings and staircases of the house, are well worth a visit. No such private buildings are erected in these degenerate days.

James N. Beck, in his pleasing little sketches of "Music by Night, and Trout in the Morning," published in 1865; eulogizes the polite old Captain; and of his charming neice, writes thus: "Luischen, modest, full orbed waiteress of the Carivansera, a comely German lass, whose good tempered nonchalance, at times recalled to my mind Johann Ludwig Glein's stanza in 'Das Maedchen vom Laude.'"

> "Wie fliesst die, du Maedchen
> So ruhig das blut!
> Du Maedchen vom Laude,
> Wie bist du so gut."

"Louisa! she of the pure German accent, ever anticipated our wishes, with a grace as charming as it was unassuming; may the murmuring, rippling waters of the Monockasy outside, serenade her for many ensuing years."

The only copy of Neuweid's work in the United States, is owned by Mr. Wm. Theodore Roepper, of Bethlehem, Professor of Mineralogy and Geology, in the Lehigh University.

Gordon's Gazetteer, of Pennsylvania, 1832, says of Bethlehem, "The situation on a rising hill is particularly romantic ; a fine mill-stream and the Lehigh Canal passing through the lower part of the town, affording considerable facilities to business. The number of private dwellings in the year 1831, amounted to 112. The public buildings consisted of a remarkably large church, a boarding school for young ladies, established since the year 1788, a school house for boys, and two peculiar establishments, in one of which a number of widows find an asylum in their old age, and in the other, unmarried women chiefly, likewise of an advanced age, board together under proper regulations, and the guardianship of the Society. The town contains 800 inhabitants, &c." The account is very long, and particularly interesting, but it contains nothing not already related and described.

On the 25th day of June, A. D. 1842, it being the *Centennial* celebration of the settlement of Bethlehem, the occasion was observed in the Moravian Church with appropriate ceremonies, of which the following is a brief account, kindly furnished by the Rev. Edwin de Schweinitz.

1. June 24, 1842. In the evening preparatory service was held by the Rev. John G. Herman.

2. June 25, 1842, at 9 o'clock A. M., the first service of the Centesimal celebration, Anthem by the choir; hymn by the congregation; reading of a salutatory letter from the Board of Elders at Berthelsdorf, in Saxony. Address in German and English, both by Rev. John G. Herman.

3. Second service, at 10½ A. M. Reading of a Historical sketch of the founding and progress of Bethlehem, in German, by Rev. P. H. Goepp.

4. Third service at 3 o'clock P. M. ; a Liturgical service; singing by the congregation, and anthem by the choir, and an address by the Rev. Mr. Hecht, Pastor of the Lutheran church at Easton, Pa. At this service, Rev. Charles F. Seidel, presided.

5. Fourth service, 8 o'clock, P. M. Held in the old burying-ground, which was illuminated by more than 1000 lanterns of colored paper, and consisting of Liturgical offices by the congregation and choir. More than 2000 persons were present.

6. Sunday, June 26, at 9 A. M., fifth service, for the children, held by the Rev. Peter Wolle, of Litz, Pa.

7. At 10½ A. M., service by the Rev. G. F. Bahnson, of Lancaster, Pa., in German. Text, John, 15, 16.

8. At 3 P. M., seventh service; sermon in English by the Rev. David Bigler, of Philadelphia. Text, Habak. 3, 2.

9. At 7½ o'clock, P. M., the eighth and last service was the ordination of four Deacons of the Moravian Church to the Priesthood, by Bishop Andrew Benade, as a fitting conclusion to so eventful an occasion.

The United States Gazetteer, printed in New York in 1843, says : " Bethlehem, which is characterized by great neatness and order, is on the north bank of the Lehigh river, at the mouth of the Monokacy creek. The ground rises gradually from the river and creek, and gives a commanding situation to the view ; it is compactly built on a street running North and South, and two other streets running east from the main street. It contains a large stone church, in the Gothic style, 142 feet long and 68 feet wide, with a small tower rising from the centre, and surrounded by a dome. There is a bury-ing ground to the north-east of the village, laid out with great neatness and taste, in which the graves have the head to the North.

"There are about 200 dwelling houses, beside other buildings. There is a bridge over the Lehigh 400 feet long. This place has long been celebrated for a female school of high order, conducted by the Moravians, in which many highly respectable ladies of the Middle States have received their education.

"The Lehigh canal passes along the river through the lower part of the place. It contains 4 stores, capital $10,500; capital in manufacturies, $88,000; 1 college, 8 students; 2 academies, 175 students; 2 schools, 169 scholars. Population, 1622."

Bethlehem was incorporated as a Borough on the 6th of March, 1845; and the first election for Borough officers, was held on the third Friday in March, 1845, and resulted as follows:—

Charles A. Luckenbach,	Burgess.
Philip H. Goepp,	Councilman.
Benjamin Eggert,	"
Ernst F. Bleck,	"
John M. Micksh,	"
Christian Luckenbach,	"
Charles L. Knauss,	"
Christian Weber,	Treasurer.
Samuel Brunner,	Clerk.
Matthew Brown,	Supervisor.
Augustus Milchsack,	"
Charles W. Rauch,	High Constable.

The late Rev. Louis David de Schweinitz, one of the most learned and eloquent divine of the Moravian Church in America, wrote some interesting and instructive little sketches for the amusement of his children; one of these, the Bethlehem alphabet, has already been inserted, and the following, relating to one of the most influential and numerous of all the families of Bethlehem, is full of wit, and proof of the assertion.

My First Visit to Bethlehem.

"On my late journey to Wilksbarre, I was pleased with the prospect of spending an afternoon at the pleasant village of Bethlehem. I had been detained at Quakertown, so as to miss the morning stage, and was upon the point of giving up my plan, when I was informed that a Mr. Luckenbach (David) from Bethlehem, who kept a hack, was ready to start for that place, having but one passenger. I eagerly embraced the opportunity, and found that passenger an old friend of mine. As my friend was intimately acquainted with Bethlehem, and its immediate vicinity, I gladly acceded to his proposal, when we reached the summit of a hill within a near view of the town, to alight and walk on foot, in order to enjoy the delightful scenery. After walking a few paces my attention was arrested by a young man in the adjoining field ploughing unusually deep furrows, and remarking to my friend that they appeared so to me, he replied that Mr. Luckenbach (George) was noted for his deep ploughing.

"Continuing our walk we soon arrived at the bridge over the Lehigh, and were civilly stopped at the gate by the toll-keeper, an old Mr. Luckenbach, (Adam) to receive the toll, and while we were making some inquiries of him concerning the rise of the river at the late freshet, a young gentleman on horseback came up, whom my friend shook hands with, informing me that he was a Mr. Luckenbach, (Charles Augustus) who had recently purchased the Mill property. I confess I began to wonder at the frequency of the name, and was just going to remark on it, when we came up with a person carrying a fowling-piece, accompanied by two dogs, whom my friend addressed as Mr. Luckenbach, (Samuel) telling me he acted as Forester to the town.

"On the bridge across the canal we stopped to admire this fine work, and were contemplating a new house just erected there, when I was surprised to hear a person call out Mr. Luckenbach! (Jacob) to the master builder, who was sitting on the rafters, and make some inquiries of him. We then went down the tow-path of the canal, and walked up to the Lock to see a couple of *Arks* just passing. The lock-keeper, I immediately understood, was a Mr. Luckenbach, (Samuel, Sr.) and I observed to my friend that it was strange that we should meet all the Luckenbachs of the town before we entered it. I found myself, however, mistaken, for the first signboard which struck my sight in town, informed me that there lived a Mr. Luckenbach, (William B.) a coppersmith. When we approached the " Eagle Tavern," we saw a number of persons assembled before it, and understood that they were the Committee, under whose care and superintendence are the various water-works, by which water is introduced, and my friend, with a smile, pointed out to me a Mr. Luckenbach, (Christian) the Chairman, as a person remarkable for his knowledge on such subjects.

" By this time it began to grow late, and the church bell ringing, I learned that a marriage was to take place in the church according to the Moravian custom. Desirous of witnessing the ceremony, I repaired thither, my friend accompanied me, and took pleasure in increasing my astonishment, by informing me that the young man who was to be married was a Mr. Luckenbach, (William Jr.) a cabinet-maker. Being invited to remain when the meeting broke up in order to be present at the ceremony which with the Moravians is in the place of a wedding dinner, I accepted. After some time, the company being seated, a middle-aged clergyman entered and occupied the usual place of the minister; after he had addressed a few words of congratulation to the young couple, he commenced singing, during which wine and biscuit were handed around. My friend told me that the clergyman was the Rev. Mr. Luckenbach, (Abraham) a highly valuable missionary among the Moravian Indians in Canada, now on a visit to his friends in Bethlehem. And I ceased to wonder at the number of Luckenbachs, and their various occupations, when I was informed that at this wedding all the relatives of the parties had been invited, and there was present on the part of the bridegroom, 1 grandfather and 1 grandmother ; 3 great uncles and 3 great aunts : 1 father and 1 mother ; 17 uncles and 18 aunts ; 10 brothers and sisters, and 21 first cousins, making 80 near relatives, members of the

Society, and all descended from old Mr. Luckenbach, who had been dead for upwards of 80 years. *God save the Luckenbacks !"*

The following *Obituary* is copied from The Moravian.

" Died; at Bethlehem, Pa., December 1, 1867, very suddenly, Mrs. Elizabeth Luckenback, relict of the late David Luckenbach, in the 85th year of her age.

" The deceased was one of the oldest members of the church at Bethlehem. For 35 years she lived with her husband on one of the river farms, belonging to the church, in the old homestead, the site of which is now occupied by the Railroad offices of the Lehigh Valley Railroad in the present borough of South Bethlehem.

" She was the mother of ten children all of whom are living, and had sixty-six grandchildren, and forty-three great grandchildren, together one hundred and nine children's children, of whom, however, thirty died before her. Direct descendants to the number of eighty-nine survive her."

The Act of Parliament of 22 George the Second, 1749, in 7th Statutes at Large, Chap. 30th, page 155, &c., hereinbefore alluded to as recognizing the *Unitas Fratrum* as a Protestant Episcopal Church, is as follows :—

" An act for encouraging the people known by the name of *Unitas Fratrum*, or United Brethren, to settle in his Majesty's Colonies in America."

" *Whereas* many of the people of the church or congregation called the *Unitas Fratrum* or *United Brethren*, are settled in his Majesty's Colonies in *America*, and demean themselves there as a sober, quiet and industrious People ; and many others of the same persuasion are desirous to transport themselves to, and make larger settlements in the same Colonies at their own expense, provided they may be indulged with a full Liberty of Conscience, and in the exercise of the religion they profess ; and several of the said Brethren do conscientiously scruple the taking of an oath, and likewise do conscientiously scruple bearing arms, or serving in any military capacity, although they are willing and ready to contribute whatever sums of money shall be thought a reasonable compensation for such service, and which shall be necessary for the defence and support of his Majesty's Person and Government:— *And whereas the said Congregations are an Ancient Protestant Episcopal Church* which has been countenanced and relieved by the Kings of *England,* your Majesty's predecessors. And whereas the encouraging the said People to settle in *America* will be beneficial to the said Colonies; therefore may it please your Majesty at the humble petition of *Abraham,* Baron of *Gusdorff; Lewis* Baron *Schrautenback* free Lord of *Lindheim; David Nitschmann* Syndic; *Charles Sebachmann* Baron of *Hermsdorf,* and *Henry Cossart,* agent, Deputies from the said *Moravian* Churches, in Behalf of themselves and their *United Brethren,* that it may be enacted; and be it therefore enacted by the King's most Excellent Majesty, by and with the advice and consent of the Lords Spiritual and Temporal, and Commons, in this present Parliament assembled, and by the authority of the same, that from and after the 24th day of June, 1749, every person being a member of the said Protestant Episcopal Church, known by the Name of *Unitas Fratrum,* or the *United Brethren,* and which Church was formerly settled in *Moravia* and *Bohemia* and also now in *Prussia, Poland, Silesia, Lusatia, Germany,* the *United Provinces,* and also in His Majesty's Dominions, who shall be required upon any lawful occasion to take an oath in any case where by law an oath is or shall be required, shall, instead of the usual form, be permitted to make his or her solemn affirmation or declaration in these words following:—

"'I, A. B., do declare in the presence of Almighty God, the witness of the truth of what I say.'"

"Which said solemn affirmation or declaration shall be adjudged and taken, and is hereby enacted and declared to be of the same force and effect, to all intents and purposes, in all Courts of Justice, and other places where by law an oath is or shall be required, within the kingdoms of *Great Bri-*

tain and Ireland, and also in all and every of his Majesty's Colonies and Dominions in America, as if such person had taken an oath in the usual form."

There are seven other sections of the Act. Penalty for false affirming. Not to extend to criminal cases. Moravians summoned to do military duty to be discharged on payment of the rate assessed; and that any person claiming the benefit of the act should produce a certificate of membership, signed by some Bishop of the Church, &c., all of which are now without interest to any one.

In a work entitled the *"Pictorial Sketch-Book of Pennsylvania,"* edited by Eli Bowen, and printed in 1853, is a note on page 306, on the Origin and History of the Moravians, from which the following extract is made; the first part of which must be taken *cum grano salis,* as no authority is given for the statement. The Ancient Brethren's Church dates only from the 1st of March, 1457.

"In the 9th century, a sister of the King of Bulgarvia, being carried a prisoner to *Constantinople,* became a Christian, and through her means, on her return to her native land, a Christian church was established in her native country, of which the king of Moravia and the duke of Bohemia were members. A part of these churches were afterwards forced into the Roman Church, but a select few still refused to be merged into it. This little remnant, adhering to the pure and simple doctrines of the primitive church, suffered a variety of persecutions for several centuries, but were at length permitted to live in a wasted province on the borders of Moravia. Here they established a church in 1457, on what they deemed the rule and law of Christ, calling themselves at first, "Brethren of the law of Christ," and finally, the "United Brethren." As there are other denominations styling themselves United Brethren, they are now usually called Moravians.

"The celebrated missionary, Count Zinzendorf, was not the founder of the Moravian church, as many have supposed; but was merely the Protector of some of the members when driven from their native land. They were allowed to settle in his village of Bethelsdorf. He assisted to reorganize their church, and after fruitless attempts to induce them to join the Lutheran church, he became himself a convert to their doctrines, and subsequently their leader and guardian, especially in temporal affairs."

The Moravians are referred to in several places in the same work, and a mythical anecdote is related of Count Zinzendorf, copied from Chapman's History of Wyoming Valley, p. 246, &c., of a rattlesnake which crawled over his feet, without harming him, while he was sitting before a fire in an Indian tent, during one of his missionary visits to the Shawanese tribe of Indians of Wyoming Valley. An occurrence not at all unlikely, as it was a cool evening, and the snake was seeking the warmth; but the story sounds very much like the account of St. Paul shaking the viper from off his hand into the fire, on the Isle of Melita. See Acts of the Apostles, 28 Chapter, and the first six verses. Chapman says in a note, that the occurrence is not mentioned in the Count's memoirs, lest the Brethren should think that the conversion of a part of the Shawanese Indians was attributable to their superstition.

The following interesting account of Hope, is copied from the "Historical Collections of the State of New Jersey," by William Barber, and Henry Howe, published in New York, in the year 1847, p. 491, &c.

"In 1769 the Moravians from Bethlehem, Pa., purchased a tract of about 1000 acres at this place of Mr. Green, who lived in a log house on the hill, a few rods from the Christian church. The Moravians who lived here were remarkably honest in all their dealings, but by trusting too much to the honesty of those with whom they had business, suffered in their pecuniary affairs. In 1805 or 1806, they returned to their settlements at Bethlehem and Nazareth. While here they erected a church and a tavern, which last stood where the Christian church is now erected, and was burnt a few years since. The annexed engraving is a representation of the Union Hotel in the village, built of limestone.

This structure was erected in 1781, and was originally the Moravian church, being surmounted by a cupola, which has since been taken down, and a portico added.

"In the village burying-ground at Hope, are the graves of about 40 or 50 Moravians; a slab of grey stone about two feet long is placed horizontally over each grave, each with a simple inscription recording the name, birth, and death. The following is a copy of two of the inscriptions.

No. 33.

CONRAD OMENSETTER,
Born December 18th, 1740,
In Germany.
DEPARTED
July 2, 1792.

MARIA SALOME BLUM,
Born June 11th, 1718,
In Hope,
DEPARTED,
August 30, 1778.

"The United Brethren, or Moravians, derive their origin from the Greek Church in the 9th century. The Society, as at present, was placed on a permanent foundation in 1722, by Count Zinzendorf, a German nobleman. At the commencement of the last century, after more than 200 of their congregations had been destroyed or dispersed by persecutions in Moravia, a small remnant found refuge on his estates in Saxony, and through his patronage built Hernhut, now their largest settlement. Count Zinzendorf, the instrument of renewing their church, was subsequently consecrated one of their Bishops, and from thenceforth devoted his life to the cause. Individuals of all religious denominations united with them, and gave rise to such a diversity of sentiment, that it was considered judicious to unite upon some general rules of agreement. Accordingly, under the guidance of the Count, certain articles of union were concurred in, which omitting the distinctive doctrines of the various Protestant denominations, adopted only the generally admitted fundamental truths of Scripture. The United Brethren, therefore, object to being considered as a separate sect, inasmuch as their own peculiarities arise principally from their social organization. Individuals of all Protestant denominations, consequently, have always been admitted into their communities without renouncing their peculiar creeds. Discussions relating to the Trinity, and other speculative truths are carefully avoided; but they make the merits of the Saviour the principal theme of their discourses, and the only ground of salvation. High wrought emotions engendered by momentary impulses, are not considered as sure tests of piety as a daily upright and humble deportment. The *Moravian Church is Episcopal*, and has a liturgy, but their Bishops possess no pre-eminent authority.

"The Brethren early turned their attention to this country, with the view of propagating the gospel among the Indians. In 1735 they temporarily established themselves in Savannah, but abandoned and *returned* (?) to Pennsylvania, in consequence of being obliged, if they remained, of taking up arms with the Spaniards against the English. Here it was, it is believed, that the great founder of Methodism, John Wesley, became acquainted with them, from whom he imbibed some of his peculiar sentiments. In 1741 they settled near the forks of the Delaware. Count Zinzendorf, then on a missionary tour in America, visited this place at Christmas, in that year, and lodged in a log hut attached to which was a stable. From this circumstance the name of Bethlehem was given to the settlement.

"The Count was undoubtedly pre-eminently fitted for a pioneer in the cause. He is represented to have been one of the most extraordinary divines that has appeared since the Reformation—a man of fervent piety, powerful imagination, original genius, and extensive requirements, and a sound, though perhaps, eccentric theologian. In his portrait he was dressed in a plain, single-breasted coat, a mantle partially thrown over the shoulder, and a white cravat, gathered in a simple fold; the hair dark, smoothly parted on the left side, and hanging in graceful ringlets down the neck and shoulders; the forehead high and even; eye penetrating; nose, long and aquiline; mouth large, but well formed, and the general expression highly intellectual, denoting purity of thought and benevolence. When here, he travelled much among the Indians, generally on horseback, but not unfrequently on foot. Once or twice he narrowly escaped being slain by them.

"No people have probably done so much in the cause of missions, in proportion to their means, as the Moravians. The sufferings and devotedness of their missionaries have been without a parallel, and many interesting anecdotes are given of them. They have gone forth single-handed and unknown, among the savage population of the West Indies, the sour, licentious hordes of Greenland, and the savages of our own country. In some instances *ten*, in others nearly *fifty* years have elapsed ere they saw any fruit; yet they continued to labor, full of faith, struggling against misrepresentations, suffering and loss of life.

"The number of missionaries, with their wives, employed in 1838, was 230. These had 51,000 souls under their care, of whom 16,000 were communicants. Owing to their simple mode of living, and the practice, in some instances, of supporting themselves by personal labor, this great scheme of missionary effort has been conducted on a very economical scale. The annual outlay of the Society for the support of their 42 stations, pensions to returned missionaries and widows, and the education and apprenticing of their children, and other expenses, amounts to about $50,000.

"There are at present in the United States several societies of Moravians, besides their independent communities; but as they do not come under their social regulations, cannot in the fullest sense be considered as belonging to them. Their communities are at Bethlehem, Nazareth, and Litiz, in Pennsylvania, and at Salem, in North Carolina.

"Bethlehem, their largest town, has about 1000 inhabitants, who are mainly of German descent, and speak and worship in that language. The village is romantically located, compactly built, and combines the attractions of both town and country. Their government is administered by a Board elected biennially. The land belongs to the Society, and is let out for building-lots, and other purposes, at a trifling annual rent. This enables them to keep their village free from unworthy persons; but they ever admit of the temporary residence of such as are willing to conform to their external regulations. The inhabitants are engaged in the usual mechanical, mercantile and agricultural employments, and some have acquired considerable property. It was formerly the custom here, and is still in Germany, to have separate establishments for such as had not families, viz, the 'Single Brethren's House,' for young men and apprentices, where they lived and carried on their respective employments; the 'Sister's House,' for the abode of unmarried females; and the 'Widow's House.' But as the Society has increased in wealth, the necessity for them has vanished, and it is believed they do not now exist any where in the Union.

"Meetings are held every evening in the week. Sunday mornings the litany is read, and a sermon delivered in the church; services are also performed in the evening. Certain festival days, such as Easter, Penticost, Christmas, &c., are celebrated. As usual among the Germans, great attention is paid to music; and almost every dwelling has its piano, and it forms one of the most interesting features of their public worship. Before the Lord's Supper they have a *Love Feast*, when all assemble expressly to listen to vocal and instrumental music, interspersed with hymns, in which the congregation join, while they partake of a cup of coffee, tea, or chocolate, and light cakes, in token of fellowship and brotherly union. Easter morning is devoted to a solemnity of a peculiar kind. At sunrise the congregation assemble in the grave-yard; a service accompanied by music, is celebrated, expressive of the joyful hopes of immortality and resurrection, and a solemn commemoration of those who in the course of the last year, have gone to heaven.

"Soon as a person dies the event is announced by solemn instrumental music, from a band stationed in the church tower. Different tunes are played, signifying the sex, age, and condition of the deceased, so it then usually is known who is dead. These death hymns, sounding as they always do, upon the still morning or evening air, must have a singularly melancholy effect upon the hearer, reminding him that he too is mortal. Their funeral services are usually performed in the Church, from thence the congregation march to the grave preceded by a band of music. If the deceased is a female, the ladies follow first after the coffin, if a male, the reverse. They consider death as no evil, but the entrance to eternal bliss, and therefore do not mourn for friends, nor wear insignia of grief. In alluding to the departed, they use the expression " heim gehen," signifying that they have *gone home*. The grave-yard, like most of this denomination, is laid out as a garden, and planted with trees, under which are seats for visitors. The graves are void of the disagreeable coffin-like shape of our own, but resemble flower-beds, and in many cases are covered with myrtle and other ornamental plants. The monuments are small slabs, laid horizontally on the graves, the inscriptions uppermost, and bearing simply the name, age, and place of decease."

BETHLEHEM.

CHAPTER X.

MORAVIAN MEMORIES.—MODERN BETHLEHEM. —THE OLD GRAVE YARD.—FUNERAL CEREMONIES OF THE MORAVIANS.—TSCHOOP.—TADEUSKUNG, ANECDOTE OF THE CHIEF, THE FIGURE ON INDIAN ROCK ON THE WISSAHICON.— DAVID NITSCHMANN.—DR. ROBERT DUDLEY ROSS.—MOURNING DRESS NOT WORN BY THE MORAVIANS.—THE PASSING BELL.—EASTER MORNING CELEBRATION.—DRIVES, WALKS, AND PLACES OF INTEREST NEAR BETHLEHEM. —DR. MAURICE C. JONES AND THE FREMDENDIENER'S.—MORAVIANS IN EARLY TIMES.

MORAVIAN MEMORIES.

BY GEN. WM. EMIL DOSTER. 1856.

There yon Church tower's summits high and hoary,
Point, like gray-mantled Prophets, up towards the sky
Where speaks yon dome Moravia's olden glory,
   Serene and high.

There sounds mysterious, soul-enthralling numbers, *
Melting in sunlight, as sad Memnon's voice of old—
Soft as the mermaid's strain that wooes the twilight
slumbers,
   Are gently rolled.

Ye have heard them blending with your matin dreaming,
Ye have caught their carols ling'ring o'er the lea,
Ye have heard them tell, in voices more than seeming—
   "'Tis well with me!"

Yet fraught, those strains, with wild and fearful meaning,
The list'ners pause, and muse with wond'ring tread—

 * The Trombone choir announcing a death from the steeple of the Church.

Hath here the reaper paused,—forever gleaning
   Amongst the dead?

Yes; to a holier, calmer meditation
Some soul has passed—some spirit of our love
Wakened amidst that wondrous revelation
   That waits above!

Gone,—gone forever! Brother! well betide thee!
Sing on where holier lays shall call thee blest;
Sing on 'till we attune our harps beside thee
   In peaceful rest.

And each departed hath its own sweet token,†
Whispered to loved ones in that trumpet tone,
Distilling dew o'er hearts with sorrow broken—
   From Heav'nly home.

Memento beautiful! that breathest consolation;
No shrieking, clanging, horror-brooding knell,
Nor hail'st despair, nor sick'ning desolation
   Like tolling bell.

O glorious ritual! Essence of Heaven's creation
In melody to mourn the sainted dead,
Pouring, like Israel's bard, his harp's oblation
   O'er Absalom's head.

Elysian lyres, ye are fountains forever flowing
O'er drooping flowers—echoes of angel's choirs,
Where white-robed souls are chanting, and forever
glowing
   With Heavenly fires!

And still sublimer far, ye sound to sad affliction
As wild as trump, triumphant o'er the blast,
Shall sound to our great final resurrection
   Creation's last!

That Grave-yard chant on resurrection morning‡
Floating like pean towards th' uprising sun—
Emblem of Christ's triumphant Earth returning—
   The slaughtered One!

 † Each class has its peculiar hymn tune performed by the Trombonists. There are eight classes.
 ‡ Easter morning celebration in the Grave Yard.

These voices, too, appear like Mary's weeping,
Her tearful off'r'ng o'er her Saviour's tomb—
Flinging above the beds of minstrel's sleeping
   In Heavenly bloom,

That grand old anthem, pride of Christmas even,*
Around yon Church's arches carolled near and far ;
Each songs sung th' angelic hosts, hailing on orient
 heaven
   That morning Star !

Shall these all perish like the dew of morning,
To vapory homes recalle ',—to Islands far away ;
Or shall their fragrance hallowed Earth adorning
   Endure for aye?

Yes, let these melodies forever breathe their numbers—
Exalt my soul to purer, nobler love,
'Till I awake the harp that never slumbers,
   In realms above !

Then sweep o'er my soul with entrancing emotion,
When they carry me there where the willow's sad wave.
O, chant one last dirge, ere I sleep in Lethe's ocean,
And dream it's last echo in the gloom of the grave.

Bethlehem is not now, as in days of old, approached from the south through a wood, by a bridle-path, or by the rough stage route, but by the more modern innovation of the "North Pennsylvania Railroad." The train, on leaving Hellertown—famous for its trout and trout suppers—winds around the eastern base of the Lehigh Mountains, on the south side of the river of that name ; and to the north-west, situated on a declivity, you see the houses, schools, and churches of that famous old town.

The first object that particularly attracts the eye, is the imposing school edifice, situated on the top of the hill. Near it looms up in the distance, the spire of the large Moravian church, and the belfry, from which the trombones sound the call to that joyous festival, the "Love Feast," or announce the death of one of the members of the brethren's church. Sounding from on high in the air, the sad, yet sweet dirges of the trombones, fill the hearer with a pleasing melancholy. It is one of those outward religious ceremonies which the Moravians still observe. May it long be cherished, and ever remain as a mark of their gentle faith, far too many of the forms and time-honored customs of the Church, have been abandoned, by the town and people becoming Americanized.

* Rev. F. F. Hagan's beautiful anthem—"Morning Star the darkness break."

It is related, "That once upon a time," when a band of hostile Indians had at nightfall secreted themselves on the south bank of the Lehigh, with the intent to destroy the place, and massacre its inhabitants, one of the brethren having died, the trombones, as usual, were sounded from the belfry of the Church, to communicate the loss to the infant settlement. Those sad, sweet dirges, three in number, announcing the sex, age, and condition in life, of the departed, breathed in mournful cadences upon the evening air, like the wailing tones of an Æolian harp, falling upon the ears of the lurking superstitious savages—who were watching the rites of their *Medicine Man*—seemed to them to be a warning from the Great Spirit. Thrilled with terror, they deserted their ambuscade, abandoned their murderous project, and with silent, rapid steps, plunged into the depths of the forest, and soon left far behind them the spot and people protected, as they supposed, by the great *Manitou.*"

The air of Bethlehem is provocative of a good appetite, and it must be confessed, that the inhabitants encourage it as much as possible, and then endeavor, with the utmost success, to gratify the desires they have excited. The housekeepers are all excellent cooks, and provide abundantly. Visions of "*apple cake,*" "*Moravian sugar cake,*" and other delicacies that continue to provoke the appetite after the solids have been eaten, still linger in the memory. For good living, better cannot be had than is obtained in the Hotels of this ancient borough.

The first visit of the stranger in Bethlehem, is naturally to the Moravian Cemetery, situated near the centre of the town, and occupying about five acres of ground. It is handsomely laid out with walks intersecting each other at right angles, having trees of various kinds planted on the borders, principally consisting of Poplar, Locust, Maple and Dog-wood.

" Beneath those rugged elms, that yew tree's shade,
 Where heaves the turf in many a mouldering heap ;
Each in his narrow cell forever laid—
 The rude forefathers of the hamlet sleep."

This sacred spot is entirely free from all

those ghastly monuments usually erected in burial grounds, to beautify them; but which render them places to be avoided by the sensitive, and fill the casual visitor with a thrill of dread in the day time, and with sensations of horror in the night; and sometimes scare the wits out of nervous people. It is said that on one occasion lately, it being necessary to change the place of repose of a departed brother, the grave-digger took advantage of a fine moonlight night to effect that purpose; it was quite late at night, and on reaching the coffin he found it would be necessary to have a rope, for which he dispatched his son, who was assisting him, but who remained away so long on the errand, the old man became very impatient; hearing at last footsteps approaching on one of the walks near him, he supposed it was his dilatory assistant; stripped of his coat, in his white shirt sleeves, his hat off, and his long white hair streaming in the wind, he raised up from the grave his tall white ghostly-looking figure, and with his deep voice sarcastically said, "*Komst den bald?*" (i. e.), *are you coming soon?* Imagine the terror of the belated wanderer, who was taking a short cut home—a yell, a rush of footsteps, and a wild jump which cleared the paling of the enclosure, was the answer to this summons from the grave.

The bravest-hearted would naturally hesitate about passing a night alone in the Cemeteries of Laurel Hill, or the Woodlands, in Philadelphia, or in any of those in our large cities, no matter how beautiful they might be in broad daylight; but in Bethlehem, the children play all day in the grave-yard, and go home at night with reluctance. Ladies sit on the benches in the shade at their sewing, at all hours of the day; and at night lovers oft wander under the trees, and linger side by side in this lovely place, forgetting all but themselves; even the fact that they are in a place sacred to the departed. All this is easily accounted for; the Moravians have striven to make their grave-yards as attractive as possible, and they have succeeded in that in which all the rest of the world

have failed; and it is very pleasant to know that it is so. Each grave is marked by a small marble slab, about a foot and a half by two feet in size, laid flat upon it; emblematic that death levels all, and that all are alike. Each stone has cut upon it the name, age, and birth-place of the departed. If a married woman, her maiden name. Sometimes a verse of a hymn, or a quotation from the Scriptures is added. Flowers are planted on many of the graves, and vases with wreaths and bouquets of flowers are common tokens of affection to be seen on the little slabs that cover the remains of some loved one, gone from the earth forever. Time soon takes off from the marble tablets their glaring whiteness; the grass grows around them, and they are almost hidden from the sight, and the visitors see only blooming flowers, trailing vines, luxuriant grasses, waving trees, and comfortable benches to sit upon. They hear the songs of the birds, see the children playing upon the walks, and lured by the beauty and novelty of the scene, forget entirely where they are, or to be sad and mournful. And thus the Moravian grave-yard becomes a place of cheerful resort to the living, and the sweetest spot on earth in which to place the remains of the loved ones who have gone home. Beneath dear Bethlehem's sky may my remains to earth committed be, when this life's weary journey's o'er.

Although HEINE has so sadly, yet so sweetly sung in immortal verse:

"Wo wird einst des Wandermuden
  Letzte ruhestatte sein?
Unter Palmen in dem Suden?
  Unter Linden an dem Rhein?

"Werd' ich wo in einer Wuste
  Eingescharrt von fremder Hand?
Oder ruh' ich an der Kuste
  Eines Meeres in dem Sand?

"Immerhin! mich wird umgeben
  Gotteshimmel, dort wie hier,
Und als Todtenlampen schweben
  Nachts die Sterne uber mir."

"Where shall then this weary wanderer,
  When the soul is parted, lie?
Under cool and dusky Lindens,
  With the blue Rhine sweeping by?
Or where stately Palms are waving
  'Gainst the cloudless Southern sky?

"Shall a grave be fashioned for me,
By a cold and alien hand—
Where no bird will sing above me
In that wild and desert land?
Or, the lonely shore receive me
'Neath the sea-coast's barren sand?

"Let me rest—God's heaven above me,
Full of love, shall ever be—
In *this* world—and that immortal.
Ah! my *Spirit* will be free—
And like Death's pale lamps will quiver,
Solemn night-stars over me."

The men and women are placed in separate divisions of the ground, in regular order, the heads to the north. The first interments of the bodies were evidently commenced at the north-west corner of the grave-yard; and one can read the names of the ancient fathers of the Church, or of some Indian convert, buried there. At first the tomb-stones were very small, and contained only the number of the interment on them

Those who love the neat simplicity of the Moravian system of burial, will perceive with regret, that in later years the Memorial Stones upon the graves are being made larger and larger; and are led to fear that the Church will at some future day depart from their ancient custom in this regard, and adopt the monumental piles of masonry used by other sects, which are only evidences of the pride and wealth of the living, and not marks of esteem for the dead.

At the eastern extremity of the Cemetery is a large grove of trees, a famous resort for flocks of birds of all kinds, but particularly the Black-birds, who make it their especial roosting-place at nights; although you may see there the beautiful Baltimore Oriole, Robins, Flickers, Thrushes, Cedar-birds and other kinds. Towards sunset they begin to arrive by flocks, squads, or in pairs, and settle in the trees, each kind of birds take possession of different trees, from which they make raids on each other, causing the air to resound with the rushing noise of their wings as they wheel in rapid flight, or with their twittering cries and songs, till the evening is far spent; in the morning the ground, and walks are covered with their beautiful feathers, which soon become the spoil of the children. Nothing in Bethlehem is more illustrative of the peaceful character of its people than this scene. The birds seem to know that they will not be harmed, and the place is always full of them, even in day time, especially the Robins, which are so tame that they scarcely seem disturbed by the presence of human beings.

Immediately adjoining this grove in the garden of Doctor Abraham Stout, stands an old majestic *pine tree*, which, although shorn of some of its lower limbs by vandal hands, and a portion of its upper trunk by the fierce storms of winter, is still a prominent object in an approaching view of Bethlehem, and a thing of great interest to the towns people. In the early Spring, flocks of Black-birds fill its branches with their nests, and the Orioles swing there their gourd-like Summer home; where high in air they are secure from molestation. A very handsome stereoscopic view of the "old Pine tree," is included in Kleckner's views of Bethlehem; and in the Moravian of March 22d, 1866, the "oldest inhabitant" thus relates its history:

"About the year 1793, two citizens of Bethlehem, viz.: the late *Joseph Horsfield* and *Frederick Fuehrer*, made a trip to the Pocono Mountains. On their return they observed many small Pine trees growing at the wayside. Mr. Horsfield said to his friend "come let us pull up a couple of these, and plant them when we come home, we may perhaps live to see them grow up large enough to furnish wood for our coffins." They brought two along, Mr. Fuehrer planted his a short distance east of the late "Old Crown Inn." He survived the tree by three days. It was blown down by a storm. The other one now standing was planted by Mr. Horsfield. The ground upon which it stands was formerly known as his nursery.

"Have pity on the Black-birds! they are becoming more domesticated than formerly. They may steal a few seeds from your gardens, but at the same time they relieve us from the thousands of insects more to be dreaded than all the harm done by the birds. Prudent farmers of the present day welcome the appearance of the Black-birds, and even entice them with food.

" May we not, with very slight change, address Bryant's words to the water fowl, to these birds in their migrations hitherward

"All day your wings have fann'd,
    At that far height the cold, thin atmosphere,
Yet stoop not weary, to welcome land,
    Though the dark night is near."

' And soon that toil shall end,
    Soon shall you find a Summer home, and rest;
And scream among your fellows,—Pines shall bend
    Soon o'er your sheltered nest."

And add the moral:

He, who from zone to zone,
Guides through the boundless sky your certain flight
In the long way we must tread alone,
    Will lead our steps aright."

In the north-western part of the Cemetery, in that portion of the ground allotted to the men, will be found the graves of many Indian converts. Among them, conspicuous by having at its head a rose bush, that in Summer bears a white rose, which was planted there by Miss Mary Eyre, a daughter of the late Manuel Eyre, lie the remains of *Tschoop*, said to be the father of *Uncas*, who, under the name of *Chin gach gook*, is one of the characters in Cooper's series of novels, called "Leather Stocking Tales." The tomb-stone bears the following inscription.

"In Memory of
Tschoop,—a Mohican Indian,
Who in holy baptism, April 17th, 1742,
received the name of
John.
One of the first fruits of the
Mission at shekomeko, *and a*
remarkable instance of the power
of divine grace, whereby he
became a distinguished teacher
among his nation.
He departed this life in full
assurance of faith at Bethlehem
August 27th, 1747.
" There shall be one fold
and one Shepherd.—*John x. 16.*"

There are altogether 58 Indian converts buried in the Cemetery. A ludicrous anecdote is told of the celebrated Indian Chief *Tadeuskung*, a Moravian convert. While the Chief was on a visit to Philadelphia, after his conversion, he was found one Monday morning, by a well known Friend, *Anthony Benezet*, sitting on a curbstone, in Market street, with his feet in the gutter—very drunk. " Why, *Tadeuskung*, I thought thee was a good Moravian?" said the Friend; " Ugh! Chief no Moravian now, Chief joined Quaker meeting yesterday," replied the facetious savage.

Tadeuskung is described as having been a tall, portly Indian Chief, proud of his position as the leader of the Delawares, or Lenni Lenape tribe; an earnest talker about his State and Nation, and over-fond of "fire-water." The Delawares once roamed over our hills in pursuit of game, or held their Councils in the valleys of the Wissahicon and *Manatawna*, as the Schuylkill was originally called. Man-a-taw-na, (*i. e.*) the place where they drank.

On the eastern side of Wissahicon Creek, nearly opposite the "Indian Rock" Hotel, may be seen the figure of an Indian chief fastened upon the face of a high perpendicular rock, which commands a fine view of the surrounding country. This rock is peculiar, having a pulpit-like recess formed by nature in its perpendicular front, with a stone table in the centre like a pulpit desk, which tradition says, was used by the Chief (*Tadeuskung*) when addressing his tribe. From the papers of Joseph Eastburn Mitchell, one of Philadelphia's antiquarians, to whom the public is indebted, in a great measure, for this memorial to that celebrated Indian Chieftain; much of the information here given concerning him is due. Mitchell spells the old Chieftain's name *Tedyuscung*, but I have preferred to follow Cranz; see his History of the Brethren, page 476. The figure of the Indian Chief was placed there on the 18th of July, 1856, in commemoration of *Tadeuskung's* last visit to the spot, which occurred just 100 years previous, and is said to be a correct representation of a Delaware Chief. This "Indian Rock" and "Indian Hill," as it is called, on which it is situated, was venerated by Indians as a place sacred

to the Great Spirit, and *Tadeuskung* and his
band of warriors often frequented the spot;
endeared to all the tribe, as the place where
their forefathers had offered up their sacri-
fices to the great *Manitou;* for the *Lenni
Lenape's* were the former owners of all these
lands, from the Delaware to the foot of the
" Endless" mountains.

Of the old Chief it may be said :

"Once a mighty Chief, whose many bands
  Ranged freely o'er these shaded lands ;
But *now* there's scarcely left a trace
  To mind us of that faded race !"

And of the Red Men who once lived here,
it truly has been written :

"———that all have passed away,
  The noble race—and brave ;
That their light canoes have vanished,
  From off the crested wave——
That 'mid the forests where they roamed,
  There rings no hunter's shout ;——
But, their name is on your waters,
  Ye may not wash it out."

Near the grave of Tschoop, towards the
west, are interred the remains of the Founder of Bethlehem, and upon the tablet dedi-
cated to his memory, is engraved :

" DAVID NITSCHMAN
FOUNDER*
of Bethlehem, who felled the first tree, and
built the first house.
Born September 18th, 1676,
IN MORAVIA,
Died April 14th, 1758.
This second
Memorial was erected
June 1853."

On the 22nd of February 1751, JOHANNA,
the first wife of the very Rev. Bishop John
Nitschman, Sr., departed this life at Bethlehem. Her husband was then the ruling
spirit here, being the successor of *Spangenberg.* She was an extraordinary woman, one
of the eighteen single women, who at Hernhut, formed that covenant, out of which grew

---

* The above, commonly known as " Father Nitschman," page 6, was the Master-builder. His nephew,
Bishop David Nitschman, was the Founder, see page
59, also the " Transactions of the Moravian Historical
Society," page 125, in a note.

the class, or choir, of " Single Sisters" of the
Moravian Church. She was buried in the
(then) exact centre of this old burial ground,
in the middle path.

The middle path was then the second one
from Market Street, running east and west.
Mrs. Nitschman was the 153rd person buried
in those grounds. The mound over the grave
was subsequently levelled, owing to the fact,
that it was in the path, and became en-
croached upon, and the tablet defaced. She
was laid there because of her exemplary
christian life and character. She was then,
and still is called " *a hand-maiden of the Lamb ;*"
and by some, " The Congregation's Mother ;"
and her memory is honored in the church.
She was thus buried, not at her own request,
but by those in authority, as an honor, and
a bright example to others. Her grave is
directly opposite (north of) No. 114, and
south of No. 169.

In the north-eastern portion of the Cemetery is a stone, on which is the following :

" LOUIS DAVID
DE SCHWEINITZ,
Senior Civilis.
He was born
The 13th of February, 1780,
at Bethlehem, Pa.
Departed this life
the 8th of January, 1834."

In the southern section of the ground, set
apart for the males, beneath the shade of the
grand old American tulip trees, which ornament this quiet home of the departed ones, lie
the remains of a boyhood friend and fellow-
student--ROBERT DUDLEY ROSS, M. D., a nephew of John Ross, the late celebrated Chief of
the Cherokee nation. The grave of the old
Chief's eldest son, James McDonald Ross, is
near by. The inscription on his tomb is very
singular.

Bethlehem was until very lately, the residence of many families, descendants of the
American Indians.

Among the Indian converts buried in this
old Cemetery, there is one particularly deserving remembrance, namely : the aged
Brother MICHAEL. In his younger days, this

old Savage, was one of the most experienced and undaunted warriors of the Munsey tribe. He was baptised in 1742, and led until his death, a consistent christian life. He was styled "The crown of the Indian Mission." The serenity of his countenance, when laid in his coffin, formed a singular contrast to the warlike characters scarified and tattooed upon his face when he was a noted Indian brave. On his right cheek and temple was the representation of a rattlesnake; from the under lip a pole was drawn, passing over the nose and up between the eyes to the top of his forehead, ornamented at every quarter of an inch with round marks, intended to represent the number of scalps he had taken; upon his left cheek two lances, crossing each other appeared; and upon the lower jaw was delineated the head of a wild-boar. All these figures were executed with a remarkable degree of artistic skill. He died July 25th, 1758.

The funeral ceremonies of the Moravians are of a peculiar character. The coffin containing the remains of the departed, is generally placed in the "Dead House," a neat little building back of the church, and in front of the "Old Chapel." After the funeral services in the church, appropriate to the occasion, the coffin is placed on a bier, covered with a white linen cloth, and taken part of the way up the path towards the cemetery, where it is then set down at the northeastern corner of a square plot of ground, in the centre of which is growing now a magnificent weeping willow; each side of this square is bounded by gravelled walks, on which the mourners take their stand, forming in military parlance, a hollow square, the family of the departed one, forming the eastern line. The Minister stands at the head of the bier, and reads aloud the following hymn, line by line, and the congregation sing it, accompanied by the trombones:

> "Oh, let me when expiring,
>   Recline upon Thy breast ;
> Thus I shall be acquiring,
>   Eternal life and rest."

When this is finished, the procession moves on to the place of interment, where the corpse being placed beside the grave the Minister says :

> "Lord have mercy upon us."

And the people respond :

> "Christ have mercy upon us.
> Lord have mercy upon us,
>   Christ hear us."

Then follows the Lord's prayer, with the solemn Litany :

> Lord God, Son, Saviour of the world,
>   Be gracious unto us,
>   By thy human birth,
>   By thy prayers and tears,
>
>   Bless and comfort us,
>   Lord and God.
>   Lord God, Holy Ghost,
>   Abide with us forever.

Then follows the prayer, beginning : " I am the resurrection and the life, saith the Lord, &c." After which the assembly sing, to the accompaniment of the trombone choir :

> "Now to the earth let these remains,
>   In hope committed be,
> Until the body changed attains
>   To immortality."

During the singing of this verse, the body is deposited in its last resting place; and after the Minister has read the remainder of the solemn service, the people sing :

> " The Saviour's blood and righteousness,
>   My beauty is, my glorious dress ;
> Thus well array'd, I need not fear,
>   When in His presence I appear."

And then the congregation are dismissed by the Pastor with the usual benediction ; and some linger long around the sacred spot, endeared to so many of them by sad and tender recollections, of their loved ones buried there.

The mournful accompaniment of the trombones on such occasions, never fails to remind the hearer of the beautiful lines of the Episcopal burial service : 1 Cor., xv, 51-2.

" Behold I show you a mystery : we shall not all sleep, but we shall all be changed, in a moment, in the twinkling of an eye, at the last trump ; for the trumpet shall sound, and the dead shall be raised incorruptible, and we shall be changed."

"I'd gladly hear the trombone's sound,
I'd gladly sink beneath the ground,
And mingle with the dead who lie,
So still beneath this Bethlehem sky."

The Moravians do not put on *mourning* for the dead, they consider it wrong in principle, deeming Heaven the final abode of all God's chosen creatures; they esteem it a blessing *"to go home."*

This is an example which it would be well for all other denominations to follow; for independent of the fact that the wearing of mourning is but an outward show, it is an useless expense, even to those in comfortable circumstances, while many others who can ill afford the outlay in this regard, spend the means to be in the *fashion*, which are needed for the common necessaries of life. The pomp, parade, and expense of funeral displays, are much to be deplored, their effect is vicious, for the poor will imitate their wealthier neighbors.

It is the custom in Bethlehem, to announce the death of a member of the congregation by the music of the trombones, performed in the belfry of the church; no matter where they may die.

" And each departed hath its own sweet token,
Whispered to loved ones in that trumpet's tone,
Distilling dew o'er hearts with sorrow broken,
From heav'nly home."

Three dirges are always performed, the first and last being the same air, (T, 151, A.) and are selected from the appropriateness of those hymns for such an occasion. The second air is varied, as it designates the sex, and condition in life of the deceased, or in Moravian phraseology, the choir to which the departed belonged. In the German Liturgy Book, where the order for these announcements of death are given, (pages 217, 218 and 219,) the hymn which suits for each choir is appended; and by the old Moravian is at once recognized. They are as follows:

   83. D. for Married Men.
   79.   "   Married Women.
  132. A. " Widowers.
  149. A. " Widows.
  185.   " The Single Brethren.

   37. A. for The Single Sisters
   23.   " Youths.
   14. A. " Maidens.
   39. A. " Little Boys.
   82. D. " Little Girls.

The following interesting account from the MORAVIAN of September, 24th, 1868, will better explain the meaning of the funeral dirges, which are as interesting to the strangers as they are dear to the Moravians:

" We will say that a brother in the middle age of life has departed. The sad event is soon after touchingly announced to the congregation, by the trombones, who ascending to the church tower, play at brief intervals, *three* solemn dirges. How affecting the soft funeral tones, attracting the attention of the most careless; the busy hum of life is for a moment arrested, as the hurried question is asked:—" Who is dead?" The notes of the music are not blown at random. They give utterance, as it were, to a living voice. Each dirge has reference to a special hymn, which is expressive of particular declarations in reference to the departed, or of the prayerful wishes of the survivors. Thus the first hymn makes the announcement of the departure, which freely translated from the original German, is:

> A pilgrim soul released
>   From sorrow, care, and pain,—
> Has e'en now left our covenant,
>   " *Gone home !*" with Christ to reign.
> The hour of consummation
>   For him has struck,—thrice blest!
> We wander still,—all weary,—
>   Our lov'd one is at rest.

The second dirge denotes the class, and period of life to which the deceased belonged, and intimates what are the sentiments of the dying Christian at the hour of departure. The tune here is varied to suit the age and sex of the person. In the present instance, that of the man of middle life:

> Jesus Christ as I go hence
>   Still is near me! This inspireth
> Ever living confidence
>   Yea,—even as his love requireth
> Hope with dust, rests on my grave;
> His full likeness I shall have.

The closing dirge is to the same solemn tune as the first, and is the believer's practical response to the sad announcement:

> Lord at my dissolution, .
> Do not from me depart;
> Support at the conclusion
> Of life, my fainting heart;
> And then, though I be dying,
>   'Midst sickness, grief and pain,
> I shall, on thee relying,
>   Eternal life obtain.

From June 28th, 1742, to February 9th, 1853, or during 111 years, 1672 persons died in Bethlehem and its vicinity.

The Moravians do not toll the bell at funerals, but before the services are held in the church, the bell is rung in the usual manner to call the congregation together.

On the tenor bell of the Parish Church of Abbott's Leigh, Somersetshire, England, are the words:

> "I to the Church the living call,
> And to the grave doth summon all."

The "Passing Bell," was so named because it was tolled when any one passed away from this life. Hence it was sometimes called the *Soul's Bell*, and was rung that those who heard it might pray for the soul of the dying person. This custom was continued till the time of Charles II.; *it arose in the darkest ages.* The ringing of bells was supposed to drive away the evil spirits which might assail the dying; the tolling of the bell, it was thought, struck them with terror.

Now the "Passing Bell" is no longer rung in England, but on the morning after the death of any person, the bell is tolled; and at the end of the tolling in Yorkshire, and Dorsetshire, 9 knells are tolled for a man, 6 for a woman, and 3 for a child. In Somersetshire, 3 knells are tolled for a man, and only 2 for a woman.

In some of the parishes of England it was customary to ring out the number of bells corresponding to the age of the person who had died. So says the author of "A BRAVE LADY," in chapter 12. And such was the custom in the parish of St. Paul's Episcopal Church at Chester, Pennsylvania, in my boyhood. So that the announcement of death by the music of the trombones, by the Moravians, is but an observance of an ancient custom of the Christian Church, although in another form. How old a custom it is, it would be difficult to say, but as horns were used before bells, it is without doubt the more ancient.

On Easter morning at sunrise, the Moravian congregations assemble in their respective grave-yards, and sing their Liturgy. A friend thus wrote on April 19th, 1867: "On Easter morning you will recollect, that we in Bethlehem generally go into the grave-yard, singing our Liturgy for the occasion. Mr. Jedediah Weiss, and Mr. Charles F. Beckel, will have played as members of the trombone choir for *fifty* years this Easter morning. This is a rare occurrence." Both of these fine old Moravian gentlemen are still living, in excellent health, and have played in the choir three Easter mornings since the above was written; may their days be long in the land.

In this connection, the following may not be without interest:

(Special Correspondence of The Press.)

BETHLEHEM, March 29, 1869.

Yesterday morning being Easter Sunday, the accustomed Litany was performed, with other services, according to immemorial local practice, in the Moravian church, conducted by the Rev. E. de Schweinetz, assisted by the Rev. L. R. Huebner. These services began at 5 A. M. in the church, with singing and the litany for Easter morning. By daybreak the whole congregation, consisting of 2,000 persons, proceeded to the burial-ground, preceded by the trombone choir, and a large open square was formed, after which, with musical accompaniment, the choir began with—

> The graves of all His saints Christ blest,
> And soften'd every bed;
> Where should the dying members rest,
> But with the dying Head.

There is another verse, after which the congregation joined in with

> Then let the last trumpet sound,
> And bid our kindred rise
> Awake, ye nations under ground,
> Ye saints, ascend the skies

Then the minister followed, with excerpts from the Holy Scriptures, the congregation giving the "Amen," the choir again chiming in, and the congregation, minister, and choir thus alternating to the close of this singularly interesting service."

The following Obituary of a departed Brother, copied from the "Moravian," is inserted here, that all may see how among the Moravians, a friend who hath left, is mourned and honored:

"IN MEMORIAM.

Departed this life at Bethlehem, Pa., October 14th, 1868, AMOS COMENIUS CLAUDER, son of the Rev. Henry G. Clauder, and manager of the Moravian Publication Office. Aged thirty-three years.

"'Our deceased brother has left behind him a record of sterling virtues, and christian goodness, which will long remain a cherished remembrance. Exemplary in all the relations of domestic and social life, of a bright and cheerful temperament, an honorable and industrious man of business, a conscientious and devoted agent of the church, his loss will be widely felt, and felt more deeply as time elapses.

* Sleep in peace!
All thy earthly toil must cease,
For death's night hath closed around thee,
And its peaceful slumbers bound thee,
'Till His voice all eyes release.
Sleep in Peace!

Sleep in peace!
'Till the eternal morn appear;
By the risen Saviour's merit—
Thou endless life inherit,
By the power of His word
Called to life.

Besides the large Moravian church, and the Old Chapel, there are Lutheran, German Reformed, English and German Methodist, and Catholic places of worship in Bethlehem. An Episcopal church is now spoken of, as intended to be erected at the corner of Market and High Streets. In South Bethlehem there is a handsome Episcopal church, and parsonage adjoining, occupying a prominent

* Sung at his funeral by the ANION Society, of which he was a member."

site; and also a handsome Catholic church, and a fine large Moravian church. The building known as "Christmas Hall," on the grounds of the Lehigh University, was formerly a Moravian church.

The Lutheran congregation have a large place of interment at High and Church Sts., adjoining Nisky-Hill Cemetery. It only needs a small expenditure, and some exercise of taste to make it a very pretty spot.

Bethlehem, proper, covers quite a large area of ground on both sides of the Manockasy Creek. That portion of the town south of the Lehigh River, being called "South Bethlehem," and incorporated under that name. The most interesting part, however, is that portion occupied by the old town, on the hill to the north of the river Lehigh, which is the old Bethlehem of history, containing the old Moravian buildings, churches, schools, stores, and the old taverns, made famous by the writings of travellers. There are many handsome residences, and many more very comfortable ones in this part of the town, nearly every dwelling has a fine yard and garden attached, containing many varieties of fruit trees. Fruit is raised in abundance in this section of the State, and in riding through the country around, and by the hill farms, the stranger cannot fail to realize the fact. In the mountains, cherry trees abound, both wild and cultivated, their fruit serving to feed the small birds that are so numerous in the hills, and the country around Bethlehem, where they are not much disturbed fortunately, for game birds are very scarce in the Lehigh Valley, and consequently the country is not infested by sportsmen, who generally, when they cannot get better game, slaughter every insectivorous bird they come across. A few partridges and squirrels, are occasionally to be seen in the fall, these, with some wild pigeons, are the only game to tempt the gunner to a "day's shooting in the country." The valley and the mountains are, however, beautiful, and the lover of nature cannot but enjoy the many beautiful walks and drives in the vicinity of the town, and

NAZARETH HALL,

NAZARETH, NORTHAMPTON COUNTY, PENNA.

REV. EUGENE LEIBERT, PRINCIPAL.

will not soon tire of the many charming views that open around him in every direction.

The favorite ride for visitors to Bethlehem, is to "*Bauer's Rock*," the highest point on the mountain range to the south of the town, and about eight miles distant. It is about 1000 feet above tide water, and from the two high rocks which crown the summit of the ridge, there is a beautiful view of Saucon Valley to the south, and with a good glass, it is said, Chestnut Hill, near Philadelphia, can be seen on a clear day; while to the north, are splendid views of the Blue-ridge, the Lehigh Water Gap, and the mountains beyond and around Mauch Chunk; the Little Gap, Allentown, and the Lehigh River winding in the distance like a silver ribbon.

From here, a ride to Allentown, and a visit to the curious spring which furnishes the town with water, is the usual programme. At the spring the water rushes out of the side of a hill in an immense volume, falling first into quite a small basin, clean, cool, sparkling and delicious, thence flowing into a small pond stocked with a large number of trout. From this pond the supply necessary for the town, which has a population of 17,-000 inhabitants, is drawn, and yet enough flows off from it to fill quite a large dam, which furnishes sufficient water power for the use of several large mills. In its way it is a greater curiosity than the spring at Bethlehem; a handsome hotel was erected in 1868, near this spring, for summer boarders.

Then there is the drive to Hellertown, about four miles from Bethlehem, where there is a hotel, with an excellent cook; parties go there to enjoy a trout supper, waffles and spring chicken. Make your first drive here, for trout are very scarce, and very expensive.

To the northeast of Bethlehem, and about ten miles distant, is the quiet Moravian village of NAZARETH. In this latter town is located the *Pedagogium*, or Boarding School for Boys, instituted by the Moravians in the year 1759. in which, now, as in many other schools of a like character in the United States, military tactics are taught; and the pupils are dressed in a grey uniform, somewhat similar to those worn by the cadets in the U. S. Military Academy at West Point.

There are some quaint old buildings in Nazareth, and a day or two can be profitably be passed there by the stranger in visiting the many places of interest in the town, and its vicinity. The drive to it from Bethlehem is through a very beautiful country, and fine views reward the beholder on all sides. The view of the surrounding country from the old Moravian grave yard, is especially worthy of note.

The *Pedagogium*, or Boarding School, better known as Nazareth Hall, stands on a commanding site in the western extremity of the village, its front having a southern exposure, with a fine large lawn in front, intersected with walks, embracing to the south a view of a landscape of exceeding beauty. In front of the Hall stands a handsome monument, erected in 1868, to the memory of the graduates of the institution who laid down their lives in the services of their country during the late rebellion of 1861-65. A fine old piece of woods to the west of the Hall, partly on the rising hill, has been reserved as a play-ground for the boys, it is neatly laid out with walks, having a spring and a small stream of water running through it, with some small ponds of water, seats and arbors abound under the old hickory, oak and chestnut trees which ornament the grounds; the Moravians beautify and adorn some such spot as this in all their towns and villages, quiet, shady retreats, attractive alike to the young and the old.

"Nazareth Hall," was erected as a Manor House for Count Zinzendorf, in hopes of his taking up his permanent residence there. It was intended to accommodate the Count and his coadjutors, and was designated as the "Pilgrim house." The corner stone was laid on the 3rd of May, 1755, and the structure completed in 1756. The Hall is a massive structure of blue limestone, now roughcast with mortar and gravel, with an unsightly brick addition, lately added to its eastern wing, out of all architectural proportion and taste. The ancient portion, with its double pitched roof and two rows of dormer windows, with the balcony and belfry which surmount it, give it a venerable appearance well becoming its antiquity. On the east side of the open square in front of the Hall, stands the old " Sisters' House."

On the 6th of June, 1759, Nazareth Hall was opened as a boarding school for the sons of the Moravian Brethren, with 92 scholars. In 1779 the school was closed, owing to the inability on the part of the Church to defray the expense of educating, as they did, almost gratuitously, so many children. The Brethren, having about this time involved themselves in so many expensive missionary enterprises, this step was indispensably necessary. But on the 3rd of October, in the year 1785, the institution was again opened as a boarding school for boys of all Protestant denominations, and has ever since enjoyed an increasing patronage, with successful results. Boys are admitted to the school from nine to fifteen years of age. The necessary expense of the scholastic year is $280. This does not include music, drawing, painting or the foreign languages, for each of which a small extra charge is made of about $20 per year.

The situation of the town, and the healthy air of the adjacent country, render Nazareth a very eligible location for a boarding school; but a more quiet country town cannot well be imagined. "Sleepy Hollow," is a lively place in comparison; by staying there a few days one gets an idea of life in Bethlehem a hundred years ago.

In the American Gazetteer, published in 1797, there is a very interesting sketch of Nazareth, to which the reader is referred. And a full account of the Boarding School will be found in William C. Reichel's " Historical Sketch of Nazareth Hall, from 1755 to 1869," published in the latter year, by J. B. Lippincott & Co., Philadelphia.

OLD NAZARETH is situated a short distance east of the present town of that name. It is still the property of the Society, but no longer the seat of a Moravian Congregation.

Christian Spring, about two miles to the south-west of Nazareth, was formerly a small Moravian settlement, and was named in honor of Christian Renatus Zinzendorf, a son of the Count. It was built in a quadrangular form. On the north were the chapel and dwelling houses; on the east the different workshops, and a grist and saw mill, propelled by the waters of the Manockasy. All the buildings enclosed are square and of considerable size. During the Indian wars of 1755-56 and 57, it was stockaded, and put into a condition of defence. The Government attached great importance to the place, it being one of the principal outposts of the white settlements. The buildings are all still standing, except the mills. It is no longer a Moravian settlement, although the property is still owned by the Society.

GNADENSTHAL, i. e., "The *Valley of Grace*," is situated about half a mile to the north of Christian Spring. It was formerly a Moravian settlement, but is now the property of Northampton County, and the County Poor House has been erected there.

Friedensthal, or " *Valley of Peace*," was another of these little settlements, with small Moravian Congregations. It is about two miles east of Nazareth; but the place is no longer owned by the Society. See Bondthaler's Life of Heckwelder, published in Philadelphia in 1847, in the notes to page 34.

The drives to Freemansburg, Bath, Catasauqua, Easton, and Nazareth, are very beautiful; the lovely scenery will alone repay the visitor to either of these places, passing as the roads do, through the " Drylands," presenting varied views of river, mountains, valleys, and richly cultivated farm lands.

On the south side of the Lehigh, near Bethlehem, situated on a plateau of the Lehigh Hills, is the celebrated " *Water Cure Establishment*," of Dr. Oppelt; during the Summer months the house is full of patients, and boarders from a distance. The situation is very retired; the grounds are beautiful, and the view of the surrounding country from the hills in the rear of the place, which are covered with fine forest trees, is exceedingly fine; near the Establishment is a never failing spring of water, gushing up out of a crevice in the rocks, around which are fixed seats; close by are swings and a bowling alley, for the amusement of the boarders. This spot would be a splendid position for a hotel. Adjoining this Establishment to the south, is the handsome residence of the late Mr. Fiot, once a celebrated music publisher in Philadelphia, now deceased. The house has been enlarged, and is now occupied as a Boarding School for young ladies, under the auspices of the Episcopal Church, with Miss Edith Chase as Principal—and is called " BISHOPTHORPE SCHOOL."

There are many objects of interest in Bethlehem worthy of a visit; and as in the days of old, the stranger was shown over the town and through the Brethren's buildings by " Father" Thomas; so in these later days, a worthy gentleman has been found to supply the place of that kind old patriarch, now departed. The writer, and so very many visitors to Bethlehem, have received so many marks of attention and kindness, from this fine old Moravian Brother, that these sketches would not be complete, without mention of his name in connection with this ancient old Burg. DR. MAURICE C. JONES, is now the *cicerone* of the visitors to Bethlehem, a self-constituted *Fremdendiener*. He is a retired physician, of ample means, a Welsh Moravian, who loves Bethlehem, his adopted country, and his ancient and honorable church, taking great interest in all the offices of the Society; and is an agreeable, estimable, and courteous gentleman, of fine conversational powers, justly proud of the venerable old town in which he lives, and its historical mementoes. The same affectionate regard is shown to him, in our modern times, by all who know him, as was formerly shown to Mr. Thomas, in the days of his usefulness.

From the early days of the settlement of Bethlehem, it has been customary for the church authorities to appoint some one to wait on all strangers visiting the town, who desire to see and inspect the schools, and the various buildings of the Society. John Etwein, afterwards a celebrated Bishop of the Church, was the first " *Fremdendiener*," or guide to the visitors, more properly perhaps translated as " The Strangers' Friend;" he served from 1776 to 1779, and was succeeded by Nicholas Garrison; how long the latter acted in this capacity I cannot say, but Chastellux mentions him in his work, which was printed in 1782. After him, John Bonn was the guide till 1788. He was better known as " *Pappy Bonn*," an affectionate appellation bestowed upon him by the young girls at the Seminary. His successor was Francis, more familiarly called " *Daddy Thomas*," at first by the girls, to whom he carried the letters from the post office, and afterwards by everyone. He was a very amiable and courteous old man, a great favorite with all who knew him, and full of old fashioned wit. He departed this life in 1822, being then in the ninetieth year of his age, and his remains repose in the old grave-yard on the Hill. He held his position as guide, and remained in the employ of the Seminary till his death; since then no one has been named to perform such duties. But courteous gentlemen are always to be found in the congregation to act as the " Strangers' friend."

The Moravians were once a very plain, unassuming people, forbidding vain show in dress, and economical in all their habits; their apparel was simple, clean and neat. The straight, unlappelled, dark brown coat, the broad brimmed, low crowned hat, the knee-buckled small clothes, the broad round-toed shoe, were consistent characteristics of a Moravian Brother; whilst the plain drab or black silk bonnet, the three cornered white kerchief, the plain silk gown, the comfortable hood furnished cloak, the stuff shoe, for comfort and convenience, were the Sisters' attire; and their manners were bland, courteous and winning. This costume was continued inviolate until about 1825;

since then the Moravians have not been distinguishable by dress from any other denomination of Christian people.

The air of Bethlehem seems not only to be very health-giving to invalids, but also conducive to longevity, of which there are many instances among the inhabitants. Eighty-four is not an unusual age for the people to attain, as may be seen from an inspection of the tomb-stones in the old grave-yard. And there are now many residents of the place whose ages exceed that number of years.

For the first twenty years after the settlement of the town, all property was held in common by the "Economy." But in 1762, the Society began to dispose of portions of their real estate, to such of the Brethren as were desirous, and able, to purchase homesteads for their families.

The number of people belonging to the Economy in 1756, was 953. They did not all live in Bethlehem, but some in *Saucon*, some at *Lisby*, and some in the other Moravian towns in the vicinity. The Indian converts, numbering 82, are not included in the enumeration, nor the young Indian women who lived with the Sisters. There was quite a falling off in the number of the inhabitants, after the abolition of the Communist system in 1762. In 1756 there were 219 "Single Brethren" living at Bethlehem, Christian Spring, Nazareth, Gnadensthal and Friedensthal; but in the year 1782, the number was reduced to 39.

But one person of each trade or vocation was permitted to settle in any Moravian town in the United States; this system was kept up till 1828, the object being to prevent rivalry in business. The secular affairs of the town were governed by a Board called the "COLLEGIUM," who regulated all matters of trade; and all members of the Society intending to commence any business, had first to get their permission to do so. The stores, taverns, and several other branches of trade, continued to be owned and carried on by the Society, until within about 25 years ago. The last business conducted by the Brethren

at Bethlehem, was the accommodation of travellers at the "Sun Hotel," which they sold in 1848, to Charles Augustus Luckenback.

" *On the other side of Jordan*," at the foot of South-Mountain, nine miles from Bethlehem, and five miles south-west from Allentown, is situated the Moravian settlement of EMMAUS; it is built on a single street; the town contains one store, about thirty-five dwellings, and a Congregation House, which is united to a Chapel. There is also a tavern in the place. The land on which the village is erected, was bequeathed to the Society by two members of the church, for the support of a minister and a school. Ogden, in his old work, already referred to, at page 55, says : " In this place was one of those accommodations for the lodging of a married couple, which cause so much conversation. * * According to constant practice, single beds are used by unmarried persons, from their youth upwards. When a couple are united in holy wedlock, and become heads of a family, these two beds and their bedsteads, are placed so contiguous to each other, that they are covered with one general blanket or counterpane. This outward covering designates the lodging of some married persons ; but this is not an universal custom, as many use the common large beds. It is convenient, in case of sickness of either party, the nursing of children, and the poverty of young housekeepers, who may not wish to be at the expense of exchanging or altering their single beds, bedding or beadsteads. The bedstead is not different from that in common use, except that it has head, foot, and side boards."

I am unable to perceive anything singular or curious in the above related custom, which it is said, excited a great deal of impertinent curiosity, and in consequence the usage was discontinued ; because I know married people who now sleep upon *single beds*, arranged just as the old Moravians fixed theirs, and for some of the same reasons, although they are persons of wealth ; besides this, it is well known, or ought to be, that in the better circles of society in England, and Continental Europe, it is customary for man and wife, although living together amicably under the same roof, to occupy separate sleeping apartments.

On the 28th of April, 1870, I received the following communication from my friend *Bertine S. Erwin*, of Bethlehem, in reference to the "Old Pine Tree," mentioned in this chapter, which had become so decayed in its upper branches, as to be unsafe; so the old land mark had to be destroyed:—

"I have a sad communication to make, inasmuch as the old pine tree departed this life, this A. M. at 8. 05. The chief mourners, the Blackbirds, are congregated in the grave-yard surrounding the garden.

"The age of the tree is 70 years, or thereabouts. It took four men 28 minutes to fell it. Knowing your interest in matters pertaining to Bethlehem antiquities, I thought it might interest you to hear of this sudden "pining" away. This old tree was only 80 feet in height, although it looked much higher, it had, however, lost about 20 feet of its top in a storm some years ago. The lowest limb was 44 feet from the ground."

In Chastellux's Travels in North America, vol. 11, page 311. The Translator in a note says: "It is remarked that on the lands within reach of Moravian settlements, the cultivation is superior, and every branch of husbandry is better carried on, first from the emulation excited by these industrious people, and secondly from the supply the countrymen procures from them of every necessary implement of husbandry, &c., fabricated in these settlements." These remarks are as true to-day, 1870, as they were in 1780. "Besides those the Marquis speaks of, I visited some others, not far from Bethlehem, at one of which called *Nazareth*, is a famous gunsmith, from whom my friend bought a pair of pistols, many of which I saw there of the most perfect workmanship. Nothing can be more enchanting than these establishments; out of the sequestered wilderness they have formed well built towns, vast edifices all of stone, large orchards, beautiful and regular shaded walks in the European fashion, and seem to combine with the most *complete* separation from the world, all the comforts, and even many of the luxuries of polished life. At one of these cleared out settlements in the midst of a forest, between Bethlehem and Nazareth, possessing all the advantages of mills and manufactures, I was astonished at the delicious sounds of an Italian concert; but my surprise was still greater, on entering a room, where the performers turned out to be common workmen of different trades, playing for their amusement. At each of these places, the brethren have a common room, where violins and other instruments are suspended, and always at the service of such as choose to relax themselves, by playing singly, or taking a part in a concert."

This old work brings us back by easy stages, from "Moravian Mill" to Bethlehem, from which we have wandered. The translator, an Englishman, who announces that he resided in America during the period of Chastellux's travels, says in a note to page 321, vol. II:—"The first time I visited Bethlehem, was from Philadelphia; and after travelling two days through a country alternately diversified with savage scenes and cultivated spots, on issuing out of the woods at the close of the evening, in the month of May, found myself on a beautiful extensive plain, with the vast eastern branch of the Delaware on the right, widely interspersed with wooded islands, and at the distance of a mile in front of the town of Bethlehem, rearing its large stone edifices out of a forest, situated on a majestic, but gradually rising eminence; the background formed by the setting sun. So novel and unexpected a transition, filled the mind with a thousand singular and sublime ideas, and made an impression on me, never to be effaced. The romantic and picturesque effect of this glorious display of natural beauties, gave way to the still more noble and interesting sensations, arising from the reflection in the progress of the arts and sciences, and the sublime anticipation of the "populous cities," and "busy hum of man," which are one day to occupy, and civilize the vast wilderness of the new world."

Speaking of the "Sun," Chastellux remarks: "This tavern was built by the Society of Moravian Brethren, to whom it served formerly as a magazine, and is very handsome and spacious;" and in a note the translator adds: "This Inn, from its external appearance, and its interior accommodations, is not inferior to the best of the large inns in England, which, indeed, it very much resembles in every respect. The first time I was in Bethlehem, we remained there two or three days; and were constantly supplied with venison, moor-game, the most delicious red and yellow-bellied trout, the highest flavored wild strawberries, the most luxuriant asparagus, and the best vegetables,

in short, I ever saw; and notwithstanding the difficulty of procuring good wine and spirits at that period, throughout the continent, we were here regaled with wine and brandy of the best quality, and exquisite old Port and Madeira. It was at this house that the Marquis de la Fayette retired, to be cured of the first wound he received in fighting for America; an accident, which I am well assured, gave this young nobleman more pleasure than most of our European *petite maitres* would receive from the most flattering proofs of the favor of a mistress."

The whole account of Bethlehem in the body of the work, and in the notes, is very interesting; but both the writer, and translator, show a lamentable ignorance of the life, manners, customs, and religious belie of the Moravian Brethren.

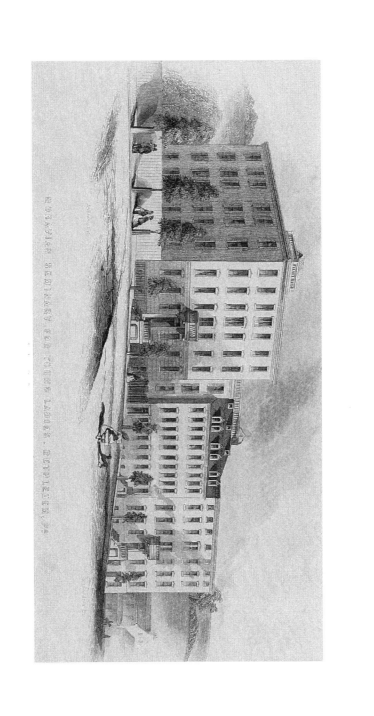

MORAVIAN SEMINARY FOR YOUNG LADIES. BETHLEHEM, PA.

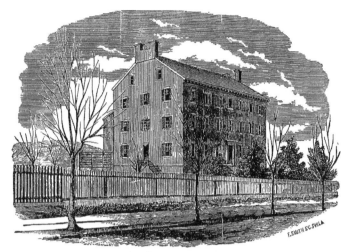

THE MORAVIAN COLLEGE,
BETHLEHEM, PA.

CHAPTER XI.

THE MORAVIAN PAROCHIAL SCHOOL.—THE
MORAVIAN COLLEGE, FOUNDED, A. D., 1807,
CHARTERED APRIL 3, 1863.—THE BETHLE-
HEM MALE BOARDING SCHOOL.—NISKY HILL
MALE SEMINARY.—THE OLD BARN OF THE
CONGREGATION FARM.—SKETCH OF THE BETH-
LEHEM SEMINARY FOR YOUNG LADIES.—THE
MILITARY RECORD OF BETHLEHEM DURING
THE REBELLION.

Issuing from the Old Moravian Graveyard
by the southwestern gate, the stranger
stands in the rear of the Moravian Parochial
School House, a very large, handsome brick
building, four stories in height, erected in
1857, and capable of holding in its recitation
rooms over 300 scholars. The upper story
is used for concerts, lectures, &c. In it all
the children of the members of the Bethlehem congregation of the United Brethren,
under 14 years of age are educated, all until
they reach that age, receive the same advantages, and at a very trifling cost. The
Moravians take an especial pride in this Institution, and very justly so, for the educa-

tion imparted in this school is of a very superior character, and well qualified to fit its
pupils for the active duties of American life ;
not professional. In proof of the above
statement the following short paragraph is
inserted from the *Moravian* of November 1,
1869. " On Saturday evening next the pupils
of the Moravian Parochial School, assisted
by the church choir, will give an entertainment in the hall of the school building. The
programme consists of recitations in concert
by the different classes of the children, in
English, French, German and Latin, and the
singing of hymns. Among the contributions
of the choir, (which need no praise from us,)
to the entertainment, is the magnificent
solo, ' I know that my Redeemer Liveth,'
from Handel's Messiah. The entertainment
commences at seven o'clock."

The Moravian College in Bethlehem, a view
of which is given at the commencement of
this chapter, copied from an old circular of
Mr. Vankirk's, is situated on Church Street,
near Nisky Hill Cemetery, it is a fine large
commodious brick building, painted lead

color, commanding one of the handsomest sites in the town, overlooking the Lehigh River and Mountain, and the rapidly increasing town of South Bethlehem. It is surrounded by a well laid out garden, and a fine large pleasure ground for the recreation of the students. This institution, in the form of a Theological Seminary, was founded in the year 1807, and located at Nazareth, Pa., and was designed not only to give the young men of the Moravian Church, desiring to enter the ministry, a complete course of Theological studies, but also to prepare them to enter upon it by a thorough classical education; hence the institution embraces two departments, a *Preparatory School*, and a *Theological Seminary*, In 1850, the Seminary was moved to Bethlehem, and the house now occupied by Adolph Conradi, in Broad Street near New Street, taken for the use of the Institution. In 1855, the school was taken back to Nazareth. And in 1858, the "Moravian Sustentation Diacony," *i. e.*, the Executive Board of the Moravian Church, purchased of Mr. Benjamin Vankirk, the present building and surrounding grounds, and the Theological Seminary was again removed to Bethlehem; its present location.

In 1851, Mr. Vankirk purchased the building in Main Street, now occupied by Charles W. Rauch, of Ernst F. Bleck, and continued there the "Bethlehem Male Boarding School," the project proving a successful one; in 1855, he purchased the grounds at Nisky Hill, and erected there the same year the present building, now known as the "Moravian College," moved his school thither, and changed its name to that of the "Nisky Hill Male Seminary;" not long after this, Mr. Vankirk was seized with a severe and long continued illness, (from which he is now happily recovered, and occupies an important position as assistant in the Seminary for Young Ladies at Bethlehem,) which compelled him to dispose of his building, as before stated, and break up his school.

In the year 1863, the Theological Seminary and its Preparatory Department, after undergoing these various changes, were re-

organized as a college, and incorporated as such, by an Act of Assembly of the Commonwealth of Pennsylvania, of the 3rd of April, 1863. See Pamphlet Laws of 1863, p. 277; and also Beitel's Index of Corporations; with the power of conferring the usual and scholastic degrees, and in 1864, thrown open to students of all other Protestant denominations. The act referred to is in these words.

An Act to Incorporate the Moravian College and Theological Seminary, at Bethlehem, Pa.

WHEREAS, The Church of the United Brethren, (formerly called Moravians,) had, for a long time, a Collegiate and Theological institute connected with the boarding school at Nazareth, but in the year 1858, removed the same to the Borough of Bethlehem, and established in said borough a college for the education of male persons in the various branches of science, literature, and the ancient and modern languages, as likewise a department of the same for training and preparing of young men for the gospel ministry. And whereas, It is deemed by the authorities of the said church, to be desirable and necessary for the convenient management of the concerns of said college, to have said college incorporated; therefore,

SEC. I.—Be it enacted by the Senate and House of Representatives of the Commonwealth of Pennsylvania, in General Assembly met, and it is hereby enacted by authority of the same. That the Right Reverend John Christian Jacobson, Bishop, and the Reverend Francis Florentine Hagen, and the Reverend Sylvester Wolle, all of the Borough of Bethlehem, duly elected by the Synod of the Northern District of the American Province of the United Brethren, a Board of Direction of the Ecclesiastical affairs of said Church, in said District, and likewise constituted by the virtue of their office, the Board of Trustees of said College, and such other persons as may be hereafter appointed their associates or successors, according to the rules and regulations of the said branch of the Church of the United Brethren, be and they are hereby constituted a body politic and corporate, in fact and in law, by the name and style of the "Moravian College and Theological Seminary," and by that name shall be capable of perpetual succession, may sue and be sued, may have and use a common seal, and alter and change the same at pleasure, and shall also be capable to accept, and take, by devise, grant, bargain, sale or otherwise, any estate, or property, real or personal, and the same to hold and enjoy, or to sell and convey, lease, or mortgage, as fully and absolutely, in all respects, as any natural person might do. *Provided*, however, That the clear annual income of the estates and properties of said Corporation, exclusive of any lands and tenements that may be occupied by said College for its accommodations, or that of its officers or professors, and exclusive of income from students, shall not exceed the sum of *Ten thousand dollars.*

Sec. II.—That the Trustees already appointed, or who shall hereafter be appointed in accordance with the fundamental statutes which govern the Church of the United Brethren in the said Northern Province of the United States of America, shall have the care and management of said College, and of its estates and properties, and shall have power to make all needful laws and regulations for the appointment of competent professors and teachers, for the fixing and payment of all salaries, for the fixing of the prices of board and tuition of students, for studies and exercises of the students, and for the general well being of said College. *Provided,* That the said statutes, by-laws and regulations, shall not be inconsistent with the Constitution and laws of this Commonwealth, or of the United States, or the enactments of the Synod of said Church of the United Brethren.

Sec. III.—That no misnomer, or misdirection of the said Corporation, in any will, deed, grant, or other instrument of writing, shall vitiate or defeat the same, but that the same shall take effect in the same manner as if said Corporation were rightly named therein. *Provided,* That it is sufficiently described to ascertain the intention of the parties.

Sec. IV.—That the Trustees, in connection with the faculty of the College, shall have power to grant and confer such degrees in the liberal arts and sciences, or such branches thereof, to such students of the College, or others, as from their proficiency in learning, they may seem justly entitled to such honors, and such as are usually granted by institutions of a similar kind, and to grant diplomas and certificates under their common seal, as may authenticate and perpetuate the memory of such graduation.

Approved April 3, A. D., 1863.

From the catalogue of the College, issued in 1848, the following additional facts are derived. "To the two already existing departments was added a third—the grammar school. The design of this branch is to prepare students to enter upon the course of study pursued in the College. In it particular attention is paid to Latin, Greek and Mathematics. The grammar school and College are in the same building, and under the same faculty, thus enabling a student to pass through the entire course with the same instructors, and rendering attention to the known wants of the individual possible to

the professors. No student is admitted into the Institution under 13 years of age."

Besides the usual course of studies in similar colleges of like character; any student can, without extra charge, take lessons in Drawing, German, French, Natural Philosophy and Chemistry; these are, however, elective studies. For instruction in vocal or instrumental music, an extra charge is made, for the number of lessons taken. The scholastic year is divided into three terms, of from twelve to fourteen weeks each. There is a short vacation at Christmas, and at Easter, and one of seven weeks in July and August. A limited number of students can reside in the College. No student is permitted to board at a hotel, and in all cases the boarding places are subject to the approval of the faculty. The expenses of a student residing in the College, including tuition, room, boarding and washing, is about $100 per term. Those boarding outside, pay only $25 per term to the College for tuition, use of room, light and fuel. Payment of the regular expenses are required in advance. The Board of Trustees is the Provincial Elders' Conference, and the members of the Faculty are the Rev. Edwin de Schweinitz, Pastor of the Moravian Churches at Bethlehem, President; Professors, the Rev. William H. Bigler, Rev. Charles B. Schultz and Rev. Edwin G. Klose.

The old stone building on Main Street, mentioned as having been first used by Mr. Ernst F. Bleck, for his "Bethlehem Male Boarding School," was originally the barn of the Society's farm. It was struck by lightning during a thunder storm in the summer of 1762, and set on fire, but it was extinguished without materially injuring the building; which was afterwards altered into dwelling houses, and occupied by three families. In tearing down the northern part of this old structure, in 1869, lately occupied by Michael Stuber, the manufacturer of the old fashioned *Bethlehem chairs,* now so much in vogue; the rafters of the old barn were found to be blackened and charred, and the evidences of the fire as fresh as on the day of the occurrence, one hundred and seven years before. Mr. Bleck founded the Bethlehem Male Boarding School in 1839, and carried it on with great success until 1851, when he sold out to Mr. Vankirk.

The old farm house was originally attached to the barn to the north, and it still stands in excellent order, quite as good as when it was first erected. It is now used by Ambrose Rauch, as a confectionery store. And but few of the gay and happy throngs of beautiful women and gallant men, who resort thither to flirt over ice-cream and cakes, know what sacred memories are connected with the old building, wherein once lay wounded the gay, noble and chivalric *Lafayette*.

On the south side of Church Street, facing Main Street, and opposite the large Moravian Church, stands the celebrated "Bethlehem Seminary for Young Ladies," where, not only the daughters of the members of the Moravian Church, residing in the town, receive their education; but hundreds of others from all parts of the United States, the West Indies and the Sandwich Islands. During the session of 1863, and 1864, this school had 263 pupils, and the total number that year attending the schools in Bethlehem, including the public school, was 985.

The Moravians make the education of the young, one of their specialties, and there are schools for young ladies in each of their principal settlements in America, namely, at Litiz, Pa.; Salem, North Carolina, and at Hope, Indiana; and at Chaska, Minnesota, for boys and girls; and one at Nazareth, Pa., for boys.

The children of the Moravians are so educated, that they are not only kind and courteous to the stranger, but they are loving, obedient children. This is not only evinced by their amiability at home, but by their correct deportment abroad. Grape vines, loaded with their treasures, (the favorite place for them seems to be over the doorways of the dwellings,) and trees whose limbs are laden with ripe fruits, stand temptingly in the streets, yet the children and people of

the town never touch them, without the permission of the owners.

This is another beautiful illustration of the character of these people, once so little understood, but now, each day becoming to be more fully appreciated by the good and thinking in all classes of society. Bethlehem has ceased to be a Moravian settlement, but it is to be hoped that their influence may long be felt among the people of this pleasant town.

The boarding school for girls consists of three large adjoining buildings on Church Street, with a handsome chapel in the rear. The centre building in front, three stories in height, with its steep roof, and two rows of attic windows, is a well preserved relic of the old style of Moravian buildings. It was originally "The Single Brethren's House," and reminds one of a first class "Man of War," (before steam came into vogue,) on the stocks, the windows resembling her open ports; it was erected before the Revolutionary War, of 1776, and was used during that period as the general hospital by the American forces. Many distinguished American officers were inmates there at different times, either as patients or visitors; among them, General Lafayette, suffering from the wounds he had received at the battle of Brandywine.

On the brow of the hill, to the right hand of the public road, leading to Allentown, and west of the Manockasy, lie the remains of about *one thousand* American soldiers, who died in this hospital during the war; no monument has been erected to their memory, and no stone marks the place of their repose.

From the annual catalogue issued by the "Moravian Seminary for Young Ladies," the following facts that cannot be refuted, are gathered. It is an establishment under the direction of the Moravian Church, and has been in successful operation as a boarding school since the year 1735, and is believed to be the oldest institution of the kind in the United States. Located in a healthful section of the State, in the midst of the charming scenery of the Lehigh Valley, among a people distinguished for a high moral tone of

MORAVIAN SEMINARY FOR YOUNG LADIES AT BETHLEHEM, PA.

character, and of a superior education, this school possesses external advantages that cannot be surpassed. The Seminary play grounds are large, and laid out with taste. The many lovely places of resort in the vicinity are frequently visited by the scholars under the care of their teachers.

Since the foundation of the Academy, more than *five thousand* of its *Alumnæ* have spread its reputation over all parts of the Union. More scholars are offered nearly every year than can be accommodated. The course of instruction, while it keeps pace with the progress of society, and the advancement of science, has in its leading principles and mode of government, been in no wise changed since its establishment, and anything that would give it the reputation and character of a *fashionable* boarding school, has been carefully avoided. Everything is done to discipline and develop the mind, to instil moral and religious principles, give a healthy physical development to the body, and fit the pupils for a useful life. The school is conducted on religious, but not sectarian principles. The scholars attend service only in their own chapel, and in the Moravian Church. The scholastic year begins in September and ends in July. The total charge for the year is about $275. The educational books are an extra charge. The foreign languages, music, drawing and ornamental needle work, are considered elective studies, for which an extra compensation is required.

One of the most interesting occasions at the Seminary, is the annual "entertainment," generally held about the 1st of July of each year, when the town and hotels are crowded with anxious mothers and fathers, and other relatives of the young ladies. The exercises were formerly held in the large Moravian Church, but are now given in the "New Chapel" attached to the school, which was built during the summer of 1868. As a matter of course, a programme of one of these great occasions is given. Bethlehemites are great on programmes, every thing is done decently, and in order, in this good old Moravian town.

ORDER OF EXERCISES AT THE

MUSICAL ENTERTAINMENT

Given by the Young Ladies of the Moravian Seminary at Bethlehem, Wednesday Evening, July 12, 1865.

Chorus—95th Psalm. Mendelssohn.
" O, come let us worship and kneel before the Lord."
Recitation—Far away. "The land that is
    very far off." Is. 33. 17.
        Mary McOrn, New York.
Song—"Rose, how enchanting art thou."
    Spohr.
        Mary Ecky, Philadelphia.
Piano Forte—Reigen der Sylphen.
        Mary Geissenhainer, Bethlehem.
Song—Das bettelnde Kind. Gumbert.
        Kate Selfridge, Bethlehem.
German Recitation—Der gerettete Juengling.
    Herder.
        Sallie Baker, Quincy, Ill.
Piano Forte—Une fleur animee. Carl Mayer.
        Jennie Senseman, Nazareth, Pa.
Trio—"Hearts feel that love Thee." Mendelssohn.
1st Soprano—Sarah Henry, N. Y.
        Ernestine Schmid, N. Y.
        May Saul, N. Y.
        Mary Chew, Millville, N. J.
2d Soprano—Marie Belloni, Harlem, N. Y.
        Jennie Senseman, Nazareth, Pa.
        Mary Holland, Bethlehem.
        Lizzie Adams, Newark, N. J.
Alto—Julia Baker, Quincy, Ill.
        Larry Belloni, Harlem, N. Y.
        Kate Glover, Harrisburg, Pa.
Recitation—The Evening Walk.
        Lizzie Mitchell, N. Y.
Quartett—Piano Forte a 4 ms., Violin. Violoncello.
        Annie Stein, Bethlehem.
        Kate Selfridge, Bethlehem.
Piano Forte—Chant du Bivouac. Ketterer.
        Mary Holland, Bethlehem.
French Recitation—Noees et Festins.
        Georgie Davy, Newark, N. J.
        Agatha Schurz, Bethlehem.
        Alice E. Pine, N. Y.
Quartett—"As pants the hart." Thomas.
        Amelia Furman, South Amboy, N. J.
        Maria Wunderling, Nazareth, Pa.
        Messrs. Rau and Goth, Bethlehem.
Piano Forte—Etude. Carl Mayer.
        Fannie Jenks, Brookville, Pa.

Song—The Wanderer. Schubert.
Julia Baker, Quincy, Ill.
Piano Forte Duett—La Balladine.   Lysberg.
Lizzie Adams, Newark, N. J.
Lizzie Renton, Newark, N. J.
Chorus—From "Paradise and the Peri."
Schuman.
Recitation—Story of Blue Beard.
Pauline Demonet, Brooklyn, N. Y.
Callie Spivey, Savannah, Ga.
Ernestine Schmid, N. Y.
Althea Schmid, N. Y,
Bertha Balmer, St. Louis, Mo.
Clara Downing, Downington, Pa.
Ada Spivey, Savannah, Ga.
Isabel Roberts, Philadelphia.
Larghetto—From 2d Symphonie. Duett with
Melodeon accompaniment.   Bethoven.
Carrie Cessna, Bedford, Pa.
Addie Mercur, Towanda, Pa.
Duett—"Speed my bark." Neukomm.
Mary Ecky, Philadelphia.
Maria Wunderling, Nazareth, Pa.
Piano Forte—Ernani. Prudent.
Nettie Corey, Newark, N. J.
Trio—"Lift thine eyes." Mendelssohn.
1st Soprano—Mary Jenks, Brookville, Pa.
Fannie Jenks, Brookville, Pa.
Jessie Davidson, Yonkers, N. Y.
Sarah Henry, N. Y.
Kate Selfridge, Bethlehem.
2d Soprano—Mary Belloni, Harlem, N. Y.
Laura Wolle, Bethlehem.
Mary Holland, Bethlehem.
Jennie Sensemen, Nazareth, Pa.
Ellen Laubach, Danville, Pa.
Alto—Kate Glover, Harrisburg.
Julia Baker, Quincy, Ill.
Georgie Benneson, Quincy, Ill.
Larry Belloni, Harlem, N. Y.
Recitation—"The Little Heartease."
Agatha Schurz, Bethlehem.
Arie—From Freischutz. Weber.
Mary Jenks, Brookville, Pa.
Piano Forte Duett—The Huguenots. E. Wolff.
Sallie Baker, Quincy, Ill.
Prof. Agtha.
Song—The Erl King. Shubert.
Jessie Davidson, Yonkers, N. Y.
Recitation—"Along the Path of Life."
Nettie Corey, Newark, N. J.
Chorus—"Come, enjoy this day of pleasure."
Concone.
Madam Dressler's Pupils.

Recitation—Midsummer's Eve.
Lizzie Arms, Philadelphia.
Piano Forte—La Juive. Prudent.
Mary Jenks, Brookville, Pa.
Recitation—The Owl.
Isabel Lange, Bethlehem.
Chorus—"O, hail us ye free!" from Ernani.
Verdi.

Hymn—

Lord, dismiss us with thy blessing,
Fill our hearts with joy and peace;
Let us each, thy love possessing,
Triumph in redeeming grace;
O refresh us, ※
Trav'ling through this wilderness.

One of the young gentlemen who was at
this entertainment, after his return home
from the visit, thus described it in the *Easton Argus*, a few days later, heading his effusion:

"'Brother Charlie's' account of his visit to
the Bethlehem Seminary entertainment.

"'The man that hath not music in himself,
Nor is not moved with concord of sweet sounds,
Is fit for treason, stratagem and spoils,'

"Shakspeare's opinion is ours also. Music
always has charms for us, and beauty invariably attracts us; therefore, we determined to attend the entertainment last week.

"About half-past six, we arrived at the
church, and found it already crowded. What
a galaxy of beauty, was there assembled!

※   ※   ※

"The stage was very tastefully decorated
with greens. At the rear sat a number of
gentlemen assistants, while on either side,
were the young ladies, looking very happy,
and very, very beautiful.

"The exercises opened with a short address
by the Principal, the Rev. Francis Wolle,
in which he gave a summary of the last
year's work, and stated the prospects of the
Seminary for the ensuing year.

"Then followed both vocal and instrumental music, interspersed with recitations.

"The pieces were all so well executed, that
to make particular mention of one, were to
do injustice to the others.

"Upon that rostrum, all the divisions of
our glorious Union were represented. Pennsylvania and her neighbors may well be

proud at being able to say, that such an institution is within their borders, and that so much beauty and talent can be displayed by their daughters: while our elegant and accomplished Western sisters can never be surpassed. The Southern States may be glad that they have yet some to show to the world, what they were, and might yet have been; while, with our Eastern friends, it were impossible to find fault.

"At the conclusion of the entertainment, we adjourned to the Eagle, where soon we were gaily tripping through the mazes of the giddy dance. Here, many of us, had the pleasure of meeting near and dear relatives, while the rest consoled themselves with the agreeable task of promenading, dancing, or chatting merrily with friends."

The Moravians were much annoyed during the Revolutionary War of 1776, on account of their refusing to bear arms, from which they were exempted by an act of Parliament of Great Britain, and because, like the Quakers, it was a part of their religious discipline at that time to do so; they considered it wrong in principle to engage in offensive warfare, they suffered in consequence on all sides, but remained firm in their determination. This article of their faith seems now to be abandoned, for a more patriotic people do not at this time exist in the United States. They proved this in the great rebellion that has been lately suppressed; when the town was almost drained of its young men, most of whom were Moravians. The 46th regiment of Pennsylvania volunteers, consisted almost altogether of men from Northampton County; one company, C, being from Bethlehem and its immediate vicinity. General Knipe was the original colonel, but being promoted for bravery, Brevet Brigadier-General, James L. Selfridge, the first captain of the Bethlehem Company, became its commander, and led it through the entire war; ending its glorious career by accompanying General Sherman on his "grand march to the sea."

There was also a part of a company from the town, in the 2nd Pennsylvania Heavy Artillery, which was commanded by my old friend and comrade, Colonel Augustus A. Gibson, of the regular army.

Bethlehem also claims amongst her heroes, Generals Schurz, Sigel, Schimmelfenning and Doster, whose families lived in the town during the rebellion. The latter is a Moravian, and now a distinguished member of the Easton bar.

Several other military organizations, besides those mentioned, had Bethlehemites among their members; and during each rebel raid on Pennsylvania, the borough furnished a full company of men on 24 hours notice, fully armed and equipped for the defence of the State.

We insert here a portion of the memorial of the Bethlehem Company in the 46th regiment, and a complete list of all the commissioned officers serving in all arms of the service, during the late civil war, a record of the bravery of her sons, of which the old town has a just right to be very proud of.

THE SOLDIERS' MEMORIAL.

Company C, 46th Regiment Pennsylvania Veteran Volunteers.

Company Officers.

William H. Stolzenbach, Captain.
    Wounded July 20, 1864.
James McQuillan, First Lieut.,
    Wounded May 24, 1862.
Owen B. Sigley, Second Lieut.,
    Wounded June 16, 1864.

SERGEANTS.

Isaac Davis.
James A. Peifer.
John J. Davis,
    Wounded and taken prisoner August 9, 1862.
William H. Eichelberger,
    Taken prisoner May 24, 1862.
Daniel Davis,
    Wounded September 17, 1862.

CORPORALS.

Levi Benner.
Hugh Lyons,
    Wounded August 9, 1862.
John C. Abbott,
    Taken prisoner August 9, 1862.
Wm. H. McMonagle,
    Wounded June 9th, 1864.
John Moore,
    Wounded July 20, 1864.
Julius A. Bealer,
    Taken prisoner May 2, 1862.

John Patrick,
  Taken prisoner May 2, 1862.
Daniel Billiard.
Edward Troxell—musician.
David Lachman—wagoner.

Transferred.

Joseph Mechett, First Lieut., to Captain of Co. I.
Edmund Cramsie, Sergt., to Second Lieut. of Co. D.

Promoted.

Horace B. Jones, to Second Lieut. Co. G.
Thomas B. Gorman, to Sergt. Major.
Levi Tice, to Reg't Quarter Master.
Charles B. McCarty, to Serg't Major.
James T. Adair, to Ass't Surgeon 77th P. V.
Franklin Weaver, Corp'l, to Veteran Reserve Corps.

Discharged.

Owen A. Luckenbach, Captain, October 29, 1862, for wounds.
William D. Thomas, First Lieut., March 4, 1862.
John C. Fetter, Second Lieut.
Robert B. Dentry, Serg't, December 15, 1862.
Henry B. Levers, Serg't, November 22, 1862.
Benj. H. Weaver, First Serg't, Oct. 21, 1862, wounds.
Rob't E. Williams, Corp'l, Nov. 10, 1862, wounds.
George A, Yohe, Corp'l, December 12, 1861.

Our space will not permit the insertion of the honorable record of the private soldiers. On the Memorial it is stated:

" The regiment arrived at Camp Kalorama, Washington, D. C., September 18, 1861, and were soon after assigned to General William's Brigade, Bank's Division, on the Upper Potomac. The regiment took part in all the campaigns of General Banks; and was in the Division when it was assigned to the army of Virginia, under General Pope, suffering severely at the battle of Cedar Mountain, losing fully two-thirds of its number. Took part in the Rappahannock campaign; also, the Maryland campaign, ending with Antietam. The old division of General Banks having been transferred to the 12th corps, under General Slocum; took part in all the varied campaigns of the Army of the Potomac, until the fall of 1863, when the 11th and 12th corps were transferred to the Army of the Cumberland.

The regiment re-enlisted in January, 1864, and returned to Pennsylvania on a 30 days' furlough. In the Spring of 1864, the 11th and 12th corps were consolidated, and formed the 20th corps, under General Hooker,

and participated in all the subsequent campaigns of General Sherman through Georgia and the Carolinas, ending with the surrender of Johnstone's Rebel Army, and the march from thence to Washington, where it participated in the *Grand Review*, May 24, 1865.

Mustered into the United States' service September 4, 1861, at Harrisburg. Re-mustered as veterans, January 15th, 1864, at Dechert, Tennessee.

Engagements.

Winchester, Va., March 23, 1861.
Middletown, Va., May 25, 1861.
Winchester, Va., May 26, 1861.
Cedar Mountain, Va., August 9, 1862.
Sulphur Springs, Va., August 27, 1862.
South Mountain, Md., Sept. 4, 1862.
Antietam, Md., Sept. 17, 1862.
Chancellorsville, Va., May 1, 2, 3, 1863.
Gettysburg, Pa., July 1, 2, 3, 1863.
Resaca, Ga., May 15, 1864.
Cassville, Ga., May 19, 1864.
Dallas, Ga., May 25, 1864.
Pine Knob, Ga., June 9, 1864.
Culps Farm, Ga., June 22, 1864.
Peach Tree Creek, July 20, 1864.
Atlanta, Ga., Sept. 6, 1864.
Cypress Swamp, Ga., Dec. 8, 1864.
Savannah, Ga., Dec. 21, 1864.
Chesterfield C. H., S. C., March 2, 1865.
Averysboro, N. C., March 14, 1865.
Bentonsville, N. C., March 19, 1865.
Coon Run, N. C., April 10, 1865.

The Soldiers' Memorial is printed on a handsomely illustrated sheet, surrounded by warlike implements and scenes, including a spirited sketch of an engagement in the field.

JAS. L. SELFRIDGE.—Captain of Co. A, 1st Pa. Vols.—three months service—April 20, 1861.

Re-entered as Lieut. Col. of the 46th regiment Pa. Vols. August 8, 1861; promoted to Col. May 10, 1863; served in the Army of the Potomac until the fall of the year 1863, when his regiment joined the Army of the Cumberland under General Sherman, and formed a part of the forces who made the grand march to the sea. He was promoted to Brig. Gen. by Brevet, March 16, 1865; mustered out of service July 16, 1865. He was afterwards Collector of Internal Revenue for the 11th District of Pa., and is now Clerk of the House of Representatives of Pennsylvania.

REV. W. HENRY RICE.—Chaplain of the 129th regiment Pa. Vols., entered the nine months' service August 16, 1862, 5th army corps of the Army of the Potomac; mustered out May 18, 1863.

The Rev. Mr. Rice was the only Moravian minister who acted as an army chaplain during the war.

CAPT. R. MOULTON GOUNDIE.—In the three months' service, Second Lieut. of Co. A., 1st regiment Penna. Vols., mustered April 20, 1861. Re-enlisted in three years' service as First Lieut. of Co. G, 2nd Pa. Heavy Artillery, promoted to Captain, and mustered out with regiment. Now civil engineer, Bethlehem, Pa.

Doctor Frickhardt had two sons in the 2nd Pa. Artillery, Augustus and Frederick, who died in the service, aged respectively, eighteen and twenty years; they were privates, unused to the hardships of a soldier's life, and died in camp before seeing active service.

WILLIAM H. STOLZENBACH.—Entered the service April 17, 1861, a private of Co. A, 1st regiment Pa. Vols., three months' service. Entered the three years' service as First Serg't Co. C, 46th regiment Pa. Vols., September 4, 1861; promoted to Second Lieut. September 5, 1861; First Lieut. March 4, 1862; Captain, November 1, 1862. Served under General Banks, Hooker and Pope, of the Army of the Potomac; and re-enlisted under Sherman with his regiment, as veteran volunteers, and was painfully wounded at the battle of Peach Tree Creek, July 20, 1864, losing all the fingers of his right hand, during the grand march to the sea. Rejoined his regiment at Raleigh, N. C., and mustered out July 16, 1865.

OWEN A. LUCKENBACH.—In the service three months under the first call. Entered the three years' service as First Lieut. Co. C, 46th regiment Pa. Vols., August 17, 1861; promoted to Capt. Sept. 4, 1861; discharged on surgeon's certificate, October 20, 1862. Having been wounded at the battle of Cedar Mountain, August 9, 1862, and his right leg amputated. Now United States Collector of Internal Revenue for the 11th District of Pennsylvania.

JOHN C. FETTER.—Entered the three years' service August 17, 1861; promoted to Second Lieut. November 1, 1862, of Co. C, 46th regiment Pa. Vols.; resigned September 10, 1863.

OWEN B. SIGLEY.—After the three months' service, entered the 46th regiment Pa. Vols., August 17, 1861; promoted Second Lieut. May 22, 1865; mustered out with his company, July 16, 1865. Now publisher of the "Weekly Progress," of South Bethlehem, Pa.

CHARLES B. McCARTY.—In the three months' service; entered the three years' service with Co. C, 46th regiment Pa. Vols.; promoted Serg't Major February 12, 1863; mustered out with regiment. He died May 20, 1867, and on his tombstone in the old Cemetery, is the following inscription.

In memory of CHARLES B. McCARTY, late Sergeant Major of the 46th regiment of Penna. Veteran Volunteers, Born March 24th, 1838, Died May 20th, 1867. Forever with the Lord.

THOS. B. GORMAN.—In the three months' service with 1st regiment Penna. Vols. In three years' service with 40th regiment Penna. Vols. Promoted to First Lieut. Co. H., February 1, 1862. Dismissed the service by verdict of a Court Martial.

ORVILLE A. GRIDER.—Entered the nine months' service August 15, 1862, as Second Lieut. of Co. C, 129th Pa. Vols.; promoted to First Lieut. March 28, 1863; mustered out with company.

ROBERT E. ABBOTT.—Entered nine months' service August 15, 1862, as Captain of Co. G, 132nd regiment Pa. Vols.; severely wounded in the face at the battle of Antietam. Honorably discharged January 13, 1863, on account of his wound. Now one of the proprietors of an iron foundry at Bethlehem.

EDWARD HAMMANN.—Enlisted as a private in Knapp's celebrated battery of Pittsburg, Pennsylvania, and rose to the rank of First Lieut. of artillery; mustered out of United States service with his company. Now a conductor on the North Pennsylvania Railroad.

DR. ABRAHAM STOUT.—Entered United States service October 1, 1862, as Assistant Surgeon of the 153rd regiment Pa. Vols., of the Army of the Potomac; mustered out July 24, 1863. Now a practising physician at Bethlehem.

DR. CHARLES E. HUMPHREYS.—Entered the service May 14, 1863, as Assistant Surgeon of the 142nd regiment Pa. Vols.; promoted to Surgeon of the 143rd regiment Pa. Vols., March 17, 1865; mustered out with regiment, June 12, 1865. Now Physician at Bethlehem.

ALEXANDER W. SELFRIDGE.—Private in Co. A, 38th regiment Pa. Vols., June, 1861; promoted Second Lieut. Co II, 46th regiment Pa. Vols., February 6, 1862. Served in the Shenandoah Valley under General Banks. Was twice captured, escaped the first time; on the second occasion, accused of violating his parole, but acquitted of the charge and sent to "Libby Prison" with the rest of General Pope's officers. Exchanged in four months, joined his regiment in the field, and was promoted to Captain of his company. Served with Sherman during his great march to the sea. At Altoona was appointed acting Commissary of Subsistence on General Knipe's staff. Then on the staff of General Broughton, in the same capacity, and afterwards on the staff of General Selfridge, (his uncle,) Breveted Major March 13, 1865, for his gallantry during the war, and honorably mustered out of service August, 1865.

HORACE B. JONES.—Entered the nine months' service September 1, 1862, as First Lieut. of Co. G, 40th regiment Pa. Vols.; resigned September 23, 1861.

JOSEPH A. FRY.—Entered the service October 7, 1862, as Captain of Co. B., 153 regiment Pa. Vols., Army of the Potomac. Mustered out July 24, 1863.

HENRY J. OERTER.—Entered the service as Captain of Co. C, 153 regiment Pa. Vols., October 7, 1862; mustered out July 23, 1863. Now deceased, and buried in the old Moravian grave yard at Bethlehem.

BENJ'N F. BOYER.—Entered the service for nine months', as Second Lieut. Co. C, 153rd regiment Pa. Vols.; resigned January 22, 1863. Now merchant in Bethlehem.

JOHN FREDERICK R. FRUEAUFF.—Entered the service April 23, 1861, as First Lieut., three months, afterwards in the nine months' service, with the 153rd regiment Pa. Vols., as Major. Assistant Inspector General for General McLaws; mustered out with regiment July 24, 1863. Now attorney-at-law, Litiz, Pa.

OWEN RICE, JR.—Entered the nine months' service in 153rd regiment Pa. Vols., as Captain of Co. A, October 7, 1862; mustered out with regiment, July 23, 1863. Wounded at Chancellorsville. Now a druggist at Lancaster, Pa.

ANDREW A. LUCKENBACH.—Entered the service as private in Co. A, 1st regiment Pa. Vols., April, 1861, three months; re-entered service August 10, 1862, as First Lieut. Co. C, 129th regiment Pa. Vols., nine months; promoted to Captain March 18, 1863, and mustered out May 18, 1863. Now miller at Bethlehem.

WILLIAM D. LUCKENBACH.—Entered the service for nine months, August 12, 1862, as private in Co. C, 129th Pa. Vols.; re-entered service September 4, 1864, as First Lieut. and Adjutant of 202 regiment Pa. Vols. for one year; promoted to Assistant Adjutant General to General Albright, of the Army of the Potomac; mustered out of service August 4, 1865. Now attorney-at-law, Allentown, Pa.

Captain JONATHAN K. TAYLOR has the following record engraven on his tomb, in the old Bethlehem grave yard:

"To the memory of Captain JONATHAN K. TAYLOR, Co. C, 129th regiment Pa. Vols., son of David and Hannah K. Taylor, who received a mortal wound at the battle of Fredericksburg, December 13, 1862, and died at George-town, D. C., March 28, 1863, aged 20 years, 11 months and 20 days. By his comrades in arms."

Cut upon a shield, surmounted by the American eagle, and ornamented by the national flag, and the batallion colors.

Lieut. Col. SAMUEL WETHERILL entered the United States service as the Captain of Co. H, which he raised by his own exertions, on the 25th of September, 1861, and served with distinction until the end of the war, when he was mustered out October 2, 1864, having attained the rank of Major. On the 13th of March, 1865. He was breveted as a Lieut. Col. for distinguished services during the war. He is a son of the late eccentric John Price Wetherill, of Philadelphia, who was

in his day a prominent man, and a popular member of the Masonic fraternity.

The REV. MR. NEVIN, late Rector of the Protestant Episcopal Church of the Nativity, in South Bethlehem, was the commander during the war, of Nevin's celebrated Battery of Light Artillery. He is now in charge of the American Chapel at Rome, in Italy.

The following short sketch of company A, 4th regiment Pennsylvania Cavalry, is inserted, to give some idea of the nature and extent of the duty performed by our soldiers in the field. It was in this company, as will be seen, that General William Emil Doster entered the service.

Company A, 4th regiment, Pennsylvania Cavalry, was recruited on the "Sand Island," Bethlehem, in August, 1861, from Bethlehem, Easton, Weissport, Summit Hill and Mauch Chunk. The company left Bethlehem 116 strong, and was mustered into Harlan's Cavalry, (afterwards the 11th Penna.,) at Philadelphia, August 15, 1861, with the following officers.

Capt. Wm. Emil Doster, Bethlehem.
First Lieut., Herman Horn, Weissport.
Second Lieut., Edward Tombler, Bethlehem.

The company was transferred to the 4th Penna. Cavalry, commanded successively by Cols. Compbell, Childs, (killed at Antietam,) Kerr, Doster, Covode, (killed at St. Mary's Church,) and Young; and served to the close of the war, in 2nd Brig. 2nd Div., Cavalry Corps, Army of the Potomac, being at different times under the command of Gens. Keyes, Stoneman, Averill, Pleasanton, Kilpatrick, Gregg, Duffie and Sheridan.

It participated in the following engagements:—Gaines' Hill; Charles City Cross Roads; Hedgeville; Antietam; Markham Station; Kelley's Ford; Chancellorsville; Upperville; Middleburg; Aldie; Snicker's Gap; Gettysburg; Sheppardstown; Bealton; Rhappahanock Station; Beverly Ford; Culpepper; Trevilian Station; Todd's Tavern; Sulphur Springs; Deep Bottom; St. Mary's Church; Ream Station; Stony Creek; Boydton Road; Wyatt's Farm, and Bellefield.

Eighteen of the company were captured at Sulphur Springs, and died at Andersonville, including A. Walton, of South Bethlehem, First Serg't, and Josiah McHose, of Hanover.

Capt. Tumbler served through all the campaign before Richmond, noted for bravery and discipline. On the march before Gettysburg, he succumbed to chronic diarrhœa, and was transferred to the Veteran Reserve Corps, of which he commanded a battalion to the close of the war, at Evansville, Indiana. Capt. Andrews succeeded Capt. Tombler, and was breveted Major, he commanded the company until the death of Col. Covode. Capt. Andrews was succeeded by Capt. Hyndman, of Mauch Chunk, who was also breveted Major.

Capt. Doster was, in October, 1861, promoted to Major, in March, 1862, assigned to duty on the staff of Gen. James S. Wadsworth, and appointed to succeed Gen. Porter as Provost Marshal of the cities of Washington, Georgetown, and Alexandria. In March, 1863, he took command of his regiment as Lieut. Colonel. During Stoneman's raid before Chancellorsville, he was put in command of the 2nd Cavalry Brigade. At Upperville, Va., during a charge on Fitzhugh Lee's cavalry, he was captured, but by killing his captor, succeeded in rejoining his command. He was subsequently transferred to the Colonelcy of the 5th Penna. Cavalry, and breveted Brig. Gen. for gallant and meritorious conduct at Gettysburg. Now attorney-at-law, at Easton, Pa.

COL. HENRY COPPEE, L. L. D., President of the Lehigh University, and now a resident of South Bethlehem, was, during the rebellion, aid de-camp to Governor Curtin, of Pennsylvania, and in that capacity, being a graduate of West Point, was of great service to the State. He also, during that time, edited the United States Service Magazine; and after the war, wrote an excellent life of our President, General U. S. Grant.

JOHN H. RICE, of Bethlehem. was the Second Lieut. of Co. H, 11th regiment Penna. Cavalry.

DAVID A. LUCKENBACH was the captain of a company of boys during the rebellion, who were handsomely equipped, and exceedingly well drilled, and deserve mention. He served as Orderly Sergeant on three different occasions in the companies of militia raised in Bethlehem during the rebel raids on the State; when he declined the office of Second Lieut. the first time, that of First Lieut. on the second, and that of Captain on the third, for either of which positions he was well qualified, saying that he could be of more service as First Sergeant. Now one the proprietors of the old Mill at Bethlehem.

From the *Bethlehem Daily Times* the following account of the proceedings on "Decoration Day" of May 29th, 1869, is copied, viz:

"DECORATION DAY.—In all ages of the world and in all nations, it has been the custom of the living to honor the memory of the dead, who lost their lives in battle for the defence of their country. Yesterday and Saturday were set apart by the highest authority in the Grand Army of the Republic for the decoration of the graves of soldiers who lost their lives in the Union armies during the late civil war, as also of those who at any time fell in the defence of the country and under her flag. In this exercise it was designed that all citizens should unite. Owing to the fact that comparatively short notice had been given for preparation for the decoration of the graves of Bethlehemites and strangers who lie in soldiers' graves in and about the town, it was feared that the turnout of citizens would be meagre; but such was not the case. A goodly number of those who thought they could spare a quarter of a day from labor to honor the graves and memory of those who died that they might labor whole days in peace and safety, were present. For some reason, to us unknown, the citizens were not marshaled in line, and therefore did not add their numbers to the line of the procession. A drum corps with fife, members of the G. A. R., young ladies with boquets for the graves, and numbers of the firemen from all the companies, formed the order of procession. We have only to add that those who participated in the decoration of soldiers' graves in and about Bethlehem, on Saturday, May 29, 1869, were abundantly satisfied with the exercises, and that, now that Post 182, Grand Army of the Republic, is fully organized, they expect on all occasions of the kind hereafter, to be fully prepared to do honor to their fallen comrades.

"When the last graves had been decorated, in the old Moravian Burying Ground, Gen.

Selfridge, the Chief Marshal, introduced Rev. Mr. Nevin, of the Church of the Nativity, of South Bethlehem, who made a short address full of comprehensive patriotism, of honor to the dead soldier and sailor, and of hope for peace and harmony in our great country, and of exhortation to be true to the spirit of our institutions, the permanence of which depends upon the citizen soldiery of the country.

"We cannot more fittingly close these hasty words concerning what Bethlehem and her surviving soldiers and citizens did to honor the memory of their dead comrades and protectors than to quote these words of the poet Montgomery:

> "Give me the death of those
> Who for their country die;
> And oh ! be mine like their repose,
> When cold and low they lie !
> Their loveliest mother earth
> Enshrines the fallen brave ;
> In her sweet lap, who gave them birth,
> They find their tranquil grave."

"The following is a list of those soldiers whose graves were decorated with flowers in the old Moravian Burying Ground.

Capt. J. K. Taylor; Capt. J. H. Rice; Lieut. Merrill; Clarence Kampman; F. Fickardt; Hiram Yohe; Henry Haas; Capt. H. J. Oerter; Lieut. E. Doster; Serg't Maj. McCarty; E. A. Slolzenbach; A. Fickardt; Jno. C. Hagen; J. B. Vail, (navy.)

In Nisky Hill Cemetery.—Albert C. Cortright; John Jones.

In the Lutheran Grave Yard.—Edward Troxell; Tobias Jones.

In the Methodist Grave Yard.—Urias Bodder; —— Hess; —— Schwabb.

In the year 1860, the Military Companies of the town, consisted of the "Bethlehem Artillery," Captain *William Wilson, M. D.,* now deceased. The company had a fine armory in the large brick structure in Broad street, east of New street on the north side; the building was erected for that purpose. The Masonic Lodge of Bethlehem now hold their meetings in the upper portion of the house. The "Washington Grays," commanded by Captain *James L. Selfridge,* now Bre-

vet Brigadier General of U. S. Volunteers, was then organized as a company of Infantry. There was also a company of Cavalry, known as the "Bethlehem Cavalry," under Col. *Geo. Wenner.*

In this connection I cannot refrain from relating an incident which occurred during *Lee's* advance on Pennsylvania in 1863, just preceding the battle of *Gettysburg.* One Sunday morning, in the latter part of June, whilst the congregation were at worship in the Moravian church, a telegraphic message was received from Governor Curtin, calling for a company of volunteers from Bethlehem. The church bell was rung, creating the most intense excitement among the congregation. The *drum corps* was ordered out, marched through the town, arousing all the inhabitants, who flocked to the "Eagle Hotel." As the people came from the church a meeting was organized, the wishes of the State authorities made known, volunteers called for, and enough men to form a company, quickly enrolled their names. As each gave his name he hurried home to equip himself for the field, and say good-bye to the loved ones there. Some, however, came ready to march; the *long roll* of the drums had told them their country called, and like most men of the day they were ready to take the field at a moment's notice, for none knew how soon they might be called. So like the old soldier all were ready to "fall in" when the order was given. A company fund was freely subscribed by the citizens and paid over to a treasurer selected by the meeting. Company officers were elected, viz., Frank C. Stone, captain; Wm. H. McCarty, 1st Lieutenant; Henry Schelly, 2d Lieutenant; together with five sergeants and eight corporals. One gentleman, *David O. Luckenback,* was nominated for 2d Lieutenant, but declined, saying, " I would rather be orderly sergeant, I know the duties of that position best." He was accordingly elected to the desired position.

In *one hour* from the time of sounding the alarm, ninety-four men fully equipped and ably officered fell in, at the order, ready for service in the field. A short, stirring, and patriotic speech was made to the company, by the eloquent physician, Doctor Frederick A. Frickardt ending, "God bless you boys! Go! we know you will do your duty to your country." Then the drums beat; parents, relatives and friends cheered, many with tears in their eyes, and choking sobs in their voices, as they heard the stern command, "shoulder arms," "right face," "forward march!" and saw those they loved going from their sight perhaps forever. So many of those who but a short hour before were engaged in the service of their God, marched ready to serve their country in the hour of her direst need.

When the company reached Reading, it was incorporated into the 34th Regiment of Pennsylvania Militia, under Col. Albright. *Abm. S. Schropp*, one of the members of the Bethlehem company, was elected Adjutant of the regiment with the rank of Lieutenant. *Edmund Doster* (now deceased) another private, was elected Regimental Quartermaster.

On a previous call for volunteers by the authorities of the State, a full company of militia was raised on a few hours notice, and dispatched the same day to the front. The company consisted of eighty-six privates and non-commissioned officers. David O. Luckenback being 1st Sergeant. The commissioned officers were Joseph Peters, Captain; F. J. Haus, 1st Lieutenant; Abraham S. Schropp, 2d Lieutenant.

It was thus all over the country, that the nation's gallant sons rushed to arms, and we astonished Foreign Nations by showing them that a free people could assemble a well-disciplined militia force in the field with the same marvelous rapidity, that they could put in motion their large standing armies; and we afterwards increased their surprise by disbanding a million and a half of soldiers in a few months; returning them quietly to the pursuits of civil life, and paying all expenses of a gigantic civil war, without foreign aid of any kind, but much opposition. It is only in a republic, such as ours, where every man is free and unfettered in mind, body and estate, that such things can be accomplished.

O, thus be it ever, when freeman shall stand
Between their loved homes, and the wars desolation,
Blessed with victory and peace, may heaven's rescued land;
Bless the Power that hath made and preserved us a Nation.'

Bethlehem was full of soldiers during the war. Recruiting offices for all arms of the service were open. Recruits, veterans, soldiers and officers, sick, discharged, on duty, or on leave, gave the place the appearance of a Garrison town; and the uniforms of the U. S. cavalry, infantry and artillery were common in the streets. And during the long winter evenings as we gathered around the fire at the Eagle, "old soldiers" of twenty-four or younger, related the stories of their battles to their friends, and to each other. May they all live long to tell their stories over again for many years to come.

THE CHURCH AND SEMINARY.—1830.
BETHLEHEM, PA.

CHAPTER XII.

THE ENTERPRISES OF THE MORAVIAN CHURCH.
—THEIR SCHOOLS.—THEIR PUBLICATIONS.—
THE TEXT-BOOK.—BIRTH DAYS, AND THEIR
CELEBRATION.—THE FIRST PRINTING OFFICE.
—THE NEWSPAPERS OF BETHLEHEM IN
THE PAST AND PRESENT.—"PENNSYLVANIA
DUTCH."—LOVE-FEASTS."—THE MORAVIAN
CHRISTMAS PUTZ.—THE "YOUNG MEN'S
MISSIONARY SOCIETY," AND CHRISTIAN AS-
SOCIATION OF BETHLEHEM.

THE enterprises of the Moravian Church, are Home and Foreign Missions, Educational Institutions, and Publications.

The Educational Institutions of the Moravian Church in America, are very justly much esteemed, and enjoy the public confidence in a high degree; their schools are liberally patronized, and many thousands of pupils not belonging to the communion of the church, have received their education in Moravian boarding schools. The Moravian College, and the Seminary for females at Bethlehem, have already been referred to. *Nazareth Hall*

Boarding School for Boys, went into operation in 1785, and and has been in successsful operation ever since, at Nazareth, Pa., with an average attendance of ninety-six pupils. *Linden Hall*, at Litiz, Pa., a school for Girls, was founded in 1794, and has an average of 100 scholars per year. *Salem Academy*, for Females, at Salem, North Carolina, where scholars were first taken in 1802, has had to this time over 4,000 pupils. *Hope Academy* at Hope, Indiana, was founded in 1866, and *Chaska Academy*, at Chaska, Minnesota, was established in 1865, both for the education of females.

The publication office, and store of the Church are located at Bethlehem, Pa., of which my good friend, Henry T. Clauder, is the amiable and efficient head, where all of the historical and religious works of the Moravian Church, can be obtained.

The publications of the Church in America are "The Moravian," in the English language, and "Der Brueder Botschafter," in the German, the former a weekly, and the latter a bi-weekly newspaper; and both now ably edited by the Rev'd Herman A. Brickenstein.

"Der Brueder Botschafter," or Brotherly Messenger, is intended for the German Moravians. It contains exhaustive reports of the Missions of the Church, and copious extracts from appropriate German publications· The first number was issued in the month of September, 1866.

"The Moravian," in 1856, took the place of "The Moravian Church Miscellany," a monthly publication of the church, which was issued from 1850 to 1855, inclusive. At first it was an eight page folio, but in 1862 it was enlarged, and then again in 1864, to its present size. Previous to "The Miscellany," the church printed "The Missionary Intelligencer," from the year 1821 to 1850.

The Provincial Elders' Conference, having been authorized by the Provincial Synod, are now erecting a building for the use of the Publication Office, in Bethlehem. The site selected is on Main Street. The building will be four-stories high ; the book-store, counting-house and editor's office being on the first floor, and the composing-room, and bindery on the fourth. The press-room will be in the basement. The middle floors not being at present required for the uses of the establishment, will be fitted up as offices. The present expenses for rent is quite equal to the interest of the money to be thus invested. And the rent of the offices will pay all the necessary outlay required for repairs to the building, insurance, taxes, &c.

The Moravians were the first people who employed the art of printing for the publication of the Bible in a living tongue. And from the Moravian Publication Office at Bethlehem, they print and issue all Devotional boooks of their Church, Sunday-Schools and Missions in the United States.

It has been the custom of the Brethren's Church, since the year 1731, to issue annually a little volume called the "Text-Book," consisting of a selection of verses from the Bible for each day, with appropriate collects taken from their hymn book. To which has been added a reference to the Bible lessons

for the day, as will be seen by reference to the "Text-Book" of 1870. The first verse or "Daily Word," contains a short sentence of prayer, exhortation or promise. The second or "Doctrinal text," is intended to enforce some doctrinal truth or practical duty. This custom arose out of another, which was observed in the first congregation of the Renewed Church, at Hernhut, of appointing for each day some persons, whose duty it was to go from house to house and greet the inmates with a text from the Bible, which was to serve as a subject for meditation during the day, and furnished the topic of discourse in the evening meeting of the congregation. This arrangement afterwards gave place to the annual issue of this little manual, which is now (1870) in its 140th year. It is thus prepared : "the Elders Conference of the Unity," at Hernhut, select each year many hundreds of suitable Texts, from these they draw by Lot, one from each Testament, for each day, of the coming year ; to each of these Texts is added an appropriate stanza from the Moravian Hymn Book. Then the Text Book for the coming year is printed and furnished at a trifling expense to the Members of the different Moravian Congregations, and Missions throughout the world. There appeared in 1869, in the German, 39,750 copies of this work. In English, 4,800 copies. In French, 5,600 copies ; Negro-English, used in Surinam, South America, 600 copies. Nearly 50,750 copies were printed. Being usually read at the early morning meal, or in connection with the private or family devotions, the texts afford food for reflection, and often prove of the most striking application, and encouragement to the pious and attentive heart, (see appendix to Text-Book of 1869.) This ancient and beautiful custom is still retained in all true Moravian households in Bethlehem. At the breakfast-table the selections from the Text-Book, are read before eating, and the "Birth-day Book" is laid beside the plate of the head of the family, with the "Text-Book." In this latter book, or on the margin of the "Text-Book, is generally entered a record of all the birth-days of the members of the family, and all of their friends, so that, if on the way to business, or during the day, the relative or friend is met, he or she can be congratulated.

As an example of the daily devotions, the following is copied from the "Text-Book" of 1870, under date of April 7th, viz:

"Thursday 7. Num. xi., 21-35.

"'He shall come down like rain upon the mown grass, as showers that water the earth.' Ps. 72, vi.

As RAIN OVERSTREAMING THE PARCHED GROUND.—WITH PLENTY NOW TEEMING, SPREADS VERDURE AROUND.—THE PROMISED BLESSING ITS INFLUENCE DIFFUSES. 739. 1.

'Take no thought for to-morrow; for the morrow shall take thought for the things of itself. Sufficient unto the day is the evil thereof.'—Matt., vi. 34.

WHAT THOU SHALT TO DAY PROVIDE,
LET ME AS A CHILD RECEIVE,
WHAT TO-MORROW MAY BETIDE,
CALMLY TO THY WISDOM LEAVE:
'TIS ENOUGH THAT THOU WILT CARE,
WHY SHOULD I THE BURTHEN BEAR?
—164. 2.

1735.—Departure of the first Missionaries to Surinam.

1735.—Arrival of Spangenberg with the first Colony of the Brethren, at Savannah, Georgia."

From Roudthaler's Life of Heckewelder, page 141, the following information contained in a note, is copied.

"The volume of 'Daily Words,' or as it is called in the German, the *Watchword* of the congregation, is published every year. Its contents are two texts for every day in the year, one taken from the Old, and the other from the New Testament. To each is subjoined a suitable verse, or part of a verse, from the Moravian hymn book. Nothing finds a place in such a volume that does not tend to real edification. All texts that might conduce to useless disputing, or subtile distinctions of doctrines, which those often understand the least who busy themselves most about them, are omitted. Inspection will show such subjects as the Love of Christ, his Sufferings and Death, his guardianship of the Christian Church, Love to Christ, Holiness of life, Surrender of the heart to him, Confidence in God, the Happiness of the life to come, &c., to form the contents. These yearly volumes have done much towards promoting unity of spirit and simplicity of faith in the church. In the earlier times of the Renewed Church of the Brethren, these 'Daily Words' were not printed, but announced every day in the different houses in Hernhut. They were to serve as a watchword in the daily warfare of the soldiers of Christ, by which to cheer, as well as exhort one another. Hence the name 'Loosung,' (Watchword,) by which they are still known in the German Congregation."

Among the members of the family and their friends in Bethlehem, it is the universal custom to celebrate all the birth-days, by presents and a little home Love-feast. The anniversary of marriages are also celebrated in a like manner. These little social courtesies render life more happy and attractive to the older ones; and to the little ones these are periods of unalloyed happiness.

Sometimes these social festivals have a deeper meaning, taking the form of a "Surprise Party," with music and singing; sometimes presents to a worthy minister, at another time to celebrate a father, mother or friend's fiftieth birth-day, or the Golden Wedding of some beloved old friend or connection. On such occasions, the friends and relatives of those to be honored or surprised, are all in the secret, a *meal* is prepared and floral tributes adorn the well loaded table. I remember such an event, a friend's fiftieth birth-day had arrived, and everybody retired to bed early, much to his annoyance, so at last, he went grumbling off to rest, as he supposed, and when the light was out in his room, busy hands prepared the festive table, with suppressed voices and half-choked laughter; at midnight, beneath his window, the old Bethlehem Band played "Should old acquaintance be forgotten;" and then, until morning, music, fun and jollity reigned supreme.

From the "Moravian" of February 25th, 1860, is inserted here, from an editorial item, a beautiful description of

"A GOLDEN WEDDING AT LITIZ, PA.—The following account of the golden wedding celebration of Brother and Sister John Beck, of Litiz, was prepared at our request. The friends of the pair are so many in all parts of the Church, that it will be read with much interest and hearty sympathy.

"*Dear Moravian.*—The name of the 'Old Schoolmaster' of Litiz, is a familiar and beloved one in many a family throughout the length and breadth of our land, and his occasional communications in our church-paper have been pursued with interest and delight, so that a brief account of the celebration of his Golden Wedding, which took place on Tuesday, Feb. 2d, in the dear old village of Litiz, may not be out of place.

"The afternoon and evening of the previous day brought children, grand-children and friends to the old homestead, where, for fifty years, from the very beginning of their married life, the now venerable couple have resided. It was a delightful reunion, and the usually quiet rooms were full of life and gladness. After the old people had retired for the night, loving hands made the preparations for the morrow's celebration. Kind friends in town had contributed freely of their floral treasures, and these, with wreaths of evergreen and ivy, were used in decorating the parlor. There were flittings in and out, mysterious whisperings, and stifled laughter, lest suspicion might be awakened. The table was draped with white and the gifts spread out to the best advantage. At last all was done, and with bright anticipations for the morrow, the company dispersed. The quiet of the early dawn was broken by the sweet strains of the trombones, arousing the dear old folks from their slumbers and calling down a benison upon their heads. The choir was led by one of the sons, and the beloved mother's favorite tunes had been selected as the first sounds which should greet her ears on this happy morning. Then followed the delighted surprise as the parlor was entered; the happy morning meal, the loving congratulations, com-

munications in poetry and prose from absent friends, and cordial interchanges of thought and feeling. There was 'holy joy and children's glee,' merry laughter, and sometimes to a brimming eye, as allusions were made to the 'loved ones gone before.' The remembrance of those sainted ones was no check upon our happiness; it only served to hallow the joy and remind us that we have a 'better country, even an heavenly,' and that *this* is not our rest.

"Then followed the grand dinner at the Litiz hotel, the dining-room of which was for the time exclusively at the service of the schoolmaster's family. Around one table the older portion of the company were gathered, children, friends, and all the resident ministers with their wives. At the other, the sixteen grand-children did justice to the profusion of good things, which bespoke not only the liberality of our venerable friend, but also the culinary skill of the hotel hostess. Before partaking of the meal, the pastor, Rev. E. T. Kluge, proposed that the company unite in singing, in the old Moravian style, a hymn expressive of our good wishes for our old friends. Accordingly all present with united voices sang,

"'Be their comfort which ne'er faileth, &c.'

"After the repast the old schoolmaster was called upon for a speech, which he made in his happiest style, relating various experiences connected with the first opening of his school, and giving God the glory for all the success with which he had met. By request, Rev. E. Frueauff replied in the German language. He had been one of the old schoolmaster's first scholars, and paid an eloquent tribute to his former instructor's faithfulness, interspersing his remarks with some incidents of the olden time, which caused bursts of merriment.

"Later in the afternoon the company gathered again in the homestead, when two little grand-children received the rite of holy baptism from the hands of the pastor.

"At 7 o'clock, P. M., the congregation had been invited to partake of a love-feast in the church, a printed psalm for which had been prepared. The pulpit and altar were tastefully decorated with flowers and evergreens, and a delightful feeling of joyousness and love pervaded the whole assembly. The relatives of the old schoolmaster occupied the front pews, while he and his beloved wife sat on the same spot before the minister, where they had plighted their troth fifty years before. We would fain speak of the beautiful humility visible in every feature of *her* face, but we know these are flowers which love best to bloom in the shade, and so we forbear. Before singing the psalm the pastor in a very neat address told the congregation why they had assembled there: then spoke to the aged couple about the faithfulness with which their Lord had led them through days of prosperity as well as adversity, and finally pronounced over them the Old Testament benediction. The congregational singing was delightful; every voice seemed tuned for the occasion. A serenade from the Litiz Sextette, later in the evening, closed the happy day, and with peaceful and happy hearts all sought their rest that night. It was a never to-be-forgotten time. Not the slightest thing occurred to mar the festivity, and the true, old Moravian spirit of unfeigned love and simplicity seemed to pervade the whole day. The Saviour's presence and His approving smile was felt throughout the day, and those who returned to their homes next morning, did so with hearts encouraged and refreshed.

"God bless the dear old couple. May the light of His countenance beam upon them, smoothing their declining years, and granting them at last an abundant entrance into His kingdom."

The first printing office was established in Bethlehem by Henry Muller, a Moravian, in 1762. His place of business was in Market Street, in one of the old log houses near the old Grave Yard. The first *newspaper* printed in the town was issued in 1845, in the German language, called "*Die Biene,*" and was edited by Dr. A. L. Huebener, and was printed by Julius Held. Commencing in the year 1853, an English newspaper, called "*Lehigh Valley Times,*" was published for five years, conducted by E. H. Rauch. After its discontinuance, a weekly paper entitled "The Bethlehem Advocate,,' was printed for several years, edited by H. Reude.

On the 27th of January, 1866, D. J. Godshalk commenced the publication of a weekly paper, called the "*Lehigh Valley Chronicle,*" of which he was both editor and proprietor. On the 22d of December, in the same year, it was discontinued. And on the 4th of February, 1867, he first printed and issued "*The Bethlehem Daily Times,*" which has been three several times since then enlarged. And it has been so successful a publication, that its editor began on the 20th of June, 1868, the publication of a weekly issue, under the name of the "*Weekly Times and Educator.*" Under the latter head embracing articles in favor of, and support our liberal principles of public school education established in this State; and of interest to those engaged in teaching. Which paper receives, as it very justly deserves, a large and increasing support. Mr. Godshalk, in connection with the issue of his papers, has a large printing office for the miscellaneous purposes of his business.

The peculiar dialect spoken in many parts of this state by those of German and Dutch descent, is called "*Pennsylvania Dutch,*" more properly it should be called, perhaps, "Pennsylvania German," in some parts. A late writer says that it "is a South German patois, a cross between the soft Allemanium or Swabian, and the hard glib low German more or less intermingled with Germanized English words; in some localities in the State there is little intermixture of English in the dialect." This may all be very true, but the name of "Pennsylvania Dutch" originated from the patois spoken by the old residents of Reading and its vicinity, and originating there. During the Revolutionary War of 1776, the American forces captured a brigade of British troops, at *Red-Bank,* below Philadelphia, in New Jersey, commanded by Count Dunop, *i. e.,* Done-up, and so pronounced, which brigade contained three regiments of Hessians, these were sent to Reading, then a depot for prisoners, and remained there ever after; the English government refusing to pay the expense of their transportation to their homes. So they settled, married, lived and died there. And their descendants mingling with the Americans, and being without education, naturally acquired the patois, which has extended over the State, and although now intermixed with German, is called "Pennsylvania Dutch," a specimen of which is contained in the following copy of an advertisement, of an old acquaintance. The first line means "Just look here once!" A favorite expression in and about Bethlehem.

GOOK YUSHT AMOHL DOH!
Monsleit un Weibsleit!!
BUWA UN MÆD YUNGY UN OLTY.
ATTENTION!!
DER EAGLE DRUG SHTORE!
Der Besht under Wholfealsht!
WM. S. SIEGER, OBBADEAKER.

In der Dritt Shtrose, Sued Bethlehem.

Olsfort uf hond, olly sorta fun de beshty Drugs un Meditziena, un on de wholfealshty prices. Also, Paint, Oehl, Glaws, Varnish, &c. Mer hen aw an neier article dos gor net gebutta konn wærra; es is de bareemt

"SALTED SODA"

uu wærd g'used for seaf kocha. Prowiers amohl—de directions wo mers braucht geana mit. Om Eagle Drug Shtore is aw der plotz for

PATENT MEDITZIENA, BITTERS, &c.,
&c., &c.,

Fun olly ort, un on de wholfealshty prices. Also, Coal-Oehl, Lompa, Waughashmoer, &c., &c.

Now mind was mer sawya; mer hen olles uf hond was mer denka konn in unser line of bisness. We g'sawt, unser prices sin wholfealer dos in ennichem onnera Drug Shtore im County. Ferges't net der platz,

IN DER DRITT SHTROSE UNNICH DER LOCUST SUED BETHLEHEM.

Now is de tseit; macht eich bei, un judg'd for eich selwer; kummt in foor weasa, uf horseback, uf em Railroed odder tsu foos—mer sin gor net particular wie, yusht so dos der kommt on

DER EAGLE OBBADEAK IN SUED BETHLEEEM.

Un bringt eier greenbacks mit. Wholfeal for Cash—sell is unser style.

WILLIAM S. SIEGER,
Obbadeaker.

August 28, 1869.

The following piece of poetry, in "Pennsylvania German," by L. A. Wollenweber, of Philadelphia, is copied from the *Weekly Progress,"* of South Bethlehem, under date of June 23rd, 1870, and will be found in one of the interesting and very amusing letters of "Danny Kratzer" (Edward Ebermann,) "*Ains fun Johnny seina boova*," which are a marked feature in the weekly issue of that paper.

"'I bin au en Pennsylvanier
D'ruff bin ich Stolz und froh.
Dass Land is shay, die Leut sin nett
Bei Tschinks! ich mach schier en'ge wett,
'S biets kay Land der Welt.'

Wir Stamme vun die Deutsche her,
Druff bin ich a recht stolz,
Die Deutsche sin arg brave Leut
Sin Sparsam, fleissig und gesheit,
Sie biet ke Folk der Welt.

Do guk nur als de Karta au,
Wie Pennsylvany haist,
Wachst do net alles shay un guth,
Un hutt net yeder g'sundes Blut!
'S biets kay Land der Welt.

Un net allainich uff der Erd
Wachst alles shay und guth,
Au drunne gebbts so fiel ihr wollt,
Kohle, Eise—may werth wie gold,
'S biets kay Land der Welt.'"

There is a very interesting article in the *Atlantic Monthly* of October, 1868, entitled "Pennsylvania Dutch," page 473, &c., which is worthy of perusal.

The ancient and beautiful Christian practice of holding *Love-feasts* as a religious ceremonial, has been continued in the Brethren's Church from the earliest days of Moravianism. *Love-feast's*, and the *Kiss of Peace*, were originally connected with the Holy Communion. Saint Chrysostom says, "Upon certain days, after partaking of the Lord's Supper, they met at a common table, the rich bringing provisions, and the poor who had nothing, being invited." The same spirit that actuated the early Christians, still animates the Brethren of the Moravian Church. All the members of the congregation are invited to the Love-feasts, of the different choirs or classes, and the expenses are defrayed by a general collection taken up after the service, to which all contribute who are able, that feel inclined. Formerly, after a Love-feast, a collector called at each house, asked how many had been to service, and collected the amount due, so much being charged for each. Now, the collection is made at the door, where the "church servants" are stationed, with small baskets in which such as choose, drop their offerings. Whatever balance remains unpaid the congregation fund is taxed to make it up.

In the case of the "Single Brethren" and "Single Sisters'" Love-feasts, at their festivals, they invite whom they choose, and pay their own expenses, so much for general expenses, and so much for each invited guest. The stated times for holding these Love-feasts, are upon festive occasions, which occur annually; the different *choirs* celebrating their own festivals, and inviting the rest of the congregation. These Festivals, Prayer-days or Love-feasts, are held in commemoration of revivals, or some other interesting events in the early history of the Brethrens' Church. The refreshments furnished on these joyous occasions, consists of Moravian sugar bunns, and coffee only.

The appointed days for the annual Love-feasts of each of the different choirs of the Moravian Church, are as follows :

    April 30th, for the Widows.
    May 4th, for the Single Sisters.
    June 4th, for the Older Girls.
    July 9th, for the Older Boys.
    August 17th, for the Children.
    August 29th, for the Single Brethren.
    August 31st, for the Widowers.
    September 7th, for the Married People (Parents.)

The widows and widowers are generally associated with the choir of the married people and parents.

These festivals are always celebrated on Sunday, and in the church. The services commencing at 2 o'clock P. M., and lasting about half an hour. If the anniversary does not fall on a Sunday, the succeeding Sabbath is the day on which the festival is held.

On the days of the celebration of the married people's festivals, that choir hold a private meeting, at 9 o'clock, A. M., in the church, at which there is generally an address by the minister, suitable to the occasion, and to the condition of those present; concluding with prayer and singing.

In the *Episcopal Watchman*, volume I, page 143, of the year 1827, is published a sketch entitled,

"A MORAVIAN LOVE FEAST."

" The following is an account of one of those feasts at Bethlehem, Pa., at 7 o'clock on Sunday morning, five musicians announced the day of the feast from the church steeple, by a solemn air on the trumpets and trombones," three airs are always played. "The ordinary Sabbath exercises were performed in the morning, and at 2 o'clock a large assemblage was collected for the festival. The church is large, containing several apartments besides the room for worship, having a lofty ceiling, and large windows hung with white curtains. One half of the church was occupied by the female part of the congregation, including more than 120 scholars of the boarding school; in white dresses and caps, trimmed uniform, the *sisters'* and *widows*.

" The other division of the church was occupied by the males, among whom were a number of school boys, arranged according to size. So large a collection, orderly seated on benches, and preserving an entire stillness, had an imposing appearance.

" During the performance of the choir, in which the organ was accompanied by violins and trumpets ; six women and four men entered the church, each couple bearing a basket of soft cakes, which they distributed to the whole congregation, commencing with the clergymen, when these were served, the same persons brought in coffee in white mugs, on wooden trays; which were distributed in the same manner, and of which all present partook; during the continuance of the services, which consisted entirely of singing by the choir, the officiating clergyman, the females, the children and the congregation, alternately in chorus, excepting two hymns, the words were German, as was all the music.

"Singular as the description of such a ceremony appears, it was conducted with so much solemnity and propriety, that no other appropriate feeling could be excited. Typical of that fellowship which is the bond of the Moravians, and from which they derive their appellation of *Unitas Fratrum.* This occasional festival is an opposite emblem of the social love which has received the beautiful ecomium of David, 'Behold how good and pleasant it is for brethren to dwell together in unity ; it is like the precious ointment upon Aaron's beard, which flowed to the skirts of his garments : like the dew of Hermon, and like the dew which descended upon the mountains of Zion ; for them the Lord commanded the blessing, even life forevermore.'"

For a more proper understanding of the exercises and manner of conducting a Lovefeast, a copy of the Fest Psalm sung at the Single Sisters' Festival in the Moravian Church at Bethlehem Pa., in the year A. D., 1870, is here inserted.

ODE

FOR THE

Festival of the Single Sisters,

IN BETHLEHEM.

Liturgus.   Mel. 90.

O Chor des Herrn, ermuntre Dich
Zu frohen Lobgesängen!

Gäste.

Preis' deinen Heiland inniglich
Mit süßen Freudenklängen,
Da Er dich abermal ein Fest
In Seinem Frieden feiern läßt.

Sisters.   T. 151 G.

Head of Thy congregation,
    Kind Shepherd, gracious Lord !
Look on us with compassion,
    Met here with one accord :
Accept our thanks and praises
    For all Thy love and care,
Which we in various cases
    Repeatedly did share.

Chor.

Freuen und fröjlich müſſen ſein in Dir, die nach Dir fragen, und
die Dein Heil lieben, müſſen immer ſagen: Hochgelobt ſei Gott: O
wer nur immer bei Tag und Nacht Dein zu genießen recht wär' be=
dacht, der hätt' ohne Ende von Glück zu ſagen, und Leib und Seele
müßt' immer fragen: Wer iſt wie Du?

Sisters.   T. 56.

Nought but blessings :||: He for us intends,
And His mercy :||: never, never ends;
Let us look unto the cross,
Where He died to ransom us,
On that offering :||: faith alone depends.

Guests.   T. 16.

Happy is the virgin's station
  Whom he kindly owns as his,
And who counts his great salvation
  As her highest good and bliss.

Happy who thus find in Jesus
  All their wishes satisfied;
Ah, to them how dear and precious
  Is that friend who for us died.

Choir.

Holy, holy, holy is the Lord God of Sabaoth. Full are
the heavens of Thy glory. Praise the Lord, O my soul, and
all that is within me praise His Holy name, Hallelujah!
Praise the Lord, O my soul, and forget not all His benefits;
praise the Lord, and bless His holy name! Hosanna in the
highest!

Gäſte.   Mel. 141.

Friede thau' von Oben
Seligs Chor, auf Dich!
  Lieben, danken, loben,
  Still und jungfräulich
    Rein vor Ihm erſcheinen,
Unter Seinem Kuß,
    Sünderſchaamroth weinen —
Sei Dein Feſtgenuß!

Sisters.   T. 168.

Unto Thee, most faithful Saviour,
  We ourselves anew commend;
O look down on us with favor,
  To our prayers and wants attend;

Grant us all a tender feeling,
Of thy love and gracious dealing,
That our hearts may truly be
Fill'd with fervent love to Thee.

Mel. 22.

Ach zieh' in unsre Herzen ein,
Und laß sie Deine Wohnung sein;
Nimm Seel und Leib zu Deinen Gnad'n,
Bewahre sie vor allem Schad'n!

Chor.

Es ist ein köstlich Ding, daß das Herz fest werde, welches geschieht
durch Gnade.

Sisters. T. 585.

Though unseen we love the Saviour,
He almighty grace hath shown,
Pardoned guilt, and purchased favor;
Hence, through mercy, we're His own.
Give Him glory :||:
Grace and glory are His own!

Mel. 119.

Führ' uns durch, :||:
Führ' uns, HErr! durch's Thränenthal,
Deiner Herrlichkeit entgegen,
In den schönen Freudensaal!
Hilf bei unserm Unvermögen,
Gib zum Treu-sein Kraft, zum Wachen Muth,
Dann geht's gut. :||:

All. T. 246.

Blessing and power and majesty
Through endless ages be to Thee,
Who us by blood hast bought,
In mercy sought,
And to Thy fold us brought.

Amen, Hallelujah!
Hallelujah!
Amen, Hallelujah!

1870.

One of the most interesting of these occasions, is when, during the evening of the day of the celebration of the children's festival, they are all assembled in the open air in front of the church at Bethlehem, and sing, to the accompaniment of the trombone choir, their Fest Psalm. Nothing can be more interesting, nor more pleasing; the sweet sounds of the voices of the little ones, the solemn tones of the trombones, breaking upon the air of a still quiet evening; the scene lit up by the torches of the choir, the streets and side walks crowded by the people, friends, parents and, relatives of the children, who join in the singing, as the minister gives out the hymns line by line. Formerly the front of the church was on these occasions hung and lit up with colored lamps, much increasing the beauty and interest of the scene.

On the last occasion at which the lanterns were used at the celebration (outside) of the children's festival, a stranger at Bethlehem, no doubt pleased with the scene, wrote a sketch of it, entitling his effusion, "The Feast of the Lanterns." The Moravian minister in charge of the Bethlehem congregation at the time, became thereupon dreadfully alarmed for fear the world would think that the Brethren worshiped the *lanterns*, so they were abolished; and their use has never been resumed since.

The lanterns used at the illumination, were made of tissue paper, red, white, blue and yellow, pasted over a wire frame, and a lighted candle placed in each, and these suspended from a long wire drawn from tree to tree in front of the church; the effect was very fine, a mellow light was cast upon the crowd of spectators, upon the neighboring houses, the street, and open square, and glimmered among the trees, while the chorus of childish voices, and the peculiar tones of the trombones filled the air, sounds, which once heard, are never forgotten, but linger still on the ear—in memory. From the *Moravian* of August 25th, 1870, I insert a description of the children's festival at Nazareth, Pennsylvania.

"A LITURGICAL SERVICE IN THE MORAVIAN CEMETERY AT NAZARETH.—On Sunday evening, 21st inst., a novel and beautiful sight was presented to the spectator, standing outside of the southern gate way of the Moravian Cemetery. I do not allude to the extensive view of the lovely landscape from the top of this hill, but to another and most lovely spectacle, which was exhibited this evening on looking down in the direction of the Moravian Church. In front of the church a large number of children, and the pupils of the Sunday school, accompanied by their teachers and many members of the congregation had assembled, who formed into a procession, which ascended the hill to the cemetery, the children going before, and singing several sweet songs of Zion. This day had been set apart for the celebration of the "children's festival." All their special services, including a Love-feast, had been held in the church. But the evening service was appointed to take place in the cemetery, as had been done last year. Punctually at 6 P. M., the procession started from the church, after singing a hymn of praise. Upon entering into the cemetery, the choir played a soul-stirring choral. The small army of children having taken their position in the avenue of evergreens, flanked on both sides by the brethren and sisters of the congregation, the service of God was opened by the singing of the verse: *Gott ist gegenwaertig,*" (God reveals his presence,) and, truly, the congregation sang with unction and deeply feeling the presence of the Lord on this solemn occasion, and standing around the graves of our sainted dead. A very appropriate air was then sung by the choir, accompanied by instrumental music, whereupon the pastor invoked the throne of grace and made a brief address. The congregation were then requested, by singing several verses, to commend our dear children to their great and best Friend and Saviour. This impressive liturgical service was closed by the chanting of the Benediction on the part of the whole congregation. When returning from this sacred spot, our children

sang with cheerful voices and happy hearts;
'Lord, dismiss us with blessing,' &c., and
' Sing Hallelujah, praise the Lord,' &c."

It is customary on the Sunday immmedi-
ately before *Christmas* of each year, to have
a Love-feast for all persons engaged in any
capacity in serving the Church. This festival is however, somewhat different in its
character from the festivals of the different
choirs or classes of the church members; as
a portion of the time is passed in social conversation, touching matters pertaining to
their several duties, the changes to be made,
and a general discussion of church affairs
within their sphere, and improvements to be
made therein. This makes the occasion one
of the most interesting kind to all those who
take any interest in the welfare of the Church.
It must be distinctly understood, however,
that the Moravian Brethren who do occasional duty in the Church, like that to be
presently mentioned, do not ask, or receive
any pay for their services, any more than
the knowledge, and the hope, that they are
performing an acceptable service to their
Brethren and their God.

It was at the close of such a Love-feast
immediately before Christmas, in December,
1868, that the following changes were made
in the "church servants." Brothers Ruben
O. Luckenbach, Christian Belling, Herman
Yost, and Edmund Peisert, having served
from twelve to eighteen years in the Church,
asked to be relieved from their positions of
"Saal Diener's." So Brothers Cornelius W.
Krause, Orlanda B. Desh, Ashton C. Borheck, and Sidney S. Schneller, were named
to take their places. Those gentlemen perform the duties of ushers, that are in other
churches filled by paid and obsequious sex-
tons, in list slippers; may they long live to
fill their positions acceptably, and to do humbly their duty in their Master's house.

There are eight "Saal Dieners" or chapel
servants in the Moravian Church at Bethlehem; four of the number did not ask to be
retired from duty, namely, Brothers John C.
Weber, William Leibert, Benjamin F. Schneller, and Isaac Walp. These gentlemen choose

their new associates in their self-imposed,
and meritorious labors; and the newly appointed Brethren entered into the duties of
their office in January, 1869.

Among the Moravians of Bethlehem, there
is still retained many of the ancient customs
and usages of the Church, and of the people
from whom they are descended. Many of
these customs are simple, child-like and
charming, making life more sweet and
pleasant, and reminding us every day, whilst
we are among them, that men and women
are but children of a larger growth. It is
this charming simplicity of character that
renders life in Bethlehem so pleasing. With
Americans, life is real, life is earnest; and we
are too apt to forget in the social circle at
home, those little tender, loving kindnesses,
and gentle attentions, that are so dear and
so acceptable to those we love.

Numbered among the many surprises that
add to the enjoyment of the Christmas holidays at Bethlehem, there is one that carries
with it pleasure both to the young and old;
for be it known, that the Moravians observe
the Christmas holidays with peculiar zest,
and great are the preparations for the enjoyment thereof. In our principal Moravian
settlements, the Christmas festival lasts a
week, or rather eight days, from Christmas
day to New Year's day, included. It is a
season of free, joyous, social intercourse, such
as no other denomination of Christian people attempts. And one of the great essential
features of every well regulated Moravian
household, is the *Christmas Putz*.

All Christendom has adopted the *Christmas
Tree*, but the Moravians have brought with
them from the Fatherland, a charming improvement, denominated "a Putz," which in
the German means an embellishment, or an
ornament, but in Bethlehem parlance, a
large Christmas decoration. It is generally
a miniature representation of some loved or
beautiful scene in nature, an entire indoor
landscape. Some of these mimic scenes
are of the most pleasing character, dis-
playing great artistic taste and talent. A
varied scenery of mountain and valley, a

tumbling water-fall, near which is often a mill, with its great wheel in rapid motion, sometimes a quiet lake, with living fish, a distant village, with its ancient church, whose tall spire is reflected in a peaceful stream flowing near, all forming a quiet summer scene; oft again, one with the snow clad mantle of winter; then again a night scene in the dear old Fatherland, lighted up by a mimic moon. These are represented with a faithfulness of detail, and a genuine skill of arrangement, that excites our admiration, as much, if not more than a beautiful picture, giving frequently a pleasure that can be exceeded only by some charming scene in nature.

Behind the bar of the Eagle tavern, at Bethlehem, in the common room, there has been a large aperture made in the wall of the house, ten feet long, by four feet high, opening into a room built outside of the house, about ten feet square, covered over with a glass roof, as in hot-houses. In this room, William W. Yohe, son of mine ancient host, Caleb, erects each fall a *Putz;* some miniature winter scene. In the spring he replaces this by a summer view, sometimes imaginary, oft times real. On one occasion he made a view of a town in Western Virginia, the scene of one of the earliest battles of the late Rebellion, which a Union refugee at once recognized as the home he had just fled from. Mr. Yohe is quite celebrated in Bethlehem as a *Putz* builder, of much good taste.

In the *Moravian* of Christmas week, 1867, a writer thus refers to "an old time *Putz.*"

"How far back they date we are not prepared to say. They were in the full tide of their glory when we were a boy, twenty-five years ago, when we were sufficiently advanced to lend a helping hand, and *then* the great *Putz*-makers were men well advanced in years, so that it is fair to presume that *Putz* making is amongst the ancient institutions of this venerable town. The taste and ingenuity displayed in these decorations was often very considerable. We use the word 'decoration' for the want of a better, though

it does not convey a correct idea of the *Putz*, which is not a festooning of the rooms with garlands and wreaths, but a miniature representation of some scene in nature, imaginary or real. As we have said, the art displayed in these mimic scenes was frequently very creditable. Mountains and valleys, tumbling waterfalls and peaceful fields, lakes and villages, in the bright green of summer, or the delicate snow covering of winter, were represented with a faithful minuteness of detail, and in really artistic groupings. Many evenings, until late in the night, were devoted to the making of them. Who will say that it was labor thrown away? Now-a-days we fear, you could scarcely gather together a dozen men who would be willing to devote themselves to the preparation of one of these grand *Putzes* of the olden time, just because they loved to do this sort of thing, and the time is now to them so precious a thing for business, that they cannot spare it for the purpose of pure and innocent amusement. Are we any the happier or better now? are boys any more frank and innocent, or the girls any more loveable and modest than they were then? When, even on a Christmas Eve, the great *Putz*-seeing evening, they came home at nine o'clock, and were thankful for the privilege of being allowed to go, and to be an hour later than usual.

"Besides these *Putzes* which were made on a grand scale, there were smaller ones in abundance; the humblest home having its little table, covered with a white cloth, and backed by branches of evergreens, from which were suspended glittering stars, wax angels, bright colored candies, &c., in pretty confusion, illuminated by many burning candles. Who, that ever saw or played at them, will forget those bright Christmas scenes? The cave from which issued the monster bear or lion, the looking-glass lake, on which ducks and geese of various sizes sat in motionless propriety, the silver-sanded road, on which was ranged the contents of a Noah's Ark, with the patriarch and his family walking first, and the animals following two by two in solemn procession; the little village with its church and rows of stiff poplar trees; the pleasant minglings of bird and beast and fish, all in perfect peace with one another, as became them at Christmas time; the stable where the 'blessed child' was born; the mill hoisting up its bags and letting them down again, as long as the hidden machinery remained in working order, whilst the miller smoked his pipe, and his dog kept up a very energetic, if somewhat methodical jumping at his feet; all these, and a thousand other recollections, rise before the memory, and force us to the conclusion that *Putzes* are a great institution, and ought not to be allowed to die out. And there are other memories associated with them, some of which are of too sentimental a character to be mentioned. The expeditions in search of moss, the pleasant preparation for the great *Putz*, the mysterious darkened and carefully locked up room, the anxious suspense, the joyous surprise, the happy hearts and smiling faces, the sweet interchange of precious presents between the juveniles, not of the same family or sex, the fortunate and often repeated meetings whilst going the rounds of visiting the many *Putzes*, which it was necessary to see. We wonder whether the young ones enjoy Christmas as thoroughly and innocently as they used to do when Bethlehem was only a little village, and the outer world was quite shut out."

The lament of our friend is uncalled for, there has been a revival in *Putzes* since he wrote, and the young still enjoy them, especially the lovers, as much as they did in the good old times of which he writes. And if my readers want to have some happy hours, just let them go and pass the Christmas holidays at Bethlehem once.

There is one institution in Bethlehem which is deserving of more than a mere passing notice. That is the "Young Men's Misssionary Society." The first stated meeting of the society was held September 7, 1840, in the old Moravian school-house, and the following officers elected. President, David Zeisberger Smith, the founder and originator of the society. Vice President, Henry J. Van Vleck. Recording Secretary,

Augustus Wolle. Treasurer, William Warner. Directors, A. A. Reinke, E. H. Reichel and Albert Butner. Soon afterwards, Dr. Maurice C. Jones was made Corresponding Secretary.

The following is the list of the original signers to the first constitution.

David Z. Smith,	L. O. Tombler,
George W. Perkin,	Christian H. Belling,
William H. Warner,	Francis D. Schneller,
Amadeus A. Reinke,	Wm. F. Ranch,
Albert Butner,	Owen J. Rice,
Andrew G. Kern,	Mortimer Warner,
Edward H. Reichel,	Wm. L. Brown,
Henry J. Van Vleck,	Maurice C. Jones,
George A. Weiss,	Wm. S. Weinland,
Augustus Wolle,	Samuel P. Geehr,
Simon Rau,	Levin J. Krause,
Joseph H. Kummer,	Benj. F. Schneller,
J. Edward Luckenbach,	Charles Schneller,
Reuben O. Luckenbach,	Reuben Clewell,
Francis W. Knauss,	Alfred Ricksecker,
	Edward C. Peisert.

Meetings are held every month; and the reading of mission reports was made the custom for several years, but has of late years been abandoned. On the 24th of January, 1841, the first annual meeting of the society was held, and an address delivered by Edward H. Reichel. Annual meetings have been held ever since that time, and the society still continues in successful operation.

In 1841, the project of forming a Museum as a source of income to the society, was first proposed, and at once adopted. In 1843, a liberal gift of books from Miss Mary Allen, formed the nucleus of the library. The association continued to hold their meetings in the old town school building till 1858, when, through the kindness of the Moravian school-board, a large, convenient room in the new school house was assigned to the society, and suitably furnished as a reading room, library and museum, and the first meeting held therein on the 17th of April of that year.

The constitution of the society, which had been remodelled in 1842, with the motto, "And above all things put on charity, which is the bond of perfection."—Colossians, iii, 14; was altered, and an entire new constitution adopted; the objects of the society being stated to be " The furtherance of the Foreign Missions of the United Brethren among the Heathen, and the Religious, Literary and Social Improvement of Young Men."

In the winter of 1858-59, the practice of having a course of lectures given by popular speakers before the society and its friends was first inaugurated. These lectures were delivered before numerous audiences in the Citizen's Hall, and the number of members increased to one hundred.

In 1862, the society removed to the building now occupied by Dr. Jacobson, for his office, in Market Street. And afterwards to Broad Street near Main, and finally in 1868, to the building in Main Street near the Moravian Church, erected by the society in conjunction with the Young Men's Christian Association of Bethlehem." This building is three stories in height, the first floor being occupied by the publication office of the Moravian Church. In the rear of the store is the Museum of the Missionary Society, very tastefully arranged, consisting of many curiosities from different parts of the world, the presents of the Moravian missionaries, and numerous ancient relics of the first settlement of the town, added to which is the fine large picture of Zeisberger preaching to the Indians, painted by Schussele.

In a note to page 232, in the History of Lehigh Valley, there is a pleasant description of the contents of the Museum, in which it is said, " Several of these curiosities deserve special mention. The old 'Sundial,' the 'old Cannon,' and the 'old Spinnet or Piano.'" To this list might be added the "old Cradle" and the "old Chairs," like those used an hundred years ago in the town, and still in use in Germany, and sometimes seen in German paintings. The collection contains many rare and curious things. The second story is occupied for the purposes of the Library, which is free to all who desire to avail themselves of its privileges, except the taking out of books for reading at their houses; that right is confined to members of the two societies. The Library is under the direction of the Christian Association, by an arrangement made between the two corporations. The third story is fitted up for, and used as a lecture room, in which the societies hold their meetings.

The thirtieth anniversary meeting of the Young Men's Missionary Society of the Bethlehem congregation, was held on Sunday evening, January 30, 1870. The Moravian report states that:

" The annual report was read by the retiring president, Brother A. J. Harwi. The total membership of the Society is 315. Monthly meetings are held, the interest of which during the past year was considerably increased by short addresses by different brethren on the history or present condition of the missions of our church. The direct donations of the society were made to the congregation at Estridge, St. Kitts, and the Missionary Home, Kleinwelke, Saxony. The officers of the Society for the ensuing year are, President, Eugene Weber; Vice President, Edwin Bishop; Secretary, Aug. Leibert; Treasurer, Aug. Bishop. The anniversary address was delivered by Bro. Wm. Vogler, of the Theological Seminary. May his earnest words find a response in the hearts of all the members of the Society."

The ceremonies attending the laying the corner-stone of the building of the Missionary Society and Christian Association, were performed on August 26th, 1867, and it was finished and occupied during the next year. The exercises were began by singing a hymn, followed by a prayer by the Rev. A. A. Reinke, a lesson from the Scriptures were read by the Rev. Mr. Kemble, and an address delivered by Henry J. Scamen, president of the Christian Association; after which, another hymn was sung. A list of the contents of box deposited in the corner-stone, was read, then followed a hymn, sung by the congregation, who were dismissed with a benediction by the Right Rev. Bishop Jacobson.

The following members of the Missionary Society were killed, or died in the service of their country during the late rebellion.

SAMUEL BEAN, of Quakertown, private in company C, 129th regiment Penn. Vols., killed at the battle of Fredericksburg, Dec. 13, 1863.

JOSEPH L. CLEWELL, of Schoeneck, company F, 132nd regiment Penna. Vols., killed at Antietam, September 17, 1862.

EDWIN PFLUEGER, of Seidersville, private in 2nd regiment Penna. Heavy Artillery, Col. Augustus A. Gibson, commanding. Wounded at Petersburg, May, 1864; died of his wounds.

CLARENCE KAMPMAN, clerk to Admiral Lee, U. S. Navy; died June 4, 1869, on board U. S. Hospital Ship "Red Rover."

JOHN C. HAGAN, private in 2nd regiment Penna. Cavalry; died August 7, 1865, at Bethlehem, of the Camp Fever, contracted in the service.

ARTHUR VAN VLECK, company C, 126th Ohio. Taken prisoner at Culpepper, October, 14, 1863. Died in Libby Prison December 21, 1863.

On the 21st of April, 1864, on application of the members of the Young Men's Missionary Society of Bethlehem, the said association was duly incorporated by the Court of Common Pleas of Northampton County, Pa. The petition was signed by Joseph A. Rice, Bertine S. Erwin, Joseph H. Treager, William A. Erwin, Herman A. Doster, Robert Rau, Geo. H. Luckenback, T. M. Rights and J. Albert Rondthaler.

The following is a list of presiding officers of the Young Men's Missionary Society, since its organization.

1840-41—President,	.	.	David Z. Smith.
1841-42—	"	.	Simon Rau.
1842-43—	"	.	Owen J. Rice.
1843-44—	"	.	Owen J. Rice.
1844-45—	"	.	Owen J. Rice.
1845-46—	"	.	Owen J. Rice.
1846-47—	"	.	B. F. Schneller.
1847-48—	"	.	Francis Wolle.
1848-49—	"	.	Francis Wolle.
1849-50—	"	.	R. A. Grider.
1850-51—	"	.	R. A. Grider.
1851-52—	"	.	L. R. Huebener.
1852-53—	"	.	R. P. Krause.
1853-54—	"	.	R. P. Krause.
1854-55—	"	.	J. Burdge.

1855-56—President,	.	.	A. J. Erwin.
1856-57—	"	. .	A. J. Erwin.
1857-58—	"	. .	A. J. Erwin.
1858-59—	"	. .	Joseph M. Leibert.
1859-60—	"	. .	Joseph M. Leibert.
1860-61—	"	. .	Edward Rondthaler.
1861-62—	"	. .	Herman A. Doster.
1862-63—	"	. .	Abraham S. Schropp.
1863-64—	"	. .	Joseph A. Rice.
1864-65—	"	. .	Joseph A. Rice.
1865-66—	"	. .	W. J. Holland.
1866-67—	"	. .	Henry T. Clauder.
1867-68—	"	. .	Henry J. Seaman.
1868-69—	"	. .	Alfred J. Harwi.
1869-70—	"	. .	Alfred J. Harwi.
1870-71—	"	. .	Eugene E. Weber.

The speakers at the Anniversary meetings of the association were:—

January 24th, 1841...Edward H. Reichel.	
" 9th, 1842...A. A. Reinke.	
" 8th, 1843...Ed. A. De Schweinitz.	
" 14th, 1844...Edwin E. Reinke.	
" 26th, 1845...E. H. Reichel.	
" 25th, 1846...Francis Wolle.	
" 17th, 1847...Bernhard DeSchweinitz.	
" 30th, 1848...Max Goepp.	
" 14th, 1849...Lewis R. Huebener.	
" 13th, 1850...Lewis R. Huebener.	
" 18th, 1851...Bishop Van Vleck.	
" 18th, 1852...Parmenio Leinbach.	
" 23rd, 1853...L. F. Kampman.	
" 28th, 1854...Clement L. Reinke.	
" 28th, 1855...Eugene Leibert.	
" —th, 1856...——— ———.	
" 11th, 1857...Clement L. Reinke.	
" 10th, 1858...Eugene Leibert.	
" 16th, 1859...Herman A. Brickenstein.	
" 15th, 1860...William Bigler.	
" 20th, 1861...Samuel Reinke.	
" 16th, 1862...W. Henry Rice.	
" 25th, 1863...J. Theophilus Zorn.	
" 17th, 1864...Edward Rondthaler.	
" 29th, 1865...Ed. A. De Schweinitz.	
" —th, 1866...J. Albert Rondthaler.	
" —th, 1867...Edw. Rondthaler.	
" —th, 1868...Eugene L. Schaefer.	
" —th, 1869...Edw. Regennas.	
" —th, 1870...Wm. H. Vogler.	

To insert a list of the active members of the society would not be interesting to the general reader, so it is omitted, but a list is given of the

LIFE MEMBERS.

James Leibert,	John Jordan,
Mrs. Jane Jordan,	W. H. Jordan,

Miss Helen Bell,
Abm. S. Schropp,
Jos. H. Traeger,
Rev. Henry Van Vleck,
Edw. Bell,
Rev. Sylvester Wolle,
Henry Coppee, L. L. D,
John C. Schropp,

Miss Sophia Henry,
Jos. A. Rice,
Ewing Jordan,
Miss Emily Bell,
Miss Laura Bell,
Bernhard E. Lehman,
Wm. Schropp,
Col. Forester.

John Hill Martin,

The society issued in 1865, an historical sketch, and an address by the Rev. Edward de Schweinitz, in a neat pamphlet, to which I am indebted for most of the foregoing information, particularly the lists; to complete them, I add that containing the names of the ministers and missionaries who are members of the association.

Rev. David F. Smith,
 " E. A. de Schweinitz,
 " B. E. de Schweinitz,
 " George Weiss,
 " Wm. H. Warner,
 " Edward Rondthaler,
 " E. H. Reichel,
 " A. A. Reinke,
 " Sylvester Wolle,
 " Francis Wolle,

Rev. E. M. Leibert,
 " P. R. Leinbach,
 " E. T. Kluge,
 " Emanuel Rondthaler,
 " C. L. Reinke,
 " A. R. Horne,
 " James Haman,
 " P. Rommel,
 " Joseph Romig,
 " W. Henry Rice,

Rev. E. E. Reinke,
 " Wm. C. Reichel,
 " E. P. Greider,
 " Joseph H. Kummer,
 " H. J. Van Vleck,
 " L. F. Kampman,
 " G. W. Perkin,
 ' H. A. Brickenstein,

Rev. Edmund Oeter,
 " H. S. Bachman,
 " S. B. Simes,
 " H. S. Hoffman,
 " Chas. B. Shultz,
 " S. M. Smith,
 " Edw. Rondthaler,
Mr. W. Spaugh.

Mr. H. Ruede,

The "Young Men's Missionary Society and Christian Association," was organized February 6, 1866, but by a resolution of September 3, 1867, became two distinct societies.

At a monthly meeting of the Young Men's Christian Association, held on Tuesday evening, September 13, 1870. The following gentlemen were elected officers of the Association to serve for the ensuing year; President, C. W. Krause; Vice Presidents, Wm. C. Ferriday, C. H. Kidder, W. R. Smith, G. V. Snyder, Michael Bitler, and H. T. Clauder; Recording Secretary, Aug. H. Leibert; Corresponding Secretary, Wm. H. Vogler; Recording Secretary, Eugene A. Rau; Treasurer, Franklin C. Stout.

CHRISTIAN ASSOCIATION AND NURSERY BUILDINGS.—1870.

BETHLEHEM, PA.

CHAPTER XIII.

THE SOCIETY FOR PROPAGATING THE GOSPEL AMONG THE HEATHEN.—STATISTICS OF THE UNITY OF THE BRETHREN, JANUARY 1, 1869. LIST OF THE CHURCHES AND MISSIONS IN THE NORTHERN DIOCESE OF THE CHURCH OF THE UNITED BRETHREN IN AMERICA.—AN OLD PASSPORT.—CHRISTIAN FREDERICK POST.— SISTER "POLLY HICKEWELDER."—REV. JOHN HICKEWELDER, AND HIS WRITINGS.— THE HORSFIELD PAPERS.—HISTORY OF NORTHAMPTON COUNTY, FROM A PAMPHLET. OFFICIAL SEAL OF THE MORAVIAN CHURCH, A CORRECTION.—TRAVELS OF THE MARQUIS DE CHASTELLUX IN AMERICA, 1780.—CHAS. THOMPSON'S THEORY OF THE FORMATION OF THE WIND-GAP.—CURIOSITIES.—THE OLD IRON STOVE PLATES.—INDIAN CORN GRINDER.—THE OLD SUN DIAL.—OLD TILES.— OLD WATER PIPES.—THE FIRST MARKET HOUSE.—OLD GRAVE YARD, SOUTH OF THE LEHIGH.—ZINZENDORF'S VISIT TO WYOMING. —FORMATION OF NORTHAMPTON COUNTY.

THE illustration at the head of this chapter, which is copied from one of Kleckner's cabinet stereoscopic views of the Lehigh Valley, presents to the right hand, looking at the picture, a representation of the southern portion of one of the old Æconomy buildings of the Moravian Society, which I have heretofore described as the "Old Nursery." It stood on the east side of Main Street, a short distance north of the Moravian church, and has just been torn down to make room for the new publication office of the Moravian church, a splendid large four-story structure, with a Mansard roof. The northern part of this old relic was demolished in 1867, to make room for the building of the Young Men's Christian Association of Bethlehem, a view of which is also given in the cut. This latter building was erected in 1867-68, at a cost of $16,500. It is 28 feet front by 70 feet deep, and three stories in height, built in the most substantial manner of brick with brown sandstone facings. On the first floor is the store and office of the Publication Society of the Moravian church, and in the rear the Museum of the Young Men's Missionary Society. On the second floor the Library of the Christian Association. And in the third-story a Lecture-room, capable of seating 400 people, and which is used by the two societies that erected the building.

Among the many societies formed by, and composed of Members of the Moravian church in America, none are more ancient or honorable, or more deserving of commendation, than the "Society for Propagating the Gospel among the Heathen," incorporated by Act of Assembly of the Representatives of the Freemen of the Commonwealth of Pennsylvania, on the 27th day of February, 1788. The first, second and fourth sections only, of said Act, are necessary to give a sketch of the purposes of the society; the others relate merely to the business operations of the corporation, and its power to hold real estate, and receive bequests.

SEC. 1st.—Whereas, it has been represented to this House, by the Rev. John Ettwein, one of the Bishops of the Church called UNITAS FRATRUM, or United Brethren, and the Rev. John Meder, Pastor in Ordinary of the said Church in the City of Philadelphia, that since the year of our Lord, 1749, when said Church began to make settlements in America, the principal aim of their members coming over from Europe, was, to carry the glorious truths of the Gospel to the Indians here; that they have without intermission continued their labors among the Indians, and notwithstanding the increase of expenses and other difficulties, are resolved to pursue and support this commendable work, and for this purpose have formed a Society for the Propagation of the Gospel among the Heathen, and entered into certain rules of association (a copy whereof they have subjoined to their Petition,) and prayed to incorporate the said Society.

And Whereas, The propagation of the Gospel among the Indians of America, is of great importance to the citizens of this and other of the United States, and may, by the blessings of God, be conducive to the peace and security of the inhabitants and settlers of our frontiers,

and by living examples of the Missionaries and the converts, the Savages may be induced to turn their minds to the Christian religion, industry, and social life with the citizens of the United States.

And Whereas, This House is disposed to exercise the powers vested in the Legislature of the Commonwealth, for the encouragement of all pious and charitable purposes.

SEC. 2nd.—Be it therefore enacted by the Representatives of the Freemen of the Commonwealth of Pennsylvania in General Assembly met, and by the authority of the same. That the Rev. John Ettwein, Bishop; Frederick William Von Marshall, gentleman; the Rev. Andrew Huebner and Paul Muenster; Hans Christian Von Schweinitz, gentleman; the Rev. David Zeisberger, Jr.; John August Klingsohr; Jeremiah Denke; Charles Gotthold Reichel; Daniel Kochler; Christian Denzien and Godfrey Brezel, the present Directors. The Rev. Benhard Adam Grube; Frederick Peter, Sr. and Jacob Van Vleck, the present Assistant Directors of the said Society. The Rev. John Herbst; John Meder; Francis Bochler; James Birkby; Lewis Bochler and Abraham Reincke, and others, the Ministers in the different Brethren's Congregations, and their Successors, and all other members of the said Society, who have and sha'l hereafter subscribe to the Rules of the said Society, be, and they are hereby made, declared and constituted, to be a corporation and body politic in law and in fact, to have continuance forever, by the name, style, and title of "The Society of the United Brethren for Propagating the Gospel among the Heathen."

The third section empowers the society to hold real estate by purchase, gift or devise, and to receive bequests of all kinds of personal property.

SEC. 4th.—And be it further enacted by the authority aforesaid, That all donations and contributions, rents, interests and profits, arising from the real and personal estate of the aforesaid Corporation, shall by the said Directors and their successors, from time to time be applied and laid out for the maintenance and support of their Missionaries and other Assistants; for building and supporting places of public worship and schools, providing books for the better educating, instructing and civilizing the children of the converts and others among the nations who shall be desirous to commit their youths to the care and instruction of the said Missiouaries, and for such other pious and charitable uses as are conformable to the true design and intent of the said Society.

The fixed seat of the said Society is at Bethlehem, Pa., where the Board of Directors meet, and the stated general meetings are always held.

Article X, of the Stated Rules of the Society, says:

"As we have no other view or aim but the furtherance and propagation of the knowledge of Jesus Christ among the poor benighted heathen, and esteem it a high privilege to support that praiseworthy work to the best of our abilities, being constrained to it by the love of Christ. All the Directors, Assistant Directors, and Officers of the Society, renounce for ever all demands and claims for salaries or compensation for their services."

The 81st Anniversary of the Incorporation of the Society was held at Bethlehem, Pa., on the 9th of September, A. D., 1869, when the following officers were elected for the ensuing year, viz :

Sylvester Wolle, *President.*

Robert de Schweinitz, *Vice President.*

Edwin G. Klose, *Secretary.*

William H. Bigler, *Corresponding Secretary.*

Ernst F. Bleck, *Treasurer.*

Charles Augustus Luckenback, Henry B. Luckenback, James T. Borhek, and John C. Weber, *Assistant Directors.*

James H. Wolle, Charles F. Beckel, and Simon Rau, *Auditors.*

Rev. Sylvester Wolle, President of the Society, conducted the introductory devotional exercises, Bro. E. F. Bleck acted as Secretary. The following members deceased during the past year, Thos. C. Lueders, of Indianapolis, Ind., George Thomas, Litiz, and Amos C. Clauder, Bethlehem. A number of new members were elected. The report of the Board of Directors, containing a review of the condition of the Indian missions in Canada and Kanzas, was read by Rev. L. F. Kampmann. The receipts of the Society last year were $11,659.64, of which amount $10,500 was forwarded to the Mission Department of the Unity's Elders' Conference. At the love-feast in the afternoon, as during the morning meeting of the Society, addresses on various subjects connected with the work of missions, were made by the Brn. Robert and Emil de Schweinitz, A. A. Reinke and Herman A. Brickenstein, late delegates to the General Synod.

In the *Moravian* of August 26, 1869, the following is given as a Roll of the Living Members of the Society for Propagating the Gospel among the Heathen, with the date of their enrolment.

1816. Peter Wolle.

1818. Peter Ricksecker, John C. Jacobsen, Samuel Reinke.

1819. Jedidiah Weiss.

1822. Charles C. Tombler, Charles F. Beckel, Henry Huebener, William F. Giering.

1824. Geo. Henry Bute.

1825. John M. Miksch, George W. Dixion, Chr. D. Busse, John Beck, Fred. Roming.

1826. George H. Goundie, Andrew G. Kern, Charles, F. Kluge, Abraham L. Huebener.

1828. John C. Brickenstein, Eugene A. Frueauff, Ernst F. Bleck, David Bigler, John J. Giering.

1830. Jacob P. Sigmund, Geo. F. Bahnson, Henry J. Kluge.

1832. Jonas Meyers.

1834. Charles B. Peter, Herman J. Titze, Wm. L. Lennert, Ambrose Rondthaler, Philip A. Cregar.

1835. Julius T. Beckler, Philip H. Goepp.

1836. Henry R. Luckenbach, Matthew Crist, Amos Bealer.

1837. John Krause, Sylvester Wolle.

1838. J. Chr. Weber, Emil A. de Schweinitz, Lewis F. Kampman.

1840. James Henry, Wm. Theodore Roepper.

1841. Simon Rau, Jos. H. Kummer, Robt. de Schweinitz, John Regennas, Francis Wolle, Ferdinand Lennert, Abr. Lichtenthaeler, Timothy Masslich, Philip Cann, Jacob Sturgis, Francis W. Christ, George Grider, Ambrose H. Rauch, John Graeff, Ferdinand Rickert.

1842. Chas. Aug. Luckenbach, F. F. Hagen, Edw. H Reichel.

1843. Reuben O. Luckenbach, Augustus Wolle, H. A. Shultz.

1844. Samuel Yost, Benj. F. Schneller, Samuel B. Clewell, C. Edw. Peisert, Oliver Tombler.

1845. Henry J. Van Vleck.

1846. Edwin P. Wolle, Nath. S. Wolle, Benj. Wilhelm.

1847. James T. Borhek, Edmund D. Schweinitz.

1848. William C. Reichel.

1849. Augustus Belling, Maurice C. Jones.

1850. William Bear, William Kreiter, Henry Rauch.

1851. Charles Sturgis, Aug. Sturgis.

1852. A. A. Reinke, Charles W. Rauch, Herm. Ruede, Alex. Sturgis, J. L. Eysenbach, Wm. N. Moench.

1853. James H. Wolle.

1856. Eugene Leibert, Herman A. Brickenstein.

1857. E. Linke, Benj. Ricksecker, H. C. Bachman, Eugene P. Greider, Henry G. Clauder.

1858. William Leibert.
1859. J. Phil. Rommel, Lewis R. Huebner, O. T. Huebner, H. T. Bachman, Owen Rice, James Haman, Albert L. Oerter, John Cennick Harvey, W. H. Bigler, Ernst Salathe, Jacob Moersch, Fred. Berger, Fred. Andreae, William Smyth, Fred. Wilhelm, E. E. Reinke.
1860. Edward Keller, Rich. W. Leibert, Samuel Weinland.
1861. Clem. L. Reinke, John F. Frueauff, J. Edw. Luckenbach, Wm. Henry Bice, G. F. Oehler.
1862. Jacob Luckenbach, Fred. R. Borhek, John J. Detterer, Gilbert Bishop.
1863. Edw. T, Kluge, Lawrence J. Oerter, P. H. Gapp, Thomas D. Luckenbach.
1864. Richard Wolff, Chas. B. Shultz, J. J. Groenfeldt, W. Herman Frueauff, Herman Yost.
1865. Ambrose J. Erwin, Allan Hamilton, M. A. Erdman.
1866. Herman Doster, Edm. A. Oerter, L. P. Clewell, H. S. Hoffmann, F. H. Holland, J. C. Israel, A. M. Iverson, F. W. Knauss, J. G. Kaltenbrunn.
1867. John Praeger, Isaac Prince, Joseph Romig, Edward Rondthaler, Henry Reusswig, Dav. Z. Smith, Stephen M. Smith, G. F. Uecke, J. E. Wuensche, Jno. M. Warman, Abr. S. Schropp, H. J. Seaman, Joseph Rice, David Rau, Cornelius W. Krause, Rud. F. Ranch, Cyrus Breder, Jos. H. Traeger, Orville Grider, Edw. T. Meyers, Robert Rau, Fred. A. Clauder, Henry T. Clauder, Theod. F. Levers, Wm. A. Erwin, John Schmid, James K. Rauch, Jacob Fulkerson, Adolph Conradi, Herm. Jacobson.
1868. Francis Jordan, Christion Neu, Charles Nagle, Joseph Ricksecker.
1869. Gustavus Feurig, Edwin G. Klose, William H. Jordan, Ludwig Scheele, Haydn H. Tshudy, Henry E. Weinland, Albert T. Doster, George W. Perkin, Alfred J. Harwi, Ashton C. Borhek, Augustus H. Leibert, Robert Peysert, Theodore Fradeneck, John Samuel Krause.

The statistics of the Unity of the Brethren, January 1, 1869.

Provinces.	Communicants.	Total.
German,	4,895	7,270
British,	3,280	5,448
American		
North,	5,860	
South,	1,088	6,768	11,885
	14,871	24,573
Missionaries among the Heathen,		305
Children of Missionaries,		100

Total of Congregations in the Foreign Mission Field,   69,123

                                              94,101

A list of the Churches and Missions of the Northern Province of the Moravian Church in America.

Bethany, Minn., .	. Henry Reusswig.
with Oakridge, Minn., .	" "
Bethlehem, Pa., .	} Edm. A. de Schweinitz and Lewis R. Huebener.
Brooklyn, N. Y. .	. Edwd. Rondthaler.
Canal Dover, Ohio,	. Stephen M. Smith.
Chaska, Minn., .	. Clement L. Reinke.
with Northfield, Minn.,	" "
Ebenezer, Wis., .	. John G. Kaltenbrunn.
Egg Harbor, N. J.,	. G. R. S. Feurig.
Elizabeth, N. J., .	. Christian Neu.
Emmaus, Pa., .	. Julius Wuensche.
Ephraim, Wis., .	. John G. Groenfeldt.
with Sturgeon Bay, Wis.	" "
Fort Howard, Wis.,	. Andrew M. Iverson.
Freedom, Wis., .	. Gottlieb Uecke.
Fry's Valley, Ohio,	. James B. Haman.
Gnadenhuetten, Ohio,	" "
Graceham, Md., .	. Henry T. Brachman.
Gracehill, Iowa, .	. Benjamin Ricksecker.
Greenbay, Wis., .	. John D. Detterer.
Harmony, Iowa, .	. Lewis P. Clewell.
Hope, Ind., .	. William L. Lennert.
with Enon, Ind.,	" "
Hopedale, Pa., .	. Charles Nagel.
with Coveville and Oakland, }	" "
Lake Mills, Wis., .	Philip F. Rommell.
. with Mamre, Wis.,	" "
and New Salem,	" "
Lancaster, Pa.,	. David Bigler.
Lebanon,	. Edmd. A. Oerter.
Lititz, Pa., .	. Edward T. Kluge.
Moravia, Iowa, .	. Francis W. Knauss.
Nazareth, Pa., .	. Henry A. Shultz.
New Dorp, S. I., .	. Francis F. Hagen.
with Centreville, S. S.,	" "
New York, N. Y. English,	Amadeus A. Reinke.
New York, N. Y. Germ'n,	Theodore Sonderman.
Olney, Ill., .	. John F. Warman.
Palmyra, N. J., .	. Philip H. Gapp.
with Riverside, N. J., .	" "
Philadelphia, Pa., 1st ch.,	Joseph H. Kummer.
Philadelphia, Pa., 2d ch.,	Herman S. Hoffman.
with Harrowgate, Pa., .	" "
Schoeneck, Pa., .	. John J. Regennas.
Sharon, Ohio, .	. David Z. Smith.
South Bethlehem, Pa., .	Henry J. Van Vleck.
with English, S. S., .	

Utica, N. Y.,	John Praeger.
Watertown, Wis.,	John C. Israel.
West Salem, Ill., English,	Joseph J. Ricksecker.
West Salem, Ill., German,	Herman J. Titze.
York, Pa.,	William Henry Rice.
INDIAN MISSIONS.	MISSIONARIES.
New Fairfield, Canada,	Edwin E. Reinke.
New Westfield, Kansas,	Joseph Romig.

In this connection, the following copy of a passport issued during the French and Indian war, by Gov. Denny to Rev. Frederick Post, 1759, will not be without interest.

WILLIAM DENNY.

To all persons whom it may concern, Greeting.
Whereas, Rev. Frederick Post, a Deacon in the Church of the Unitas Fratrum, has signified to me that now peace, through the Divine Blessing, is likely to be established between his Majesty and the several Indian Nations with whom we were lately at war, he has an earnest desire to go amongst them with some of the Brethren of the said Church, in order to publish the glad tidings of salvation obtained by our Lord Jesus Christ, and whereas, I have had good experience of the loyalty, integrity and prudence of the said Frederick Post, having employed him on several important occasions during the war in negotiating with the Indians; I do therefore very readily grant him my authority and full licence and permission, together with one, or more, of the said Brethren, to pass and repass as often as he shall think fit in the Indian country, unmolested and for the purpose aforesaid, that is to say, to preach the gospel amongst any of the said Indian Nations, in alliance with his Majesty, he continuing to demean himself well, and giving me in every journey, or immediately on his return home, an account of his doings amongst the said Indian Nations, to whom he is hereby heartily recommended for a kind reception and good treatment.
Given at Philadelphia November 5th, 1559.

By his Honors command,

RICHARD PETERS, *Secretary.*

Christian Frederick Post, was a Moravian Missionary among the Indians, a very courageous man, undertaking the most dangerous journeys cheerfully. He assumed during his travels, the dress of the Indians, and was much beloved by them. His journal was in possession of the late departed Sister "Polly" Heckewelder.

Johanna Maria Heckewelder was an inmate of the Sisters' House, in Bethlehem, Pa., where she departed this life on the 19th of September, 1868, aged eighty-seven years, five months and two days. She was the only daughter of the famous Moravian Missionary to the American Indians, the late Rev. John Heckewelder, and was born on Easter Monday, April 16, 1781, at Salem, a village of christian Indians on the Muskingum River, and was baptized the next day by the Rev. William Edwards, minister at Gnadenheutten. She was the first white child born in what is now the State of Ohio. A few days after her birth, occurred the events which ended in the breaking up of the Indian congregations on the Muskingum. The Wyandotte Nation took all the settlers prisoners, and they were compelled to march on foot to Detroit, which they reached after many hardships. In 1785 she was sent to the Female Seminary at Bethlehem, where she was educated, and in her twentieth year became a teacher in the Moravian School for Girls, at Litiz, Pa.; five years afterwards her loss of hearing compelled her to resign her position. Her father died at Bethlehem in the year 1823, and having then no home, she found a safe retreat in the "Sister's House," where she lived a quiet, peaceful life, and passed her allotted time on earth. She was a great favorite with the people of the town; and many visitors to the place called on her, to hear her recount recollections of the past.

Her father, the Rev. John Heckewelder, was even more celebrated as an author than he was as a Missionary.

In the first volume of the transactions of the Historical and Literary Committee of the American Philosophical Society, held at Philadelphia, for promoting useful knowledge, published in 1819, will be found the following works of Rev. John Heckewelder, "An account of the History, Manners and Customs of the Indian Nations who once Inhabited Pennsylvania and the Neighboring States," occupying 350 pages. In the same volume, will also be found 100 pages devoted to the correspondence between Mr. Heckewelder and Peter S. Duponceau, Esq., respecting "The Languages of the American

Indians." And an article No. III, entitled, "Words, Phrases and Short Dialogues, in the Language of the Lenni Lenape or Delaware Indians," by the Rev. John Heckewelder, of Bethlehem, these take up the rest of the volume, 12 pages. Preceding these works, which are invaluable to the historian, is "The Report of the Corresponding Secretary to the Historical Committee, on the Languages of the American Indians," and a "List of MS. Donations to the Committee, concerning the Indians and their Languages." Among these donations are the following, by Mr. Heckewelder.

1. A vocabulary of the *Machicanni*, taken down from the mouth of one of that nation, born in Connecticut—by the donor.

2. A vocabulary of the *Shawano*, taken down from the mouth of a white woman, who had been 20 years a prisoner with that nation—by the donor.

3. A vocabulary of the *Nanticoke*, taken down from the mouth of a Nanticoke chief in 1785—by the donor.

4. A comparative vocabulary of the *Lenni Lenape* and *Algonquin*—by the donor.

5. Same of the *Lenni Lenape* proper, the *Minsi* dialect, the *Mahicanni*, *Natik* or *Nadik*, *Chippeway*, *Shawano* and *Nanticoke*—by the donor.

6. Same of the *Lenni Lenape* and *Miami* or *Twightwee*—by the donor.

7. Names of the various trees, shrubs and plants, in the language of the *Lenni Lenape* or *Delaware*, distinguishing the dialects of the *Unamis* and *Minsi*—by the donor.

8. A short account of the *Mengwe*, *Maqua* or *Mingoes*, (as they are called by the white people,) according to the sayings and reports of the *Lenni Lenape*, *Mahicanni*, and other tribes connected with these, 4 to 25 pp.—presented by the author.

9. A short account of the emigration of the nation of Indians calling themselves *Lenni Lenape*, and improperly called by the whites, *Delawares*, as related by themselves, 4 to 28 pp.—presented by the author.

Among the books in the Library of the Philosophical Society at Philadelphia, there are numerous works "*deposited* by the Society of United Brethren at Bethlehem." why they do not reclaim them and keep them in their own church Library, is a mystery, they would be much safer in the church, than in the old building in Fifth Street below Chestnut, in Philadelphia.

"The Horsfield Papers, a large collection of original documents and letters from the principal characters in Pennsylvania, relating to Indians business, at and about the period of the war of 1756, *deposited* by Joseph Horsfield, Esq., of Bethlehem," are also in this Library. They ought to be withdrawn and put in a place of safety.

The Rev. Mr. Heckewelder also wrote "A Narrative of the Missions of the United Brethren among the Delaware and Mohigan Indians," which was published at Philadelphia in the year 1820.

From a small business pamphlet published by Frederick & Co., at Lancaster, Pa., in 1869, the following brief "History of Northampton County," is extracted, viz:

"NORTHAMPTON COUNTY, FORMED IN 1751, is bounded north by Carbon and Monroe counties; east by the river Delaware, separating it from New Jersey; south by Bucks county; west by Lehigh county.

"The southern portion is mountainous and uneven, being traversed by the irregular chain of hills called the South Mountains. These are chiefly composed of gneiss and other primary rocks, which are overlaid by limestone in some of the narrow valleys. Magnetic iron ore is found in several places on the hills associated with the primary rocks. North of these hills is a broad belt of the great limestone formation of the Cumberland or Kittany valley; which stretches from the Delaware south-westward into Maryland and Virginia, having a soil of the most productive character, and a comparatively level surface. Iron ore of the brown argillaceous and hematite varieties is abundant along the south side of the Lehigh, near the junction of this limestone with the primary rocks, and is mined in many places. It is also occasionally found within the range of limestone further north. On the Delaware, above Easton, the limestone belt is divided by a high ridge of primary rocks, called Chestnut Hill, having along its southern side serpentine and other magnesian rocks, associated with which are found talc, asbestos, tremolite, arogite, nephrite, zircon, tourmalin and a variety of other interesting minerals. There are few places in the State which offer so inviting a locality to the mineralogist as the neighborhood of Easton. About three miles north of Bethlehem is a small insulated ridge of primary rock, protruded through the limestone, and nearly in line with the range of Chestnut Hill. Between Allentown and Bethlehem, along the north side of the Lehigh, is a hill in which these rocks also appear, having on its northern side some detached portions of sandstone between the primary rocks and the limestone. The northern border of the limestone formation extends eastward from the Lehigh at Siegfried's Bridge, by Bath and Nazareth to the Delaware, at the mouth of Martin's Creek, appearing also on the north side of the river, to a point nearly opposite Belvidere. From this line to the base of the Blue Mountains the country is composed of a slate formation, with the exception of a narrow point of limestone on the Delaware, about the mouth of Cobus Creek, below the Water Gap, which, after extending a short distance westward sinks beneath the overlaying slate. The surface of this slate region is generally hilly, and the soil but moderately productive; being, however, susceptible of great improvement by the use of lime as a manure, when aided by judicious cultivation. Extensive slate quarries have been opened at different places, and an extensive business is carried on. Roofing slate of a superior quality is obtained in large quantities, and school slate manufactories have been established, in which, by the aid of ingenious machinery, slates of neatness and excellence are produced at a moderate price. Some of the lower strata of the slate formation, near its junction with the limestone, yield an excellent hydraulic cement, which is manufactured on the Lehigh. These strata are finally exposed on the east side of Martin's Creek, near its mouth.

"The Blue Mountain now forms the northern boundary of Northampton, and is capped by the compact gray and reddish sandstones of the formation next above the slate last mentioned. The Delaware and Lehigh rivers both pass through this mountain by gaps apparently torn by the mighty force of the gushing waters from the country above; with high and precipitous cliffs rising almost perpendicularly from the water, and presenting magnificent views of wild and romantic scenery on the rivers, as well as a widely extended and beautiful prospect from the top of the mountain. Near mid-way between

these two rivers is a singular opening called the Wind Gap, through which no stream passes; but the almost level crest line of the mountain is here depressed nearly as low as the country on each side; forming a notch in the mountain of peculiar convenience for the passage of travelers and teams, and towards which the leading roads on both sides converge and pass through in one great thoroughfare.

"The Delaware river flows along the eastern side of the county, in a direction nearly south, but with a meandering course. The Lehigh runs south-eastward along the western boundary to within about five miles of Allentown, where it passes into Lehigh county, one township of which lies east of the river. At Bethlehem it again enters into Northampton county, having now a north-eastern course to the Delaware at Easton. Bushkill creek is a considerable stream, rising by several branches near the Blue Mountain, and flowing southward to the Delaware at Easton. Its mouth is but a short distance above that of the Lehigh. This stream supplies power to a great number of mills throughout most of its course. Martin's creek runs southward to the Delaware, seven miles above Easton. The Monocacy has also a southward course, falling into the Lehigh at Bethlehem. Saucon creek flows north-eastward from the southern part of Lehigh county, and empties on the south side of the Lehigh below Bethlehem. All these streams, together with a number of smaller creeks in different parts of the county, supply abundance of water power for mills and manufacturing purposes. In addition to this, the surplus water from the dams and canal of the Lehigh Navigation Company, is let for uses requiring water power.

"Easton, the county town, is beautifully situated at the confluence of the two rivers, surrounded by picturesque hills, having on the east the majestic Delaware, on the south the wild and rapid Lehigh, and on the north the little Bushkill, winding its way through the green meadows, and having its banks studded with busy mills and substantial farm houses. This town is favorably located for business, being in the midst of a fertile, well cultivated and populous region, and at the junction of the Delaware Division of the State canal, with the works of the Lehigh Navigation Company. It has communication with New York by several rail roads and the Morris Canal on the opposite side of the Delaware. The town is rapidly increasing in wealth and population, containing about 14,000 inhabitants. The Court House is in the centre of the town, and other fine public buildings, and a number of churches, some of which are spacious and handsome edifices. Lafayette College is a noble building, situated on the hill north of the Bushkill creek, and commanding a fine view of the town, the rivers, the canals and the picturesque and flourishing country around for miles in extent.

Bethlehem, on the Lehigh, eleven miles above Easton, was founded at an early day by the Moravians or United Brethren, and the town is still chiefly inhabited by their descendants. They have a large church, a female seminary, a school for boys, a widows' house for the support of indigent widows, and a sisters' house for the support of indigent unmarried females, &c. All these institutions are admirably conducted, and a degree of neatness and order is everywhere observable which is highly creditable to that church. The schools enjoy a high and deserved reputation, and have a great number of pupils from the city and various parts of the country. The delightful situation of this place, the charming country around it, and above all, the quiet and order observed by the inhabitants, with their politeness and general attention to the convenience and comfort of strangers, have rendered Bethlehem a favorite place of resort during summer months. The day may be pleasantly passed in riding through the beautiful country around, in walks among the hills, in boating or fishing on the river, while the evenings are enlivened by music, the inhabitants being distinguished for their attention paid to music, and the excellence of their performance in this art. Bethlehem, or old Bethlehem, contains about 6,000 inhabitants.

South Bethlehem, opposite Bethlehem, on the south side of the Lehigh, is a very enterprising town, containing about 4,000 inhabitants. There are zinc works, rolling mills and numerous other works of note; also, an extensive mercantile business, conducted chiefly by young and enterprising business men. The Lehigh University is in its limits, it is an edifice that has but few equals for beauty, health, &c., and bids fair at no distant day to be one of the greatest institutions of America.

The public improvements of most importance to the country are the Delaware Division of the State Canal, and the canal and slackwater navigation of the Lehigh Navigation Co. The Delaware Division extends from tide-water, at Bristol to Easton, about eight miles of the canal being in Northampton county. At Easton it connects with the Lehigh Navigation, which extends up the river to the north-western corner of the county. The benefits received by the people of this region from the construction of these works will be perceived when it is considered, that before they were undertaken the Lehigh was useless for the purpose of navigation—produce being sent from Easton in long narrow boats, which descended the Delaware at high water by hazardous voyages through the falls, and were pushed back against the current by the incessant and fatiguing operation of "setting" or propelling the boat by means of long poles pointed with iron.

The roads are generally kept in good condition for traveling, and bridges are built across the Lehigh at important points. The inhabitants are mostly of German descent, and in their familiar intercourse with each other generally use their own language, though there are few who do not understand and speak English sufficiently well for the common purposes of conversation. We cannot make this history complete without giving a passing notice of some of the principal business houses of Bethlehem and South Bethlehem. In the dry goods business we find C. M. Knauss & Borhek, Bethlehem; Dr. J. K. Roney, of Pennsylvania Dental College of Philadelphia; the Photograph Gallery of Messrs Osborne & Malthaner; taking pictures from *carte de visite* to life size, they do work equal to New York or Philadelphia. E. C. Ricksecker's spacious music store, where a full assortment of musical instruments and sheet music is always kept on hand. Again: the jewelry establishment of James K. Rauch, which is equal to any in the larger cities. To those contemplating going to housekeeping, or wishing fine furniture, will find it at Messrs. Zimmele & Harwi. Any person wishing anything in the hat, cap or fur line, can find a well selected assortment at John B. Zimmele's. F. E. Luckenbach, dealer in stoves, tin and house furnishing goods; H. M. Krause, dealer in hardware; Jos. A. Weaver keeps constantly on hand books, stationery, &c., and the daily papers, opposite the Sun Hotel. Anthony Goth, dealer in wall paper, and paper hanger. Any person wishing a fine suit of clothes, can be accommodated at Messrs. Nickum & Derr, merchant tailors. Geo. Jones, manufacturer of spirit vinegar and bitters. J. H. Lilly, dealer in grain, flour, feed, liquors and wine. Transue & Buss, planing mill; and the Monocacy Brewery, In South Bethlehem we find the enterprising druggist, William S. Sieger."

SEAL OF THE MORAVIAN CHURCH.

At page 60, of these sketches, the official Seal of the Moravian church is spoken of as the "official *Episcopal* seal," which is erroneous, as the Bishops of the Moravian church are not clothed with any pre-eminent authority. They do not govern the church, and the Seal not being used by the Bishops exclusively, is not an Episcopal Seal. For this correction I am indebted to the "Memorials of the Moravian church," vol I, p. xiii, where the following description is given of the Seal of the church, viz: "On a shield sanguine a Paschal Lamb argent, passant, carrying a cross resurrection argent, from which is suspended a triumphal banner of the same."

I beg to observe that the color *sanguine*, murry, or a dark red, is in heraldy a *stained* or *dishonorable* color, see the Encyclopedia Metropolitana; the color should therefore be *gules*, red, expressed by lines perpendicular from top to bottom, in a drawing of the Seal. The color represented by the book-plate of "The Moravian Book Association," is argent; the banner is without the cross upon it; the staff is entirely too long, and improperly drawn, neither extremity of it should touch the edge of the shield.

It has always been my intention to place upon the title page of this work, the official Seal of the Moravian church; and with all due respect to the association, I shall carry out my original design; although the wood-cut will not express any colors, because the impression which I have of the "official Seal" (furnished me by the proper authorities of the church,) does not bear the heraldic marks of colors. The true blazon of the Seal, furnished me by Mr. Charles J. Lukens of Philadelphia, a member of the Historical Society of Pennsylvania, and the well known expert in heraldic art, is "Gules, a Paschal Lamb, (or holy lamb,) proper, upon a Mount Vert. Motto:—*Vicit Agnus, noster, Eum Sequamur*, 'Our Lamb is victorious, let us follow him.'"

In an old work entitled, "Travels in North America, in the year 1780, &c," written by the Marquis de Chastellux, will be found an interesting account of the author's visit to the "Moravian Mill" and Bethlehem, commencing at page 306, of vol. 2nd, and ending at page 334.

And in a note to page 401, of the same

volume, will be found Mr. Charles Thomson's interesting account of the formation of water-gaps in our mountains, in which particular mention is made of the Wind-gap; which he thinks was formerly the bed of the Delaware, or rather an earlier outlet for a vast inland lake, once existing to the north of the Blue Ridge; but that afterwards the waters of the lake having freed another and easier opening in the ridge at the Delaware Water-gap, which entirely drained what was once the great inland sea, the Wind-gap became what it now is, a dry thoroughfare, about one hundred feet higher than the present bed of the Delaware.

Among the books written by Mr. Charles Thompson, afterwards secretary of the Continental Congress, is a rare work, a copy of which I have in my possession; showing the manner in which the Minisink and Munsey Indians were defrauded of their lands, having the elaborate title of "An Enquiry into the Causes of the Alienation of the Delaware and Shawanese Indians from the British Interest, and with the measures taken for renewing their Friendship.

"Extracted from the Public Treaties and other authentic papers relating to the Transactions of the Government of *Pennsilvania* and the said Indians, for near forty years; and explained by a *Map* of the country.

"Together with the remarkable Journal of *Christian Frederic Post*, by whose Negotiations among the *Indians* on the Ohio, they were withdrawn from the Interest of the *French*, who thereupon abandoned the Fort and Country.

"With Notes by the Editor, explaining sundry Indian Customs, &c.

"*Written in Pennsylvania.*

LONDON.

"Printed for J. Wilkie, at the Bible in St. Paul's Churchyard.

MDCCLIX."

On an old cast-iron oven plate, taken from the cellar of the former residence of Christian Lange, deceased, the following words are cast, "*Richte nicht Auf Das Ihr*," i. e.,

"Judge not least ye be judged." The sentence is not complete, as will be perceived, the words "*Nicht gerichted wird*," being omitted. On the lower part of the plate is the date of its casting, 1756. I deposited this old relic in the Museum of the Young Men's Missionary Society, where there are several others of a like character. These plates are about 22 by 26 inches. On one of them there is the picture of a minister in a pulpit, having a book in his hand, with a crown in an arch above his head, the arch being supported by columns on either side of the pulpit, on the right is a female figure, apparently entering the church through an open door, to the left is the figure of a man, also entering, this representing, I presume, a marriage ceremony; below on the plate is the inscription.

" WER DAR IBER NUR WIL LACHEN,
  DER MAG ES BESER MACHEN,
  TATELEN KENEN IA SER VIL,
  ABER BESER MACHEN IST DAS RECHTE SPIL."

That is to say :
" Whoever chooses to laugh over this picture, He shall make a better one. Anybody can make fun, but to do better, that is the right way."

There is another plate, bearing the date 1756, on which is the following distach, "*Las dich das bese nicht*," meaning, " Don't let your anger overcome you," or in the vernacular, keep cool! a cool proverb for the cook, on a hot plate; for these plates were used on the front of the ovens, and the sides of fire places in old times, to ornament them, while being useful. There is one side plate in the museum, taken from the " old Family House" or "Nursery," as I have called it, on which is the figure of a stork drinking out of a high, long necked urn, while a thirsty fox looks on disgusted. Another front plate, dated 1751, is so broken that the inscription cannot be deciphered, although the plate is the most interesting of the whole collection, being ornamented with arches, columns, festoons, boquets and flowers in pots; in the upper dexter corner is the following name, in large capital letters, joined together, forming a kind of monogram,

IAHN POT.

Meaning JOHN POTT, who was one of the first iron founders in Pennsylvania, and the manufacturer of these cast-iron stove plates. He lived at that time in Germantown, and was of German descent; his father, Wilhelm Pott, having emigrated to this country in 1734, and settled at that place, see Rupp's History of Schuylkill County, &c., page 272, in a note. From this family the town of *Pottsville*, Pennsylvania, takes its name. The Germans pronounce the name *Putt;* I have this from John Vogel, of Philadelphia, late of Bath, who is of German descent, and was well acquainted with some members of the Pott family, and like them, is engaged in the same business that they were then. Mr. Vogel says he has one of the old stove plates above described, of a very large size, bearing the date of 1745. Nearly every one of these old plates have the representation of flowers in pots, on them; this seems to have been the trade mark, or the crest of the family of Pott.

Mr. Edward H. Rau, showed me one of these old relics, now in possession of his family, on which there is the representation of the temptation of Joseph. Potiphar's wife is in the act of springing out of a high-post, curtained bed, clutching with both hands the flying cloak of the rapidly departing Adonis; below the picture are the words,

" DAS WEIB DAS SVCHT
  JOSEPH ZV ENTZVNDE.
  IM. I B. MOSF 13 C 1749."

Meaning literally, " The woman she seeks Joseph to inflame." In the first Book of. Moses, chapter 13, 1749."

Among the numerous curiosities in the Museum are some that are rare. I purchased of a lad, Thomas A. Milchsack, a few years ago, a large stone, pear shaped, resembling in form a *pine apple cheese*, only in size a trifle larger, which had formerly been used by the Indians to grind corn with, the under side, or larger end, is polished smooth from constant use. It was found in the old Indian House, on the west bank of the Manockasy, when they tore down that old building.

A gentleman at Nazareth has a large and valuable collection of Indian relics and curiosities, numbering 6,000 pieces.

The "Old Sun Dial," made of soap-stone, is another curiosity, this was formerly on the south side of the Brethren's House, it has on its face the date, MDCCXLVIII, at the bottom of the stone, and at the top the words "GLORIA PLEURÆ," i. e., "Honor to the pierced side of Christ."

In the Museum there is also many old *Tiles*, made in Bethlehem, a part of one has burnt in on its face, 174 the rest of the date being broken off. These tiles were used for floors, mantels, stoves, and roofing. Some were colored, and highly ornamented with figures and flowers, impressed on them and burnt in. A specimen of mantel brick or tile, black in color, and ornamented, is among those preserved in the Museum. Some specimens of the roofing tile formerly used in the town, are also carefully treasured.

In tearing down the old residence of Mr. Lange, above referred to, to make room for the erection of the large building and handsome drug store of M. M. Selfridge, on Main Street, opposite the Eagle Hotel, he discovered under the pavement in front of the dwelling, two sections of the old pitch pine water pipes, laid down there in the year 1766, to supply the Sun Hotel with water. One section of it was carefully removed, and found to be in a perfect state of preservation. He had it sawed into short lengths, one of which is deposited in the Museum at Bethlehem, and another portion sent to Frederic C. Graff, the engineer of the Fairmount Waterworks, Philadelphia. This latter piece has still attached to it the original iron connection or hub, by which it was fastened to the next section. The wood, after having been in the ground one hundred and five years, emitted a strong smell of turpentine when taken out. This section appeared to have been made from the trunk of a pine tree,

with bark on it, and the branches still remaining some three inches in length, with a hole bored through the trunk. The hole had become much enlarged by the action of the lime water, which had eaten out the heart of the tree. The bark helped to preserve the wood, which is sound and perfect, except the heart, although the bark crumbled to dirt on being exposed to the air and handled.

In demolishing the old Œconomy Building on Main Street, to make room for the erection of the new Moravian Publication Buildings, the rafters of the old structure were removed sound and in good condition, they were of oak, of large size, 24 feet long, each, and six by eight inches in thickness; and were sold for joists, to be be used in another building about to be erected in the town

There were some curious customs in the town in the old days of the Œconomy, one of which would sound singular in these times. The store belonged to the Society, and when any one called for an article, sugar for example, the person was asked: How much do you want? If, six pounds, was replied. How many have you in your family? Or if the storekeeper knew, he said, you have only six, you must do with three pounds, we have others to supply beside you, we don't get goods from town, (Philadelphia,) every day.

In the open space of ground to the south of the Eagle Hotel, now an open green, there stood in the early part of the present century, an enclosed frame MARKET HOUSE, which was torn down about the year 1824; and an open Market House, with brick pillars erected in its stead, on Market Street near to, and east of Main Street, here meat only, was sold every morning to the people. Shortly after the incorporation of the borough, it was determined to grade the streets; in doing this it was necessary to cut down Market Street at that point very considerably, so the market had to be demolished. Since then there has been no public market in Bethlehem, although one is sadly needed. The stone Water Tower, which stood further east on Market Street, opposite the present residence of Ambrose J. Erwin, was also torn down about the same time, and for the same reason.

There was a grave-yard laid out on the south side of the Lehigh River, in the year 1747, for the interment of persons attached to the Brethren's Church, who lived in Saucon. It was on the hill near the ferry and Crown Inn, on the spot now occupied by the hot-house of Mr. E. P. Wilber.

The town of Easton, Pa., the seat of justice of Northampton County, was laid out in 1737, by Hugh Wilson and Col. Martin, commissioners, and Wm. Parsons, surveyor. The Moravians had at this place, at an early period of its settlement, a Brethren's House, a large stone edifice, now one of the oldest buildings in the town, forming a portion of John Bachman's hotel, but it was never used for the purpose for which it was erected. It was rendered famous in the Colonial times by the councils held there with the Indians and the treaties concluded with them, especially those made with *Cau-nas-sat-e-go*, the chief of the Six Nations, and *Teducscung*, the celebrated king of the Delawares.

ZINZENDORF'S VISIT TO WYOMING.

" Zeal for the propagation of the Gospel, caused the foot of the first white man to tread the soil of Wyoming. Long the residence of kings, it may not be improper to relate that the first white visitor should have been of noble birth, and of kingly* (?) extraction." So admirably is the event related by Mr. Chapman, that I copy his original and well authenticated narrative entire. Wm. Penn Miner's History of Wyoming, page 38, &c. See also Wm. L. Stone's History of Wyoming, page 100.

" Soon after the arrival of the Delawares at Wyoming, and during the same season (the summer of the year 1742,) a distinguished foreigner, Count Zinzendorf, of Saxony, arrived in the valley on a religious mission to the Indians. This nobleman is believed to

have been the first white person that ever visited Wyoming. He was the revivor of the ancient church of the United Brethren, and had given protection in his dominions to the prosecuted Protestants who had emigrated from Moravia, thence taking the name of *Moravians*, and who, two years before, had made their first settlement in Pennsylvania.

"Upon his arrival in America, Count Zinzendorf manifested a great anxiety to have the Gospel preached to the Indians; and although he had heard much of the ferocity of the Shawanese, formed a resolution to visit them. With this view, he repaired to *Tulpehocken*, the residence of Conrad Weiser, a celebrated interpreter, and Indian agent for the government, whom he wished to engage in the cause, and accompany him to the Shawanese town. Weiser was too much occupied in business to go immediately to Wyoming, but he furnished the Count with letters to a missionary of the name of Mack,* and the latter accompanied by his wife, who could speak the Indian language, proceeded immediately with Zinzendorf for the projected mission.

" The Shawanese appeared to be alarmed on the arrival of the strangers, who pitched their tents on the banks of the river a little below the town, and a council of the chiefs having assembled, the declared purpose of Zinzendorf was deliberately considered. To these unlettered children of the wilderness, it appeared altogether improbable that a stranger should have braved the dangers of the boisterous ocean, 3,000 miles broad, for the sole purpose of instructing them in the means of obtaining happiness after death, and that too, without requiring any compensation for his trouble and expense; and as they had observed the anxiety of the white people to purchase land of the Indians, they naturally concluded that the real object of Zinzendorf was either to procure from them the lands at Wyoming for his own use, to

---

* I never before heard that Zinzendorf was of kingly descent.

* John Martin Mack, a missionary then, and afterwards a Bishop of the Moravian Church. The idea of Weiser introducing Zinzendorf to one of his own people, is absurd

search for hidden treasures, or to examine the country with a view to future conquest. It was according resolved to assassinate him, and to do it privately, least the knowledge of the transaction should produce a war with the English, who were settling the country below the mountains.

"Zinzendorf was alone in his tent, seated upon a bundle of dry weeds, which composed his bed, and engaged in writing, when the assassins approached to execute their bloody commission. It was night, and the cool air of September had rendered a small fire necessary to his comfort and convenience. A curtain formed of a blanket, and hung upon pins, was the only guard to the entrance of his tent. The heat of his fire had roused a large rattle-snake, which lay in the weeds, not far from it; and the reptile, to enjoy it more effectually, crawled slowly into the tent, and passed over one of his legs undiscovered. Without, all was still and quiet, except the gentle murmur of the river at the rapids, about a mile below. At this moment the Indians softly approached the door of his tent, and slightly removing the curtain, contemplated the venerable man, too deeply engaged in the subject of his thoughts to notice either their approach, or the snake which lay extended before him. At a sight like this, even the heart of the savage shrank from the idea of committing so horrid an act, and quitting the spot they hastily returned to the town, and informed their companions that the *Great Spirit* protected the white man, for they had found him with no door but a blanket, and had seen a large rattle-snake crawl over his legs without attempting to injure him. This circumstance, together with the arrival soon afterwards of Conrad Weiser, procured Zinzendorf the friendship and confidence of the Indians, and probably contributed essentially towards inducing many of them, at a subsequent period, to embrace the Christian religion. The Count having spent twenty days at Wyoming, returned to Bethlehem.

"Count Zinzendorf learning the supremacy claimed and exercised by the Six Nations,

applied to their chiefs for leave to visit the Indian villages, and instruct the natives in the doctrines of repentance and salvation, through the merits of the Saviour. He could not have been received and replied to with more politeness, at the most refined court of Europe. The answer is so beautiful in its simple, yet dignified eloquence, that I take pleasure in translating it.

"'Brother, you have made a long journey over the seas to preach the gospel to the white people and to the Indians. You did not know that we were here, and we knew nothing of you. *This proceeds from above.* Come therefore to us, you and your brethren; we bid you welcome among us. Take this fathom of wampum in confirmation of the truth of our words.'

"The Moravians who had established themselves at Bethlehem, were indefatigable in their labor of love to christianize the Indians. Neither the heats of summer, winters storms, the dangers of the entangled forests, nor the toil in ascending precipitous mountains, could check the holy enthusiasm of the missionaries. Eight or ten made themselves masters of the Indian languages, with their kindred dialects, that they might be understood. Two bishops, Camerhoff and De Watteville, traversed the wilderness on foot, visited the various tribes and settlements on the Susquehanna, preaching the Saviour, and exhorting to repentance; the former sacrificing his life by exposure to the behests of duty."

By virtue of an Act of Assembly of March 11, 1752, the County of Northampton was formed. By the Act, Thomas Craig, Hugh Wilson, John Jones, Thos. Armstrong and James Martin, were authorized to purchase land at *Easton*, on the *Leheitan*, to build a court house, &c., for the public service.

The first court was held at Easton, June 16, 1752, in the 26th year of the reign of George 2d, &c., by Thos. Craig, Timothy Horsfield, Hugh Wilson, James Martin and Wm. Craig, justices of the Lord our King.

Previous to this time, Bethlehem was within the limits of Bucks County, which formerly contained all of Northampton, Lehigh, Carbon, Monroe, Pike, Susquehanna and Wayne, and parts of Schuylkill, Northumberland, Luzerne and Columbia.

See I. D. Rupps, History of Northampton, Lehigh, Monroe, Carbon and Schuylkill Counties; copyrighted in 1844, and printed at Harrisburg in 1845. G. Hills, proprietor, Lancaster, Pa.; also, the History of Lehigh Valley, page 31.

THE WIDOW'S HOUSE.

BETHLEHEM, PA.

CHAPTER XIV.

The Litany of the Moravian Church.—"Bartow's Path."—Nisky Hill.—Friedenshuetten.—The Indian House.—The German Barns.—Tecumseh.—The Indian Missionary Stations.—Haidte's Painting of the First Fruits.—Scheussle's Picture of Zeisberger Preaching to the Indians.—The Islands.—The Lehigh, its Freshets and Fisheries.—A Ride on the Switchback.—American Tea.—The Old Perseverance and the Fire Apparatus of Bethlehem.—The Hotels.—The Streets.—The Old Tannery.—Social Life.—Census of 1870.—Powder Magazine.—Height of the Lehigh Hills.—May-day.—The Masonic Societies of Bethlehem.

The first Litany that was used in the Renewed church of the Brethren, was Luther's, which was compiled by him from the ancient forms. This same Litany was used previously by the *ancient Unitas Fratrum*, and will be found in their hymn book, printed in 1566. It is also to be found in the first hymn book of the Renewed church, published at Hernhut, in 1735, (for a translation, see the *Moravian* of August 3, 1865.) As the congregation at Hernhut began to assume a more assured position as a church, it was felt that a Litany more expressive of the special wants and freedom of spirit of the members of the congregation, ought to be substituted for, or added to the ancient Litany. *Leonhard Dober*, while "General Elder," was the first to give expression to this desire, and John de Watteville, (Langut,) one of the moving spirits of the church in his day, made the first draft of the new Litany, under the direction and dictation of Zinzendorf, who is to be considered as really the author. In its first form, as it appeared in the appendix to the hymn book of 1742; and printed in almost the same form in the book of common prayer, edition of 1744, the evidences of Zinzendorf's style, and his peculiar method of expression, are quite perceptible; while the spirit and main portions of Luther's Litany remain. This first Litany of the Renewed church, is essentially the same in arrangement and substance as that now in use.

"The *Wunden Litanie*, which was composed later, in 1744, at the commencement of the "time of Sifting;" is of an entirely different character. The Litany was not altogether uninfluenced by the spirit which prevailed during that period of fanaticism, as will be seen by reference to the Liturgy book, edition of 1755-57. But it also received some improvements at the same time, one of which was the introduction of the Lord's prayer. The unhealthy elements were, however, afterwards removed from the Litany, during a revision of it, which took place under the direction of Bishop Spangenberg. The Liturgy book of 1790-3, contains the Litany as now used, almost *verbatim*.

"The names of Luther, Zinzendorf and Spangenberg, are connected therefore indissolubly with the history of the Litany of the Moravian church. Traces of the style and mode of expression of thought, common to each of those great minds, can easily be distinguished in this beautiful service, whilst in its general form and spirit, it is similar to the more ancient Litanies of the earlier Christian churches. In point of excellence and beauty, it compares very favorably with the Litany of the Episcopal church, to which it assimilates in its Catholic Spirit; its petitions for all classes of mankind, and in its intercessions for all the daily needs of the individual, and the church, and protection from all dangers that encompass life. In it the Brethren's church have an especial treasure, beautiful and precious, and of which they are justly proud. The *Kyrii*, "Lord have mercy upon us," at the opening, and the *Agnus Dei*, "O thou Lamb of God," at the conclusion of the Litany service, should both

be sung, not spoken, as is the custom in the Moravian church in America."

Bartow's path, frequently alluded to in these Sketches, was a lovely walk a mile and more in length, along the banks of the Lehigh River, commencing a little westward of where Doster's saw mill now stands, continuing eastwardly, and overshadowed by the cliffs of "Nisky Hill;" seats were placed along the path at intervals under the fine old trees that lined the river's edge, for the promenaders to rest upon. The walk was partially natural, and the remainder along the foot of Nisky Hill was laid out and constructed by a gentleman from Philadelphia, whose name it bore; and extended to the foot of "Jones' Ledge," from the summit of which there is a magnificent view of the winding river, Bethlehem and its vicinity to the west. But this beautiful work like many others, has disappeared before the destructive march of commercial enterprise; it was destroyed by the construction of the canal of the Lehigh Navigation Company; the ornamental in this country has to give place to the useful; and but lately the Lehigh and Schuylkill Railroad has been cut through the eastern part of Nisky Hill Cemetery, a desecration which might have been avoided by making a slight curve in the road.

Freight and produce, to and from Philadelphia, before the Lehigh Canal was constructed, were carried by the way of the Lehigh and Delaware rivers in *Durham* boats. In olden times the country people called the canal boats,—arks.

Situate in the southeastern part of Bethlehem, overlooking the Lehigh River and canal, South Bethlehem and the Lehigh Mountains, is the famous "Nisky Hill," once a beautiful park, now a cemetery, a portion of the grounds being retained by the Bethlehem Congregation for the interment of its members, the remainder sold out or for sale to any who choose or buy, and many not Moravians, have availed themselves of the privilege of purchasing lots in this lovely spot, and already some ghastly monuments, in execrable taste, disfigure the grounds.

One tomb looks like a fire plug,
And another like a lounge;
One, a large slab of marble,
Sticking in the ground.

These form a strange contrast to the old Moravian style of memorial stone, laid flat upon the grave, which is rectangular in form, the stone being only twelve inches in breadth, and eighteen inches in length. The church Diary of the Philadelphia Congregation of June 28, 1757, gives this as the size of the tombstone, and says, " *Et ist so in Bethlehem aus gamacht.*" It is so made in Bethlehem.

It ought to have been made a condition that all graves should have been marked in the simple Moravian style, and no enclosed marks of ownership erected around the lots sold in the cemetery.

Nisky Hill is a charming place, laid out with walks in good taste, and thickly planted with trees, some of the original forest trees have been preserved, and add much to the beauty of the grounds. The original tract extended down to the Lehigh River, and along its banks for nearly half a mile, but the Lehigh Canal cuts off the approach to the river. A few years since, a long serpentine path, similar to the "Lover's Walk" on the bank of the Hudson River at West Point, ran along the banks of the canal, the entire length of the grounds, from which there was a fine view of the river, and the Lehigh mountains to the south; but even that has been partially destroyed by the track of the Lehigh and Susquehanna Railroad, made in the year 1868. Nisky is one of the most delightful spots it is possible to conceive, in which to take a quiet ramble; seats are fixed on the borders of the paths at intervals, on which to rest. On Sunday afternoons the walks are thronged with crowds of the young and old people of the town, that is the only day on which they make it a place of resort, during the fine weather of the summer, the young ladies from the school, under the care of their teachers; and the visitors stopping in the town, add largely to the gay throng.

There are some beautiful views of the surrounding country from different parts of the Hill, but the most attractive of all, is from the western walk, looking to the southwest the Lehigh River is seen in the distance, winding on its course like a silver ribbon, with its lively islands, and in the further distance the outline of the mountains covered in summer with verdure, adds to the beauty of the prospect. In the fall of the year, when the trees put on their autumnal livery, the variegated colors of their leaves make the scene one of gorgeous beauty.

In a note to p. 227, "History of Lehigh Valley," the reader is informed that *Niskeu* is a Delaware Indian word, implying a swamp, or a wet place, in allusion to the swampy grounds at the foot of the hill. If this were so, then "Nisky Hill" would be an anomaly; but the simple fact is, the place was so called by the Brethren, in remembrance of the village of *Nisky,* a settlement of the Bohemian Brethren in upper Lusatia.

On the same page of the same work, it is stated that, "Along the brow of this hill was the Indian town of Friedenhutten, &c." This statement is erroneous. *Friedenshuetten,* or "Tents of Peace," was built on the flats below the hill on which the Gas Works of Bethlehem are now located, on the banks of the Manokasy. And the Lehigh Canal now covers a portion of the former site of that old Indian town, erected by the Brethren in 1746, as a temporary home for their Indian converts who came to Bethlehem in that year from *Shekomeko* and other places. But soon finding it inconvenient to maintain so large an Indian congregation near the town, the Brethren some months later, purchased a tract of land near the junction of the *Mahony* creek with the Lehigh river, and the Indians were removed to that place, and the huts on the Manokasy flats torn down. The settlement on the Mahony was called *Gnadenhuetten,* or "Tents of Grace ," and was deemed a more suitable residence for the Indians, who could there build, plant, hunt and live in their own way. Their Missionary, John Martin Mack and some white Brethren accompanied them, laid out their town, and remained with them until the terrible massacre on the night of November 24th, 1775, when the settlement was attacked and burned by the savage Indians under the French, and eleven of the inhabitants, all white Moravians, were murdered, viz.: Gottleib Andreas, his wife and child, Martin Nitschman and wife, Catharine Senseman, George Sugart, Christian Fabricius, Leonard Katermyer, Martin Presser and Frederick Lesley. The Indian congregations on the Mahoning and Lehigh were afterwards collected together and removed to Bethlehem for protection; the number of Indian refugees soon became very large, and their presence very inconvenient, so in 1758, *Nain* having been built, they were all removed to that place.

The *Indian House*, which has been before described as situated on the west bank of the Manokasy, was located in what is now the barn-yard of *Levin J. Krause*, where he found this summer (1869) the fire-place, composed of quite a number of the large bricks, such as were made for that purpose in Bethlehem in those days, and specimens of which may yet be seen by the curious on the entries of the first floor of the "Sister's House."

In the first volume of the Memorials of the Moravian Church, page 230, it is stated, "the *Indian House*" that had been built in October, 1752, on the west bank of the Manokasy, for the entertainment of visitors from Gnadenhuetten and elsewhere, just above the stone bridge that crosses the creek at Water Street. It was 52 by 40 feet, of one story, and of stone; and yet within those narrow limits *"the above seventy* who escaped" were domiciled. In the summer of 1756, a log-house, 63 by 15 feet, containing a chapel, besides apartments, was built due south of the other. * * * It was removed in the early part of the present century. The spring that empties into the creek immediately above the bridge, rose then in the cellar of the "*Indian House.*"

The spring referred to is a curiosity; it rises, or rather the water bubbles up from the bottom of the Manokasy into a well formed of planking in the bed of the creek, which keeps the clear cold waters of the spring from mingling with the waters of the stream. Some good Samaritan keeps a tin cup placed on a post near by, so that the thirsty travellers may drink of the cooling waters and be refreshed.

As a specimen of the splendid barns erected by the Germans of Pennsylvania, that of Mr. Krause, above referred to, is a fair sample in size and color:

These large red barns always remind me of the story about the Fairmount Engine of Philadelphia. At one of the Company's meetings, preparatory for a grand parade of the Firemen, a discussion was entered into as to what *color* the "FAIRY" should be painted for the occasion. One of the members, a genuine *B'hoy*, arose and said: "Fellers, I'm willin' to paint her any color, so its red."

The bodies of the Hessians who died in the General Hospital of the American army at Bethlehem during the Revolution, were buried on the left hand, or south side of the road leading to Allentown, and on the west side of the Manokasy; the place of their interment is now partially covered by the barn and house of Mr. John Krause. Many remains were found while digging the foundation of the barn; they were decently gathered up and carefully buried elsewhere. The statement made before, that these remains were found on the right hand side of the the road in digging the foundation of Levin J. Krause's barn (a son of the venerable John Krause) is an error, growing out of the fact that the father's barn is on one side of the road, and the son's on the other. The remains of the American soldiers are buried on the *right* hand side of the road, opposite, but further west.

The Indian converts spoken of as residing for awhile in Bethlehem, were chiefly of the Delawares, or the *Lenni Lenape* tribe, *i. e.*, the "*Original people*," as they have always called themselves. The only remnant of this once great and powerful tribe, whose subservience to the *Six Nations* has always been a great mystery to all interested in the Red men, now live at MORAVIANTOWN, or New Fairfield, on the river Thames, in Upper Canada, seventy miles from Detroit, a place made memorable by the death of the celebrated *Shawnee* Chief, TECUMSEH, shot to death there in the Battle of the Thames by Col. Richard M. Johnson, now deceased, late Vice President of the United States. Tecumseh, at the time of his death, was about 46 years of age, six feet in height, erect and lofty in his deportment, with a penetrating eye, and stern of visage, artful, insidious and bold. He was the pride of the Indian warriors of the west.

This, and two others, are the only Missionary establishments of the Moravian Brethren among the American Indians. The Mission was formerly under the direction of the Rev. Abraham Luckenbach. They worship from printed books in the Delaware Indian tongue, translated by that Missionary.

I have in my library a book, printed in New York in 1838, the title of which is *" Forty-six Select Scripture Narratives from the Old Testament, embellished with Engravings; for the use of Indian Youth. Translated into the Delaware Indian by A. Luckenbach."*

The Rev. E. E. Reinke is the present Missionary in charge of the Station. One of the other Indian Mission Stations is among the *Cherokees*, at Spring Place, near Marysville, Arkansas; and the third at New Westfield, Kansas. A concise account of the past and present Missions of the Moravian Brethren among the American Indians can be found in De Schweinitz's Moravian Manual, (2nd Edition) page 44, &c.

Crantz, in his History of the Brethren, says, (page 333) "About this time, (1747) *John*, the first fruits of, and a teacher among the *Mahikanders*, departed this life. This gave occasion to reckon up all the first fruits of the heathen that were brought to Jesus Christ through the ministry of the Brethren, and, to the year 1747, were fallen asleep in the faith; and to represent them in a picture in their natural colors, and in the dress of their country. They are painted as standing before the throne of Jesus Christ with palms in their hands, given to them by an angel, with the superscription out of the Revelations, Chap. xiv., 4. *' These were redeemed from among men, being the first fruits.' "*

The names of all the converts—heathen in all parts of the world—represented in the picture are given, and the account is of much interest. This ancient painting is carefully preserved among the Church Archives at Bethlehem. It was the work of HAIDT, a Moravian artist; a valuable relic of the olden times, and of the success attending the Moravian Missions among the heathen.

There is now on exhibition in the Museum of the " Young Men's Missionary Society" of Bethlehem, a splendid painting of " Zeisberger—the Moravian Missionary—preaching to the Indians," by C. Schüssele, of Philadelphia.

There was formerly many lovely walks in the vicinity of Bethlehem, on the banks of the Lehigh, some of which have been already described; but none were more attractive than the upper and lower paths on the south side of the river, west of the old bridge; these extended to the brook running down by the Water Cure Establishment, and emptying into the Lehigh; and around which there reigned an undisturbed forest stillness. The spring was a favorite spot near which to loiter on a warm summer's day; now it is arched over, and the hundred trains of the Lehigh Valley Railroad daily thunder over what was once the quiet haunt of the old Moravians; yet the stream still trickles down to the Lehigh; a few noble forest trees rear their heads over the small reservoir beside the tract on the river bank; and the curious visitors who read about the beauties of the spot in days long past, visits in one of FAN's boats the spring, to taste of its cool and limpid waters, hunt for the remains of the famous cavern, and view the ruins of what was once a sylvan haunt of peculiar loveliness.

Of all the former quiet retreats around Bethlehem, the only one left to remind us of the old times, are the beautiful and famous " Islands" in the Lehigh, a short distance above the North Pennsylvania Railroad Bridge. There are three Islands in the group; the two smaller are seldom visited; but the larger, *Calypso Island*,* is a famous place of resort for old and young; every visitor to Bethlehem makes the necessary pilgrimage to its quiet shades, and lingers long beneath its grand old shady trees, wanders through its open glades, its sheltered coverts, and at last with lingering looks cast behind, sighs to think they must leave so much quiet loveliness of Nature. What a hidden, quiet place it must have been fifty years ago, we can well imagine, when it is so beautiful to-day, although to the north and to the south the screaming whistles of the locomotives, and the heavy thundering thud of laden cars, bearing the wealth of Lehigh Valley, and the treasures of the " Blue Hills" to a market, disturbs its former calm repose.

The Island belongs to the Bethlehem congregation, and it is there that the Moravian schools hold their annual Pic Nic's, and nearly every Moravian family take their annual *meal* on the Island, to which their friends are invited, and only those who have attended these kindly festivals of the Brethren, can tell how pleasant they are, or how dear is the remembrance of such quiet, happy, joyous hours. To the children these are periods of unalloyed joy, thought of for weeks beforehand, and enjoyed on the day of the festival, with games and song, laughter and childish shouts of pleasure, mingling their happiness with the rippling flow of the river, and awakening the echoes of the hills. And the parents and friends must be old indeed if they do not join in all the youthful sports, for our German Brethren do not look on and sigh over the pleasures of childhood, but enjoy the present while recalling the past. But the great event of the year is the annual Pic Nic of the Sunday Schools of the Bethlehem congregation. On that day every true hearted Moravian visits the Island; it is an occasion

*The name of the larger Island is properly *Catalpa*, not Calypso, and was so called by the old Moravians, from the great number of Catalpa trees which were then, and still are growing, upon it.

of innocent enjoyment for old and young, and those who care not to play, can talk, feast, drink coffee, row in the boats on the river, or recall together with their old friends the past days spent on the Island. An evening on the Lehigh, after a day at the Island, has its charms, floating lazily on the river, surrounded by our friends, music and song naturally following; such are the happy moments of life. The charms of Bethlehem's Islands, and the beauties of the Lehigh, are still unsung; but the dear remembrance of hours passed there are engraven on the memory of many with an impression that can never be effaced, but will remain a joy forever.

The following items are copied from *The Weekly Progress*, of South Bethlehem, August 18th, 1870 :

"THE CHILDREN'S FESTIVAL.—On Sunday next, the ' Children's Choir' of the Moravian church, will celebrate their festival according to a time honored custom yearly observed from the earliest days of Moravianism to the present time. Each distinct ' choir' of the church celebrate their festivals at different periods during the year, being divided thus : first, the ' Married Choir,' to which have been combined in later years the ' widower's' and ' Widows' Choir,' ' Single Sisters' ' Single Brethren,' ' Children's' and ' Dieners' —or ' Servants of the Church,'—all celebrating their respective festivals with a ' Love Feast.' Several of the festival days of the church are being observed during the present month. The ' Gemein Fest,' or ' Love Feast', for all ' choirs' or classes of the congregation united, having been celebrated last Sunday afternoon preparatory to Communion services held in the evening, and attended by communicant members of the church only. Next Sunday the children will celebrate their love feast in the afternoon, and in the evening the beautiful and attractive open air exercises will be held at the west end of the large Moravian church immediately after the evening services have ended within the sanctuary. These open air services consist entirely of singing selections of such anthems and hymns, which have been committed to memory by all members of the congregation, the officiating clergy merely giving out the opening lines. A full attendance of instrumental and vocal music by the Moravian Church Choir is also given on this occasion, which renders the effect more soul inspiring and impressive, blending in sweet unison with hundreds of youthful voices out in the free open air of a calm and quiet Sabbath evening. In former years lighted lanterns of paper in variegated colors were strung up in front of the singers, which added considerably to the effect, but the custom has been abandoned. The simple and beautiful ceremonies on Sunday evening next, should the weather prove propitious, will be largely attended, as they have been in the past, by various denominations within and without the limits of our town."

"THE ISLAND.—The 'Old Bethlehem Island,' or 'Calypso,' as it is perhaps more familiarly known by hundreds of visitors to Bethlehem, has this year been more frequently visited by Moravian families, and members of families of other denominations of this place, than has been the case for the last few years. We think no better enjoyment, for one day in the heat of summer, can be better appreciated, than by members of a family, or a group of friends congregating in good old pic nic fashion in this cool, shady and secluded spot.

Above the "Old Bridge," leading west, are yet to be seen traces of a handsome walk, that leads along the banks of the Lehigh to a fine grove of trees. The path formerly extended a mile or more along the stream, and a walk along the tow-path of the Lehigh Canal as far as the first lock above Bethlehem, shows the visitor how beautiful the promenade once was, and how charming the scene still is. Along the edge of the swiftly flowing river grow fine large tree of various kinds, but many of these were blown down in a terrific gale in the summer of 1869. The disastrous flood on the Lehigh, of June 5th, 1862, brought down the river large quanti-

ties of drift timber, trees, houses, and canal boats, these destroyed the walk, left by the erection of the canal; wounded the fine old trees along the water's edge by striking and tearing off the bark, so that now some old patriarch yields to every severe gale, and soon none will be left, for all were injured more or less, about twenty feet from the ground, and the large scars on their sides give evidence of internal decay. Many new trees had been planted to the north of the pathway, and in the grove. Seats were placed on the river side of the walk for the promenaders to rest upon, but all these were damaged or carried away by the flood. In 1868, the bridge connecting the North Penn, as it is called, and the Lehigh and Susquehanna Railroads was built diagonally across the river, completing the destruction of the *Path;* and in the grove where the younger trees that had been uninjured by the flood, were growing beautifully, they are now landing from canal boats, sandstone curb-stones, and cutting them on the ground. It is thus all the beautiful walks around Bethlehem have been eradicated by combined attacks from land and water. It was along this path, in the river, that in former times were moored the pleasure boats, owned by nearly every Moravian family, each gaily painted and bearing on the stern some historic name; now few are left, except those of Mr. Fahs, who hires his boats out by the hour to such as desire to visit the "Islands," or row on the river.

The Lehigh is a broad and shallow stream of clear, cold water, flowing over a rocky bed, from springs in the different spurs of the Blue Ridge mountains, in Luzerne county, near Wilksbarre, and flows one hundred miles to its entrance into the Delaware at Easton. In its upper part it is a rapid, mountainous stream, with many falls; and like all others of a like character, is subject to floods after all heavy rains. The destructive flood of June 5th, 1862, was not the first by any means, that caused great suffering to the inhabitants along its banks, and destroyed much valuable property, but it was the most severe; at Bethlehem the water rose to the height of twenty-one feet, and the back-water flowed up the Manockasy to the mill dam back of the "Eagle Hotel;" it tore away one half of the northern portion of the 'Old Bridge" over the Lehigh, and covered the "Islands" with sand, logs, trees, and all kinds of debris, to the height of twelve or fifteen feet, so that it took over a year to clear them off again; it entirely devastated the upper end of Calypso Island, leaving only a sand bank, where once had been beautiful trees, waving grasses, and lovely wild flowers. It will be many years before the slow growth of Nature restores the island to its pristine beauty.

The mode of catching fish in the Lehigh in olden times, is thus described in the *South Bethlehem Conservative:*

"The mode of catching fish was borrowed from the Indians. The Indians ran a dam of stones across the stream where the depth would admit of it, not in a straight line, but in two parts, verging towards each other in an angle. An opening is left at the point in the middle for the water to run off—at this opening they place a large box or basket, the bottom of which was full of holes. They then make a rope of wild vines, reaching across the stream, upon which boughs some feet in length were fastened at the distance of two fathoms from each other. Then a party is sent about a mile above the dam with this rope and appendages, which there begins to move gently down the current, some guiding the ends while others keep the branches from sinking by supporting the rope in the middle with wooden forks. Thus they proceed, driving the fish before them, while other Indians with poles and noise drive the fish through the opening into the box, where they were caught and put into canoes. This method of fishing was adopted and long continued by the settlers. Strangers often inquire what these angular stone dams are for, and few are aware that they are the remains of the ancient fish dams, repaired time and again, by the fishermen of modern times.

"Various laws were passed before the Revolutionary War, tending to the preservation of the fish in the Delaware and Lehigh Rivers; one of which had a singular penalty attached—in subjecting the seller of rockfish under twelve inches in length, to a fine and the forfeiture of the fish. In the early period of the settlement along the Lehigh, before the erection of dams to render it available for the transportation of coal to Philadelphia, it was the resort of shad, which found their way from the ocean up into its fresh waters to deposit their spawn.

The Lehigh in the vicinity of Bethlehem, has many of these fish-weirs, or *fish-karbe*, built in different parts of the stream; they are formed by long dams built with the numerous pebble stones which form the bed of the river. A line of stones are erected diagonally across the stream, from each bank, down the river, and converging to a point, in the manner described above, where the weir is placed to catch the fish; the weir resembles in form the body of a cart, the hinder part up stream, and the bottom formed of lathes, placed close together, so as to admit of the water passing freely, but retaining in it the fish. In the spring and fall large numbers of *suckers* and *eels* are caught in these weirs. But the dams on the Lehigh and these fish-korps have destroyed all other kinds of fish; and there is nothing to be caught by the angler on the river, except some small chub and sun-fish, and an occasional stray trout. When Bethlehem was first settled, and for many years afterwards, trout were plenty in the Lehigh and Manockasy, and in season, shad and herring were numerous, there was a fishery near the town and on the 10th of May, 1752, for instance, 1,000 shad were caught with the seine. Now these kinds of fish are not to be found in the river at all; the dam at Easton interrupts their upward course from the Delaware. The people living on the Lehigh ought to petition the legislature of the State for an Act, compelling those who have obstructed the course of the stream, to put up schutes, slopes or steps, at the breast of every dam erected on the river, to facilitate the free passage of the fish up stream to spawn, and their return to the ocean afterwards; and to remove the fish-weirs, or fish-baskets. Such an Act has been already passed, relative to the Susquehanna river, since when, the shad, herring, and many other kinds of fish have returned in large numbers to that stream to spawn. A great many counties have also had protective acts passed in regard to game and fish, and it is time Lehigh and Northampton followed suit.

The Act referred to, that of March 13th, 1866, (See Pamphlet Laws of 1866, page 370,) and its supplements, are very stringent; in general terms the provisions of the law are, that there shall be made at all dams, or weirs, or other artificial obstructions in the river, sluices, schutes, slopes, steps or other devices, for the free passage of the fish, and their fry up and down the stream. The dams are to be deemed nuisances unless the devices are made, and a failure to comply with the conditions of the Act is to be deemed a misdemeanor and subjects the owner to a fine of $10,000; and it is made unlawful for any person or persons to place any fish-basket, fish-trap, or any like device, either permanent or temporary across the river, or to draw any seine or net within half a mile of any of the sluices made for the passage of the fish, either above or below the same, or to fish with any seine or other device for catching fish in numbers, within a given distance mentioned, of the sluices or passage-ways over the dams, or in any manner to frighten the fish, or spawn, (?) or fry, or in any manner to prevent their passage up or down the stream in any part thereof, under the penalty of a heavy fine, of not more than $1,000, and imprisonment not exceeding one year, at the option of the court. Some of the counties make it unlawful to fish their streams at certain seasons; others to fish otherwise than with a hook and line; and some put a heavy fine on the use of poisonous bait, cast nets, or any other device to catch the fish in numbers. The right of fishery, over half a mile from the schutes, is not taken away by

Act of March 13th, 1866, from the owners of real estate bordering on the Susquehanna.

On the 16th day of April, 1858, an Act of Assembly was passed prohibiting fishing with *gill-nets* in the river Lehigh, between Bethlehem and its junction with the Delaware at Easton, (See Pamphlet Laws of 1858, page 305.) During the session of 1869-70, I endeavored to get the legislature to pass a Bill for the protection of the fish in the Lehigh river, for the removal of the *fish korps*, and the erection of sluices or fish passages over the dams; but it was objected to, First, on the grounds that it would be impossible to raise fish in the Lehigh, as the sulphur water from the coal mines destroyed the fish; but as they are caught daily in the river that objection is evidently subservient to the Second: That the Lehigh Navigation Company would not like it.

The cobble stones with which the "cart-ways" of the streets of the city of Philadelphia are paved, were, and still are taken from the beds of the rivers Delaware and Lehigh, without any perceptible diminution of the quantities contained in them. The stones are rounded and *water-worn* into many curious shapes, such as geese eggs, bird's eggs, cannon balls, and marbles. I have one the size and shape of a loaf of domestic rye bread just out of the oven, with the marks of the pan, in which it was baked, apparently marked on it; and another in the form and likeness of a jewel case, for which it is often mistaken, as it lies on my table for use as a paper weight.

The Lehigh Canal which passes through the lower part of the town of Bethlehem, formerly connected the head waters of the Lehigh river, with its mouth at Easton, where it empties into the river Delaware, and by the means of dams, locks, and canals, navigation was open to White Haven, in Luzerne County, eighty-four and a half miles; thirty and a half miles consisted of pools; thirty-nine and a quarter of canals; two and a half of locks, and the remainder of sluices. The freshet of June 5th, 1862, destroyed all the canal, most of the dams, and all the improvements above Mauch Chunk; and the canal now only extends from that place to Easton. It forms a most important communication with the coal regions of this section of the State, to which railroads are continued. At Lehigh Gap, where it passes through the Blue Ridge, the mountains rise on each side of the river to the height of 1200 feet, and the scene is very grand and beautiful.

The Blue Ridge, or South Mountains, are the eastern range of the Alleghanies, branching off from the main range in North Carolina, crossing the State of Virginia and extending to the Highlands on the Hudson river. The Indian name of these mountains in Pennsylvania was the *Kittocktinny*, now called *Kittatinny*, meaning the endless mountains. The common name they now bear is the Blue Mountains.

Mauch Chunk has been called by some writers, " the Switzerland of Pennsylvania," which means that it is well worthy the visit of the tourist. The ride over the Gravity Railroad, or " the *Switch-back*"as it is called, although there are no switch-backs on the Railroad now, is one of the most exciting and beautiful rides in America. At the foot of *Mount Pisgah*, the visitors enter small passenger cars, each holding twelve persons, and the cars are drawn up the ascent by a stationary engine on the top of the mountain. This plane is a formidable looking affair, the track seeming to be nearly perpendicular; it is 2,322 feet in length, with an elevation in that distance of 664 feet. A *sharp grade*, railroad men call it. Every precaution is taken to prevent accidents; the train is pushed up by a *safety car* fastened behind it; the conductor sits on the front car, where he mans a patent safety brake. The safety car is made fast to two steel bands, each seven and a half inches wide, either strong enough to hold and draw the train, which never exceeds ten cars; should both bands break, the safety car has attached to it two immense steel arms with sharp points, which, an arrangement made for the purpose releases from their horizontal position on the side of the car, should it start backwards these points would then enter the earth and keep the train stationary. These arms are also assisted by a rachet provided for the same purpose, to prevent the descent of the train in case it should break loose. This ascent takes eight minutes. Mount Pisgah is 1000 feet above the bed of the Lehigh river at its foot. The view from the mountain top is very fine, extending on a clear day to Schooley's Mountains in New Jersey. From here the train starts on the gravity road, on a down grade of fifty feet to the mile; after a swift and exhilarating ride of six miles, the foot of Mount Jefferson is reached. The ascending plane here is 2,070 feet long, overcoming a height of 462 feet. The train is again attached to a safety car, and drawn up to the top of the mountain, 1,144 feet above the Lehigh; and after a short ride of a mile, the cars arrive at Summit Hill, a drearylooking town of 7000 inhabitants, with a dismal Town Hall, which looks like a French Bastile. The once celebrated switch-back railroad begins here, and runs through *Panther Creek Valley* to the many different coal mines. Leaving here, the cars descend at the rate of 221 feet to the mile. The descent was formerly made by switch-back changes from one track to another, but now the track is continuous; instead of a switch-back the cars are carried around a curve by their own momentum. At the bottom of the Valley the train generally stops long enough to permit the passengers to visit the coal breakers and the mines. The grade of the track through the valley is sixty feet to the mile. The immense mountains of useless coal dust fill the visitor with surprise and regret; it is to be hoped that some inventive genius will soon suggest a mode by which this can be used with profit, so as to enable it to be transported to a market; it is a great waste and loss at present, and gives a dreary look to the valley where these mounds are piled up, killing the trees, and causing the creeks to run streams as black as ink. Leaving here, the train soon reaches the foot of *Panther Creek Plane* No. 2, 2,030 feet in length, with an elevation of 250 feet; being drawn up this, the cars go several miles further by gravity, through mining villages, and past mounds of coal dust to *Panther Creek Plane* No. 1, in length 2,436 feet, with an elevation to be overcome of 375 feet. After ascending this plane, the train arrives again at Summit Hill, having made a circuit of eight miles. It was near here that coal was first discovered by a man named GUNTHER, in 1791; and it was also here that the first mine was worked by the Lehigh Coal and Navigation Company. They supplied the market without opposition till 1847. From Summit Hill the cars run by gravity nine miles back to Mauch Chunk, without any stoppage; that distance has been made in thirteen minutes. The cars descending on an acquiring impulse of a down grade, averaging ninety-six feet to the mile. The train, however, seldom makes the distance in less than thirty minutes, giving the passengers time to enjoy the beautiful distant views, and magnificent scenery all along the route. One of the coal mines near Panther Creek Valley, has been on fire now for over thirty years, and all efforts to extinguish it have failed. As an effort of engineering skill the planes are unsurpassed, but I am at a loss to understand why the fact that the cars descending the grades by the impulse of their own weight, or in other words, run down hill rapidly, is considered so very wonderful a feat. The ride, however, up the planes, down the grades, over the mountains, and through the coal regions, is one no visitor to Bethlehem should miss; the trip can be made in a day without fatigue, leaving that place at seven and a half A. M., and returning at six P. M. to supper, which will be very heartily enjoyed, and the day's trip will be an episode in the most adventurous life. A few years more and all this cannot be seen or enjoyed, as it is the intention of the Company to cut a tunnel through the mountain; it will be 3,900 feet in length, and the work has already been commenced.

The Moravian, in its issue of January 20th, 1870, had the following interesting item.

"The *Slatington News* reports the re-discovery of a valuable mineral spring, about a mile from Lehigh Gap, and four miles from Slatington. The spring was known to the Moravians at Gnadenhütten a hundred years ago, and the water was hauled to Philadelphia at one time, to cure an epidemic which was then raging in that city. Dr. H. O. Wilson, by means of an old draft, succeeded in again finding the spring, which had been quite covered with stones and earth. The spring is marked on the original map of the Province of Pennsylvania, made by Nicholas Scull, Surveyor General, in the year 1759. Dr. Franklin mentions having camped at this spring on his way to Fort Allen. The plot of the property on which it is situated, contains a certificate from Thos. C. James, dated Philadelphia, February 24th, 1806, in which the statement is made that the water is "a pure Chalybeate, the iron being held in solution by carbonic acid and fixed air.'"

In the first volume of the "Memorials of the Moravian Church," issued at Philadelphia, in 1870, at page 30 it is stated that, "This spring was visited as early as 1746, by the Brethren, and its waters bottled by them for the use of invalids in Philadelphia."

One evening, in the latter part of August, 1863, we had on the supper-table at the Eagle Hotel, in Bethlehem, an infusion of "*American* tea." This tea was made from the leaves of a plant, or shrub, which is indigenous on the mountain's side, in the vicinity of the town, and in other parts of the State; it has been sometimes called "New Jersey tea," and was so named when used during the Revolutionary War of 1776, as a substitute for the Chinese tea, which was then an expensive luxury; it is still used by many persons in the country, who consider it quite equal to the imported article. I am informed that it is prepared in Massachusetts in large quantities, and sold to whaling ships; it consists, however, only of the dried leaves, which are not properly prepared. The botanical name of this plant is *Ceanothus Americanus.*

The tea which we drank was, however,

made *secundum artem*, in the true Chinese style; that being the only way in which the real virtues of the leaf can be retained in perfection. It had all the appearance, taste, and aroma of the finest imported tea, with the exception of a slight herby flavor, in consequence of its newness, not being quite three weeks old. This peculiarity, we were informed, would leave it when it acquired age.

A choice sample of this tea was deposited in the Museum of the "Young Men's Missionary Society," in Bethlehem, for preservation, as a specimen of the first and finest American Tea ever manufactured.

This tea was made by Dr. Spencer Bonsall in the early part of August, 1863, at a place called "China," in the mountains, near Lock Haven, Clinton County, Pennsylvania, under the auspices of the "American Tea Company," incorporated by an Act of Assembly of this Commonwealth, of April 14th, 1863, which had for its object the cultivation and manufacture of tea on an extensive scale. At the time the tea manufactured was made, Dr. Bonsall was the Chief Superintendent of that company, but the undertaking was not successful. That gentleman was for several years engaged in the manufacture of tea in the Valley of *Assam*, situated to the west of the Province of *Yunnan*, in China; and on his return to this country, he wrote an interesting article on the subject, which was published in the Agricultural Report of the United States Patent Office, for the year 1860.

Prominent among the ancient relics and curiosities, so abundant in Bethlehem, there is one of which the citizens are very proud. It is the "*Old Perseverance Hand Fire Engine*," which is preserved, very properly, with much care. It is one of the oldest apparatus of the kind in this country, having been built in London, by Brooks, in the year 1698, and was purchased there by Captain Christian Jacobson for the "American Moravian Society," for the sum of £77 12s. 2d., and brought by him to America at an expense of £6 18s. 3d., and delivered in Bethlehem December 10th, 1763. It is not, how-

ever, the oldest hand engine in the United States, for the "*Fellowship Steam Fire Engine Company*" of Philadelphia, have an old Hand Fire Engine, six feet long, and five and a half feet high to the top of the gallery, which runs on wooden wheels, and can throw a stream of water through a three-quarter inch nozzle, one hundred and fifteen feet high. It was made in London, by Ham & Rag, in the year 1694, and is, therefore, four years older than the Old Perseverance. Nor was the Perseverance the first Hand engine imported into the United States; for the City Councils, of Philadelphia, imported two Hand Engines from London in 1730, where they were first invented in 1663. And previously, on 14th of December, 1719, the city purchased from Abraham Bickley, a Fire Engine, which was also, no doubt, imported from England. See Wescott's History of Philadelphia, Chapter 66, *Sunday Dispatch* of April 5th, 1868.

The Perseverance Fire Engine Company, No. 1, of Bethlehem, was re-organized in 1848. They have also a fine Hand Fire Engine, made by Agnew, of Philadelphia, and an excellent Hose Carriage.

The first hose used in Bethlehem was made of hemp, and was brought from Germany, in 1818. The first leather hose was purchased by the Reliance Fire Company, No. 3, in 1838; this latter company had the first Hose Carriage in the town. The only other Fire Company is the "Diligent Steam Fire Engine Company, No. 2."

There is also in the town a handsome Hook and Ladder Company, called "The Niskey."

The Borough authorities own all these different fire apparatus but one.

Bethlehem is well supplied with Hotels, of which the "Sun," and "Eagle" have already been described; there still remains unnoticed the "American," situated at the north-east corner of Broad and New Streets, the highest elevation in the town. It is a fine large building, formerly a private house, but with very extensive back buildings now added to it; its rooms are quite large and airy, and the view of the surrounding country from the windows of the upper stories of the house is very fine; from them the entire range of the Blue Mountains is distinctly visible. The scene from the top of the house, at sunset, on a summer's evening, presents a panorama of exceeding beauty.

The "Union Hotel" is situated one square further east, at the north-east corner of Broad and Centre Streets. It is a fine, large house, and seems to be the resort of the people from the surrounding country, whilst on their visits to the town; in fact, a veritable country tavern, in all its outward surroundings.

The "Pennsylvania Hotel" is a large brick building, on the banks of the Lehigh Canal, in what was formerly called "Old South Bethlehem," in Lehigh County; the road in front of the house runs along the banks of the Lehigh, and leads to the old Bethlehem bridge, over which all travel passes to reach the "Union Depot" of the "North Penn and Lehigh Valley Railroads."

There is also a good House kept by Mr. John Schilling, in the north-western part of the town, attached to which there is a fine Lager Beer Brewery, and if you wish to taste that article in all its purity, you must go to "Schilling's."

There are several Restaurants and Ice Cream Saloons in the town, which do quite a large local business. "Rauch's" is the favorite resort of all strangers and people of the town who desire to enjoy Ice Cream and cakes. It was in this House that Lafayette lived whilst in Bethlehem. In the saloon there is a small fountain, whose marble basin is surrounded always by flowers, kept fresh by the falling spray of the flowing stream, which is continually thrown up; it is a tasty little affair, and attracts universal attention and admiration. Mr. Ambroise H. Rauch, the owner of this large confectionary establishment, resides in a fine old mansion on Market Street near Main; attached to which he has a handsome conservatory filled with rare and beautiful flowers and plants. And although there are many fine, large stores of all kinds in the town, where all the necessary comforts and luxuries of life can be obtained, there are no market houses, either public or private, in the place, and the inhabitants are compelled to buy their meats from the butcher wagons that drive around each day, and their poultry, butter and eggs from the farmers, or from the stores, where such things are taken in trade, as is usual in our country towns. There are some small "Provision stores," where vegetables only are sold. The town does not need market houses so much as provision stores where everything necessary for the table could be kept for sale. The expenses of living in Bethlehem, before the Rebellion, were very moderate; but for the last few years they have been nearly equal to those of a city life.

The streets of Bethlehem are lighted by gas, but the lights are extinguished at ten o'clock, P. M., a capital arrangement for thieves of all kinds. Until quite recently it was the boast of Bethlehemites, that they never had more than one *Watchman* in the town at a time; those halcyon days are, alas! no more; the town has been divided into Wards; they have now a High Constable and several Policemen, whose presence seem to excite in the unruly a desire to keep them employed. In old times in this ancient borough, "the night-watch patrolled the town with a *spear* in his hand;" this continued till about the year 1804 or 1805. Rose was then the Watchman, who on leaving his beat in the morning, called, "*Der Glock hat Sechs Schlag*," i. e., Die Glocke hat 6 geschlagen! Brother Rose superceded Brother Stolz in 1801, as Watchman."

The streets were lighted at nights with lamps before the year 1800, and so continued to be until Thursday evening, July 13th 1854, when they were first lighted with gas. The expense of lighting with lamps was borne and paid by private subscription. The lights were put out at ten o'clock, as they still are. Each housekeeper had then, and still has, a lantern for use on dark nights.

There are some queer old streets in the town, that branch off from the main thoroughfares at an angle, winding around the hill-side, and ending very abruptly against it, or turn off by some unexpected outlet into another winding street or road, or by-path. Those streets were once evidently foot-paths in the earlier days of the settlement, and are on the western declivity of the hill on which the town is built, and nearly all lead down to the Manokasy. There are many pleasant old "short-cuts," or by-paths in other parts of the town. Market Street used to end at *John Oerter's* house, thence east a lane extended, on both sides of which very large apple trees were growing. Church Street formerly ended at the "Sister's House;" and from there a lane called the "Sister's lane" extended eastwardly to *Roth's* farm; on both sides of this lane cherry trees were planted, which bore excellent fruit. Fruit trees of all sorts were more plentiful in those good old times than at present. Apple and cherry trees are indigenous to America.

Water Street was so swampy when the *Tanner's House* was about to be erected, that it was necessary to lay large logs of wood on the surface, then stones, and earth on top of these, to form a firm sub-stratum on which to build the foundation walls; these were six feet thick, and immense labor was required to complete the building. The whole vicinity then being a swampy wilderness, full of large rocks, brush and trees, amongst which the wild rose grew in great abundance, and the "Cats-tails" so much used in making beds, in profusion.

The splendid old willow trees, formerly growing near the Old Stone Bridge on the Manokasy, were cut down in January, 1855, to make way for the new stone one erected during that year.

In olden times the inhabitants of Bethlehem were early risers, as many of them still are, they took breakfast at six o'clock, and as they then all worked together, they were summoned to their meals by the church bell; at nine o'clock they had their *make-peace*, a light repast of Moravian cake and beer, on the principle of our *lunch*. The dinner hour was, and still is, twelve o'clock M. At two o'clock P.M., " *Vesper*," cake and coffee. At

six P.M., supper. These customs are not yet abandoned by all the Moravians.

The census of 1870 having been completed, gives the population of Bethlehem and its suburbs as follows :

Bethlehem, ...	4,512
South Bethlehem, ...	3,556
Old South Bethlehem and West Bethlehem, ...	890
* Hottlesville, ...	200
Outside borough limits of South Bethlehem, ...	450
	———
Total, ...	9,608

The Old Water Works, illustrated and mentioned before, were used during the Revolutionary War as a powder magazine for the American Army.

The Lehigh Hills, where the Old Philadelphia road crosses the mountains, is 430 feet above low water mark on the Lehigh River. The highest point of the mountain is 700 feet above low water mark of the river. The Canal level is 200 feet above the sea; and Market Street, at the corner of New Street, is 110 feet above the Canal.

Bishop De Schweinitz, in his "Life and Times of David Zeisberger," in the glossary says, "the Indian name of Bethlehem was *Mena-gach-suenk*; of the Lehigh River, *Lech-au-week*; of Nazareth, *Wela-ga-mika*." See also Heckwelder's Indian names in the Bulletin of the Historical Society of Pa., 1 vol., 121.

Among the days formerly celebrated and made a holiday of in Bethlehem, was "May Day;" but of late years the weather has been unsuitable for out-door enjoyment; this year, however, the weather was so delightful on the first of the month of flowers, that the Editor of the *Moravian* thus grieves "for the good old days of Adam and of Eve."

"It has been many a year since we have had such delightful weather at this season as during the past three weeks. 'May Day'

* Hottlesville is a new town that is springing up just outside of the northern limits of the old borough of Bethlehem ; from the Nazareth road westward, to the road leading to Bath. Pronounced *Bass* by the country folks.

has got to be one of the things of the past, an imaginary season of flowers, warm vernal airs and sunshine, on which the young people kept holiday, and chose their queen, and had a procession. This year the boys and girls might have celebrated it without any risk of catching colds or making themselves ridiculous. Bethlehem used to have such a spring-flower festival,—a good many years ago it was, and many of the flower-crowned girls are now substantial matrons, with boys and girls of their own old enough to go maying, and the grass has been growing for many a year over the graves of others. But alas! with our railroads and miscellaneous other 'improvements,' the old village has grown into a miniature city, and who thinks of 'May Day' now?"

In the Chapel of the Young Ladies' Seminary, I noticed this summer at the entertainment, that the bellows of the organ were blown by *water power*, the machinery being the invention of the Principal, the Rev. Francis Wolle; and I noticed also that the organist was a very handsome woman. She is a "Single Sister," from Salem, North Carolina, I believe.

The following Masonic Societies hold their regular meetings at the Masonic Hall, in Bethlehem, Pa.

A. L. 5870,

BETHLEHEM LODGE,

No. 283, A. Y. M.

Meets Wednesday, on or before Full Moon.

OFFICERS.

Bro. Morris A. Borhek, W. M.
" Homer Stanley Goodwin, S. W.
" Allen J. Lawall, J. W.
" Marcus C. Fetter, Treasurer.
" Bernhard E. Lehman, Sec'y.

PAST MASTERS,

Samuel Wetherill,   C. M. Knauss,
Nathan Bartlett,   Marcus C. Fetter,
Jesse H. Morgan,   Bernhard E. Lehman
Ernst F. Bleck,   Abraham Stout, M. D.,
Richard W. Leibert,   Adolph Conradi,
       Louis F. Beckel.

CONSTITUTED 1854.

A. I. 2400.

ZINZENDORF CHAPTER.

No. 216, H. R. A. M.

Meets Second Monday of each Month.

OFFICERS.

Comp. A. N. Leinbach, M. E. H. P.;
" C. C. Tombler, King;
" H. A. Wiltberger, Scribe;
" C. M. Knauss, Treasurer;
" Bernhard E. Lehman, Secretary.

PAST HIGH PRIESTS.

Jesse H. Morgan,   Bernhard E. Lehman.

CONSTITUTED 1868.

ANNO DEP. 2870.

BETHLEHEM COUNCIL.

No. 36, R. S. E. and S. M.

Meets First Thursday in each Month.

OFFICERS.

Ill. Comp. R. W. Leibert, T. I. G. M.;
" M. C. Fetter, D. I. G. M.;
" Jesse H. Morgan, P. C. of W.;
" C. M. Knauss, G. M. of Exch.;
" Theodore F. Levers, Recorder.

PAST T. I. G. M.,

Bernhard E. Lehman.

CONSTITUTED 1868.

The town of Bethlehem was formerly within the limits of Bucks County; and on the 10th of March, 1746, the inhabitants presented a petition to the court for the formation of a township, which was granted; although it was not surveyed and laid out until the year 1762. When it was done by GEORGE GOLKOWSKY. The names of the petitioners were NATHANIEL SEIDEL, HENRY ANTES, JOHN BROWNFIELD, SAMUEL POWELL, MATTHIAS WEISS, JOHN OKELY, FREDERICK CAMMERHOFF, GEORGE NEISSER, CHRISTOPHER PYRLEUS, JAMES BURNSIDE, JOSEPH POWELL, JASPER PAYNE and JOSEPH SPANGENBERG.

After the dissolution of the "Æconomy," in 1762, lots in Bethlehem were sold to the following individuals, each of whom erected dwellings thereon for the use of their families, viz:

ANDREW BORHECK, Weaver; WILLIAM BOEHLER, Wheelwright; LUDWIG HUEBNER, Potter; DANIEL KUNKLER, Shopkeeper; GEORGE SHINDLER Carpenter; FRANCIS THOMAS, Joiner; DEWALT KORNMAN, Skindresser.

Some of the houses already erected by the Society, were also sold, HENRY KRAUSE, Butcher, and GOTTLIEB LANGE, Saddler, and some others, each purchased a house.

THE SINGLE BRETHREN'S HOUSE.—1814.

BETHLEHEM, PA.

CHAPTER XV.
MUSIC IN BETHLEHEM.

THE illustration at the head of this chapter, presents a view of the "Single Brethren's House," as it appeared previous to the erection of the adjoining buildings, to the east and west, which now detract from its ancient appearance. It was made from a drawing especially executed for this work, by my brother, William Martin, Jr. Originally, the two entrance doors were put in the centre of the building; because one-half of the house, (the eastern,) was intended for the "Single Brethren," and the other half, (the western,) for the "Single Sisters." On the marble slab indicated over the doors, were the words:

"*Vater Mutter und Lieber Man
Habt Freud an unserm Jünglings plan.*"
"Father and Mother and Worthy Man,
Take pleasure in our Youthful plan."

The inscription was put there when the house was erected in 1784. When it was plastered over is not known. The porch was taken away, and the doors changed to their present position about 1814, so say Jedidiah Weiss and Charles Schneller, two of the oldest inhabitants of Bethlehem. To the west of the Brethren's House, there was a one-story stone building, used as a Hatter's Shop.

In wandering about the town of Bethlehem during a summer evening, the visitor to the place, is surprised, to hear the sound of a piano or some other musical instrument, issuing from nearly every house, no matter how unpretending its external appearance. The inhabitants say, however, that there is not as much attention given to music now as in former times, although it is still taught in all the schools.

Mr. Rufus A. Grider, who may be justly styled one of the antiquarians of Bethlehem, has a fine collection of views of the town, twenty in number; also, views of many of the old buildings, and the plans upon which they were erected; all full of interest. Being an artist of no mean merit, his pencil and brush have enriched the collection with views, taken in the streets of the town, and in the vicinity. His journals are full of interesting records of past events; and he has a valuable accumulation of poetry, both in German and English, descriptive of life and events in the history of Bethlehem. Free use has been made in this work of Mr. Grider's ancient treasures, by his kind permission; and from his "Historical Sketches of Music in Bethlehem," written in 1870, at my request, for this history, the copious extracts have been made which compose this chapter. The beautiful and quaint language needs no apology, but his sketches are entitled to the highest praise.

Mr. Grider has been connected with the church and concert choir at Bethlehem for more than twenty-five years, having been in former years the leading tenor, and a performer on one of the flutes in the orchestra, and is therefore, entirely competent to speak on the subject about which he writes.

In a sketch written in 1854, Mr. Grider states that:

"Bethlehem was perhaps, the most musical of all the Moravian Congregations in America, in proportion to its inhabitants. There was no place in the United States that could compare to it. Music was one of the institutions which gave character to the town, afforded intellectual amusement and pleasure, both to the performers and hearers; the children imbibed the spirit, and the influence of it could be distinctly seen in the inhabitants.

"The Brethren's House was the great nursery where the males received their education, and although kept very strict in many things; in music full scope was given, and was indulged in by both young and old; and if ever democratic principles were practised, it was in the Moravian towns; all were alike, respect was paid to the office and not to the man. The Bishops of the Moravians were nearly all musicians, and many of the Ministers took their part therein, frequently playing the first violin in the orchestra. The musical performances were either in church or concert music, but one was distinct from the other.

"In the Brethren's House, and the 'Sisters,' music was the principal amusement. The Single Brethren had music every evening, the married people went there to enjoy it, and to assist in the performances.

"As an evidence of the love of music, and the simplicity of the early Moravians, it is recorded in the *Church Diary* of July 8, 1754, that, 'Our musicians of the church choir, performing hymn tunes, accompanied the harvesters as far as the river, on their way to cut the rye on the new farm, which was put under cultivation last fall near the *Crown;* as the weather was fine, all who could assist, repaired to the fields, men, women and children.'"

In his later and more extensive work, entitled, "Music in Bethlehem," written in 1870, Mr. Grider thus discourses at large:

"It is not known when music in an organized manner was first performed here. It is recorded that instruments were used by the Moravians in Bethlehem in their religious services, in 1743, and that the noted Indian chief *Tschoop,* was buried amidst strains of music, in 1746. An attack by Indians was unintentionally averted about 1755, by playing a dirge on the *trombones,* the Indians supposing it meant an alarm. Thus, music may possibly have saved the town, and the lives of its inhabitants.

"Benjamin Franklin, in a letter to his wife in 1756, says, that he heard very fine music in the church; that 'flutes, oboes, French-horns and trumpets, accompanied the organ.' Hence, we may infer that music formed, previous to his visit, an essential part of Divine worship and social entertainment, and was cultivated to a great extent by a well organized body of musicians.

"The first organ was obtained when the present chapel was built, in 1751.

"The first orchestra performers, whose names are known to us, existed in 1780 :— Rev. EMANUEL NITSCHMAN, *Leader;* Rev. JACOB VAN VLECK, *1st violin;* ABRAHAM LEVERING, MATTHIAS WITKE, *2d violin;* FREDERICK BECK, *viola;* DAVID WEINLAND, JOSEPH TILL, *violencello's;* WM. LEMBKE, TOBIAS BECKEL, *French-horns;* SAMUEL BADER, JOSEPH OERTER, *flutes;* DAVID WEINLAND, TOBIAS BOECKEL, *trumpets;* JAMES HALL and FREDERICK BOECKEL, *oboes.*

"In 1795, a select party, consisting of Rev. JOHN FEDERICK FRUEAUFF, *1st violin;* GEORGE FREDK. BOECKEL, *2nd violin;* JOHN GEORGE WEISS, *viola,* and DAVID WEINLAND, *violencello,* constituted an organization for performing *Jos. Haydn's Quartettes,* then quite new. It will be perceived that the music of that period, though lacking the variety existing at the present day, included all the instruments then used by European orchestras. The trombone, double bass, fagotto or bassoon and clarinet, not having been generally introduced. It can be truly said that instrumental music here, has kept pace with that in Europe; the various new instruments being introduced as soon as used in the latter country.

"As constant accessions were made to the colony from Europe, the same statement is true as to compositions; no opportunity was neglected to obtain all the newest music which the Brethren in Europe possessed It is known that the Rev. Emanuel Nitschman, when he came from Europe, brought the first copies of *Haydn's Quartettes* and *Symphonies.* It is said that Joseph Haydn, if not directly, was at least, indirectly, in communication with the musicians of this place. JOHN ANTES, born in Frederictrop, Montgomery Co., Pa., where the Moravians had a preaching station, was apprenticed to a wheelwright in Bethlehem; being a youth possessing much talent, he devoted himself also to the study of music; performing on all the stringed instruments; he also studied it as a science. The Musical Library contains fourteen of his compositions. He was a skilful workman also, and partially supplied the then existing want of instruments, by constructing a viola,

violin and violincello; they were used at *Christian-Spring.* The viola with his name inscribed on it, still exists at Nazareth, and the latter is now in the church at Bethlehem. Having gone to Europe, he was sent out as a missionary to Egypt, where the Turks punished him with the *Bastinado,* from the effects of which he never entirely recovered; while laid up in that country, he consoled himself by composing quartettes; when convalescent, he returned to Europe. In Vienna Antes made the acquaintance of Haydn, who, together with other musicians, performed his compositions.

"In the year 1800, FEDERICK BOURQUIN, a new-comer, and a performer, brought with him the first bassoon. In 1806, a double bass was added, it cost sixty-eight dollars, it was paid for partly by a donation from the church funds, and by proceeds obtained at a benefit concert. The Rev. John C. Beckler performed on it the first time, but as he resided at Nazareth, JACOB WOLLE, one of the violincellists, became the player; who, after having perfromed on that instrument, both at concert and in the church, for a period of fifty-seven years, was called home in 1863.

"Haydn's greatest work, the *Creation,* was obtained in 1810, and partially performed in 1811. It is believed that was prior to its performance in any other part of the United States. This was the case also with his *Seasons,* the *Song of the Bell,* the *Seven Sleepers,* *Paradise and the Peri,* and other German compositions. The copies of the *Creation* were made in 1810, from the score, by John Federick Peter, and are still preserved. When the piece was first performed here, the orchestra was thus constituted : *1st violins,* DAVID MORITZ MICHAEL, Leader, JOHN FREDERICK PETER; *2nd violins,* JOHN CHRISTIAN TILL, JOHN FREDERICK RAUCH; *viola,* WILLIAM BEALER; *violincello,* DAVID WEINLAND; *contra-bass,* JACOB WOLLE; *flutes,* JOSEPH OERTER, J. F. BOURQUIN; *clarinet,* JOHN RICKSECKER; *bassoon,* J. SAMUEL KRAUSE; *horns,* JOSEPH TILL, DANIEL KLIEST; *oboe,* JAMES HALL; *trumpet,* FREDERICK BOECKEL. Soon thereafter, were added as new members, Jedidiah and Timothy Weiss, Charles F. Beckel, Jacob C. Till, George Fetter, Christian F. Luck, and others.

"The separation of the sexes was a distinguishing feature in Moravian Congregations, until about the beginning of the present century. We now regard it as an error. Its effects upon music were such, that no vocal performances could take place in the concert room, except those in which male voices alone took part, until its abolishment. It exercised considerable restraint even upon the performance of church music, since the female singers were required to occupy the northern part of the church, the present chapel; while the male performers gathered around and in the rear of the organ in the gallery, situated at the southern end.

"From existing printed and written psalms and music, used on festal occasions, dating from 1768 to 1795, it is evident that *two choirs* of singers existed, a male and a female, each complete in itself. Some pieces were sung by the first, others, entirely by the latter; in some compositions they were made to respond to each other.

"The building of the new church in 1803, ended this exclusiveness. It was no longer deemed improper for Sisters to sing at concerts. At first, the married alone were allowed to sing solos, but in time these gave way to the Single Sisters.

"While the former strict rules were in force, the Single Sisters had in their house, for many years, a complete string quartette, consisting of first and second violin, viola and violincello. The performers were members of their own choir, they performed for their own amusement, and assisted at the music in their own Prayer Hall.

"The sources from which the young people received their musical knowledge, were, the Boarding School for Females, the Sister's House and the Single Brethren's House. Instruction was generally imparted free of charge. Talent was sought for, and when found, was developed. Persons who practised music were looked upon as servants of the church; every one was expected to assist in performances, whenever called upon to do so, by the director of church music.

"*Practisings* were first held in the Brethren's House; after it was abolished as an institution of the church in 1814, they were held in the large room in the west end of the new church, now used for keeping the archives of the church. In 1824 they were removed to the present dwelling of the Principal of the Moravian Day School; after that place was required for school purposes, they were moved to the old chapel; at present they are held in the hall of the Moravian Day School.

"*Whit-Monday* has ever been held a holiday in this community. It became the anniversary day of the "Philharmonic Society" in this manner; among the accessions to the colony, was a professor of music, a member of the church, named DAVID MORITZ MICHAEL; he was a *virtuoso* on the violin, and performed well on the French horn, clarinet and other instruments. The young players all took lessons of him, and were greatly benefitted. He was a composer also, noted more particularly for compositions for wind instruments, then in vogue, called *Parthien* or Harmony Music, composed for five or six instruments, generally two clarinets, two French horns and two bassoons. Such music was generally performed in concerts from the balustrade on top of the Brethren's House, on week day evenings, in the summer, for the entertainment of the town's people.

"One of these compositions was especially composed by the professor for a diversion on the river on Whit-Monday afternoon, when the whole population could enjoy it. This was called, "*Die Wasserfarth*," or the *Boat Ride*. The idea was practically carried out for a number of years, and resulted in making it the musical day of the year.

"The inhabitants assembled on the river bank, west of the old bridge, about 1 o'clock, P. M., a large flat bottomed boat or *flat*, propelled by four men with long poles, and provided with seats and music stands, received the musicians. A procession was formed by those who intended to participate in the pleasures of the occasion. When all was in readiness, the boat started, the music began; the party moved up the Lehigh, accompanied by hundreds of listeners, enjoying the music, social concourse and delightful prospect. The scenes on that part of the Lehigh were truly beautiful; the banks were studded with buttonwood, oak, hickory, water-birch, and other trees whose graceful branches extended beyond, and dipped into the silent stream. Islands covered with vegetation, trees and shrubbery, whose shadows were reflected in the water, added to the attractions.

"The walk was level, bounded on the north by fruitful meadows, and cultivated fields and orchards, on rising grounds; on the south by the river and adjacent mountains. The season of bloom then often at its height, the apple, peach, cherry and other trees, being then in full blossom, the meadows covered with violets, the river bank with honeysuckle, lupin, and other flowers. The party continued westward one mile, to an eddy caused by a turn of the river, forming a miniature whirlpool.* The poles no longer touched bottom, the waters being too deep. The composer, poet like, supposed a case of great peril, caused the music to convey the idea of fear and terror; the boat was kept in the whirlpool long enough for the musicians to act out their part, when it emerged from the eddy into the placid stream; the sounds changed to lively airs and graceful melodies. The boat meanwhile glided with the current, and the party wended their way homeward.

"My principal authority for the foregoing, was the late Mr. Jacob Wolle, who said, 'that about the year 1809 to 1813, he assisted as a performer of the Boat-ride, and on one occasion, the performers were JOHN RICKSECKER, *1st clarinet;* DAVID MORITZ MICHAEL, *2d clarinet;* CHRISTIAN LUCKENBACH, PETER SCHNELLER, *French horns;* SAMUEL KRAUSE and JACOB WOLLE, *Bassoons.*'

"Things have greatly changed since then, the walk has been entirely obliterated, a canal has been scooped out on its site. The river, then considered gentle in its character, has, owing to the construction of dams used in feeding the canal, become violent

*Called the deep hole.

and noted as a destroyer; its floods tearing away the sodded river banks, uprooting the beautiful shade trees, and at times causing scenes of desolation, over which the lover of the beautiful laments.

"That a musical community existed here, may be inferred from the following circumstance; about the year 1800, the town contained about 500 inhabitants, yet that small number furnished six persons as organists, who were able to serve the congregation, and did so, without recompense. Such organists were required to know about 400 church tunes, and be able to play them in any key the officiating minister might start them. (The minister generally commenced the singing of the hymn without announcing the words, the organist and the congregation joined in as soon as they could catch the words and the tune.) They were required to perform concerted music at sight. Now, the congregation is about three times larger, and but three persons are found able to do so. It was deemed not only an honor to be able, but a great privilege to serve the congregation in that manner. The names of the organists of that time, as well as the business each followed, are here given.

JOHN GEORGE WEISS, Watchmaker.
JOSEPH OERTER, Bookbinder.
JOHN FREDERICK PETER, Clerk.
JOSEPH HORSFIELD, Nurseryman.
ANTON SMIDT, Tinsmith.
MARCUS FETTER, Blacksmith.

The organist of the large Moravian church, at this time, is ERNST F. BLECK, and of the Old Chapel, THEODORE F. WOLLE. The organists of the Lutheran is CHARLES SWARTZ, of the Reformed church, GEORGE K. HESS; and of the Catholic, Professor WILLIAM F. GRABER. The vocal performers are now well drilled, resulting from weekly practisings, which have been held for a period of several years by Ernst F. Bleck.

"The Moravian church has adopted choral tunes, deeming them the best suited for congregational singing, 'and although there is much sameness in style, yet, they are capable of much variety in expression, and indeed many portray in peculiarity of cadence, or in combined melody and harmony, a diversity of emotion suited to the expression of those feelings in which a believer delights. Their beauty exists not so much in the melody as in harmony, hence they should be sung in four parts. Their tune books contain about 495, of which about 400 are used. They have been gathered from many countries, from every available source; they use ten of Luther's and fourteen of J. C. Latrobe's composing; the church owes the latter a debt of gratitude, not only for his compositions, which are truly devotional, but for the impulse which he gave to many musical members of his church, in guiding and elevating their taste.' See Lecture on Church Music by the Rev. Lewis West, of Brockwier, England, *Fraternal Messenger*, February number, 1858.

"Here in Bethlehem it has been customary for the organist to play interludes between the lines, which custom has grown from a simple turn, into elaborate and highly colored passages. Such interludes not only tend to obscure the melody, but those features which caused the adoption of choral music by the churches,—its grandeur and simplicity. Many object to their use, and they are now frequently omitted by the present organists.

"Interludes between the verses were first introduced here by one of our present organists, Mr. ERNST F. BLECK. It was a decided improvement on the former method of passing from verse to verse without any relieving separation. It is not customary here for the choir to lead in congregational singing, the organ alone leads. Every member of the church who is able, is expected to sing loud and heartily. The choir sings only concerted music, and alone. Anthems are sometimes sung by the choir, and by the congregation.

"*Concerted Church Music*, with organ and orchestra accompaniment, was performed here soon after the settlement began. It was at first, very simple in its style, being chiefly the compositions of their own people, who composed under instructions of those in authority, requiring them to simplify. As the style changed in Europe, the Moravian composers were allowed to furnish compositions of a higher order; the tastes of their people gradually improved, until the elaborate productions of the best masters were regarded as appropriate.

"*The Musical Library* of the Moravian church at Bethlehem, contains about 750 compositions, 146 with English text, and 611 with German; composed by 89 different authors, all are in manuscript, the greater part having organ and instrumental accompaniments. Besides which, there is a large collection of bound books some containing collections of pieces, and others containing Masses, by various authors; the latter have English and Latin texts, and have been more recently obtained. Among the manuscript music composed by members of the church, or by others not members, but at the request of the church, and not known outside of a few Moravian congregations, there are many that may be classed among the gems of musical compositions. The favorite authors are Bishop Gregor, J. Christian Geissler, Dr. Soerensen, Graun, Bergt, Naumann, Freydt, Reissiger and Spohr, of Germany; Bishop J. C. Latrobe, of England, and Bishop Herbst and Bechler, of the United States.

"Before the choir sings, it is usual for the minister to rise and announce the piece, and read the text of the composition. It has been, and is at this time, customary for the choir to sing at every funeral; several times at every Love-feast, and on other festal occasions, such as Christmas, Easter, Thanksgiving, &c. Recently, the choir sings every Sunday evening at the opening of service. In addition, there are *Musical Singing Meetings*, where no addresses are usual, the choir and the congregation singing alternately; these are delightful occasions, there is no rule as to the compositions and hymns, the officiating minister selecting such as suit the occasion. There are also *Liturgical Singing Meetings*, where the choir, the various classes, and the congregation, sing alternately or all altogether. These are in print, and are only with organ accompaniment;

and are in the German language. Such services are generally held in the evening.

"The attractions of the services of CHRISTMAS EVE are made more interesting by music. Many suitable compositions exist here. For a series of years, the services on this occasion have been opened by singing that gem, 'Stilly night, silent night,' by the choir, a sweet composition, calming, and preparing the large audiences for what follows. The service lasts about two hours, during which the Rev. F. F. Hagen's 'Morning star the darkness break' is sung, alternating between the choir and the children, always to the great delight of those present. The anthem, although simple, and intended for children only, has taken deep root in the hearts of the congregation, who never seem to tire of its performance.

"'For unto us a child is born,'—Handel. 'Sey Wilkommen,'—by Haydn. 'Lift up your Heads, O ye Gates,'—Handel. 'Gloria,' 12th Mass,—Mozart, and other compositions, are sung.

"At this time the church choir numbers sixteen female and eight male singers. The accompaniment to the singing consists of the organ, two first and two second violins, viola, violincello, double bass, two French-horns, two trumpets, trombone and flute, clarinets are not represented for want of competent performers.

"New Year's Eve, in Moravian congregations, has ever been the occasion of special services. Formerly the adult portion of the congregation assembled in the early part of the evening to hear the *Memorabilia* read. This was a statement made by the minister of matters of public interest, or such, relating to the congregation, which transpired during the year, and were worthy of record. The paper is made up from the diary kept by all Moravian clergymen. The subjects treated of, embrace the general features of the seasons, harvests, health, peace and war, losses by fire, new buildings. All births, deaths, marriages, removals and accessions, each name being fully recorded. The number of each class, the losses and accessions, together

with a general review of the whole congregation, and a comparative statement, as to its numbers, its increase and decrease. The reading of the *Memorabilia*, at this time, takes place during the first week in the New Year. At 11½ o'clock, P. M., the congregation assembles for watch meeting. After the officiating minister enters, the choir sing Bishop Gregor's solemn composition, 'Lord! Lord! God,' and then the congregation sing; after which the text for the day is read from the text-book, and is the subject of the discourse which follows. Meanwhile the musicians in the choir consult their time-pieces, and quietly assemble in front of the organ. The organist also watches the hands on his time-piece, and sits ready with his feet poised. As the Year expires, the New is welcomed by a loud crash of melody from the organ, and a double choir of trombonists, by playing tune 146, Text, 'Now let us praise the Lord.' The performance generally leaves the sentences of the speaker unfinished, but 'Time waits not.' The congregation rise and join in singing, followed by prayer, the reading of the text for the first day, and the singing of a hymn. These meetings are always largely attended.

"*Passion Week Services* begin on Saturday evening preceding Palm Sunday, with an introductory address and prayer, and with the reading of the history of the incidents of our Saviour's sufferings. Upon which occasion Dr. Soerensen's exquisite composition, 'O Bethany, thou Peaceful habitation,' is generally performed. It was specially composed for the services on that evening. It ought to serve as a model in refined taste, in simplicity, in accompaniment, and in melody.

"In the services on *Maundy* Thursday *Good* Friday, *Great* Sabbath, and *Easter*, music forms a prominent part, most of the compositions then used were composed to suit the occasion by devoted Christian men; many of them persons of high musical culture, whose works have borne the test of time, and are greatly esteemed by Moravians, who always look forward to their performance with pleasure. Although various composers have written for the same occasions, and changes are sometimes made in those usually performed here during a number of years, we will notice the favorites! For *Maundy Thursday*, 'I see thee in thy soul's deep anguish,'—*di Freydt*. Soprano solo, and chorus, with Obligato Bassoon, carrying a mournful melody, an accompaniment to the soloist. On *Good Friday*, 1. 'Jesus bow'd his head and died,'—*di Gregor*. 2. 'The story of his passion,'—*di J. C. Geissler*. 3. 'The Lord of life! now sweetly slumber,'—*di Latrobe*. The *first*, is for Soprano Solo and Chorus, tenderly accompanied by the organ and orchestra, while an Obligato Flute continues its mournful strain uninterruptedly throughout the entire performance. The *second*, opens with a *duett* for Soprano and Alto, and ends with full chorus and orchestra accompaniment. The *third*, is for Tenor and Basso Solo, duett and chorus. This is one of Bishop Latrobe's best compositions. The instrumental accompaniment is very fine. Two Obligato Clarinets and two Flutes are prominent features therein. The services on Good Friday evening are intended to be a spiritual gathering of mourners around the grave of the buried Saviour. The three compositions have been performed here for many years, and have become precious to those who have heard them once each year since childhood.

"In the Love Feast on Great Sabbath afternoon, three musical compositions are performed by the choir, among which is Bishop Latrobe's 'Holy Redeemer,' for Tenor Solo, Chorus, and double Chorus. This composition, good judges of music deem equal to the best of Handel's works.

"The Sabbath evening services are similar in character to those of the evening previous. The assembled worshippers are supposed to be gathered at the Saviour's grave, and give expression to their feelings by strains of sorrow. The choir usually performs two pieces, one for female voices in two parts; the other, one of Latrobe's compositions, for the same, considered the best of all his works. Text, 'With thy meritorious death, &c.' Both Friday and Saturday

evening meetings, close with congregational singing without organ accompaniment, the organ after starting the choral, gradually ceases playing, this is an impressive feature. On Easter morning, the church services begin at 5 o'clock, A. M., and will be fully described hereafter.

"By the Moravians music is regarded as suited to every occasion in life, the last moments of the dying are soothed by the singing of hymns at the bedside, oft-times selected and joined in by the departing one. After death the *departure* is made known to the congregation by the performance of a trombone quartette from the church spire; at the funeral, when the congregation leave the church, the trombonists head the procession, who perform while marching, and lead the singing at the grave.* The trombones produce a peculiarly solemn effect when performed upon, better and softer melody could be produced by more modern keyed instruments, the Cornet and Alt-horn, &c., but the trombone was originally selected as the symbol of 'the last Trump,' and on that account has held its place. Four different sizes are used, known as the Soprano, Alto, Tenor and Basso. The two smaller have Trumpet Tones.

•"Trombones are also used on festal occasions, to announce the festival, from the church steeple, the time being about 7½ o'clock, A. M. Again at the opening of the service at the Love feast, at 2 o'clock, P. M., and at night, if open air, meetings are held, as upon the occasion of the children's festival. The tunes are varied to suit the occasions.

The services on Easter morning without the accompaniment of the trombonist's, would lose much of their solemnity and interest. On that occasion the choir is often increased. Formerly all the instrumental performers, whether string or wind, took part; latterly trombones only are used. The musicians pass through the principal streets of the town, beginning about 3 o'clock, A. M., in order to awaken the members of the con-

* A full description of the funeral ceremonies will be found in chapter 10th, and are theref re omitted here. —J. H. M.

gregation, greeting them with Hymn, No. 945, represented by Tune 83. The text:—

" ' Christ is risen from the dead,
Thou shalt rise too, saith my Savior,
Of what should I be afraid?
I with him shall live forever,
Can the dead forsake his limb,
And not draw me unto him?'

" Half an hour before service the spacious church is usually filled with the congregation and visitors, who engage in praying the ' Easter Morning Litany,' which embraces the creed of the church. At the passage, ' Glory be to him who is the resurrection and the life,' the minister dismisses the assembly with the announcement that the rest of the litany will be prayed in the burial ground. The musicians having left previously, greet the people as they leave the church, with appropriate hymns suited to the occasion. A procession is formed, led by the children of the schools and their teachers. 2d, the church choir singers. 3d, instrumental performers. 4th, the clergy. 5th, females. 6th, males. They then move on to the grave-yard. The males then occupy the first path running parallel to Market street. The clergy and all the musicians the second path. The females the third path, and part of that extending north and south from Market street. It is so timed, that as the procession enters the grounds, it is met by the brilliant rays of the rising sun, emblematic of the time of the Saviour's rising, and our resurrection. As soon as the multitude have reached their appropriate places; the services are continued to their close. The singing is led by the instrumental performers. In case of a fair mild morning about 2000 persons usually attend this really grand and impressive service. The grounds, which are always kept neat and tidy, shortly before Easter, receive a special refit. New tombstones are placed on the graves of the newly buried, old ones are cleansed, other graves are newly sodded, and many are decked with wreaths and boquets of blooming flowers, as tokens of endearing affection.

" Trombones were formerly used to greet celebrated persons. When General Washington visited Bethlehem, he was welcomed by the trombonists, as a mark of respect. They were also formerly blown upon the arrival or departure of clergymen, and distinguished members of the Moravian church. General Sullivan of the Revolutionary Army was so greeted when he visited Bethlehem during that war.

" It requires not a little self-denial to serve as a performer of the trombone choir. He is required to attend all the services when they are used. He is obliged to assist in announcing every death which occurs in the congregation, to play at the funerals, to play on every festal morning and afternoon, to perform before the celebration of the Lord's supper. He is in duty bound to go to the grave-yard, or climb to the church belfry at all seasons, and in every kind of weather; cold or rain must not be heeded, he goes through all. Oft-times the intense cold congeals the moisture of the instrument, and renders playing almost impossible. Yet he is ever ready. This is done for the love he bears the church. Although much is required, the congregation has never been without such a choir.

" We cannot dismiss this subject without citing the distinguished services of several who are still serving the congregation in this capacity. There exists a photograph, called the ' Three Trombonists,' the fourth, being represented by his instrument, he having ' gone home.' The three entered the service as trombonists, on Easter morning, in the year 1818, having served without interruption, to this date, a period of 53 years. The names of the surviving three are, Jedidiah Weiss, Charles F. Beckel, and Jacob C. Till, the missing brother, Timothy Weiss.

"The trombones are not, we believe, used in the religious services of any other denomination of Christians in the United States. Those in use here, were made in Neukirchen, Germany. The Brethren who constitute the performers at this time, are, AMBROISE H. RAUCH, ROBERT RAU, *Soprano*, or *Discant;* CHARLES F. BECKEL, GEORGE M. BECKEL, *Alto;* HENRY D. BISHOP, JAMES H. WOLLE,

Tenor's; JEDIDIAH WEISS, and CHARLES N. BECKEL, *Basso's.*

"Serenades have been customary here from the founding of the town to the present date. During former times more frequent than now. Visitors to the town were formerly greeted with a serenade. Birth-days were so celebrated. The date of the birth of each individual in the community was formerly known to all the inhabitants by a custom which existed, and which is still observed in Moravian congregations. We refer to the keeping of a *Birth-day-Book,* a record containing a blank page for each day in the year. In it was recorded the names of every member of the congregation, and friends, and relatives in other places; distinguished members of the church both here and elsewhere—both living and deceased—all such as they desired to remember, often also, distinguished names in the history of the world, such as Luther, Melancthon, Gallileo, Columbus, Washington, the Presidents of the United States and others were found therein.

"The *Birth-day-Book* and *Text-Book* were placed on the breakfast-table each morning; after the text was read, and while the family were being served, the record was generally consulted in order to ascertain whose birthday it was. This custom served as a bond which held the inhabitants in social union. No one, no matter how poor or humble was forgotten, every one was greeted with good wishes and attentions. Such books of record also suggested subjects for conversation often tending to entertaining and useful information, particularly so, to young persons. Distant persons were greeted by letter, those near were visited during the day, and saluted with kind wishes, sometimes by the singing of hymns ere they left their bed-chambers. Poetical effusions were composed and sent; many specimens of which, still exist in this community. The best composition of this class was written by Bishop Gregor, while residing in America to his daughter in Europe, giving a description of his American experiences, it is in the German language, and consists of thirty-six verses, the first verse is as follows:

"'Aller liebste Christal
    Hente kriegst du zwar,
    Keine Fest epistel,
    Wie die vor'ge war
    Die ich du vor'm Jahre
    Aus der See gesandt
    Denn fur die zeit fahre
    Ich auf trockenem Land.'"

"It was written in 1771, and contains an account of Bethlehem, Nazareth, and other Moravian congregations, but the most attractive portion, is the description of his visit to the Indian congregation on the Susquehanna river, called *Friedenhutten,* now Lawrence County, Pennsylvania.

"Special pains were taken when the 51st birth-day came, then surprise followed surprise. Serenades were a part of the programme. Formerly hymn tunes were performed, such music being constantly practised, the musicians were at all times ready to perform them." Here follows an interesting account of the celebration of the Golden Wedding of our friend, Jedidiah Weiss, and his wife, which occurred on November 26th, 1870, copied from the next issue thereafter of the *Moravian,* which is very pleasing but too long to be included in this brief chapter.

"The first special organization for serenading, which we can trace, existed here in 1840. It continued during many years, and produced some sweet music; mostly familiar airs, arranged by three of the members, viz.: CHARLES F. BECKEL, E. F. BECKEL, and MATTHEW CHRIST. Their collection embraced about thirty pieces. The members—CHARLES F. BECKEL, *first violin;* CHRISTIAN F. LUCH, *second violin;* MATTHEW CHRIST, *clarinet;* JOHN SIGLEY, *bugle;* LEWIS F. BECKEL, *flute;* ERNEST F. BLECK, *violincello;* HENRY D. BISHOP, *trombone;* and at a later day, the same music was rendered, existing vacancies being filled by AMBROISE H. RAUCH, *bugle;* JAMES H. WOLLE and CHARLES N. BECKEL, *trombones;* and RUFUS A. GRIDER, *flute.*

"When the era of brass music came, another club was organized, and performed for several years, during the existence of the older; and then finally took its place. It was known as the "Sextett Club." The instruments used were cornets and tubas. It was constituted as follows :—LEWIS F. BECKEL, *Leader,* GEORGE M. BECKEL, CHARLES N. BECKEL, BERNHARD E. LEHMAN, MATTHIAS WEISS, JULIUS N. WEISS, and WILLIAM H. BOEHLER. The music performed by them was mostly of Professor Grafulla's arrangement. This organization did the community good service—the inhabitants of the town received many a musical treat between their dreams.

"*Vocal serenades* have been customary here from the town's commencement. One organization for that purpose existed here about 1850. Another called the 'ARION' existed here for several years, using the Arion collection for männerchoir It sang its 'last lay,' at the funeral of Amos Commenius Clauder, one of its members, who died October 14th, 1868. Lately the members of the Moravian Church choir have serenaded several of its prominent members upon their entering the choir of the 'married people.'

"*Military music* took its rise here in 1809. Under the existing military laws, all males between the ages of 18 and 45 years were required to exercise in military tactics, twice each year, or pay a fine. The first was called *Exercising,* it embraced one of the districts of a brigade. The second, included the entire brigade, and was called 'Battalion drill.' On such occasions nearly all the males reported for duty. Females also came as spectators; it was the gala-day of that period. Shows or circus performances did not then exist. Fairs also were of a later date. A nodding plume was an admirable appendage in those days. To be an officer of the brigade was deemed a great honor. Persons attaining such positions endeavored to excel each other in display. Fine uniforms, bright buttons, large epaulets, plumes, cocked hats, and attractive music were required.

"The formation of the '*Bethlehem Band*' was the result of the militia system of that period. In the book in which the members recorded their names is found the following 'Preamble to the Constitution' of the Musical Society of the 97th Regt. Pa. Militia. As this society has been offered by the brigade inspector and colonel of the 97th Regt. Pa.

Militia, that if the Society will furnish the regiment with military music on the occasion of Battalion parades, the said Musical Society shall not be subject to any military fines, and as said Society has accepted said offer, they agree to be bound by the following Constitution. *Article* I. The Company shall be known as the *Columbia Band,* &c. To this instrument are attached 52 names, some of them, among the most prominent citizens of the town. In the early part of its formation the band numbered 12 performers, but it afterwards increased to 24 members.

The following is a list of the names of the members, as they stand recorded in rotation in the book :

Samuel Luckenbach	Christian F. Luch,
John Rickseeker,	Benjamin Eggert,
Jedidiah Weiss,	William Rice,
David Peter Schneller,	Charles F. Beckel,
John F. Ranch,	Samuel Luckenbach,
John Oerter,	son of Adam,
Christian Luckenbach,	George W. Dixon,
Timothy Weiss,	Charles Williams, Jr
Jacob Till,	David Weinland,
Daniel Luckenbach,	Charles C. Tombler,
Gottlot Guetter,	Samuel Shultz,
John G. Fetter,	John C. Weber,
Ernst F. Bourquia,	Charles Neisser,
Samuel Weinland,	Charles L. Knauss,
Christian Lange,	George H. Goundie,
Henry Hillman,	John G. Clewell,
Samuel R. Eggert,	Jacob Luckenbach,
Charles F. Kremser,	Samuel Brunner,
Phillip Bealer,	Michel Kreider,
William B. Luckenbach,	William Luckenbach,
Herman Hillman,	Aug. Belling,
Charles S. Bush,	Jos. O. Beitel,
Benjamin Whitesell,	Lewis S. Knauss,
Francis Lennart,	Matthew Christ,
Augustus Milchsuck,	John David Weiss,
Andrew Vognitz.	Francis Knauss,
John Alex. Bourquin,	Jacob Wolle,
William Neisser,	Wm. C. Luckenbach,
John M. Miksh,	C. Jacob Till.
C. F. Youngman,	

"At the beginning of the present century Military Bands were rare; few existed outside of our large cities; performers were few; it was difficult to obtain instruments and suitable music. The present great city of Philadelphia had at that time but one Band. Frank Johnson, a noted Bugler, a colored resident, had organized a Band from among his own race; it was *the Band* of that city for a long time. During the earlier part of its existence it accompanied the *Fencibles,* commanded by Col. JAMES PAGE, when on a visit to Bethlehem, which they reached *via* the Lehigh Canal by boat. On that occasion the *Bethlehem Band* assisted in welcoming the visitors to the town. Many of the members of the *Bethlehem Band* were skilled orchestra performers; some of them able to compose suitable music. Their most effective composition at that time was a *Grand March*, composed by their leader, C. JACOB TILL, the skilful rendering of which did them great credit. The band was successively led by JOHN RICKSECKER, C. JACOB TILL, CHARLES F. BECKEL, SAMUEL LUCKENBACH,[*] and again during a short period by MR. BECKEL, until it was disbanded. It existed during a period of thirty years. The excellence of its music, and the high social and moral standing of its members, gained it great celebrity; its services were sought for in distant parts; and it was regarded as equal to any Band in the Atlantic cities.

"The first Brass Band was organized in the year 1839. It was led by JOHN SIGLEY on the *Bugle*, and existed only during a short time, about four years. In 1845 an excellent Brass Band, led by PETER POMP, of Easton, visited the town; they performed with much taste, the well known *Love Not Quickstep*. The visit was long remembered by the people of Bethlehem. The immediate effect was to arouse a spirit of emulation; it was remarked by the young musicians here, 'Easton shall not outshine us long.' An organization was formed at once by young persons; an existing *Reed Band* was converted into one for *Brass* instruments, with the following performers:

AMBROISE H. RAUCH,　HENRY D. BISHOP,
AMOS BEALER,　CHARLES N. BECKEL,
WM. H. BOEHLER,　HARRY BOURQUIN,
LEWIS F. BECKEL,　JULIUS N. WEISS,
MATTHIAS WEISS,　HENRY I. OERTER,
　　JULIUS W. HELD.

This organization was continued under the lead of LEWIS F. BECKEL for about 15 years. After it was disbanded, several attempts were

* Samuel Luckenbach was not a performer, he was the captain of the band, *i. e.*, Drum-major. He always dismissed the performers with the remark, "Gentlemen, the band is dismissed I think."

made to re-organize, but without permanent success. At this time another attempt is being made by persons who have not belonged to other organizations of the town.

"*The Philharmonic Society* of Bethlehem was the result of previous musical culture, and former organization. There was a prior organization known as the *Collegium Musicum of Bethlehem*. Music had been practiced in the town during a period of seventy-eight years; as an *art era* the new name was assumed. About the year 1806 an effort was made to revive the flagging musical spirit. A benefit concert was given in 1807, after which $19.15 was collected, which at that time was deemed a large sum. No tickets were sold, and no admission fee charged; persons deposited their gifts at the door in a tin box, painted green, and marked 'For the Support of Music.'

"The Treasurer's accounts, which have been preserved, show the number and date of the Concerts given during a number of years, and the amount received after each Concert. From them the following information is gathered, viz:

Date.	Concerts.	Amt's rec'd.
1807,	17,	$31.47.
1808,	28,	32.00.
1809,	36,	42.86.
1810,	24,	32.00.
1811,	24,	32.60.
1812,	16,	25.58.
1813,	24,	42.00.
1814,	14,	16.41.
1815,	12,	7.28.
1816,	10,	12.50.
1817,	12,	10.63.
1818,	11,	10.50.
1819,	13,	8.20.

In 13 years, 241 Concerts, $301.73; averaging about one dollar and thirty cents for each Concert. The Society paid no rent, and paid for no fuel. It had no other resources except the free will offerings of its own people, and yet it was sufficient to purchase candles, violin strings, and instruments, make needed repairs, pay for music paper and copying music, and the Society had $4.42 in the treasury when it assumed a different organization, and a new name, in the year 1820.

"Leading members of the Musical Society and learners practised daily on their respective instruments from fifteen to sixty minutes after dinner and at night. Quartette Clubs also existed, which met regularly at the houses of members and at the *Brethren's House.*

"On the 19th of May, 1823, *The Creation* was performed by the Philharmonic Society, on a larger scale than ever before in Bethlehem. Seventy performers took part. It was sung in the original German text, and the Concert was deemed a great success. In 1824, eight Concerts were given. On Whit-Monday, in 1832, Schiller's 'Song of the Bell,' with Romberg's music, was rendered for the first time here, to the great delight of the public. The person representing the part of *Master*, was our present veteran *Basso*, JEDIDIAH WEISS, now seventy-four years of age. The *Tenor Soloist* was TIMOTHY WEISS, whose fine voice, and skilful rendering is still remembered with pleasure by those who heard him. The soprano soloists were, Miss Susan E. Stotz and Miss Lizzette Bleck. The alto soloists, Miss Charlotte Beckel and Miss Caroline Brown.

"Things went on prosperously under the direction of CHARLES F. BECKEL, MATTHEW CHRIST, JACOB WOLLE, ERNEST LEHMAN, and JEDIDIAH and TIMOTHY WEISS. Perfect unity of action existed, and rapid progress was made. The compositions given for a series of years at the annual festivals were, viz:

1833,.........The Creation,..............*Haydn.*
1834,.........Spring and Summer,.... "
1835,.........Winter and Autumn,.... "
1836,.........The Song of the Bell,...*Romberg.*
1837,.........The Seven Sleepers,.....*Dr. Löwe.*
1838,........ "   "   "   ..... "
1839,.........The Creation,..............*Haydn.*

"The Society was now in the zenith of its glory; 'The Seven Sleepers,' then quite new, was repeated at public request. The representations of the Seven Brothers was deemed highly interesting; but more particularly the part of the boy, *Malchus,* performed by Miss LIZETTE BLECK, who possessed the rare faculty of forgetting self, and throwing her whole soul and feelings into the part she

represented; yet so modest and childlike, that she has been regarded by those who heard her, as unequalled in the part in this place. The Bishop of Ephesus was represented by the Rev. JOHN G. HERMAN, a Bishop of the Moravian Church, whose deep, rich bass voice, had a great effect upon the audience. His official position was poetically true. It was also a pleasing and unusual feature.

"In 1840, William T. Roepper, a skilful piano-forte, organ, and violin performer, and a good tenor singer, became an active member of the Society; and soon thereafter was elected Conductor, which station he filled for about thirteen years; during which time greater efforts were made than ever before to improve the quality of the music rendered. The practice of music, however, like all other undertakings, is subject to *ebb and flow.* The Bethlehem public had been surfeited with music; the audiences became slim and indifferent; under such circumstances it was but natural that the performers should lose their interest also, and practicings ceased for a time.

"In 1858, an effort was made to revive the dormant Society. J. P. E. WINDEKILDE, a violinist, was elected leader, FREDERICK AGTHE, LOUIS F. BECKEL and RUFUS A. GRIDER, Directors, and JAMES H. WOLLE, Secretary. Miss ERNESTINA HAHN (afterwards married to Julius N. Weiss), a noted soprano singer, and a Teacher in the Boarding School, gave instruction to the male and female singers of the Society, using the 'Social Glee Book.' It was intended for open air recreations on the river in the evenings.

"In May, 1863, the Society again performed *The Seven Sleepers,* and repeated it the following month. Three Concerts were given in 1864, and the same number in 1865. In 1866, Mr. Roepper reappeared, after a retirement of several years. He gave the vocal performers an opportunity to practice SHUMAN's *Paradise and the Peri,* in order to gratify a taste which he had acquired for the works of that author, and the pleasure it would afford others. The offer was eagerly embraced. Mrs. JANE R. KRAUSE (the eldest daughter of Mr. Roepper) took the difficult and prominent part of the *Peri*, and sustained it with great success. Miss ANNIE STEIN, Miss ELLEN LICHTENTHALER, Miss KATE SELFRIDGE, and Miss EMILY SIEGER, also sang solos; ROBERT RAU was tenor soloist, and JEDIDIAH WEISS and ANTHONY GOTH, bassos. The accompaniment was performed on the piano, by Mr. Roepper. It was intended for social recreation only; but the performers desiring to sing it in public, for the benefit of some charitable object; a Concert was given in February, 1867, and with such success, that the public required two repetitions.

"In 1869, a re-organization was effected. The Society was placed under the direction of Professor WILLIAM K. GRABEB, as leader; during that year, Rossini's *Stabat Mater*, and Spohr's *Last Judgment*, were performed here for the first time. We copy from the Moravian, of March 6th, 1869:

"'The Concert on Saturday evening last was in every respect a gratifying success. The programme was a choice one, the rendering of it admirable in every particular, and there was a crowded house. Part I., of the programme embraced the following: Overture, La Cenerentola; Fantasie, Piano, Chopin (Prof. W. Warner); Trio, Piano, Violin and Violoncello, Mendelssohn, (Messrs. Wolle, Graber and Bleck); Marchia, Piano, Raff (Prof. Warner); Quintette, Larghetto and Rondo, Bethoven (Messrs. Wolle, Graber and Bleck, Charles W. Roepper, and B. E. Lehman); Prof. Warner received a well-deserved *encore*, to which he responded by playing the L'Ecume du Mer. It is seldom, indeed, that more finished and brilliant performing on the piano is heard than that with which the audience were favored on this occasion. The 'Stabat Mater,' which formed Part II., was never sung better. The parts were distributed as follows: 'Cujus Animam,' Mr. R. Rau; 'Quis est Homo,' Miss Kate Selfridge and Miss Otelia V. Clauder; 'Pro Peccatis,' Mr. Anthony Goth; 'Eia! Mater,' Mr. Jedidiah Weiss; 'Sancta Mater,' Miss Ellen Lichtenthaler, Miss Mary Ann Rice, Messrs.

Robert Rau and Edwin G. Klose; 'Fac ut Portem,' Mrs. C. W. (Jane) Krause; 'Inflammatus,' Miss Ellen Lichtenthaler. A repetition of the last was enthusiastically called for. It was superbly sung. The solos and choruses were each given with admirable precision and expression. It was a most enjoyable evening. Why cannot the Concert be repeated? We believe the public would heartily welcome a repetition, and we have no doubt that all the performers and singers would enjoy it as well. It is certainly a gratifying circumstance that there is still so much musical taste and ability amongst us, and it will not be questioned that both ought to be cultivated. It is a pleasant thing to see, and a hopeful symptom of the healthiness of social life in Bethlehem, when citizens of all ages and classes meet together to rehearse such classical music as that embraced in the above programme, and when without any parade or affectation, the same is publicly rendered for the enjoyment of others and for a charitable purpose. The Philharmonic Society has a mission to perform, which we trust it will not neglect.'

"The first Concert for the benefit of the Young Men's Christian Association's course of *Winter Evening Entertainments*, was given on Saturday evening, November 27th, 1869. The musical reporter of the *Moravian*, in the issue of that paper of December 2d, writes enthusiastically of the performance, thus:

"'The Philharmonic Concert on Saturday evening last was a delightful success. We have seldom had a Concert in which the programme was so uniformly well carried out. The selections were all more or less familiar, at which some may be disposed to cavil; (to our taste this was one great merit of the programme), but no one could have failed to be entirely satisfied with the manner in which they were rendered. Excepting our memorable 'Paradise and the Peri' experience some winters ago, we have not, for many years, had so full and well drilled an orchestra and chorus. Very great credit is due to the conductor, Prof. Graber, and to the members of the Society, who have suffered themselves to be drilled—a rather rare virtue in volunteer performers, be it remembered. The evidences of careful rehearsing were manifest throughout, and there was a promptness and correctness in time and expression in which our orchestras were formerly rather deficient. We welcome this Concert as the beginning of a new musical era in Bethlehem, which shall do more than restore its ancient renown, and as for ourselves we vote for dispensing with the lectures announced in this course of 'Winter Evening Entertainments,' and substituting Concerts, even though these could only be had by repeating some of the previous performances. Music that is worth hearing at all, has nothing to lose, but much to gain by repetition, and that not only once, but many times.

" 'The orchestral contributions to the programme were the Overture to La Dame Blanche, Op. 44, Kalliwoda, Heimweh (Jungman), and some of Strauss' Waltzes, (the latter, the only portion to' which we take slight exception). The Quartette, from Oberon, was sung by Mrs. Jane R. Krause, Miss Otelia V. Clauder, Messrs. Robert Rau and B. E. Lehman. The Flute Obligato was finely performed by Mr. Charles W. Roepper, accompanied on the piano by Prof. Wolle. The duett from Mendelssohn's 'Hymn of Praise,' was sung by Miss Annie Stein and Miss Kate Selfridge, the chorus being very full, about thirty singers. This was unquestionably the gem of the evening, and so the audience seemed to think, but it failed to accomplish a repetition. The 'Glockentoene,' (Proch), was sung by Miss Kate Selfridge, Mr. B. E. Lehman accompanying on the French horn, and Prof. Graber on the piano. It deserved the *encore* it received. The Trio, 'Die Sanften Tage,' was very beautifully sung by Mrs. Krause, and Messrs. Robert Rau and Anthony Goth. The chorus was composed of male voices. It, too, we want to hear again. 'The Heavens are Telling,' was splendidly given by the full chorus, at first a little too slow in time, but the Conductor speedily remedied this. Altogether the Concert was an event, and the public asks for many more like it.'

" In the *Moravian* of May 12th, 1870, the following interesting notice and statement will be found, viz :

" 'The *Philharmonic Society* will this evening render the Oratorio of ' The Seven Sleepers.' It has been performed several times by the Society, the first time being in 1837, when the solo parts were distributed as follows : Miss Lizette Bleck (afterwards Mrs. Israel Ricksecker), Miss Susan Stotz (afterwards Mrs. Rev. H. J. Titze), Miss Phoebe Bleck (now Mrs. Wm. Brown), Miss Louisa Pietsch, Mr. Chas. F. Beckel, Mr. Timothy Weiss, Rev. John G. Herman; Rev. Julius Bechler, Rev. J. C. Brickenstein, Mr. Jedidiah Weiss,. Mr. Beckel being also leader of the orchestra. As the text of the oratorio will be for sale at the Concert, we need not give the plot. The distribution of the solos is as follows : Sopranos, Mrs. Laura Clauder, Mrs. C. W. Krause, Miss Kate Selfridge ; alto, Miss Cornelia F. Boner ; tenors, Mr. Robert Rau, Mr. Henry T. Clauder, Mr. Bertine S. Erwin ; Bassos, Mr. Jedidiah Weiss, Mr. Edwin G. Klose, and Mr. Anthony Goth. The choruses are numerous.'

"At a meeting of the ' Philharmonic Society,' of Bethlehem, held on Tuesday, Oct. 6th, 1870, the following gentlemen were elected officers of the Society for the ensuing year :

President,, CHARLES F. BECKEL.
Treasurer, JAMES H. WOLLE.

Directors,
THEODORE F. WOLLE, ROBERT RAU, CHARLES W. ROEPPER.
Conductor,
Prof. WM. K. GRABER.

" The society seems to have taken a new lease of life. Efforts are now being made, not only to improve the rendering, but also to bring in new material ; much progress has already been made, under the industrious and genial new conductor, Prof. Graber. The number of vocal performers at this time, belonging to the society, is 62, consisting of 33 males and 29 females. The orchestra numbers 26 performers, viz :

Conductor, Prof. WM. K. GRABER.

First violins. {
Prof. Theodore F. Wolle.
Mr. S. Erastus Pettee.
" Charles F. Beckel.
" Emanuel C. Ricksecker.
}

Viola, Robert Rau, Matthew J. Schmidt.

Second violins {
Alfred C. Roth.
Charles Reigel.
Charles Luch.
Augustus Gugatsh.
}

Violincello, Ernst F. Bleck, John Luch.

Contra-Basso, George M. Beckel.

Bassoon, Jedidiah Weiss.

Trombones. {
Charles N. Beckel.
James H. Wolle.
Augustus H. Leibert.
}

Cornets, Lewis F. Beckel, Adolph Degelow.

French Horns, Ambrose H. Rauch, Bernhard E. Lehman.

Flutes, Charles W. Roepper, Harry H. McNeal, Rufus A. Grider.

Kettle Drums, Frank A. Stuber.

Organ, Mrs. Louisa Huebener.

"Although the state of music in Bethlehem, embracing a period of 128 years, has been sometimes over-rated by visitors, we believe that up to the year 1825, the Bethlehem orchestra compared favorably with any other amateur organization of a like character in the United States. When the 'Musical Fund Society of Philadelphia,' performed the *Creation,* for the first time, about 1819, the trombone parts could not be filled there, the performers were from Bethlehem; Mr. Jedidiah Weiss being one of the three who performed on that occasion. Mr. Richard S. Smith, the well known veteran Underwriter of Philadelphia, lately remarked, 'I was one of the originators of the 'Musical Fund Society,' when we gave our first *grand concert,* in which Trombones were necessary, we had to send to Bethlehem for the performers. They, and their large instruments were the centre of attraction. Trombones were a novelty in our orchestra, few in the audience had ever seen or heard one.' After the concert, one of our members said he thought he could learn to play on one of those big things, if he had one, so one was accordingly purchased for him, and he took it home to practice on it. At the next meeting he was called upon to report progress;

which he did as follows: 'I took the *trombone* home, and when I got there, the sitting room looked very cozy; the cat was curled up in front of the fire; my wife was up stairs, and the baby was asleep in her cradle. I sat down to try my new instrument; I blew vigorously, a discordant blast was the result, the cat sprung to her feet in affright, with her hair on end, and her tail much enlarged, she gave me one astonished look, then tore furiously out of the room. I made another attempt, with the same result as to sound, which awoke the baby, she screamed with terror, I laid down the *trombone,* and walked the floor for an hour, with Miss Roberts in my arms.' The report created great laughter."

These brief extracts from Mr. Grider's interesting work, will give some idea of *Music in Bethlehem,* and of his interesting work.

In 1859, Mr. Lewis H. Weiss began to write 'The Annals of the Music of Bethlehem." But as he had removed from the town, he abandoned the work; being too far from the necessary materials, which is much to be regretted. I have a copy of his unfinished manuscript, and the ability displayed, leads those who have read it, to hope, that at some early day, Mr. Weiss will complete a work so well begun.

In 1870, a new band was organized under the name of the *Bethlehem Cornet Band,* with the following named persons as performers. EDWARD BENNER, Leader, *E cornet;* GEORGE BEERS, *E cornet;* GEORGE J. MALTHANER, *E clarinet;* WILLIAM M. SIGFRIED, *E cornet;* HENRY SLIDER, *E cornet;* OTTO GROVNER, *B cornet;* LEWIS S. LILLY, *alto;* EDWARD HUNT, *solo alto;* BENJAMIN WEBER, *alto;* MATTHEW WEISS, *solo tenor;* W. BACHMAN, *tenor;* PHILLIP SINK, *barritone;* GEORGE M. BECKEL, *solo barritone;* SAMUEL SIMMS, *bass;* WILLIAM ORTT, *bass;* ROBERT HECKMAN, *bass;* EUGENE JACOBY, *bass drum;* EDWARD CLEWELL, *snare drum;* JACOB VOGNITZ, *snare drum;* STEPHEN KOMMILLER, *cymbals.*

The *Bethlehem Liederkranz* held its first meeting on Saturday evening, October 29th, 1870, in the hall of the Moravian Day School, agreeable to a call of Charles W. Roepper, the original founder of the "Kranz." Twelve persons were present, and the society was duly organized by the election of the following officers.

President, CHARLES W. ROEPPER.
Sec'y and Treas., GEORGE H. LUCKENBACH.

Directors.

MATTHEW J. SCHMIDT, GEORGE H. LUCKENBACH and FREDERICK J. RICE.

Conductor, WILLIAM K. GRABER.

Owning to the bad health of the secretary, of Matthew J. Schmidt, a director, the resignation of the president, and the insertion of a new clause in the constitution, authorizing the election of a vice-president, a meeting of the society was called, and a new election was held to fill the vacancies, which resulted in the following choice of officers.

President, ABRAHAM S. SCHROPP.
Vice President, HENRY G. BORHEK.
Sec'y and Treas., AUGUSTUS H. LEIBERT.
Directors, FREDERICK J. RICE, THEODORE F. LEVERS and JAMES T. BORHEK, Jr.

The following is a full list of the members of the society.

Charles W. Roepper,
Abraham S. Schropp,
William K. Graber,
James T. Borhek, Jr.,
George H. Luckenbach,
Benjamin Riegel,
Frank L. Wolle,
Samuel Solt,
James M. Schnabel,
Augustus H. Leibert,
Theodore F. Levers,
Caesar Spiegler,
Charles Prosser,
Joseph A. Weaver,
George Hess,
Charles Schwartz,
Clarance Crist,
Clarance A. Wolle,
Frederick J. Rice,
Joseph J. Beahm,
Quintus Jacoby,
Franklin L. Sussdorff,
Frantz Koegler,
Cyrus E. Breder,
Henry G. Borhek,
Frederick Miller,
Edward Welden,
Oliver A. Clewell,
Ammon Gardiner,
Milton J. Hess,
Adolph Degelow,
Matthew J. Schmidt,
Bertine S. Erwin, M. D.

The society meets every Friday evening for practice, and frequently serenades its members and friends. It assisted at the concert of the Philharmonic society, which was given on March 2nd, 1871, singing the following German songs, *Abschied vom Walde,* "Farewell to the Forest," by Mendelsshon; *Die Wacht am Rhein,* the German campaign song, which took the audience by storm, an encore was demanded, but instead of repeating it, the society sung *Mein Wunch, i. e.,* "My Wish," which gave great satisfaction.

This brings the history of music in Bethlehem down to the present day, imperfectly, it is admitted; but full enough to show how deeply the love of music is inherent in its people.

THE LEHIGH UNIVERSITY.
SOUTH BETHLEHEM, PA.—1871.

CHAPTER XVI.

BOROUGH AUTHORITIES.—LAWYERS AND DOCTORS.—THE CHOICE OF BISHOPS BY LOT.—AN ACCOUNT OF A "VESPER" OF THE MORAVIAN HISTORICAL SOCIETY.—OLD MAP OF BETHLEHEM IN THE HISTORICAL SOCIETY OF PENNSYLVANIA.—THE MARRIED PEOPLES' HOUSES —MANOKASY.—THE APOTHECARY SHOP.—POTTERY.—TOBACCO.—SILK.—PUBLIC BUILDINGS.—THE VINEYARDS.—THE PENNSYLVANIA AND LEHIGH ZINC CO.—SOUTH BETHLEHEM.—THE PAPER BAG MANUFACTORY.—NEW STREET BRIDGE.—VOLUNTEER COMPANIES.—THE LEHIGH UNIVERSITY. — THE FRESHET OF OCT. 4, 1869.—THE FIRST PUBLIC ROADS.—DAVID NITSCHMAN AND HIS COMPANY.—THE GREAT MINNISINK TRAIL.— THE FIRST POST OFFICE.—THE MODE OF TRAVEL IN THE OLDEN TIMES.—THE "CROWN INN."—STAGE ROUTE FROM THE WIND GAP TO PHILADELPHIA.

List of CHIEF BURGESSES of Bethlehem, since the year 1845.

Chas. Aug. Luckenbach,
John Matthew Miksch,
Ernst F. Bleck,
Jacob Wolle,
Jedidiah Weiss,
Phillip H. Goepp,
Benjamin Van-Kirk,
Edward H. Rauch,
Ira Cortright,
Nathan Bartlett,
Charles F. Beckel,
C. Edward Peisart,
Ambrose J. Erwin.

SAMUEL BRUNNER has been clerk of Councils since 1845, previous to which time, the municipal affairs of the town were under the direction of the Moravian Church.

LIST OF COUNCILS.

Philip H. Goepp,
Henry G. Guetter,
Benjamin Eggert,
Lewis Doster,
Ernst F. Bleck,
William Luckenbach,
John M. Mik ch,
Charles L. Knauss,
Christ'an Luckenbach,
Joseph H. Taylor,
Matthew Krause,
Charles Aug. Luckenbach,
John F. Rauch,
William R. Huffnagle,
Jacob Luckenbach,
Matthew Brown,
James T. Borhek,
Aaron George,
Ambroise H. Rauch,
Christian F. Luch,
John C. Malthaner,
John Krause,
Charles F. Kremser,
Dri Abraham H. Huebener,
William Bush,
Christian Lange,
Charles B. Daniel,
William F. Ritter,
John Berger,
Simon Rau,
Edward Weinland,
Peter Kleckner,
Aaron W. Radley,
Charles Edward Peisert,
Charles F. Beckel,
John Walp,
Ruben O. Luckenbach,
Nathan Bartlett,

Charles W. Rauch,
Louis F. Beckel.
Solomon Steckel,
George Steinman,
Henry T. Milchsack,
Jacob H. Lilly,
Jonas Snyder,
Merritt Abbott,
William Leibert,
Josiah George,
Charles Blank,
Ambrose J. Erwin,
Charles Bodder,
Henry S. Sellers,
Francis E. Huber,
Lewis Doster, Jr.,
David O. Luckenbach,
Isaac Walp,
D. Henry Bishop,
John K. Dech,
Richard W. Leibert,
Charles Fred'k Eberlin,
Wm. Frankenfield,
John Opp,
Jacob J. Hoffman,
Samuel Snyder,
Rufus A. Grider,
John H. Yost,
Charles E. Shoemaker,
John B. Zimmele,
Erwin Mushlitz,
Simon Kemmerer,
Louis Gerlach,
David H. Taylor,
Joseph Wendell,
Jeremiah Bieber,
William B. Rice,
Jacob Fries,

Daniel Desh.

CONSTABLES.

Chas. W. Rauch,
George Reigh,
Augustus Belling,

Permania Ricksecker,
Gilbert Van Fradeneck,
Chr. Lewis Kidd,

Joel Shitz.

JUSTICES OF THE PEACE, from 1741 to 1871.

Timothy Horsfield,
William Okely,
David Kliest,
Joseph Horsfield,
Jacob Wolle,
Joseph Rice,
William Rice,

John F. Rauch,
Reuben S. Rauch,
Samuel C. Shimer,
James T. Borhek,
Benjamin F. Schneller,
Samuel Brunner,
Abraham Myers.

LIST OF LAWYERS.

Charles Brodhead, Esq.,
William Emil Doster, "
Alfred Christ, "
William F. Hackett, "

J. Howard Burke, Esq.,
Lewis H. Stout. "
Frank Reeder. "
Walter S. Heilner, "

In March, 1871, ADOLPH CONRADI was appointed one of the *Saal Diener's* of the Bethlehem Moravian Congregation.

At page 131, it is stated that Polly Heckewelder was the *only* daughter of the famous Missionary to the Indians, which is erroneous. He had two younger daughters, one of them married Joseph Rice, the other married Christian Luckenbach. Nor was she the first white child born in Ohio, as stated, but she was the first white *female* child born in that State.

The Physicians of Bethlehem, in the past,

as well as those of the present day, have been noted for a high degree of professional skill in their calling. Some of those now departed, were not only eminent in their profession, but were celebrated for their witty sayings, or eccentricities, which have caused their names to be household ones in the place. Among these old time doctors may be mentioned:

Dr. Matthew Otto,
" John Fred'k Rudolphy,
" Jno. Fred'k A. Steckel,
" Eberhardt Freytag,
" Daniel Green,

Dr. Abraham Stout,*
" Frederick Martin,
" Abraham L. Huebener,
" William Wilson,
" Benjamin Wilhelm.

The following Physicians are at present located in the town.

Dr. Maurice C. Jones,
" Fred'k A. Fickardt
" Augustine N. Leinbach,
" Abraham Stout,
" Edward H. Jacobson,

Dr. Charles E. Humphreys,
" John H. Wilson,
" John J. Wilson,
" Bertine S. Erwin,
" George S. Engler,

Dr. John R. Goodman.

Among the notables of Bethlehem there is an artist of no mean merit, DE WITT C. BOUTELLE; his picture of Niagara is the best representation of that famous natural curiosity yet painted. It embraces a view of the *entire* Fall, presenting a truthful picture, faithful to nature, and is exquisitely beautiful.

The celebrated German painter, GUSTAVUS GRUNEWALD, resided for many years in the town, but has now returned to his native country.

Mr. REUBEN O. LUCKENBACH, who is a native of Bethlehem, and has his residence there, has painted many beautiful pictures of the charming views in the vicinity. He is teacher of Painting and Drawing in the Young Ladies' Seminary.

The following official notice will serve not only to complete the list of the Moravian Bishops, but also to show that the use of the LOT is still continued in the Church.

" We are officially informed by the Unity's Elders' Conference, that on the 7th day of July, 1870, that body took into solemn consideration the request of our late Provincial Synod to have two new Bishops appointed for our Province, and that after mature de-

---

* Dr. Stout, the elder, was an uncle of the present Dr. Stout, and of Lewis H. Stout, Esq. Dr. Maurice C. Jones studied medicine in his office, and was his assistant.

liberation it had been resolved to make use of the Apostolic lot in deciding which of the four brethren who had been nominated should be appointed as Bishops. Accordingly, after fervent prayer, the names of the four candidates, viz: the Revs. L. F. Kampman, F. R. Holland, E. de Schweinitz and A. A. Reinke, were submitted to the Lord's decision by lot. The first name drawn was that of the Rev. Edmund de Schweinitz, and then followed that of Rev. Amadeus Reinke.

" These two brethren, Revs. E. de Schweinitz and A. A. Reinke, having therefore been constitutionally elected and confirmed as Bishops, they will, (D. V.) be solemnly consecrated to their sacred office, here at Bethlehem, on the evening of Sunday, Aug. 28, 1870.

" We hereby cordially commend them to the prayers of the Church. Let it be our united petition to the throne of grace that our Episcopacy may remain precious in the sight of the Lord, and that He may endow these brethren, with a large measure of His Holy Spirit, to the end that ' they may hold fast the faithful word, and be able by sound doctrine both to exhort and to convince gainsayers,' (Titus I. 9.) and that they may ' feed the Church of God which he has purchased with his own blood.' (Acts 20. 28.)

" In the name of the Provinical Elders' Conference.

ROBERT DE SCHWEINITZ,
President.

Bethlehem Pa., August 27, 1870."

On Thanksgiving Day, November, 24, 1870, the Right Rev. John C. Jacobson, one of the senior Bishops of the Moravian Church in the Northern Province in the United States, departed this life at his residence in Bethlehem, Pa., in the 76th year of his age. In Bishop Jacobson the Church loses one of her most devoted and active servants. He had consecrated himself in early life fully to the work of a minister of Jesus Christ in the Moravian Church, and the completeness of this devotion kept him during the long service of more than fifty years always active and diligent, always cheerful and hopeful.

He was consecrated a Bishop of the Church

at Litiz, Lancaster County, Pa., September 15, 1854, in which office he served for the last time at the consecration of Bishops, in August of the present year.

The funeral of the departed Bishop took place on Sunday, the first in Advent. The solemn services were conducted by the Bishops, De Schweinitz and Shultze. The choir of the church at Bethlehem performed with wonderful power and pathos, " Blessed are the dead which die in the Lord," from Spohr's " Last Judgment." The coffin was borne to the grave by six clergymen of the Church.

In the *Moravian* for October 27, 1870, will be found the following interesting account of an ." Annual ' Vesper' of the Moravian Historical Society."

" Many an uncertain mind was gladdened as the morning of the 19th of October, 1870, dawned bright and clear, and the sun poured forth its cheering rays over the varied autumn landscape. This was the day on which the annual ' Vesper' of the Moravian Historical Society was to be held, and whose advent had so long been awaited by all those who love to spend an afternoon in the old fashioned Brethren's style; in talking over the scenes of former days, and learning from the experience of the pioneers of our church in this country. Already in the forenoon the familiar faces of brethren and sisters from other congregations could be seen in the streets of Nazareth, all wending their way to the old church edifice, where the rooms of the Society are located. After spending some time in examining the museum, with its numerous and interesting relics of ancient times, whose history alone would fill volumes, our thoughts were suddenly called away from this subject by the ringing of several of the old bells, mementoes of some of the first Moravian settlements in America. This was the signal for all to repair to the tables, and there to enjoy all the pleasures of a genuine ' vesper.' A few minutes after two o'clock, the sixty-two members present were called to order by the President, Rev. Eugene Leibert, and after singing a hymn, were informed that every one should help himself. Never was business more heartily and cheerfully engaged in. With such tempting pieces of real Moravian sugar-cake, bona fide rye bread, and fresh apple butter before him, how could any one be backward?

"While the vesper progressed, various subjects of interest to the Society were discussed, and under the blue clouds of smoke that soon overhung the assembly, many a peal of laughter resounded, as some gray-haired sire recounted some adventure that he had had many years ago. Nor was more important business neglected. The proposed purchase of the old 'Ephrata property' occupied a considerable part of the attention of those present. This, comprising as it does, the venerable Whitefield House, would be a most desirable relic for the Society to possess, both to preserve it from the impious hands of modern 'improvement,' and as a suitable place in which the Historical Society could have its museum and rooms permanently situated. Although all appeared to appreciate the liberality of the price at which the property is offered ($1,500) and the appropriateness of our having this interesting property in our hands, no further action was taken than to recommend the subject to the favorable consideration of the Board of Managers.*

"While this question was being discussed, a cable dispatch received by the Provincial Elders' Conference was passed around, and perused with great interest. It contained a laconic announcement that Bro. Augustus Schultze had accepted a call as Professor in the Moravian College at Bethlehem: 'Shultze hat angenommen.'

"Several relics also were at this time presented to the Society. A nicely framed photograph of the old 'Kingsly House' at Wyalusing, built in 1768, by Moravian Indians, under the direction of Heckewelder was, presented by Bro. Ed. Welles. Bro. Wm. Jordan presented a smaller copy of the same, while Dr. Maurice C. Jones donated a

piece of wood and some mortar from this ancient structure. The latter gentleman likewise donated some Indian relics found in Wyalusing, and Miss Clara Henry, several wild plums, plucked from a tree in the settlement. A photograph of the Whitefield House was presented by Bro. Wm. Jordan. Another very curious relic, presented by Mr. Lehr, was a Moravian catechism of the year 1736, as the title says, 'for the use of teachers who do not know better.' In reading the list of contributions of the last year, the President remarked that their number seemed to grow less and less as the Society grew older, and urged each member to strive to add to the museum by his personal exertions.

"As Dr. Jones had, during the course of the year, made a visit to Wyalusing, he was called upon to give an account of his trip. He said that his party had explored the old 'Kingsley House' from cellar to garret, and, that nothing had escaped their curiosity. From a tree which Heckewelder had planted, they gathered some apples, which they pronounced excellent, but Dr. Jones, as he did not get any, considered them rather sour.

"A very interesting account of the fire department of former times in Moravian settlements was given by Bro. Jedidiah Weiss, who had himself risen from the ranks of a common fireman to the distinguished office of Fire Inspector. At first, he said, all the responsibilities of this office rested on the clergy; but later, when ministers were no longer as "smart" as formerly, a special officer had to be elected, whose duty it was to visit every house in the settlement, to inspect all the stoves, chimneys, &c., and to advise all the house-wives to maintain constant caution and vigilance.

"Thus, divided between pleasure and business, interspersed with a plentiful supply of wit and anecdote, the afternoon passed swiftly by, and after a resolution had been passed, requesting the President to appoint some person or persons to prepare papers on historical subjects, to be read at the next annual Vesper, the meeting adjourned. Slowly and

* The property has since been purchased by a well-known Moravian gentleman, and presented to the Society.

reluctantly each one prepared to leave for his home, and as we separated, there was none who did not say that the afternoon had been pleasantly and profitably spent, God willing, there should not one such anniversary be held in the future at which he would not be present."

At this meeting Part IV. of the "Transactions of the Moravian Historical Society" was issued. It contains a "Sketch of the History of the Bible in Bohemia," by William G. Malin, a very interesting and valuable paper, and "The Establishment of the Moravian Congregations in Ohio," by Jesse Blickensderfer, a sketch that contains much new and interesting information. All members of the Society are entitled to a copy of the Transactions.

The town of Bethlehem was founded within the limits of *Bucks County*, and on the 10th of March, 1746, the inhabitants presented a petition to the Court for the formation of a Township, which was granted, although it was not surveyed and laid out till the year 1762, when it was done by GEORGE GOLKOWSKY. The names of the petitioners were, NATHANIAL SEIDEL, HENRY ANTES, JOHN BROWNFIELD, SAMUEL POWELL, MATTHIAS WEISS, JOHN OKELY, FREDERICK CAMMERHOFF, GEORGE NEISSER, CHRISTOPHER PYRLEUS, JAMES BURNSIDE, JOSEPH POWELL, JASPER PAYNE, and JOSEPH SPANGENBERG.

After the dissolution of the "Œconomy," in 1762, Lots in Bethlehem were sold to the following individuals, each of whom soon erected dwellings thereon for the use of their families: ANDREW BORHEK, *Weaver;* WILLIAM BOEHLER, *Wheelwright;* LUDWIG HUELBENER, *Potter;* DANIEL KUNKLER, *Shopkeeper;* GEORGE SHINDLER, *Carpenter;* FRANCIS THOMAS, *Joiner;* DEWALT KORNMAN, *Skindresser.*

Some of the houses already erected by the Society were also sold; HENRY KRAUSE, *Butcher,* and GOTTLEIB LANGE, *Saddler,* and some others, each purchased a house.

There is a very valuable and excellent old map of a part of Bethlehem, drawn on the 12th of January, 1757, now in the possession of the Historical Society of Pennsylvania,

hanging in a conspicuous place in their Library rooms in Philadelphia. The houses and farm buildings on the west side of Main Street, and the mills on the Manckasy are not represented on the plan; it contains only that portion of the town situated on the east side of Main Street, together with some projected buildings, including the Tavern, (now known as the "Sun Hotel,") which were afterwards erected, but not altogether in accordance with the plan. It is quaintly written in German on the western side of the map, that "The rest of Bethlehem is down below here."

The chief point, however, in connection with this old relic, is the fact, that upon the lot where the large Moravian Church now stands, there was, as appears on the map, two large log houses, and not one, as has been hereinbefore stated, at page 19. One stood at the south-east corner of the lot, near the Gemein Haus, and was called the *Married Men's House;* the other stood at the north-west corner of the church lot, and was known as the *Married Women's House.* These houses were used by, and called *The Married People's Houses.* Having sought for more light on the subject, I received a note from Mr. John Jordan, Jr., of Philadelphia, the well known Antiquarian and Bibliographer, in which he says, "You are correct in your surmise in regard to the occupance of separate houses by the married people after the time Bethlehem was settled, and I think the custom continued until the change of the Œconomy in 1762, or thereabout. The separation was of course but partial, and worked well so long as the enthusiasm which distinguished our early settlers lasted."

This explains the foot note to page 189 of the History of Lehigh Valley, which is as follows: "Married people met together only once or twice a week. The Brother lived in the Men's House, and the Sister in the Women's House. For some years there was a lack of dwelling houses."

The Rev. Wm. C. Reichel, who is now engaged in writing a full and exhaustive history of Bethlehem for the Historical Society of Pennsylvania, a Moravian minister, a resident of Bethlehem, the author of the "Bethlehem Souvenir," and of the "Historical Sketch of Nazareth Hall," who examined the old map with me, says, "The practice of keeping the married people separate was abolished about 1747 or 1748.

On the map it will be noticed that Main Street, as now laid out, is called *The new road to Burnside*, and that *The old road to Burnside* is also indicated. JAMES BURNSIDE was born in Ireland, in 1708, emigrated to Georgia in 1734, and in August, 1746, became a member of the Moravian Church. His farm (now BENJAMIN C. UNANGST's) was situated near Bethlehem, and the road led to it. He was the first member from *Northampton County* in the Provincial Assembly. He died at his farm-house on the 8th of August, 1755.

The illustration heading Chapter 3rd, page 19, represents the "Water Tower," as attached to the west end of the "Married Men's House," which was not the case, it only appeared so in taking the view. The Tower, in fact, stood in the centre of the church lot, and between the Married Men's and Women's Houses.

There was a bird's eye view of Bethlehem, dated 1755, published for sale at the Fair of the U. S. Sanitary Commission, in 1864, held in Logan Square, Philadelphia, which gives a correct representation of the two old buildings referred to, and their position on the Church lot. The "Married Women's House" was in 1754 used as a school-house for the boys. (See Life of Heckewelder, page 33, showing that Mr. Reichel is correct.)

The building on the old map, referred to in the "Explication" thereon, as the "Boy's Institute," and which I have called the "Nursery," was, so says Mr. Reichel, "built for the use of the *Married Men*, and was at one time occupied by *five divisions* of them." During the Indian Wars, all the children were gathered together from Nazareth, and the other Moravian towns, and brought to Bethlehem for protection; the smaller children were placed in this building in charge of some of the Sisters of the Bethlehem Congre-

gation, detailed for that purpose; hence the common name of the old House, torn down during the summer of 1870, to make room for the new Publication Office of the Moravian Church. All the old residents of the town called it "The Nursery;" I have followed their example. It was sometimes called the "Old Œconomy Building."

Mrs. Friday says, "The Nursery was an institution which was formed by the necessity of circumstances. The great amount of labor to be done in the building of houses, clearing the lands, farming, procuring building materials, &c., besides keeping constant watch night and day, made it necessary that every means should be taken to bring all the recourses of the inhabitants to bear. The females could assist in farming, such as rake hay, spread grass, plant and hoe potatoes and corn, husk corn, load hay, &c.; but mothers were prevented by their children. A NURSERY was thereupon instituted, where children two years of age were taken and raised under the supervision of the Church. To this institution many objections were found; it did not work as well as desired, and as soon as the *Œconomy* was abolished, (having things in common), the Institution was discontinued. It must be said however, that although the children so raised had not the parental feelings as those raised by the affectionate mother, yet some of the best citizens Bethlehem ever had were so brought up. In those days Economy ruled; in order to save paper, pen and ink, the children were taught at school to write with uncut quills on pressed sand."

In the same "Explication," on the old map, "The Corpse House" is called "The House for the bodies of the Lambs of God," at least that is the literal translation of the sentence, for the "Explication" is written in the German language. Near the corner of Main and Market Streets, standing in the street, is an erection marked O, which was the "Watch Tower," built during the first Indian Wars, in 1755.

A company of gentlemen have recently purchased the high hill and plain west of

Bethlehem, which is separated from the town by the Manokasy Creek, and have built a handsome iron bridge across that stream at Broad Street, connecting their land, which is now being laid out in lots, with the town. This new part of the town is called West Bethlehem.

The MANOKASY (this mode of spelling is my own, and is in accordance with the pronunciation of the name) Creek runs through the town and empties into the Lehigh at the foot of Nisky Hill. The old Moravians called this creek the *Manakes*, with an acute accent over the second a. Heckewelder says the Indian name was *Menagassi*, with an acute accent over the first a, meaning "a creek with many bends." The Rev. Wm. C. Reichel, the well known Moravian author and antiquarian, writes the name MANAKASY, with an acute accent over the first two a's in the name, this gives the word in the German pronunciation the same sound as my spelling, MANOKASY. The name has of late been rendered MONOCCACY, while it is pronounced Manokasy, which is absurd. There is a river in Maryland, and an Island in the Susquehanna, near Wilks-Barre, both called the *Monoccacy*, and I hope the Bethlehemites will call their creek by its proper name hereafter, and write the name as it is pronounced in English and German, *Manokasy*.

Manockissee, is another erroneous mode of spelling the name of this creek. Almost always during the summer months, the bed of the creek, a few miles north of Bethlehem, becomes as dry as the surrounding "Drylands," through which it has its course. It owes its existence entirely to the springs in its vicinity, many of which are in its very bed, as can easily be seen during the dry spell of any one of our summers. *Monockicey*, is the way Rupp, in his History of Northampton County, page 79, spells the name of the creek.

There was an old Indian Chief, called *Monokghichan*, living about 1737, it may be possible that the name of the creek has some connection with him.

"The Apothecary Shop," or first Drug Store in Bethlehem, was kept in the house now owned and occupied by Simon Rau, on Main Street, near the Moravian Church, and which he uses for the same purpose. Dr. Matthew Otto was the first Apothecary in the town, and in the County. He established his Laboratory about 1745. The medicines were prepared with great care, and were sent to Philadelphia, where they were in much demand. The profits from this source by the Œconomy were larger than from any other kind of manufacture carried on in the village. In 1782, Timothy Horsfield is spoken of as having been in charge of the Apothecary Shop, and after him, Eberhard Freytag conducted the business for the Society. There are now many very handsome Drug Stores in the town; the most extensive of which is owned and conducted by Matthew M. Selfridge, on Main Street, opposite the "Eagle Hotel." His business is both by wholesale and retail. Edward T. Myers owns also a fine Drug establishment on Main Street. He occupies a portion of the building as his residence. His lot was formerly included in the "Sun Hotel" property, and was purchased by him only a few years ago.

The manufacture of Pottery was extensively carried on by Lewis Huebener, about the year 1782, and previously. It was one of the first branches of industry carried on in the town. Apple-butter making in those days was universal in the vicinity, and when the fruit was abundant, the demand for the earthen crocks, in which it was put, was often so great, that all could not be supplied. A most excellent preserve is apple-butter; but nothing like the quantity is made now, the apple trees seem to be dying out in Pennsylvania; ploughing up the apple orchards injures the trees and retards their growth. There are in the old gardens in Bethlehem, apple trees still bearing immense quantities of fruit; the size of those old patriarchs is something astonishing.

Mr. Huebener manufactured tiles for the floors in houses; some can be seen in the "Sister's House;" also tiles for the large stoves, made after the fashion of those still in use in Germany. Tiles were also made for roofing purposes; and the hardware store of HENRY S. KRAUSE, in Main Street, is roofed with some of them, which are as perfect as when first made. Some other ancient structures are also covered with these old tiles. Pipe heads were also made in large quantities. Occasionally small quantities of tobacco are raised in the vicinity of Bethlehem, and the manufacture of segars engages the attention of a large class of people on the line of the North Pennsylvania Rail Road, at the present time.

In 1771, the Society for the Culture of Silk, located in the city of Philadelphia, awarded the premium of £10 for the greatest quantity of cocoons above twenty thousand, to *Joanna Etwein*, of Bethlehem. Reeled silk was extensively manufactured in Pennsylvania about this time, and sent to England to be woven and returned. The Society prepared during this season, one hundred and fifty pounds of reeled silk of such quality, as sold in England for twenty and twenty-five shillings per pound, exclusive of the Parliamentary bounty.

The following article, cut from the *Easton Sentinel*, for June, 1834, introduces a well known inhabitant of Bethlehem and "*a mammoth trout*. General Cadwalader and lady, of Philadelphia, being on a visit to Bethlehem, Pa., Mr. George H. Goundie presented to Mr. Zeigler, of the *Eagle Hotel*, one of the largest *brook trout* perhaps ever known in this country, which was served up in his best style, at a dinner on last Monday to the General and lady, and a party of ladies and gentlemen of Bethlehem. The trout measured 22 inches in length, 19 inches in circumference, and weighed 7½ pounds; it was raised by Mr. Jacob Schneider, of the Lehigh Water Gap, who has kept it for the last six years in a trough in the second story of his house. We understand Mr. Goundie, of Bethlehem, has about 400 fine trout yet in his trout house, measuring from 10 to 17 inches in length."

Dr. JOHN FREDERICK AUGUSTUS STECKEL,

was a Swedish Physician, who resided for a number of years in Bethlehem. He was full of *fun*, wit and anecdote. His language was an odd mixture of Swedish, German and English, and it was said that " Dr. Steckel spoke no language." The following lines are attributed to him, or what is more probable, are written in imitation of his peculiar mode of speech.

FAREWELL TO BETHLEHEM.

By Dr. John Frederick Augustus Steckel, November 24th, 1826.

Oh Bethlehem dou'rt not the leasht,
In Judas Coundry in de Easht,
Dou Bethlehem here in Immidashon,
Were Bilgrims come from every nashon
To see the wonders dat are dolt
Wit dose gued friends I oft did go
To show and dell them all I know,
Of Judas lant I could not dell
Where Sheperds mit dere sheep did dwell;
But as dis is a new creashon
Of harmless lambs of every nashon,
Who know dere Sheperd's voice and view
De Bath he leads, and him persue
Dat Basture wich did feed dat Flock
Bermitted friends at tree o'clock
Do witness all dere Educashon
Dere science great and recreashon
Mit music charms—Angelic strain
Were Joy and bleasure banish Bain,
All dose enjoyments I dit view
Must leave them *all* and bit Adieu
Oh Lehigh! dou shweet stream dat rolls,
Enlivent by dine *Arks* wit Coals
May prosperous dy commerce free
Dy floating arks returning be,
Wit passengers from ev'ry nashon
To visit Bethlehem's situashon;
No more dose scenes I shall survey,
Dy burling stream dat flows so gay,
Dy Croves, dy Isle, dy Cryshtall Spring
We wistom shtrength and beauty sing,
Where *Choirs* of Angels by us glite
Wit dere fair *Nurses* by their side
Embark in safe Abbottos' barge
And on *Kallibso's* Island march,
Enjoy dere habbiness and sing,
Make rocks and vales shweet echoes bring
Dose shweet delights I oft dit view
Must leave dem all and bit adieu
And since stern fate has bit me go,
Do all my friends I bit adieu;
I leave you all wit great regret

Your blessing shall attend my speed
Your symbathetic sorrows klaim
My warmest tanks, accept de same.

Farewell my friends, fate bits me go,
Farewell my neighbors all—Adieu
No more I'll see dose tender scenes
Were lovely youts widen dere deens
Mit dears of Joy dere frients did meet
Or part wid dem wit sore regret
My heart dit melt wit tenderness
Do see their Joy or sore regret
From scenes like dese I now must go,
And bit my dear young friends adieu;
Your joyful hearts wid mine dit glow
On all cecashons you dit show
When joyfull med on feshdel days
To celebrade our Saviour's praise
Wit music, joyful hymns dit sing
De glory of our heavenly King,
But all is lost! Fate bits me go
Farewell fair sisters all—Adieu,
Now Flora, beautiful and gay,
De dime is come, I musht obey,
I worshib'd dee all day and night,
Dy fragrant blushns were my delight
Not mine alone, but all mankind
Did by dere bresence pleasure fint
But fate decrees dat I must go,
And leave you now, and bit adieu,
No more I hear the serenading,
Mitin thy Bowry consecrating,
Mit soft harmonious symphony,
Mit bleasing notes and cheerful glee.
No more dose airs, dat gentle dell,
De shweetest sound, De Convent Bell;
From all dose scenes mit grief I go
And bit fair Flora now adieu.
De signal sounts, it calls me fort,
It points to Sout, I have de Nord;
Perhaps to Easht, perhaps to Wesht,
Wich bleases God is for de best,
No wife, no child, laments for me,
From dose afflicsions I am free,
Farewell my frents, fate bits me go
Farewell! Farewell! once more adieu.

On the 2nd of January, 1871, "THE WIDOW'S SOCIETY, of *Bethlehem*," celebrated its 100th Anniversary, at that place. *One hundred* members of the Society from Nazareth and Bethlehem, were present at the meeting and partook of a social Love-feast; the Right Rev. Brother, Bishop Edmund de Schweinitz, presiding.

The name of the Society does not fully express its object, which is, to insure to the widows of the deceased members, a yearly dividend, the income being divided pro rata among the claimants. Members are received at any age, the custom has, however, been to permit young men to become members upon their marriage, on their paying a subscription fee of fifty dollars. There are no other payments to be made to the Society, except by such as join after they are fifty years old, in that case, they pay annually, in addition to the entrance fee, one dollar.

The Society was organized January 1st, 1771. The first payments amounted to £950, Pennsylvania currency. That sum was loaned to JAMES BURNSIDE, on a mortgage on the *Nain Indian Mission property*, which had been purchased by him.

In 1821, the Society was chartered by the Legislature. The invested assets of the corporation now amount to the sum of $32,000.

Any male member of the *Moravian Church in America*, being in sound health, may become a member of the Society, and his widow after his death, will receive her pro rata share of the yearly income of the Society during the remainder of her life.

The present officers of the Society are :

JOHN MATTHEW MIKSCH, *President.*
RUDOLPH RAUCH, *Treasurer.*
Rev. AMBROSE RONDTHALER, *Secretary.*

Bethlehem has some few public buildings viz :—The *Citizen's, Concert, Masonic,* and Christian Association Halls, used for the meetings of the respective societies, and for such other societies as are common in American towns.

The first National Bank of Bethlehem has a handsome banking house on Main Street, nearly opposite the Sun Hotel, with a fine dwelling attached for the cashier. Charles Augustus Luckenback is the President of the Institution.

The *Vineyards,* on the west bank of the Manokasy Creek, where the attempt was made to cultivate the grape, and failed; has been cut up into building lots, and is now covered by the houses and gardens of the thriving village of West Bethlehem.

In 1853, the Pennsylvania and Lehigh Zinc Company's works were erected on the lands of the "Crown Farm," and have become the nucleus of quite a large town. It was first laid out by Charles Augustus Luckenback, in 1849, and called *Augusta*, the name was after changed in 1854, and the town called *Wetherill*, out of compliment to Col. Samuel Wetherill, one of the projectors of the place. Subsequently the name was again changed to *Bethlehem South*, and finally, in 1865, it was incorporated as a borough under its present name of SOUTH BETHLEHEM, and Louis F. Beckel, elected Chief Burgess. At the present time, Elisha P. Wilbur is the Chief Burgess; and the town contains a population of about 3,556 souls.

The Zinc Works were put in operation in the fall of the year 1853. These works were built by Col. Samuel Wetherill, for the purpose of making the White Oxide of Zinc under his Patents. *Spelter* was first made here from Lehigh ores, in 1854, and for several years thereafter costly experiments were made by Col. Wetherill, to discover mixtures of refractory clay which would stand the heat required to make zinc; in 1858, he discovered a satisfactory mixture, and adopted a plan, which was not completed when the "Great Rebellion" broke out. Then the man of science, like a gallant gentleman, dropped his crucibles and retorts, and entered the service of his country, as a Captain of cavalry in the 11th regiment of Pennsylvania volunteers, September 25, 1861, with a company raised by his own exertions, and served with distinction until he was mustered out as a Major, on October 1, 1864, after having participated in forty-two battles and skirmishes, without having received a wound. On the 13th of March, 1865, he was brevetted a Lieut. Colonel for his services before Richmond, Va.

In the meantime, the Zinc Company had imported skilled laborers from France, and put in practice the French process with great success.

In 1864, they erected the first sheet zinc rolling mill in the United States. And on the 1st of April, 1865, the first sheet zinc ever made in America, was rolled there under the direction of Professor Alexander Trippel.

The Company's mines are situated near the village of Friedensville, in Saucon Valley, about four miles south of Bethlehem, on the old Post Road to Philadelphia, and close to the southern side of the Lehigh Hills. The ore is hauled to the works, over the hills by horse-teams. The largest mine is known by the name of the *Ueberroth* Zinc Mine. This deposit of zinc ore was first discovered by Wm. Theodore Roepper, (Professor, now, of Mineralogy and Geology, in the Lehigh University,) in the year 1845.

The structures erected by the "Bethlehem Iron Company," in South Bethlehem, for their Iron Works, are a splendid series of buildings, of magnificent proportions, and attract great attention. The works have now been in successful operation for over ten years, under the very able superintendence of Mr. John Fritz, of Bethlehem.

A Paper Bag Manufactory was started in Bethlehem in 1854, by Mr. Francis Wolle, the inventor, and is called the *Union Paper Bag Machine Company.*

Bethlehem baskets, very handsome and very strong, are a specialty with some Moravian folks in the vicinity of the town; they make them all sizes, and being very durable, they find a ready sale.

There are some comfortable old fashioned chairs manufactured in the town by *Michael Stuber*, called Bethlehehem chairs, which have quite a reputation in Philadelphia and New York, and are in much demand. Some of the queer old chairs made and used in Bethlehem when it was first settled, are still to be found in many old residences, and in the Museum of the Missionary Society; being made of boards, they look stiff, and are hard and uncomfortable to sit upon. They are of the kind quite common to be seen in German paintings, even of the present day, and are still in use in some parts of Germany.

Bethlehem has many handsome private residences, but the most deserving of notice in that respect, is the one erected by Dr. Frederick Martin, at the northwest corner of Market and High Streets. Dr. Martin, also built afterwards a very handsome house on the highest point in South Bethlehem, now owned and occupied by Robert F. Packer. John Lerch has erected a very fine private residence for his family, on Market Street; as have also Owen Mack, and John B. Zimmele. Weston Dodson, Augustus Wolle, Abraham S. Schropp, Cornelius M. Knauss, Charles Brodhead, Esq., Ambrose J. Erwin, Richard W. Leibert, and others, have handsome residences.

There are but few indications now of Bethlehem being a Moravian settlement, In 1842, the "lease system" was abrogated, and the land sold on irredeemable ground rents. In 1845, the town was incorporated as a borough; and in 1851, the ground rents were made redeemable; since then the town has rapidly increased in size and population. Portions of the old town alone retain in some degree its ancient characteristics; the manufactories being mostly confined to the vicinity of the river, railroads and canal, while on the Hill are built the residences of the increasing population.

In 1867, the "New Street Bridge Company" was incorporated, and the bridge, 1170 feet in length, was constructed of wood, standing on eight piers, spanning the Lehigh and Susquehanna Railroad, the Lehigh Canal, the Manokasy Creek, the Sand Island, the Lehigh River, and the Lehigh Valley Railroad, and connects the two towns of Bethlehem and South Bethlehem. It was first opened for travel on the 21st day of August, 1867, although no tolls were taken till the first of September. The toll-house, erected in 1869, is a fine brick office, with a comfortable dwelling attached, for the family of the toll-keeper, it stands on the east side of the northern extremity of the bridge. The bridge is a very handsome and graceful structure; and the fine views from it of the surrounding country, make it a place of frequent resort for all visitors to the town. The original cost of this bridge was $65,000.

The Broad Street Bridge, which was completed and opened for travel in the month of April, 1871, connects the old portion of the town with the new part, now rapidly building, called West Bethlehem. The new structure is of iron, extending across the deep ravine down which the Manokasy flows in its course through the town. The bridge is a very high and graceful affair, with a roadway for vehicles, and side walks for passengers; and from it there are extensive views up and down the Manokasy. This bridge was constructed by Samuel R. Dickson, of New Haven, Connecticut. It is 400 feet in length, and 70 feet above the water. The superstructure is of wrought iron, upon cast iron piers, the parts are fastened together with hot rivets, of which there were 38,000 used. The entire cost of the erection was about $50,000.

The handsome Episcopal church in South Bethlehem, was built in the year 1864, and the Rectory in 1866. The Rev. E. N. Potter, son of the late Bishop Alonzo Potter, of Pennsylvania, was the first rector, and was succeeded by the Rev. Mr. Nevin, better known during the Rebellion as the commander of " Nevin's Celebrated Battery of Artillery." The Rev. Cortland Whitehead is the present incumbent.

Since the insertion of the Military Record of Bethlehem, there has been quite a revival in martial affairs in the vicinity. Gen. James L. Selfridge, having been appointed by Governor Geary, Division Commander, with the rank of Major General, and several volunteer companies formed, viz:—Selfridge Guards, Company A, organized Dec. 15, 1870, James R. Roney, Captain; C. O. Zeigenfuss, 1st Lieut.; Millon A. Beahm, 2nd Lieut.; Sergeants, Frederick J. Rice, Orderly, Clinton T. Weaver, George, D. Myers, Ammon A. Gardner, Victor A. Desh ; Corporals, Geo. B. Fickart, Joseph P. Miller, William F. Beckel, George M. Wilhelm, Charles Keller, Albert Kleckner, Edward Borhek, and 48 privates.

Selfridge Guards, Company B., J. Alfred

Mohr, Captain; *Daniel Fatzinger*, 1st Lieut.; *Francis Engle*, 2nd Lieut., and 49 men.

And in South Bethlehem the *Wilbur Guards*, organized in August, 1870, *M. J. Whertie*, Captain; *Michael Boyle*, 1st Lieut.; *M. J. Ryan*, 2nd Lieut., and 45 non-commissioned officers and privates.

The LEHIGH UNIVERSITY is located in South Bethlehem. The college went into operation on Sep. 1st, A. D. 1865, with a class of forty-three students, (See programme of Examination of June 25, 1867,) with COL. HENRY COPPEE, L. L. D, a graduate of the U. S. Military Academy at West Point, as President.

This magnificent institution owes its existence to the generosity of ASA PACKER, who of his own volition, in the year 1865 appropriated out of his large private fortune, the sum of $500,000, and fifty-six acres of land on the north side of the Lehigh hills, for the purpose of founding this educational institute.

The design of the founder in making this munificent endowment, was to provide for the young men of Lehigh Valley the means of acquiring such a complete professional education, as would fit them for the practical and active pursuits of this country. This view is to be kept continually in mind, so that civil engineering, mining, chemistry, metallurgy, agriculture and railway contruction, are to be the chief branches.

"University Day," June 24, 1869, was held in the chapel of the magnificent pile known as "Packer Hall," where the first pupils of the college graduated, their names were J. Haynes Corbin, Barbadoes, W. I.; Miles Rock, Lancaster, Pa.; Chas. E. Ronaldson, Philadelphia; Charles W. Roepper and Clarence A. Wolle, Bethlehem, Pa.

Previous to the erection of Packer Hall, the lecture rooms and students' quarters, were located at "Christmas Hall," once the Moravian Mission Chapel in South Bethlehem, now included in the grounds of the University. Charles Brodhead, Esq., of Bethlehem, presented the University with seven additional acres of ground, and Mr. Robert

H. Sayre erected at his own expense, an Astronomical Observatory on the grounds of the Institute, for the use of the students.

The course of study lasts for four years. The first two years of the student are devoted to such elementary branches as are needful to fit a young man for any profession or business in life he may afterwards see proper to follow. The last two years are given to the study of any particular branch the pupil may decide upon as the one necessary to success in the business he intends to pursue during life. The approximate expenses for tuition,* board, books, and washing, may be set down as a maximum of $350 per year. There are two competitive scholarships in each class, which entitle the gainers to room rent, board and tuition, free for the successful academic year. It is to be hoped that the college may be endowed by men of wealth with more such scholarships; the rules of the Institute permit it, and the scholarship will bear the name of the person making the endowment. Partial courses may also be taken by such as desire to study only some particular branch taught in the College, in which they desire to become proficient.

The faculty of the University consists at present, of

HENRY COPPEE, *President*,
Professor of History and English Literature.

PROFESSORS.

Rev. ELIPHALET NOTT POTTER, M. A.,
Professor of Moral and Mental Philosophy and of Christian Evidences.

CHARLES F. CHANDLER, successor to
Charles Mayer Wetherill, Ph. D., M. D.,†
Professor of Chemistry.

HIERO B. HERR, in place of

* By a late further gift of Judge Packer, tuition is given free of charge.

† Dr. Charles Mayer Wetherill, Ph. D., Professor of Chemistry in the Lehigh University, died suddenly on Sunday morning, March 5th, 1871, of disease of the heart, at his residence, in South Bethlehem, Pa. He was a son of the late Charles and Margaretta S. Wetherill, of Philadelpdia.

Edwin Wright Morgan, LL.D., deceased.*
Professor of Mathematics and Mechanics.
ALFRED MARSHALL MAYER, PH.D.,
Professor of Physics and Astronomy.
WILLIAM THEODORE ROEPPER, Esq.,
Professor of Mineralogy and Geology, and Curator of
the Museum.
H. STANLEY GOODWIN, C. E.,
Demonstrator of Civil Engineering.
BENJAMIN W. FRAZIER, Professor, and
RICHARD P. ROTHWELL, C. E.,
Demonstrator of Mining and Metallurgy.
CHARLES F. KROEH, A. M.,
Instructor of French and German.
Mr. WALDRON SHAPLEIGH,
Instructor in Chemistry.
J. N. BARR, S. B.,
Instructor of Mathematics and Drawing.
WILLIAM A. LAMBERTON, A. M.,
Instructor of Greek and Latin.
Founder of the University,
Hon. ASA PACKER.

Board of Trustees.

Right Rev. Wm. Bacon Stevens, D.D.,
Bishop of Pennsylvania, *President.*

Hon. Asa Packer, Mauch Chunk.
Charles Brodhead, Esq., Bethlehem.
W. F. Conyngham, Esq., Wilks-Barre.
Franklin B. Gowen, Esq., Philadelphia.
Mr. George W. Childs,   "
H. Stanley Goodwin, Bethlehem.
Rev. Cortland Whitehead, "
Eckley B. Coxe, Philadelphia.
J. I. Blakslee, Mauch Chunk.
Chas. O. Skeer,   "
Rev. L. Coleman,   "
Hon. I. W. Maynard, Easton.
Mr. Robert H. Sayre, South Bethlehem.

* On April 16, 1869.—Colonel Edwin Wright Morgan, Professor of Mathematics and Mechanics at Lehigh University, died at the Sun Hotel, Bethlehem. He entered the U. S. Military Academy at West Point in 1833, and graduated third in his class in 1837. Served as Lieutenant-Colonel of the Eleventh Infantry U. S. A. in the Mexican War, after which, he accepted the Superintendency of the Kentucky Institute, which post he filled to the opening of the civil war. Colonel Morgan, by his high attainments and skill, did much to produce and give excellence to the public works of Pennsylvania and Kentucky and other States.

Mr. Wm. H. Sayre, Jr., South Bethlehem.
Mr. Robert A. Packer, *Secretary,*   "
G. B. Linderman, M.D.,   "
Mr. John Fritz, Bethlehem, Pa.
Mr. Harry E. Packer, Mauch Chunk.
Mr. Joseph Harrison, Jr., Philadelphia.
Mr. Elisha P. Wilbur, *Treasurer.*
Mr. Ed. Tuckerman Potter, *Architect.*
Capt. James Jenkins, *Constructor.*

Homo Minister et Interpres Naturæ.

The Lehigh University is now under the auspices of the Protestant Episcopal Church, and the buildings are handsome and in good taste, except the wooden erection covered with slate, forming a kind of a steeple on the stone tower at the western end of " Packer Hall." This should be torn away, and the top of the stone tower, which is a model structure ; should be embattled, like those of ancient castles, from which on "High-days" and holidays, our starry banner could be given to the winds. Why a university should have a steeple like a church, as was the original intention, I am sure I don't know, unless it is because there is a chapel connected with it. It was once the intention to put a steeple on the Masonic Temple at Philadelphia, as will be seen by the original plan, fortunately a protest in the *Sunday Dispatch*, prevented the Temple of our Honorable and Ancient Order, from being mistaken for a church.

STUDENTS OF THE FIRST CLASS.

From the fourth page of the Programme of the LEHIGH UNIVERSITY.

First UNIVERSITY DAY, June 25, 1867.

Including those who have been in attendance from Sep't 1; 1866 to Sep't 1, 1867.

Howland L. Ashmead, *Philadelphia.*
Lehman Preston Ashmead, *Philadelphia.*
Edward C. Boutelle, *Bethlehem, Pa.*
Richard Brodhead, *South Bethlehem.*
William R. Butler, *Mauch Chunk, Pa.*
Richard J. Carter, *Tamaqua, Pa.*
J. Haynes H. Corbin, *Barbadoes, W. I.*
George L. Cummins, *Louisville, Ky.*
Milton Dimmick, *Mauch Chunk, Pa.*
E. Albert Dobbins, *New York City.*
J. T. Reynolds Evans, *Fort Wayne, Ind.*
Frank E. Forster, *Muncy, Pa.*
Charles W. Forster, *Mauch Chunk, Pa.*

John Hunt, *Catasauqua, Pa.*
George A. Jenkins, *South Bethlehem.*
Henry C. Jenkins, *South Bethlehem.*
William H. Jenkins, *Wyoming, Pa.*
William J. Kerr, Jr., *New York City.*
A. Nelson Lewis, *Havre-de-Grace, Md.*
Peter D. Ludwig, *Tamaqua, Pa.*
Lawrence B. McCabe, *Havre-de-Grace.*
Charles McKee, *Princeton, Ill.*
George McMullin, *Mauch Chunk, Pa.*
Asa A. Packer, *Nesquehoning, Pa.*
Harry E. Packer, *Mauch Chunk, Pa.*
William L. Paine, *Wilkes-Barre, Pa.*
Joseph M. Piollet, *Wysox, Pa.*
Harry R. Price, *St. Clair, Pa.*
Henry B. Reed, *Philadelphia, Pa.*
Richard H. Roberts, *Bethlehem, Pa.*
Charles W. Roepper, *Bethlehem, Pa.*
Wm. R. Donaldson, *Philadelphia.*
Jeremiah Ryan, *South Bethlehem.*
James K. Shoemaker, *Mauch Chunk.*
John M. Thome, *Palmyra, Pa.*
Josiah Wertz, *Bethlehem, Pa.*
Barnet West, *Bethlehem, Pa.*
Robert P. Weston, *Mauch Chunk, Pa.*
Charles Wetherill, *Phœnixville, Pa.*
William C. Wetherill, *Bethlehem, Pa.*
Clarence A. Wolle, *Bethlehem, Pa.*
Russel B. Yates, *Waverly, N. Y.*
Miles Rock, *Lancaster, Pa.*

During the Summer of 1821, JOSEPH BONA-PARTE visited Bethlehem for the benefit of his health, and put himself under the medical care of the late Dr. DANIEL GREEN, an eccentric and noted physician of that day. The doctor and the pure mountain air effected a speedy cure of the ills of the former king of Spain, and he paid his physician what was a handsome fee in those days, a golden *Joe.**

ʻ The incident was thus recorded by JUDGE FRANKS, under date of August 23, 1821.

King Joe, it is said, took it into head,
    To Bethlehem air to repair, Sir;
To exhibit his wealth, and to better his health,
    Under Doctor Green's medical care, Sir.

Next morning at dawn, king Joe gave a yawn,
    And expecting his aches—ope'd his eyes, Sir;
But noble Green's skill had cured every ill,
    And the monarch rose up in surprise, Sir.

* Johannes—a Portugese gold coin of the value of about ($8) eight dollars.

For the doctor he call'd—for the doctor he bawl'd,
    To be knighted at once on the spot, Sir;
But the doctor was wise, and cast down his eyes,
    And the honor of knighthood declined, Sir.

Said, "a boon will I crave, with your majesty's
    leave,
    And a grant of it hope I will find, Sir;
In the course of my life, and that too without a wife,
    I ne'er could save a poor shilling, Sir.

"Now, a *great* JOE I have saved, and the boon I crave,
    Is a little *Joe*, if you are willing, Sir!
The king in amaze, at the doctor did gaze,
    And soon cross'd his hand with the gold, Sir—
Then packed up his purses, went off with his horses
    Leaving naught but the tale to be told, Sir.

Among the many illustrious travellers who, about this time, visited Bethlehem, may be mentioned the Duke of WEIMER, then a fine, handsome looking man, who was entertained by Dr. Steckel, at the "Eagle Hotel," and was serenaded by the "Old Bethlehem Band." The Duke wrote his travels in America, and mentions Bethlehem, LEIBERT'S TANNERY, its steam engine, and Dr. Steckel. A copy of this work, in the German, was presented to the *Bethlehem Library Company*, but I have been unable to find it. I came across in the library, however, an old and valuable History of London, presented to the Library Company in 1847, by Dr. THOMAS HORSFIELD, a former resident of the town.

It was not until 1745 that the first public roads in this part of the State were laid out; yet, even after that, for many years the former mode of travel remained the same; in fact, until 1782, all business was carried on by expresses on horseback. A visit by any of the people of Bethlehem to Philadelphia, was an event of rare occurrence, and was only undertaken once or twice a year, and then only by those whose affairs rendered such a trip absolutely necessary.

David Nitschman and his company, consisting of about one hundred persons, came to Bethlehem in the year 1742, on foot, having pack-horses carrying all their worldly goods; along what was known in those days as the *Great Minnisink Trail*, which had been used for many centuries by the *Min-*

niɯɯi tribɔ of Indians, (who lived in the regions beyond the Blue Mountains,) in their journeys to the Delaware. This trail or path crossed the Lehigh River at "Jones' Island,' about one mile east of Bethlehem; and passed through the Blue Ridge at the Wind-gap, into the wilderness to the north.

Jedidiah Irish built the mill at Shimersville on Saucon Creek sometime prior to the year 1740. It is the oldest mill in Northampton County, of which we have any record. In the year 1743, the Moravians of Bethlehem petitioned the court of Bucks County for permission to lay out a road from their settlement to Saucon Mill. The mill and land attached to it was not long afterwards purchased by John Curry, a Philadelphia lawyer, who resided at the mill for many years, and established a ferry over the Lehigh River near by, which retained the name of "Curry's Ferry," until the year 1816, when Henry Jarret built the bridge over the Lehigh at Freemansburg. Conrad Omensetter was the Ferryman at Curry's Ferry during the Revolutionary war.

The following interesting event is copied from the *New York Gazette and Post Boy*, of June 19, 1849.

" The beginning of this month three natives of *Greenland*, two young men and a young woman, converted to the Christian religion by the Moravian Missionaries in that country, were in this city on a visit to the Brethren here. They left their own country about two years since, in the ship belonging to that Society, which had carried a ready made framed church to be erected there, Greenland offering no wood for building. *This vessel sailed from this port a few days ago for Davis' Straits, with some of the* Greenlanders *on board*, who have visited Brethren in several parts of *Europe*, as England, Holland and Germany. They were clad in seal skins, with the hair on, after the manner of their own country, their eyes and hair black, like our Indians, but their complexion somewhat lighter. The Moravians, it seems, have a Mission also at *Barbill*, near *Surinam*, and two Indian converts from thence, with these Greenlanders, met lately at Bethlehem, in this province, (a settlement of the Moravians,) with some of the *Delaware* Indians, and some *Mohickons*, converts also of the Moravians; and though their native lands were so vastly remote as the latitude 5.41 and 65 N. yet they observed that each others hair, eyes and complexion, convinced them that they were all of the same race. They could find, however, no similitude in their several languages." See the first number of the *Unitas Fratrum*, Philadelphia, July, 1870.

On the first of July, 1792, the first *Post-office* was established at Bethlehem, and JOSEPH HORSFIELD appointed Postmaster, a line of stages was then started to run between the town and Philadelphia; the trip occupied then nearly two days, but the time was afterwards reduced, (in the year 1798,) to one day, by the *mail stage*. The stages continued in use until the month of January, 1857, when the North Pennsylvania Railroad Company commenced to run regular passenger trains.

An old writer discourses on this subject as follows:

" In regard to travelling by private members of the Bethlehem Moravians, the rules of the Society made it incumbent upon them to have the consent and approval of the clergy to leave the town for even a day's time; and the undertaking a journey to Philadelphia or New York, was first taken into serious consideration by the Overseer's College, as well as by the clergy in general conference assembled.

" Very few of the Moravians availed themselves of the public stages in the early period of their use. Their retired habits made it very uncongenial to them to be in the company of strangers; and in fact the Moravians of Bethlehem from 1742 to 1800, whilst they lived in the world, were not of the world. Therefore, a more congenial method was adopted. There was a private stage in Bethlehem, owned and conducted by one of the Church members; this was hired by parties for the purpose. It was customary whenever any person had a business call from any town, to defer the attending to it till others had similar motives inducing them to take a journey; in this wise, six or eight persons associated themselves, and hired friend Adam Luckenbach and his stage. To carry out this intention, frequently required several weeks' negotiations until the company was formed. Before starting, several days more were consumed to make the needful preparations for the journey. All manner of cakes and pies were baked, hams boiled, coffee ground, &c. The event created great interest in the town; and in the families of the men of the party, a commotion was observable that portended an unusual occurence. This preparation was necessary. Our travelers did not stop at any of the taverns along the road. The stage driver took with him a bag of oats, which was safely stowed under the seat of the stage, a bucket for watering the horses, swung under the body of the vehicle; and a trough for feeding them, was tied on behind. Thus provided, he fed his horses at a spring or brook alongside the road; whilst the passengers regaled themselves out of the store of provisions in their baskets. Upon arriving at a tavern or a farm-house, in the evening, they asked the use of a coffee or a tea-pot, the exhilarating beverage being prepared by them; each recurred to his or her basket, and appeased their appetites out of it. This manner of travelling was consonant to the feelings of the Moravians."

The Moravians were always careful in former times, to locate their taverns at some distance from their settlements, to keep their people free from contract with the world; and to avoid as much as possible the prying curiosity of travellers. At Bethlehem, the first inn, "The Crown," was erected on the south bank of the Lehigh. And at Nazareth the first tavern was built at the distance of a mile from the town.

In the *Northampton Conservative*, of February 16, 1870, a weekly newspaper published by Milton F. Cushing, in South Bethlehem, which at that date had reached its seventy-third number, we find the following interesting account of the "CROWN INN."

"In 1743, one hundred and twenty-seven years ago, the first tavern was built near the river, where now stands the fine Union depot. We will picture the place as it then stood, in all its rural simplicity. Toiling over rough roads for many days, indeed, a three days' journey from Philadelphia, the eye was gladdened on coming down the mountain, and following a small silvery brook, shaded by overhanging forest trees, and on taking a short turn to the west, this old hostelry came in view, an old log house, two stories high, with those small windows so common in that day, the low porch with carved pillars, the peaked roof, the well sweep, and many different objects that met your eye on approaching this old retreat, gave a charm to the landscape around. Down by the river stood a large sycamore tree, and upon a hook driven in the tree, hung the horn to summon the ferryman, if you desired to visit the Moravians on the other side. In those days of loyalty to the house of Brunswick, it bore the crown of George II, on the panel of the double door of the main entrance to this humble hostelry. On the conclusion of his lonely forest journey, the traveller could enjoy the frugal hospitalities of the house, at the following rates:

Breakfast, with tea or coffee, 4 pence; dinner 6 pence, and with a pint of beer, 8 pence; supper 4 pence, or if hot, 6 pence; lodging 2 pence; night's hay and oats, 12 pence. In the long, low reception room, at the farther end of which was the bar, with its few decanters and glasses, among the rest of bar room furniture found about the bar in those days, were powder horns, bullet-pouches, guns, deer horns, &c. In a little 6 by 9 frame, hung the License, which was granted in 1746, in the 33rd year of the reign of the Sovereign Lord, George the Second, by the Grace of God, king of Great Britain, France, Ireland, &c., to the Moravian congregation of Bethlehem.

It was at this house George Washington stopped over night with his staff on a visit to Gen. LaFayette, who lay wounded in Bethlehem.

We have still in our possession the old front door of this house, and the door of the room in which Washington slept. The different landlords, who acted both as landlord and ferryman at different times, were Ephraim Culver, in 1763—Valentine Feuhrer, in 1782; and in 1794 the tavern was converted into a farm house— the old Sun Hotel being built at that time.

Several years ago the house was bought by our townsman, D. J. Yerkes, who removed it to make room for the North Penn. Railroad, but the old structure still remains as the Continental Hotel of this place."

In the 1st volume of the "Memorials of the Moravian Church," beginning at page 262, will be found the following interesting statement relative to the old Inn.

"The Crown (Die Krone,) originally the cabin of a Swiss squatter, Ruetschiby name, who settled on the south bank of the river, in 1742. In February, 1743, the tract of 274 acres on which he was seated, was purchased by the Brethren of Wm. Allen. They bought the squatter off and out, leased the premises to one Anton Gilbert, from Germantown, then to one Adam Schaues, and in 1745, after having enlarged the building, opened it for public entertainment. It was stocked in May of that year with gill and half-gill pewter wine measures, with 2 dram glasses; 2 hogsheads of cider; 1 cask of metheglin; 1 cask of rum; 6 pewter plates; iron candlesticks, and whatever else could minister to the creature comforts of the tired traveller. Here he was served with a breakfast of tea or coffee at four pence, a dinner at six pence, a pint of beer at three pence, a supper at four pence, or if hot, at six pence; with lodgings at two pence, and a night's hay and oats for his horse at twelve pence. *Jost Vollert* was the first landlord for the Brethren. The succession of publicans to the end of this piece of history were as follows : — Hartmann Verdries, J. Godfrey Grabs, Nicholas Schaeffer and Ephriam Culver. In 1794, the sign-board, emblazoned with the British Crown, that had often served as a mark for the arrows of the wild Indian boys of *Tredyuscung's Company,* was taken down, and the old hostelry converted into a farm house.   *   *   *   *   *   * At an early day the Brethren built several houses near the Crown, and thus a small

settlement sprang up on the south side of the river. A school for girls, and subsequently one for boys, *Auf der Geduld,* was temporarily conducted here."

When the Moravians first settled at Bethlehem, Loskiel states that there was but two houses in the vicinity inhabited by white people. It is said that the two families referred too, were the *Kieslsteins,* and the *Lee's.* The former lived at the foot of the Lehigh mountains, south of Bethlehem, not far from the present Zinc Works. Some of the family were buried at the foot of the mountain on the north side, and the graves covered by a large heap of stones, on the place now called the *Trone* property. The Lee's lived on the top of the mountain, south of Bethlehem, their former residence is called *Billard's place.* Mrs. George Keisling and Mrs. Levi Fenner, of Bethlehem, are both descendents of the Lee family.

It is said that a family named *Jennings,* owned and lived upon the property now known as *Geissinger's,* above Bethlehem, at the time of the first settlement of the place, and may be one of the families referred to. See Lewis H. Weiss' Annals of the Music of Bethlehem, and a note by Rufus A Grider, in his History of Music in Bethlehem.

South Bethlehem has two weekly newspapers. *The Weekly Progress* made its first appearance during the week ending March 19, 1870, it was edited by Daniel E. Shoedler, and published by O. B. Sigley & Co., it became a daily in April, 1871. The other paper is called *" The South Bethlehem Conservative,* and its first number was issued sometime in 1870.

The difference between the mode of travel in the last century and the present, is admirably illustrated by an old advertisement, which hangs framed in the office of the Eagle Hotel, at Bethlehem, cut from the pages of the *Philadelphia Advertiser,* of April 5th, 1793, with the insertion of which a labor of love is ended.

" PHILADELPHIA, ALLENTOWN, BETHLEHEM and WINDGAP STAGES.

" The subscribers respectfully inform the

public that they will start a line of stages to set out at the Wind Gap at Mr. Jacob Heller's, on Saturday, the 18th of April, 1798, at one o'clock in the afternoon, and arrive at Bethlehem said evening. Another stage will start from Bethlehem at five o'clock next morning, at which time an extra stage will start from Allentown, from the house of Mr. Jacob Hageback, and fall in with the line at Mr. D. Cooper's; then proceeding to Mr. Samuel Seller's, where another stage will set out immediately, and arrive at Mr. Ely Chandler's, Franklin Head, Philadelphia, same evening. Set out from E. Chandler's (Franklin Head), Philadelphia, on Wednesday morning at five o'clock, and proceed the same route back, and arrive at Allentown and Bethlehem same evening. Another stage will leave J. Heller's at one o'clock said day, and likewise arrive at Bethlehem same evening; set out from Bethlehem Thursday morning at five o'clock, and both stages take their respective routes, and arrive at Philadelphia same evening, and at Mr. Heller's at nine o'clock the same morning; set out from Mr. Chandler's on Saturday morning at five o'clock, and arrive at Allentown and Bethlehem said evening, and so alternately twice a week from the Windgap to Philadelphia.

"The fare for passengers from Mr. Heller's (Windgap) to Bethlehem, for each passenger, seventy cents; from Bethlehem or Allentown to Philadelphia, three dollars. Way passengers, six cents per mile, fourteen pounds of baggage allowed each passenger, 150 cwt. the same as a passenger, and the same for returning.

"Parcels taken in at the Stage Office at Mr. Chandler's, Philadelphia, at Mr. Laverings, Bethlehem, at Mr. Hageback's, Allentown, and at Mr. Heller's, Windgap. The smallest parcel twelve cents; two cents per pound that exceeds fourteen pounds, for which the subscribers will vouch for their delivery at their respective places, if properly directed.

"The subscribers, from the liberal encouragement received from the public last season, and now by providing several sets of the best horses and commodious stages, sober and careful drivers, they flatter themselves that the public will continue to give them the preference, as the line will run through from Bethlehem to Philadelphia in one day.

GEORGE WEAVER,
SAMUEL SELLERS,
PHILIP SELLERS,
ENOCH ROBERTS,
JACOB HELLERS.

April 5th, 1798.